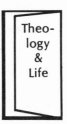

Theo-
logy
&
Life

THEOLOGY AND LIFE SERIES

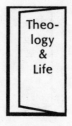

Volume 1

Infallibility

The Crossroads of Doctrine

by

Peter Chirico, S.S.

Foreword by

Bishop B.C. Butler

Michael Glazier, Inc.
Wilmington, Delaware

ABOUT THE AUTHOR

Peter Chirico S.S. is widely known as a writer and lecturer on theological topics. His work is marked by an ability to open new approaches to basic theological tenets and topics, a talent that is demonstrated in this present study. He is presently professor of systematic theology at St. Thomas Seminary in Kenmore, Washington.

Second Printing

First published in 1983 by Michael Glazier, Inc., 1723 Delaware Avenue, Wilmington, Delaware 19806. Distributed outside U.S., Canada and the Philippines by Dominican Publications, St. Saviour's Dublin, Ireland.

Nihil Obstat: Rev. Melvin L. Farrell, SS, STD
Censor Deputatus

Imprimatur: †Raymond G. Hunthausen, DD
Archbishop of Seattle
5 September 1982

©1977 by Peter Chirico, S.S. All rights reserved.

Library of Congress Catalog Card Number: 82-84593
International Standard Book Number:
0-89453-296-0 (Michael Glazier, Inc.)

Cover design by Lillian Brulc
Printed in the United States of America

Contents

Acknowledgments

I wish to thank the following authors and publishers:

for permission to quote from *Documents of Vatican II*, ed. Walter M. Abbott, S.J., AMERICA, all rights reserved. © 1966 America Press, Inc., 106 W. 56th St., N.Y., N.Y. 10016;

for permission to quote from *L'Infaillibilité: Son Aspect Philosophique et Théologique*, ed. Enrico Castelli, Éditions Aubier;

for permission to utilize material from my article "Religious Experience and Development of Dogma," *American Benedictine Review;*

for permission to cite Brian Tierney, *Origins of Papal Infallibility, 1150–1350*, E. J. Brill;

for permission to quote from "L'Infaillibilité de l'Église du point de vue d'un théologien orthodoxe" by Nicolas Afanassieff in *L'Infaillibilité de l'Église*, ed. Olivier Rousseau, Éditions de Chevetogne;

for permission to cite Daniel Maguire, "Morality and Magisterium," *Cross Currents;*

for permission to cite from *Theological Investigations*, Vol. IV by Karl Rahner © 1966 and 1974 by Darton, Longman & Todd Ltd., used by permission of the publisher, The Seabury Press, New York;

for permission to cite from Hans Küng, *Infallible? An Inquiry*, Doubleday and Company;

for permission to cite Maurice Blondel, *The Letter on Apologetics and History and Dogma*, Harvill Press Ltd.;

for permission to cite Brian Tierney, "Origins of Papal Infallibility," *Journal of Ecumenical Studies;*

for permission to cite Jerome S. Bruner, *The Relevance of Education*, W. W. Norton & Co.;

for permission to cite from R. G. Collingwood, *The Idea of History*, Oxford University Press;

for permission to cite Bernard J. F. Lonergan, *Insight: A Study in Human Understanding*, Philosophical Library;

for permission to cite Reginald Fuller, *The Foundations of New Testament Christology*, Charles Scribner's Sons;

for permission to cite *The Church Teaches*, trans. John Clarkson, John Edwards, William Kelly and John Welch, Tan Books and Publishers;

for permission to cite Gerard Hughes, "Infallibility in Morals," and John Sheets, "Teilhard de Chardin and the Development of Dogma," and Avery Dulles' review of *Dogma in Geschichte* by Josef Nolte, *Theological Studies.*

Foreword

The invitation to contribute a Foreword to this second printing of Fr. Chirico's study of infallibility is something that I accept with gratitude but with a sense of my own inadequacy. In a review of the first edition of the book I wrote: "The dominant feeling left on the mind by this book is one of grateful relief: at last someone has written an intelligent book on the subject of infallibility." (The Tablet, 7 January 1978). I retain that sense of gratitude; but I would now remark that the book calls for careful and reflective reading. Having myself read it for the second time (and after reading with particular interest its revised Introduction) I recognise that a third reading would be desirable.

I think it possible that some readers might find it helpful, after reading the Introduction, to begin with an examination of Fr. Chirico's sharp distinction between truths and their verbal expression. He argues forcibly — and I am sure he is right — that truth (and therefore infallibility) is a quality of mental judgments, and that verbal "expressions" do not "contain" (or "incarnate") truth but, at best, refer to it. The same point was made by Pope John XXIII in his inaugural address to the first Session of the Second Vatican Council. It is endorsed by Fr. Bernard Lonergan, S.J., and, in passing, I note with deep satisfaction Fr. Chirico's tribute to the thought of that great philosophic theologian.

After realising that infallibility is a quality not of dogmatic statements but of personal judgments, the reader is in a position to understand Fr. Chirico's main argument. His study of universal (and therefore "transcultural") meanings is fundamental. I am not aware that his conclusions have encountered any significant destructive criticism.

I venture to mention some issues on which I should appreciate further enlightenment:

(1) Fr. Chirico's central concern is infallibility consequent upon acceptance (by faith) of the risen Christ, in whom human-ness is brought to total fulfilment and becomes uniquely and universally relevant. Such *Christian* infallibility is thus founded upon faith. As I understand it, faith is essentially a grace-gift of God. But it actuates

itself in human persons as belief. Following Fr. Lonergan I should sharply distinguish "belief" from the "immanently generated" knowledge that is available also to the unbeliever. An unbeliever who accepts the answers and postulates of Euclidean geometry can achieve certain knowledge that the square of the hypotenuse of a right-handed triangle is equal to the sum of the squares of the other two sides. He does not have to rely upon the consensus of other mathematicians on this issue. A believer, however, depends for his beliefs on such a (relative) consensus. Lonergan infers that belief presupposes a judgment of value: Not, simply, X is true because I "see" it to be true, but X is true because I "see" that it is *good* to believe that it is true. It should be added that a Christian holds that he "ought" so to affirm. But "oughtness" takes one beyond and above the three cognitive levels (experience, understanding and consequent judgment) to the level of responsible decision; and responsible decision *presupposes* experience, understanding and judgment. Faith, therefore, or belief is something of a paradox: it is cognitive, yet it appears to commit us to something *more* than pure cognition has provided. (I am sure that there is a correct answer to my puzzlement on this issue. Perhaps Fr. Chirico has already provided the answer and I have overlooked it. Should one distinguish infallible "knowledge" from infallible "belief"?).

(2) Infallibility is a property of the Church. Will Fr. Chirico tell us how he understands Vatican II's statement that the Church "subsists" in the Roman Catholic Communion? And is infallibility a unique endowment of the Church as thus subsisting, rather than of the Church as existing in every person and in the "churches and ecclesial communities" outside the subsistent Church?

(3) Does Fr. Chirico agree that, since the Church "militant here on earth" is made up of fallible persons, it is because we believe in the abiding assistance of the Holy Spirit that we are *sure* that what the Church affirms to be infallibly true is in fact so?

Bishop B. C. Butler
15.9.82.

Introduction

IMPORTANCE OF THE ISSUE TREATED

A well-known American Protestant theologian once stated that he could not understand how so intelligent and knowledgeable a man as Hans Küng could have written a book on so unimportant a subject as infallibility. From personal experience I can verify that his opinion is by no means rare. With the world in such turmoil, it would seem that we cannot afford to spend time on such theoretical non-issues as infallibility.

My own contention is that we cannot afford *not* to spend time on the issue of infallibility. I believe it has extraordinary relevance to the Christianity of our own day for a number of reasons. First of all, for Roman Catholics infallibility is an element of their past that continues into the present in the attitudes and concepts of many Church leaders and ordinary people. It will not go away even if it is ignored by theologians. No sane person can ignore anything in her past, whether good or bad, if she is to grasp herself and live healthily in the present; for the past continues into our present reality whether we acknowledge it or not. The elements of one's past must be understood, complemented, challenged, corrected, and fulfilled. For a Church which is traditional and which recognizes that it depends upon the witness of the past for its very identity, this is doubly true. The problem of infallibility will not go away. As Church, we must come to terms with it.

Second, the personal and corporate identification of Christians in a rapidly changing age can be accomplished only by the identification of elements that endure despite all changes. It is these enduring elements that enable the leadership and the membership of the Church to see themselves as possessing something in common with their own past lives as well as with the lives of the great Christians who preceded them. The name "Christian" is totally ambiguous if it does not refer to basic elements that persist in the Christians of all times and at every stage of the development of each Christian of any given time. Since infallibility has to do with the process by which these enduring elements are definitely identified, it is of no little importance in promoting the identity of Christians of all ages and especially of an age of change such as our own.

Third, the identification of what is enduring by the exercise of ecclesial infallibility fosters a genuine pluralism in the Church. The establishment of the limits of what is enduring also establishes that many things by their very nature are dependent upon accidental cultural factors and are therefore subject to legitimate pluralistic variations. Once one knows what cannot be given away or changed, one is more easily able to accept and appreciate differences which do not deny these essentials but fulfill them in a unique way. Only a person who is sure of the basic things a good human being must have — a capacity to love, to be open, to understand others, and like characteristics — can readily and wholeheartedly accept the variations in race, color, customs, and culture which do not attack these basics. Once one has identified what is common to Christian development in any age or culture, one will more easily accept the infinite number of possible variations the richness of Christian faith permits. The antidote to the harsh dogmatism which condemns all who differ is not the wishy-washy toleration of every variation, but the firm anchoring in enduring universal truth which permits one to accept readily every new fulfillment of the old truth.

Fourth, infallibility has vast ecumenical significance. It is not just that the infallibility of the pope appears to be an insurmountable obstacle to Christian unity. We must also recognize that there are Orthodox stresses on lasting truth and Protestant notions of an enduring Gospel message that parallel the Roman Catholic doctrine of infallibility. These cannot be lightly brushed aside but must be accounted for in any genuine unity. It is the contention of this book that we can now propose a fulfilling doctrine of infallibility, one that will preserve and complement basic Roman Catholic, Orthodox, and Protestant notions by incorporating them into a single all-encompassing higher viewpoint. In this viewpoint, infallibility ceases to be an obstacle to unity but becomes the very means of identifying and deepening unity.

How does infallibility promote unity among the various Christian Churches? My contention is that the unity of persons and groups depends upon the perceived sharing of common values, that is, upon the recognition of common elements of experience, understanding, judgment, decision-making, and implementation. A *Christian* ecumenical unity appears when members of various groups recognize that they share common *Christian* elements of experience, understanding, judgment, decision-making, and implementation. Now the key element here is judgment. When persons share common judgments, they must have already participated to some extent in like experience and understanding. Further, they are prepared to share, at least to some extent, common decision-making and implementation.

I shall claim that there are aspects which constitute essential identifying traits of all Christian groups and that these aspects alone are the object of the exercise of infallibility. Other aspects at different times and places may constitute elements of unity *de facto*. Thus, the use of Latin unified the Roman Catholic Church for centuries. But infallibility refers only to judgments on factors which are demanded as an essential of Christian existence in every time and place. Hence, the operation of infallibility in the whole Church (and it must be stressed that infallibility is in the first instance a possession of the Church as a whole) identifies the sole necessary constituents of Christian unity — those universal factors which characterize Christian identity forever.

Fifth, a true notion of infallibility has relevance for the world in which the Church lives. It is not an "in house" teaching that pertains to Christians alone. This follows from the fact that, correctly seen, infallibility is *not* a super-human capacity purportedly given by God to the Church as a unique quality having no connection with the endowments of non-Christian human beings and groups; rather, it is an extension of a universal capacity of the human mind. One need not be a Christian to make a series of infallible judgments such as the following: all persons are historically conditioned; all persons are shaped by their own decisions within their unique environments; each person present at a concrete event experiences it in a way that is partially different from the way it is experienced by the other persons present. A Christian can make such judgments; but because the Christian believes in the all-encompassing presence of the risen Christ and his Spirit, he/she can also make the infallible judgment that every person is shaped not just by the surrounding physical environment but also by the outreach of Jesus Christ.

Sixth, a correct notion of infallibility does not box off and limit the Church, does not confine it to a past. Rather, such a notion opens the Church to a limitless future. This follows from the fact that the universal aspects of reality that constitute the sole object of infallibility are by their nature open-ended. To know that human beings are called to ever increasing love of all men and women, that the goal of life toward which all must move is total communion with one another and with the risen Christ in openness to the Father and the Spirit, that the truth of God has unlimited dimensions which will never be exhausted by us, that God in Christ loves us all unconditionally and that his forgiveness is ceaselessly offered no matter how often we reject it — to know these and like truths is not limiting but freeing.

Finally, the doctrine of infallibility indicated here casts light on what is meant by the saving nature of Christian truth. It shows that the kind of truth infallibility makes explicit is directly connected with the personal and Christian development of all persons. Infallibility deals with the truth that makes human beings free. It is in this light that one can begin to see morality as the rendering operative of the enduring content of doctrine in ever changing contexts; and from this follows the necessity of teaching doctrine not just in terms of abstract concepts but also in terms of the attitudes, operations, symbolic expressions, and feelings which doctrine implies. Hence, the hypotheses here proposed have far-ranging practical implications for moral theology, ascetics and catechetics.

PURPOSE AND SCOPE

Infallibility can be treated in a number of ways. In the textbook tradition which marked Roman Catholicism in the century before Vatican II, infallibility was considered in the light of the definition of papal infallibility at Vatican I and also in view of the defensive posture of the Church before Protestants, secularists and atheists. It was explained as a special privilege given to the Church enabling it to preach divine truth in the world without fear of error; the conditions for its exercise as taught by Vatican I were indicated; charges that the Church had erred in intended infallible definitions of the past were refuted.

In the second half of the present century historians began to investigate not only the immediate background and formative process out of which the definition of Vatican I emerged but also the centuries long earlier history of the doctrine. History became a tool for explaining what the doctrine meant and also for questioning or denying its validity.

The present work does not deny the conciliar-apologetic or the historical approaches. It goes another way. It attempts to integrate infallibility into the whole range of theology, to see its meaning within the context of the emergence of Christian reality and understanding. In other words, it tries to situate the doctrine within the life process by which the Church moves forward in the world toward the eschatological fulfillment which is the final gift of God to humankind.

The approach is basically philosophical, although it is rooted in dogma. It starts from the notion highlighted at Vatican II that all revelation is in Christ and that there is no revelation not reflected in his humanity. From this flows a conclusion that will sound startling to some, namely, that all doctrines, including the doctrine of infallibility, must reflect or be related to aspects of the humanity of Christ. There can be no revelation, no doctrine, that goes beyond reflection in the true humanity of the Saviour. There can be no special privilege given to the Church that is not manifested in Christ's earthly and risen humanity.

Hence, the infallibility given to the Church is rooted in the human nature we share with Christ. This suggests that there is a human infallibility which needs to be investigated, an infallibility that grace can build upon. Accordingly, a portion of this book investigates the human process of knowing and the human tradition within which that knowing occurs for the purpose of uncovering the conditions under which a human being can be infallible. The results obtained are then shown to be reconcilable with the conditions set forth at Vatican I for papal infallibility.

This work, then, is an attempt to look at infallibility from a new perspective, to ask a new set of questions, to preserve the old doctrine not by repeating it but by attempting to fulfill and enrich it with the insights of a Church on the move. Therefore, it is not intended to be a polemical work. I am not against anyone. I believe that most disagreements spring from the clash of incomplete positions. I believe that the cure for such disagreements is not a stubborn repetition of long-held positions; nor is it a debate of contrary positions coupled with a refusal of each to recognize the valid aspects of the other's position; nor is it the denial of one's own tradition. Rather, in the long run the majority of disagreements are resolved by a new creation which preserves both the valid aspects of older solutions and the genuine contributions of the present by lifting the level of discourse to a higher plane.

By its very nature a new viewpoint cannot be summarized easily for the reader; for it presupposes a host of assumptions and perspectives that must first be set forth; and this can be done only in the body of the work. Yet an attempt must be made to give the reader an overall picture of the landscape that is to be unfolded before him/her. Hence, I would say that *this book is an extended unifying hypothesis which envisions infallibility as the recurring generic process by which the Church, because of the nature of the witnessed saving reality which dogmatic statements express, can come to certitude in judgment about that reality.* It remains to unpack the meaning of this brief statement.

First of all, I am proposing *a unifying hypothesis,* not an established dogma. I make no claims that what is here advanced is the *asserted* doctrine of the past. I look upon the past — both the statements of the Church's past and her activities — as so many pieces of data to be clarified rather than as finished explanations to be repeated. I am advancing an hypothesis that purports to unify these data. This hypothesis is largely new; for unifying hypotheses are inevitably new when first propounded. Yet if the evidence indicates that the new hypothesis does unify the old data, then it may be said to be old and traditional. Thus, the declarations about Christ at Nicaea went beyond the affirmations of Scripture by unifying their meanings; and so we can call Nicene affirmations traditional.

We should not be surprised that a unifying explanation comes last. This is inevitable by the very nature of human understanding. First, one grasps the particular; later one makes minor generalizations; only at the end does one grasp the overarching unifying explanations. Hence it is that the Scriptures contain many particular affirmations; the councils make abstract generalizations that unify these affirmations; the great scholastics unified these explanations in systems; and the modern age has begun to explain the method by which one unifies all prior modes of acting theologically.

Second, I am proposing an *extended* hypothesis. This hypothesis attempts to account for many facets of the old infallibility data. Thus, it takes into consideration such Roman Catholic data as the conditions governing the exercise of papal infallibility, the assertion of Vatican I that when these conditions are fulfilled the pope's definitions are irreformable *ex sese* and not from the consent of the Church, and the notion that whenever the pope speaks infallibly he is inseparable from the Church. Further, it accounts for the Orthodox stress on the primacy of truth as the basis of infallibility and on the Orthodox demand for reception by the Church of purported infallible decrees. Finally, it meets the Protestant objections that only God is absolutely infallible and the Protestant fears of an arbitrary pope or council shutting off further development in the truth.

Third, I am hypothesizing that the *reality expressed by dogmatic statements is of such a nature that it can be infallibly grasped.* I am asserting that there are universal transcultural meanings that are, at least potentially, aspects of the genuine development of all peoples. Some of these universal aspects can be known through reflection on ordinary human experience; others can be known only by reliance upon the apostolic witness. The enduring symbiosis of these two aspects constitutes the field in which ecclesial infallibility operates. Because these aspects are universal, they can be identified and verified within the whole Church, especially by its leaders; their very universality makes such verifiability by large numbers possible. Further, because these aspects are universal, they endure; their universality gives them stability throughout time.

Since I claim that it is the nature of the reality expressed by dogma that permits infallibility, I find it necessary to examine that dogmatic reality. Hence this book contains a great number of statements about the nature and interrelationship of the realities pointed to by various classical doctrines. The reader will find the interpretations of the transcultural meaning of the Resurrection, the Mass, the Communion of Saints, the general area covered by moral theology, the development of dogma, and a host of other teachings.

I have not attempted to justify these transcultural interpretations by comprehensive historical investigations because such investigations were both practically impossible and, at least at this stage of the endeavor, unnecessary. On the one hand, they were practically impossible. To examine the history of a single doctrine from what purports to be a new viewpoint is an immense task. One cannot merely review the work of established historians of the doctrine. One must go over the primary material oneself. An historian is influenced, whether he or she knows it or not, by personal concerns and presuppositions. He or she is sensitized to certain aspects of reality and it is these aspects that are noted in the evidence. Thus, the modern scripture scholar readily recognizes artificial groupings of events in the Gospels because he or she has been sensitized to this factor; his or her predecessors hardly saw these groupings at all. The point is that the historian or interpreter comes at the evidence with certain questions in mind, and it is to these questions that answers are usually found. This does not necessarily mean that the interpreter reads things into the texts; it does mean that he or she usually finds only those aspects which are sought. The past reality is so vast and so much of it is contained in various ways in the evidence left behind that no historian can capture it all. Instead, what is found is that which is sought, at least as a general rule. Hence, if I intend to justify what purports to be a new and higher level hypothesis about the transcultural meaning of a doctrine, I would have to examine the historical evidence on the doctrine from the perspective of that hypothesis. I would have to ask questions of the evidence that were not asked before. I could not simply examine what other historians, no matter how skilled they might have been, have said. Thus to establish even one of the transcultural hypotheses that I have advanced would require a lifetime of work. To establish all of them would require personnel and resources that no one now has available.

On the other hand, such historical investigations are unnecessary, at least at this stage of the endeavor. The first moment of scientific progress in the area of overarching principles is the proposing of an hypothesis. Such was the case of Einstein with regard to relativity. He proposed a theory that purported to unify the data. He did not prove the theory, though he did indicate how it might be supported. I have attempted something similar here. I have proposed a unity in the reality behind all dogmas which makes the dogmas at the level of transcultural understanding to be so many aspects of the Resurrection of the Lord. I have tried to show the coherence brought about by viewing doctrines in this way, and I have made some elementary soundings that support my contentions. This, I submit, is sufficient for advancing an hypothesis. Its initial explanatory capacity justifies it for the moment; it also invites others to take up the work of proving or disproving the hypothesis by detailed studies in their various specialties.

Fourth, I am proposing an hypothesis which sees *infallibility as the recurring generic process by which the Church arrives at certitude with regard to universal transcultural meanings.* Hence I examine through a large portion of this book the process of human understanding. My basic point is that there is a natural infallibility of the human mind which operates in certain limited cases of universal meanings. When large numbers of persons with varying backgrounds become conscious of the recurring processes by which they grasp the universal meanings characterizing all human existence, then the possibility of making explicit the doctrine of natural infallibility arises. When the person of faith who accepts the apostolic witness about the Resurrection utilizes this process and becomes conscious of its elements, then the possibility of making explicit an ecclesial doctrine of infallibility arises.

Fifth, I am proposing an hypothesis that sees *dogmatic statements as expressing infallible judging.* Infallibility resides in the act of judgment alone. Statements are neither fallible nor infallible; rather, they are more or less adequate expressions of the judgments they reflect. As such they are of minor moment with regard to the purposes of this book. Hence, I assign to such statements a modest and secondary treatment in chapter 16. Of course, I do not deny that such statements are of crucial importance in theology since they are the primary means by which we can attain our own understanding of what the past said and meant.

Sixth, I am proposing an hypothesis which treats of *a saving reality that has been witnessed by the apostolic Church* upon whose witness we depend. I do not try to prove that witness; for a Christian that witness is a given which can be verified only in the concrete self-validating experience of faith; in biblical terms, flesh and blood cannot prove the validity of the witness, but only the interior action of the Father and the Spirit. However, that witness needs to be understood, and to understand it we must interpret documents which record the original witness. In turn, interpretation is itself a venture in understanding, and the exercise of interpretation implies a host of ordinarily unuttered presuppositions which shed light on the understanding process that lies behind infallibility. It is for this reason that the first two chapters explore the process of interpretation. That exploration reveals that the very attempt to understand and interpret past documents presupposes as factual certain dynamics which pertain to the theory of infallibility I am proposing. Therefore, the first two chapters on interpretation constitute an integral part of this work.

The rather broad scope of this work indicates the reason for its title, *Infallibility: The Crossroads of Doctrine.* The contents of dogmatic theology, moral theology, hermeneutics, theological method, Christian growth and spirituality, and liturgy *in their universal aspects* all meet in the doctrine of infallibility; for all of these disciplines treat of aspects of the one saving reality; and insofar as the aspects treated by each are universal they compenetrate and can be brought together in the collective consciousness of the Church. That bringing together of universal saving truth in the collective consciousness of the Church is the very process that we thematize as infallibility.

I might add that I give only select historical "proof" for the basic thesis on infallibility which I advance. The justification for being selective is not only the justification given for my failure to redo the history of the dogmas I cast in a transcultural mold. There is an added reason why hypotheses on infallibility need not be subject to the same historical support as other hypotheses. Infallibility refers to the generic process by which the Church comes to certitude about saving reality. It is a continuously recurring process. Hence it appeared over and over again in the history of the Church; it appeared in the past and led to the historical dogmas. As I will try to show, it is appearing in the present and will appear in the future because it is part of the dynamism of persons in general and Christian persons in particular. Now because it is a doctrine which thematizes a recurring reality that appears in the present, it is a doctrine that can be detected not only in the past but also in the present. And because our consciousness has been heightened in modern times, it becomes easier for us to detect this recurring process in our own experience than it was for the people of the past to detect it and report it on the basis of their experience. Hence, throughout this book I directly or indirectly appeal to the reader to look into his or her own experience for the recurring elements which I thematize. To put this another way, the history of any doctrine in the Church is unique, and the only way to show how the doctrine reached the present stage is to follow its unique development by an historical investigation. However, if one wishes an account of the generic process by which the Church arrives at certitude in its teaching, one can (1) trace the history of various doctrines and then note the common process that characterized the genesis of each or (2) directly examine the generic processes by which modern persons at different levels of development and in different cultures come to definitive understanding of the faith. Basically, I have followed the second alternative, although I have indicated in many instances how the proposed theory meets the historical data.

I have treated several key questions in a number of complementary ways. My hope is that the return to basic ideas at a deeper level and with terminology which brings out other aspects will assist the reader to grasp the new framework within which I am casting the old problem. I am aware of how inevitably we tend to cast what wnother says into our own traditional categories. I have utilized new and varying terminology in the hope that it will challenge the reader to find those elements in his or her experience which underlie the new framework I am attempting to convey.

Since the first printing, however, I have come to regret the use I have made of the phrase "infallible understanding." I assumed it was evident that this phrase meant a certitude without fear of error in the correctness of an act of understanding. "Infallible understanding" is thus the equivalent of "infallible judgment." Unfortunately, this equivalency was not apparent to all readers. As a result, it was not clear to some readers that my focus is *not* so much how the initial proposal of universal hypotheses occurs but how we judge that such proposals are irreformable. To grasp that a certain proposition is universal and to propose it as such is an "inspired" act. It cannot be planned and a method for attaining such propositions cannot be taught; one can only indicate the presence in the life of the faithful of the meanings thematized by such propositions. Moreover, it is the presence of these meanings in the life of all the faithful that provides the only test of the correctness of the pur-

ported infallible judgment. When a proposition "rings a bell" in the
lives of all the faithful, when it articulates in a recognizable way the
sensus fidelium, then one knows an infallible judgment has been
registered. There is no other way in which the infallibility of such
judgments can be ascertained.

SUMMARY OVERVIEW

This book is divided into two unequal parts. The first part,
consisting of chapters 1 and 2, treats of the implications and presuppositions of the interpretative process. Christianity is a traditional
religion, and the knowledge of the tradition comes to a great extent
through the use of texts. However, the examination of the process
of interpretation reveals that it presupposes a commonality of
experience and possible understanding between persons of the
present and persons of the past. This finding, first of all, implies the
existence of the universal meanings that the second part of the
work indicates are at the basis of infallibility. It implies, secondly, a
host of implications about the basic functions of texts in theology,
about dangers and mistakes to be avoided in the process of interpreting past texts, and about the practical training of exegetes and
the practical conduct of theology.

The second and larger part of the work deals directly with
infallibility. The opening chapter (chapter 3) treats the simple experiential level of existence. Its main point is that even apart from the
acceptance of Christian faith human beings experience the possibility of infallibility. This occurs because there are universal meanings, that is, differentiations of experience that exist or can exist as
moments of the legitimate and ultimately necessary development
of every person of every age and culture. Next, such universal
meanings can be infallibly grasped precisely because of their universality. Finally, the infallible judgment of universal meanings can
be expressed in statements which point to these meanings. Hence,
the basic division of this chapter is (1) universal meanings, (2)
infallible judgment of such meanings, and (3) subsequent expressions of these meanings.

The rest of the book follows this threefold division and applies it
to the Church and its faith. Chapters 4 through 8 deal with universal Christian meanings; chapters 9 through 15 treat the infallible

judgment of these meanings; chapter 16 takes up the analysis and functions of expressions and applies this analysis to the expression of infallibly judged universal meanings. Finally, the epilogue indicates (1) the value of infallibility in meeting the modern problem of vast pluralism, (2) the continuing need for dogmatic definitions, and (3) the broader function of the magisterium under the conditions of our times.

Chapters 4 through 8 constitute the heart of this work, for they deal with the universal Christian meanings upon which infallibility rests. Chapter 4 treats the basic Christian fact of the incarnation, life, death, and resurrection of Christ in transcultural terms. It brings out what is universal in the faith acceptance of the risen Christ. Chapter 5 shows why the universal meanings experienced by all human beings compenetrate the universal meanings deriving from the faith acceptance of the witness of the apostles about the risen Christ. Both meanings exist in an enduring symbiosis in the person of Christian faith. This chapter also brings out why much of the Church's past teaching was particular and culturally conditioned and not universal and transcultural. Chapter 6 explores the nature, importance, and necessity of univeral Christian meanings. Chapter 7 explains the process by which these meanings historically emerge. Finally, chapter 8 clarifies some characteristics of these meanings: their hierarchical nature; their relationship to theology; their stability; their mysterious and eschatological nature.

Chapters 9 through 15 construct the basic hypothesis about the infallible judgment of universal Christian meanings. In chapter 9 the official teaching of the Church is outlined and affirmed; lacunae in that teaching are indicated. Chapters 10 through 15 attempt to complete and fulfill the official doctrine by placing its affirmations in a larger context. In terms of this larger context, chapter 10 treats the nature of infallibility; chapter 11 takes up the object of infallibility, the risen Christ; chapter 12 clarifies the source, the goal, the practicality, and the necessity of infallible judgment; chapter 13 discusses the bearers of infallibility in general and the place of the infallibility of the faithful in particular; chapters 14 and 15 treat respectively the pope and the bishops as the official bearers of infallible judgment. In these last two chapters the conditions under which these official teachers achieve infallible judgment are examined and the findings are incorporated into the overall hypothesis which I have proposed. Throughout, the effort has been to remain faithful to the Roman Catholic tradition by advancing a theory which prolongs it, develops it, and integrates its various elements.

I wholeheartedly accept the teaching of Vatican I on infallibility; however, I recognize in accord with the document *Mysterium Ecclesiae* issued by the Sacred Congregation for the Doctrine of the Faith with the approval of Pope Paul VI on June 24, 1973 that "it sometimes happens that some dogmatic truth is first expressed incompletely (but not falsely), and at a later date, when considered in a broader context of faith or human knowledge, it receives a fuller and more perfect expression." [A. A. S., 65 (1973) 402-3.] I believe that Vatican I expressed incompletely, but not falsely, the doctrine of infallibility. I believe, further, that in our time we have a broader context of human knowledge within which to consider that doctrine. Accordingly, I have attempted to serve the Church by proposing a way to carry forward and extend what was declared by Vatican I. How well I have succeeded remains to be judged by my theological peers and ultimately by those who are entrusted with the guardianship of the faith.

It will become obvious to the reader that this is not intended to be an erudite work; it is more reflective than scholarly. I have read much of the literature and profited by that reading. However, I have decided not to clutter this book with citations from the host of men upon whose shoulders I stand. To go into the opinions of others in a fair way that would set forth the contexts in which they operated would have intolerably lengthened this work. I have preferred to keep the main lines as clean as possible so that the basic theory might have a chance to be appreciated. Moreover, the context in which I have cast the theory proposed here makes it quite difficult to cite others honestly. I have become too aware in the process of writing this book that the citation of another who works in a different context from one's own is often unfair and misleading. In addition, it is often impossible to cite the true source of one's thought or even to locate it. There are books which have been formative of my own thinking in ways of which I am only peripherally aware; and it may well be that these books have influenced my thought far more than any I cite. I have come to the conclusion that in complex matters footnotes are really only symbolic gestures which say in a mythological way that the author recognizes that much of his thought comes from others. For an author to pretend that he can pinpoint those sources is for him to indicate that he knows little of the processes of human understanding.

Finally, I am well aware that there is a christological view now being advanced in some quarters which would stress the exemplary and symbolic meaning of Christ and eliminate his presence in power. While the view obviously contradicts the one I support in this volume, I would point out that its acceptance would not destroy the basic form of the infallibility argument advanced here. It would, of course, severely modify the meaning of many doctrines that flow from the understanding of Christ's being and resurrection presupposed in this book. My opposition to this exemplary and symbolic view of Christ stems not from my notion of infallibility but from my belief that it contradicts the two thousand year old faith experience of the Roman Catholic Tradition.

CLARIFICATIONS

Reactions of reviewers to the first printing give me the opportunity to correct what I now consider inadequacies, to develop further what I now see as incomplete positions, and to rectify misunderstandings. My purpose in this section, therefore, is not to refute critics but rather to utilize their criticisms to advance the discussion on infallibility.[1]

Avery Dulles makes a number of significant criticisms.[2] First, he is puzzled by my tendency to identify certitude with universality, "as though the particular and the concrete were necessarily tentative and dubious" (p. 506). Actually I concede in my text (p. 59) that

---

1. I shall ignore misunderstandings in matters I consider secondary. Thus in his review in *Theological Studies*, 40 (June, 1979), 303 John T. Ford states that my retention of secondary objects of infallibility is unwarranted. The fact is that I explicitly state that the so-called secondary objects of infallibility are not objects of infallibility at all (p. 288). I see little value in correcting misunderstandings in such minor matters.

2. *Commonweal* (August 4, 1978), 504-6.

we need "not rule out practical infallibility regarding specific aspects of a given object or situation." What I did not make clear is that the points I make about infallible judgments have to do with judgments that are to be shared among many persons. I may have personal certitude about this or that concrete event witnessed by me. However, once I try to share that certitude with those not present difficulties arise. The insertion of a witness or a chain of witnesses which distance one from the actual event makes infallible certitude problematic. Hence, there is never infallible certitude about the concrete past matters treated by the historian.

Second, Dulles contrasts my view that "the magisterium must increasingly move from a prophetic manner of speaking, which addresses particular situations, to a strictly dogmatic and universal mode of speech" with the view of authors such as Rahner and Lindbeck who claim "that since the Church has become conscious of the culturally limited character of all formulations, the leadership should generally be content to address specific situations, speaking in a prophetic rather than dogmatic style" (p. 506).

Let me respond that in the text I do advocate a place for a magisterial prophetic style. "I am not saying the Church must pronounce only at the level of universal meanings. It must engage in the function of articulating those meanings as they apply to concrete contexts. However, this articulating for concrete contexts can no longer be done by a pope whose task is to unify the whole Church. Because there is no longer a single universal concrete context, he can no longer unify by statements which pertain to concrete contexts, but only by statements of the abstract universal kind that characterize the whole Church. The lesser and more particular statements about concrete contexts can emanate only from those who are actively present in those contexts. The bishop and the local pastor are the official Church figures for this task, not the pope" (pp. 217-18).

I would now qualify and differentiate my view. I would still maintain that in the area of *doctrinal teaching* the universal (papal or conciliar) magisterium should largely restrict itself to universal principles. However, I would assert that the universal magisterium also has a distinct role in calling attention to world situations which touch upon human and Gospel values. The arms race, unequal distribution of the world's goods, the deprivation of human rights, massive state fostered abortions, and the breakup of the family trouble humankind on a massive scale; as such they should be addressed by prophetic statements of the Church's universal magisterium. I affirm the immense value of a universal spokesman prophetically proclaiming the Church's concern in these areas.

Nevertheless, there is another prophetic function, that of proclaiming ways to alter evil situations. It is this prophetic function that I would increasingly remove from the universal magisterium. I would claim, for example, that popes should not as a general rule attempt to propound concrete plans for a new and more just economic order or suggest ways that individual nations can concretely bring about a reduction of the arms buildup. The world situation is too complex and too diversified for a reduction of Gospel principles to concrete solutions applicable to the hundreds of nations of the globe.

Yet the Church should not abdicate ministering to a concrete world. It must seek out concrete solutions. These, I believe, are more the province of local Churches operating collegially in utilizing persons who are at once experts in various fields and steeped in Gospel values. Such local Churches, through their bishops or through properly designated competent bodies (which do not exclude individual prophetic figures acting in freedom within the Church) can suggest solutions to concrete problems that represent their best effort — never binding as infallible or even authoritative teaching, of course — to apply the Gospel here and now. Thus, I believe that the national hierarchy and local bishops in the United States are in a better position to make statements challenging the concrete operation of our government in the matter of disarmament than is the pope.

In short, the universal magisterium of the Church unifies by proclaiming what is of universal import. On the one hand, it teaches universal principles; on the other hand, it calls attention to world situations which touch upon universal human and Gospel values. However, the more concrete solutions to problems in each nation and area are more properly addressed by lower levels of the magisterium and, of course, by the whole membership of the Church.

Third, Dulles states that in view of "the inevitable tensions between the divine meaning and the human understanding and between the human understanding and the verbal formulation, the multiplication of dogmas often serves to divide rather than to unite the Christian community and to burden inordinately the task of Christian mission. Generally speaking, the church is more effectively united by shared symbolism and lived communion than by dogmatic definitions." Dulles suggests I might concur in this judgment (p. 506).

I do concur to an extent, but I would amplify my views. Unity in the Church is a unity of persons as Christian. Such unity is *potential* to the degree that persons possess the same Christian feelings, attitudes, emotions, desires, understandings, and judgments and also to the extent that they perform the same activities. Thus, there is greater possibility for union between persons who feel the same feelings, desires and emotions, have the same attitudes, understandings and judgments, and do the same activities, than between those who possess only a few of these elements in common.

Unity is *actual* to the degree that the *potential* elements of unity are perceived as shared. When persons know intellectually that they share certain aspects of their Christian being, a degree of Christian unity actually occurs. When they know intellectually that they share additional elements of unity, greater unity occurs. And when their knowledge of all these shared elements surpasses the purely intellectual realm and enters into the whole fiber of their beings so that they "know" with their whole humanity that they share what constitutes them as persons, the Christian unity becomes most profound.

Potential unity becomes actual unity through expressions which make known and deepen the Christian elements persons have in common and which foster new sharings of elements until then not possessed in common. Some expressions facilitate minimal sharing because they engage only a thin range of the humanity of the sharers. Highly abstract principles divorced from concrete contexts are an example of this. To share acceptance of the second of the two great commandments apart from a concrete context does not promote unity over a wide band of the spectrum of human existence. Other expressions engage many facets of the participating persons and can lead to deeper sharing. Common activities in crisis situations such as occur with soldiers at the front can promote deep bonds. Common symbols which unlock deeper levels of the conscious and the unconscious can, when participation is more than perfunctory, bind persons profoundly together. Even a highly abstract principle such as the second commandment can lead to a deep bond *if* its common acceptance is seen within the context of concrete problems calling for the love of the neighbor here and now.

This brief analysis explains, in the first place, why shared symbolism and shared lived communion do more to promote Christian unity than do the multiplication and sharing of doctrines. The former lead to more profound sharing of Christian persons than do the latter, as a general rule. This analysis also indicates why the possibilities of unity in depth are greater at the local level than at the international level. Far more can be shared by those who live close to one another, share the same environment, use the same language and symbols than by those who live thousands of miles apart.

Finally, and perhaps most importantly, the analysis clarifies why dogmas can be divisive in the ecumenical venture. I begin with a few definitions and qualifications. A dogma is a formula solemnly sanctioned by the Church as an expression of a definitive judgment regarding an enduring aspect of Christian existence. A dogma is thus a composite of an enduring dogmatic judgment and a more or less adequate culturally conditioned expression of that judgment. A dogma is irreformable though developable in its judgmental component; it is subject to a wide variety of revisions in its expressive component.

Next, dogmas have at least two distinct uses which concern our problem. The first use is to express for the issuing Church the principal elements which constitute its enduring make up. This is the self-identifying usage of dogma. The second use is to set forth the formulated beliefs which must be accepted by other Churches as a condition for Christian union. This is the ecumenical litmus test usage of dogma.

The use of dogmas to self-identify a Church is generally good in itself and indirectly a help in the ecumenical movement. The more clearly a Church knows and expresses what it stands for, the healthier it is and the more honest and fruitful can be its dialogue with other Churches. It is the litmus test usage of dogma that can cause ecumenical divisiveness.

There is obviously a legitimate test usage of dogma since there must be some basic minimal sharing of belief if Church unity is to be a reality. Belief constitutes the heart of a Church's existence; so unity among Churches necessitates shared recognition of basic common beliefs. To demand as a condition of union of Churches a sharing in basic beliefs is not a divisive tactic. Rather, it is a demand which sets forth conditions essential to the very existence of such union. Such demands are divisive only in the sense that they make evident an underlying separation in Churches which already exists.

Having conceded this, I would state that the litmus test usage of dogma can cause, not just manifest, divisiveness in a number of ways. First, divisiveness can be caused by the demand that certain doctrinal *formulae* be accepted by another Church as a condition of unity. The problem here is that the formulae in which doctrinal judgments are couched are invariably historically conditioned. By their nature they only more or less adequately convey that judgment. In addition, the words involved may have changed their meanings over time so that they convey a different meaning to the persons upon whom they are now being imposed. Further, words often have different connotations for different persons. To impose a formula that conveys distasteful overtones and connotations on another Church as a condition of union can interpose a divisive obstacle that is not contained in the judgment component of the dogma. And it is the judgment component that needs to be shared. The verbal component is of value and should be employed only to the extent that it conveys the dogmatic judgment which is the heart of dogma. Thus for a Catholic to demand that as a condition of union all Protestants must accept the statement that the pope has full and supreme power of jurisdiction over the whole Church in faith, morals, discipline, and government would be disastrously divisive. This way of formulating the primacy (basically the way it was formulated by Vatican I) cannot but give rise to an image of the pope as absolute dictator over the whole Church — an image that is both dangerous and false. One may set acceptance of the primacy as a condition of unity; one need not and must not demand that offensive sounding formulae which do not adequately convey the dogma to others must also be accepted.

The litmus test use of dogma can be divisive in a second way. This occurs when we impose upon another Church certain dogmatic *judgments* whose positive acceptance is not necessary for dogmatic unity and whose imposition causes further division. That *some* Roman Catholic dogmatic judgments may be unreasonably imposed as conditions for unity, at least at given points of history, flows from the following factors: (1) There is a hierarchy of doctrines; some are central and basic; others, though integrally connected with the basic doctrines, are less central.[3] (2) Dogmas perform their function when they thematize common elements of faith experience. Thus they have meaning only for those who have participated in the requisite underlying faith experiences through concrete traditional life, participation in the liturgy, etc. (3) The development of differentiated faith experiences underlying various dogmas follows the law of election in the economy of salvation. This means that some persons or groups achieve the requisite differentiation of faith experience first; for these persons and groups a dogma thematizing this experience makes sense.[4] The primary example of this law is Israel itself. It was the group that first perceived the basic biblical truth about the God of history; only later was it able to share that truth with others because only later did these groups participate in the experiences that undergirded Israel's truth. Similarly, within the chosen people prophets first saw many social moral demands; only long after did the people follow.

Applying these notions to the Roman Catholic participation in the ecumenical venture, we may say that the unity of the Churches depends upon unity in the basic truths of faith. With regard to the secondary dogmas that we hold, however, it will be unreasonable and divisive to require that these be accepted as a condition of unity, if the Church upon which the demand is made lacks the underlying liturgical and ordinary life faith experience which the

3. The hierarchy of truths is mentioned in *Unitatis Redintegratio*, #11. For a concise discussion on the import of the existence of a hierarchy of truths for the litmus test use of dogma in the unity of Churches see Avery Dulles, *The Resilient Church* (Garden City, N.Y.: Doubleday, 1977), pp. 45-62, especially pp. 55-57. See my own treatment on pp. 125-27 in the text.
4. For the process by which dogmas emerge see Chapter 7.

dogmas rest upon. To impose such dogmas would be to impose acts of understanding not rooted in experience. It would be analogous to my demanding as a condition of friendship that another person who has never exercised the sense of smell must accept as a condition of friendship my definition of smell. Even if my definition is correct, the demand would be seen as unreasonable and as such will cause greater divisiveness.

This does not mean that secondary dogmas can be disregarded or pushed into the background. What would be required of another Church would be respect for the dynamism of election. This means that other Churches must at least accept the possibility that there is enduring meaning for all in the secondary Roman Catholic dogmas; it means, further, that the Churches work together to share as far as possible the faith experiences and reflection which undergird the doctrine. The rest can be left in the hands of Providence. This mode of activity is not merely a manner of respecting the sensibilities of other Churches. It is also dogmatically based. It takes into account the hierarchy of truths, the factor of election in the economy of salvation, and the necessity to ground dogma in faith experience.[5]

Having conceded these limitations to the multiplication and imposition of dogmas, I would still insist that the dogmatic area of universal Christian meanings is the only necessary constituent, at least as a goal, of the unity of the worldwide Church. Common liturgical rites will unify some Christians; such rites in all their specific concreteness cannot be reasonably demanded of all Christians. Common strategies for helping the neighbor may unify Christians of one nation; they should not be imposed on all Christian nations. The more the world divides into diverse cultures and subcultures, the more symbols proliferate, the more problems differ from place to place, the more it will become impossible to structure worldwide unity on the basis of the more concrete and profoundly engaging expressions of unity. Certainly interaction

---

5. For a more comprehensive treatment of the way in which Roman Catholics should act with regard to demanding acceptance of their secondary dogmas by non-catholics as a condition of union see my "Dogmatic Definitions as Ecumenical Obstacles," *Journal of Ecumenical Studies*, 14 (Winter, 1977), 51-65.

between Christians will always be necessary as a pre-condition for unity. Yet Christians will recognize that they are profoundly one only if there rises to some clarity amidst all the recognition that all share certain abiding Christian meanings and values.

Thus while I recognize the supreme practical importance of shared symbolism and lived communion, I believe that only those symbols and actions which incarnate universal Christian values, and only to the extent that they incarnate such values, can be mandatory. This is true of the symbols we call sacraments. It is also true of the symbol which is the papacy. In fact, I would state that only as the papacy limits its definitive claims to the universal values imbedded in the whole Christian tradition will it be progressively accepted as a necessary Christian symbol by other Churches. In all areas other than that of universal values, the exercise of papal authority must be admitted to be provisional, subject to error, bound to encourage free input and response from local Churches, open to revision.

Geoffrey Wainwright is surprised that I "do not draw more directly on the Church's liturgical experience in...(my) argumentation for infallibility in matters of faith."[6] I would agree with his stress on the importance of the liturgy but I would further qualify the matter. I believe that the experience of liturgy constitutes perhaps the most important way in which the concrete faith of the Christian community develops. In turn, this corporate faith is, as my text indicates, the matrix of implicit universal meanings from which can be quarried infallible judgments. Liturgical texts and actions, therefore, do not furnish direct support for infallible judgments; one cannot easily read off such judgments from liturgical books and liturgical practices. Instead, liturgy directly shapes the faith of Christians, and Christians so shaped can come to infallible judgments by detecting the universal Christian meanings occurring in their corporate faith life. Hence, liturgy has a most powerful influence on infallible judgments, but that influence is more mediate than immediate.

Michael Vertin claims that I confuse the risen Christ (an empiri-

6. Geoffrey Wainwright, *Doxology: The Praise of God in Worship, Doctrine, and Life* (New York: Oxford University Press, 1980), p. 577.

cal content) with the presuppositions of the knowing process (an *a priori* content).[7] Vertin is correct in asserting that the risen Christ is an object over and against us whereas the characteristics of the knowing process are presupposed internal factors within us. They are different kinds of reality without doubt. However, the risen Christ in his presence and activity touches every aspect of creation. And the human knowing process possesses aspects which are enduring and universal to every knowing subject. Hence, these two different kinds of realities share the quality of universality, even though one is what Vertin calls an *a priori* content and the other is what he calls an empirical content. They come under the same treatment as objects of infallibility because they share the single trait that pertains to such objects, namely, universality.

John T. Ford claims, first, that I have missed the fact that Vatican I "did *not* reject the notion that the pope has to consult the Church before exercising infallibility; what the Council rejected was any specification of what form such prior consultation must take."[8]

The problem here revolves around the meaning of the word "consult." In the narrow sense the word refers to an active procedure by which the pope asks the various Churches for their views on a proposed definition of faith. In the broad sense the word refers to any effort by the pope to contact the faith of the universal Church. This effort may involve studying the Scriptures and the Fathers or reading the past documents of the magisterium or reflecting on what has been taught in the Churches around the world or direct consultation of the bishops of the world or a combination of these. In this broad sense consultation refers to any and all efforts to contact the faith of the universal Church.

My view is that the Council did not reject consultation in the broad sense. However, I believe that it rejected the very necessity for consultation in the narrow sense and not just "any specification of what form such prior consultation must take." This is the mean-

---

7. Michael Vertin, "Infallibility and the Demands of Epistemology: A Review Article," *The Thomist*, 43 (October, 1979), 637-52. I summarized my views and responded to Vertin in "Infallibility: A Reply," *The Thomist*, 44 (January, 1980), 128-35.

8. Review in *Theological Studies*, 40 (June, 1979), 303.

ing of my statement that Vatican I "rejected the notion that... (the pope) *had to* consult the Church beforehand" (p. 224), as a reading of the context surrounding this statement will make clear (pp. 224-25).

Second, Ford has a comment on my method. He sees my work as an "attempt at modernizing infallibility by constructing a currently compatible conceptualization and then superimposing it on conciliar documents." This is "from a methodological viewpoint, a Procrustean fitting of the past to the exigencies of a modern schema."[9] I welcome this comment because it allows me to clarify my method and to indicate what I believe is a profound difference between my approach to theology and that of a number of my colleagues.

Ford does not see that this book is *not* an attempt to re-interpret Vatican I. Rather, it is an attempt to examine faith realities and to establish with the aid of modern tools what infallibility might mean in itself as an aspect of the process of living faith. Perhaps an example will clarify what I have tried to do. Suppose I have before me the text of a classic description of a certain kind of rose by a great biologist named Jones. Although I have read his description, I prefer to examine the rose myself and to utilize equipment and methods not available when Jones wrote. As a result, I note a number of aspects of the rose that Jones missed; and I come to an overall view of the rose that differs from his although I agree with all the specific observations that he made. Notice that my view can be partially verified by what Jones stated because it does not disagree with his observations. At the same time it is not his view; nor is it an interpretation or re-interpretation of his view. Rather, it is an interpretation of the reality Jones tried to describe by one who stands on the shoulders of Jones and his successors. It would be mistaken to object to my study of the rose that "the attempt at modernizing our understanding of the rose by constructing a currently compatible conceptualization and then superimposing it on Jones' document is, from a methodological viewpoint a Procrustean fitting of the past to the exigencies of a modern schema."

In short, I have not attempted to impose a modern construct on Vatican I for the simple reason that I have not set as my goal the re-interpretation of Vatican I. My goal is the understanding of the

9. *Ibid.*, p. 305.

reality that is infallibility. That reality transcends any and all interpretations, including that of Vatican I (and, of course, my own). I
have attempted a fuller view of that reality by utilizing modern
cognitional tools. At the same time, I have not ignored Vatican I. I
have utilized standard interpretations in order to make sure that
my own theory does not contradict what Vatican I defined.

Behind Ford's misreading of my method lies, I believe, a tendency
to think that the *only* way to theological progress is the study of
theological documents of the past and the unearthing of all the
meanings buried therein. With this view I am in profound disagreement. I believe that the great documents of the past — the Scriptures, the writings of the Fathers, the books of the classic
theologians, and the teachings of the magisterium — are important
theological sources precisely because they reflect the understanding of living faith reality at the point in time when they were issued.
They are more than a restatement or re-interpretation of the texts
that preceded them; they are to some extent a new grasp of a
present relationship to God, the relationship articulated from a
different viewpoint by earlier texts.

Now if the documents of the past to some extent take their
validity and importance from the fact that they spring in a fresh
way from the living relationship of faith, then documents of the
present can also aspire to do the same thing. They, too, can examine
the living faith with modern tools in an effort to capture new sides
of the old faith reality. They, too, can ask new questions, questions
never dreamed of by the authors of the old texts. They, too, can
make new discoveries which build on the older understanding of
reality.

My own belief is that theology stultifies when one thinks that
the only path to growth is the interpretation and re-interpretation
of the documents of the past. One must also examine present faith
reality with all the means now available. This is true of any area of
theology. It is especially true of infallibility because of the increased
modern understanding in cognitional process, in the relationship of
understanding to faith development, and in the meaning of symbols and language.[10]

---

10. I have indicated new possible approaches to the infallibility question in my "Directions
for Future Research on the Infallibility Issue," *Proceedings of the Catholic Theological Society of*

Finally, I am visibly indebted to friends and colleagues who assisted me in the preparation of this book by their criticisms and suggestions. My special thanks go to William Thompson, to Richard Basso, to Leo Stanford, and to Maurice Duchaine.[11]

America, 35 (June, 1980), 240-43. A more comprehensive criticism of Küng's views and the possibilities of further developments from the many good elements in his vision of infallibility appears in my "Infallibility: Rapprochement between Küng and the Official Church?" *Theological Studies*, 42 (December, 1981), 529-60. The connection between infallibility and spirituality is taken up in my "Spirituality and Infallibility," *Spirituality Today*, 31 (June, 1979), 109-120.

11. I have attempted to avoid sexist language in this new introduction. However, because of technical difficulties I have not been able to rectify the use of such language in the body of this work which was composed before my consciousness had been raised in this matter.

The Definition of Papal Infallibility at Vatican I

(D.S. 3073, 3074)

...sacro approbante Concilio, docemus et divinitus revelatum dogma esse definimus:

Romanum Pontificem, cum ex cathedra loquitur, id est, cum omnium Christianorum pastoris et doctoris munere fungens pro suprema sua Apostolica auctoritate doctrinam de fide vel moribus ab universa Ecclesia tenendam definit, per assistentiam divinam ipsi in beato Petro promissam, ea infallibilitate pollere, qua divinus Redemptor Ecclesiam suam in definienda doctrina de fide vel moribus instructam esse voluit; ideoque eiusmodi Romani Pontificis definitiones ex sese, non autem ex consensu Ecclesiae, irreformabiles esse.

...We, with the approval of the sacred Council, teach and define that it is a divinely revealed dogma:

that the Roman Pontiff, when he speaks *ex cathedra* — that is, when in the discharge of the office of Shepherd and Teacher of all Christians, he defines in virtue of his supreme Apostolic authority a doctrine of faith or morals to be held by the universal Church — enjoys, through the divine assistance promised to him in Blessed Peter, that infallibility with which the divine Redeemer willed to equip his Church when it defines a doctrine of faith or morals; and therefore such definitions of the Roman Pontiff are irreformable of themselves, not however from the consent of the Church.

Part One

Interpretation

Factors Involved in Interpretation

INTRODUCTION

In 1958 Gustave Thils published an account of the basic tendencies and directions of the theological enterprise as it then existed.[1] In the previous year two large tomes had been published in which the *status quaestionis* in each of forty representative areas of theology was concisely presented.[2] What marked both publications, despite the differences in their approaches, was a recognition that the decisive characteristic of modern theology was its return to the sources. Close examination of the traditional texts—biblical, patristic, and liturgical—was proclaimed to be the basic requirement of the modern theologian's work. Theology by then had become recognized as basically an exegetical or interpretive science.

This view of theology has in the main prevailed operationally to the present. In the treatment of many particular doctrines, Catholic theology has advanced relatively untouched by the philosophical debates on historical method and on the very meaning of human understanding that have been conducted in areas of basic methodology.[3] The hallmark of technical theological work is still the ability to marshal an impressive array of textual sources that support a given point of view through depicting its genesis as represented in ancient texts.

I believe that the theologian's operative interpretative method and the epistemological presuppositions that undergird that method condition to a large extent the results obtained. Further, since infallibility deals with the knowing process by which the Church comes to certitude about its past heritage, the views a theologian takes on this subject will be even more closely determined by his interpretative and epistemological stance.

Accordingly, in this first part I shall attempt to clarify what is presupposed in the very effort to interpret past documents and the consequently limited, though indispensably important, place these documents have for the theologian. I will try to indicate some of the complexities which arise in interpreting documents, the various degrees of interpretation possible, and the kinds of nonexegetical

requirements demanded of the interpreter. The preceding will be
the burden of this first chapter. In chapter 2 of this first part I will
summarize the results of this analysis for the theologian and indicate
some of the practical implications these results have for theology in
the present and in the future.

In the second and far larger part of this work I shall apply the
findings of the first part to the specific question of infallibility.

THE INITIAL ASSERTION

The analysis which follows is but a clarification and extension
of a single initial claim: that the starting point for *any* understanding
and interpretation of the past *must* be an understanding of the present. Consequently, the starting point for the understanding of the
meanings represented in theological texts of the past must be our
present theological understanding of faith. To grasp why this is so
we must elucidate what is involved and presupposed when we understand and interpret the past through documents that record its
meaning. This analysis will reveal that the interpretation of texts
of the past presupposes that the present generic process of understanding is identical with the process operative in the past; further,
such interpretation also presupposes that within certain limits the
content of present acts of understanding can be identified with
aspects of the explicit or implicit content of past acts of understanding. Therefore, if we are to arrive at the meaning of past texts (the
meaning that existed in the men who authored them), we must
anchor ourselves in present understanding.[4] Present understanding
is the only existential contact we have with meaning.

To make it easier to follow the analysis I have divided it into a
series of twelve assertions that constitute the remainder of this
chapter. The succeeding chapter will indicate the results of this analysis and some practical conclusions that follow from these results.

MEANING OF HISTORICAL INTERPRETATION
AS IT AFFECTS THEOLOGY

1. *Uniqueness of Each Experiential Continuum*

First of all, *each man's experience, his personal experiential con-*

tinuum, is unique and practically incommunicable. In this statement "experience" refers to the actualization of any human potential. To have a discrete experience is to have actualized a combination of one's physical, psychological, intellectual, or volitional
capacities within the context of definable circumstances. If no capacities are actualized, then no experience can be said to have taken
place. Thus, a blind man does not experience sight despite all the
potential occasions for sight experiences that surround him.

An experiential continuum is the totality of actualization undergone by an individual during his lifetime. That totality is not the result of an addition of countless discrete experiences to an original
tabula rasa. Rather, it is the result of a cumulative development in
which the subject as constituted by his initial potential and modified
by all subsequent experiences is now further modified by the present experience. Thus, a person begins with certain basic potentials
that constitute him as a human being. At the first instant, these
potentials are actualized by an experience which changes the person
and his potentials. In the next instant, the already changed individual is further modified by a new experience; and the process continues indefinitely.

This account of the nature and genesis of an experiential continuum is a restatement and extension of the classical axiom that
"whatever is received is received according to the mode of the receiver." What I would stress, however, is that the quality of any
given experience is to be measured not just by the nature or basic
potential of the *kind* of individual involved (in this case, a human
being) but also by the past cumulative development of this concrete
individual. Thus, at the age of two a child can look at a motor;
thirty years later, after obtaining his degree in engineering, he can
look at the same motor. The two experiences are vastly different
because the concrete experiential continuum which is modified by
the same external reality is vastly different. In turn, the two experiences differently modify the experiential continuum in which they
occur.

It is apparent that a number of factors contribute to the development of each human experiential continuum. First, there is the basic
initial potential of the individual by which we denominate him as
human. This potential differs concretely in all due to genetic factors.
Secondly, there are the quality and quantity of the situations in

which the individual is placed as well as the order of those situations.[5] Thirdly, there is the internal response of the individual at each moment of his history to the external phenomena which confront him. To some extent consciously, and to a large extent subconsciously, each individual selectively responds to partial aspects of the external world that appear before him at each instant. Thus, the rabid football fan sees a beautifully executed tackle; his wife notes senseless brutality; or, because she recoils from violence, she consciously shifts her attention from the physical contact of the sport to the brightness of the players' uniforms. Fourthly, there is the effort of the individual with varying degrees of implicit or explicit consciousness to alter the shape of the external phenomena which reach him or her. The wife in the instance cited turns away from the television set and glances out the window. Fifthly, either concurrently with the experience of external reality or in isolated moments of almost exclusive introspection, there is a turning of the subject upon himself to make explicit his experience, to analyze it, to detect its unities, and to compare it with past experiences. This heightening of consciousness is in itself an experience that modifies the prior existing experiential continuum.

The combination of all these factors renders each man's individual experiences and his experiential continuum unique and incommunicable. No two men have ever faced the same external event in the same way; for their genetic constitutions, their present experiential continua, their conscious selectivity, and their degrees of internal awareness will markedly differ. No two men ever encounter the same sequences of external events throughout their lives. Because of the immense number of possible differences, it is statistically impossible for two concrete experiences or, *a fortiori*, for two experiential continua to be identical or even remarkably similar in their total concreteness. Hence no man ever feels concretely the way another man feels. No man can ever experience the life of another individual of his own epoch; much less can he experience the life of an individual of a past epoch exactly as it occurred. The result of all this is that each human experiential continuum is practically incommunicable as a concrete whole.

2. Experience as the Basis of Understanding

Secondly, *acts of human understanding are possible only on the basis of an underlying experiential continuum.* An act of understanding represents a grasp of the unities inherent in a given continuum. It is a differentiation of that continuum, a heightened consciousness of the relationships embedded within that continuum; and it deepens the quality of that continuum. Because understanding is an aspect of a concrete experiential continuum, it never exists apart from it. Thus, greater understanding inevitably implies either a broader and richer human experience or a greater reflective grasp of the unities inherent in similar experiences. Hence children, despite great native intelligence, cannot be made to understand certain complex human realities such as the adult relationship of love of husband and wife. They lack the kind of adult experiential continuum that would enable them to make sense of the verbal explanations of even the most articulate of parents.

3. Understanding Exists Only in a Mind

Thirdly, *understanding can, therefore, exist only within a human mind.* It does not and cannot exist on paper, stone, or tape. On paper, one finds only black marks; on tape, recorded sounds; on stone, chiseled indications. These are not acts of understanding; for they are not embedded in living experiences; they are simply means of representing or pointing to acts of understanding or to a continuum of experience that once existed in a human mind. Of themselves they are inert and lifeless.

Of course, I refer here only to the kinds of markings and sounds that directly reflect understanding when I speak of them as inert and lifeless. Recorded musical sounds and depicted shapes and forms on paper and stone, although they do not contain living understanding, are "alive" in the sense that they can provide the basis of an experience even to a man who has no prior understanding—something which words simply reflective of prior understanding can never do.[6] Thus, the word "dog" on paper or tape simply refers to an act of understanding in a mind, and that word has no meaning of itself apart from that act of understanding. However, a picture of a dog has direct experiential value for the human

being seeing it and indirectly has the value of provoking understanding through that experience. Similarly, a musical notation
carries no inherent meaning or understanding, but the recording of
a symphony provides an immediate experience for the present listener and through that experience the possibility of subsequent
understanding. To put this in another way, some indications on
paper and stone are largely only referents to past acts of understanding, and in this sense they have little significance apart from
those acts of understanding. However, there are other indications
on paper, stone, or recording that are more than referents to past
acts of understanding. They are also carriers of that understanding
in a more or less implicit way in some medium of experience.

4. Diverse Experiences Can Ground Like Understandings

Fourthly, *the same act of understanding can arise from a different set of experiences in the same experiential continuum or in
different experiential continua.* On the one hand, the same man
can come to the same conclusion or act of understanding out of
different aspects or sets of experiences in his own experiential continuum. It is this fact that permits a scientist to prove to himself
that his theory is correct; for the test of a theory is its capacity to
unify or explain varying sets of data. And this is only another way
of saying that the same act of understanding grounds each of the
sets. Thus, the only reason why one can test the so-called law of
gravity on earth is that the same act of understanding underlies the
free fall of various objects dropped from varying heights in a
vacuum. On the other hand, the same act of understanding can
ground different sets of experiences in different experiential continua. Despite the fact that each person is different and the accompanying fact that his experiential continuum is inevitably different
from that of his peers, it is still possible for varying sets of experiences in these varying continua to ground the same act of understanding. Because of this fact, scientific collaboration and generalization are possible. Different men with different experiential continua operating at different times and in different places are still able
to arrive at the same act of understanding as grounding our experience of the universe.[7]

What is here said of science also applies to everyday life. Despite differences in experience that are undeniable, it is possible for men to arrive at the same act of understanding. Though no two men have experienced the identical green objects, yet they can come to a common notion of "green." Though no two men have the same concrete experiential continuum, yet they can come to the same understanding of the process of abstraction. In both cases—the detection of the color green and the process of abstraction—there has taken place a heightening of consciousness that has underlined aspects of likeness in dissimilar concrete experiential continua.

Why is such common understanding possible? In the first place, men live in the same objective world although they face that world in different aspects and at different stages of its development. Though that world varies and changes, yet some aspects remain constant, as the search for invariant laws in the sciences implies. Secondly, though men differ immensely, yet they have certain basic similar capacities to be actualized; hence we can speak of them as belonging to the same race. Thirdly, in the various experiential continua that exist as a result of the encounter of individual men with the world, similarities exist amidst vast diversity. These similarities occur precisely because each experiential continuum is a product of the meeting of a similar world with a similar set of basic human capacities. Fourthly, each man has in varying degrees the capacity to highlight or underline aspects of his experiential continuum. He can abstract. Thus, he can notice that the unique leaf he holds in his hand is actualizing his capacity to detect color; he isolates, as it were, its greenness. Or he can review a mental process he has concretely undergone and isolate its essential recurring processes; and thus he grasps the process of abstraction. Fifthly, he can recognize that in the context of different experiences the same abstract element appears. He notes that other things are green besides leaves, and he abstracts greeness again and again in different concrete circumstances. Finally, he can begin to see that, just as he can come to the same abstraction on the basis of different experiences within his own experiential continuum, so too can other men come to these same abstractions on the basis of their different experiential continua because all the continua are the result of a meeting of common capacities with a similar world.

This explanation of how we can come to common understanding on the basis of different experiential continua clarifies a number of points. First, it demonstrates the truth of the axiom that we understand only on the basis of experience, that when we understand there is always a reversion to the phantasm, or mental image. In the present analysis all understanding involves a heightening of aspects of the experiential continuum; to re-understand is to heighten once more certain aspects of one's continuum. Without that heightening, one may recall verbal explanations of the past, but one is not actually understanding. Secondly, this explanation enables us to see how we go about classifying objects or experiences into categories. What we do is to advert to the fact that a certain group of objects or processes actualize the same set of potentialities within us. Subclassifications emerge in our consciousness when we recognize that some of the objects or processes within the larger group actualize in us a further common set of capacities.

5. The Meeting of Minds is Possible
Despite Diversity of Experiences

Fifthly, *it is the fact that the same act of understanding can be made on the basis of different sets of experiences in different experiential continua that grounds the possibility of a meeting of minds, of human communication.* If it is true that one's personal experiential continuum is unique and practically incommunicable, it must be recognized that there are abstract aspects of each man's continuum that *are* communicable. I do not mean, of course, that I can transfer my act of understanding (which is an aspect of my experiential continuum) to you. But I can utter sounds or write words you are capable of recognizing as pointing to an act of understanding that has taken place in you and in me. When that recognition occurs, then real communication has taken place. Unless that recognition occurs, however vaguely and implicitly, no significant human communication has taken place.

One may argue that we have no proof that we actually can make the same acts of understanding. One may say that we think we both understand "green" or "generalization" in the same way; but the fact is that we have no superior vantage point from which we can compare independently the two sets of understanding; we cannot directly prove by empirical methods that these acts of understanding are the same. Hence we cannot prove that communication is possible.

While it is true that we cannot place two acts of understanding under a microscope for comparison, we can still be certain that different sets of experiences can ground the same act of understanding and thus make communication possible. On the one hand, each of us is conscious of the fact that he has changed his experiential continuum and his personality over the course of his life. In this sense, each of us has been many different persons. Yet, at the same time, each of us can recall having made the same act of understanding from different sets of experiences occurring during many of the lives he has lived. On the other hand, our lives of attempted communication with others about what we have understood have led to vast external co-operative ventures involving an immense number of activities together. That these external activities succeed in producing a business that functions as a unit, an airplane that flies, or an intricate and detailed scientific explanation that actually makes sense to one's peers constitutes a cumulative proof that men do make the same acts of understanding, at least on a fairly frequent basis. If men did not make individual acts of understanding like those of their peers, it is almost a mathematical impossibility that enterprises requiring a vast number of acts of understanding contributed by different people could ever have any external effectiveness or coherence at all. The situation is analogous to that of the deciphering of a code in which some arbitrary symbols stand for the letters of the alphabet. One becomes certain that one has correctly identified the symbols with the letters precisely because a consistent replacement of the same symbols with the same letters leads to coherent messages in each case. In similar fashion, when the consistent assigning of given acts of understanding to the words and gestures of others leads to global coherence in case after case, we are assured that the constituent acts of understanding that enter into the global coherence appreciated by all of us must with illimitable certitude be the same.

6. Man Regularly Symbolizes All Areas of his Experience

Sixthly, *man regularly represents in words uttered and written, in sounds recorded on tape, and in marks on stone, his undifferenti-*

*ated experiences together with his acts of differentiated under-
standing.* These media are pointers to the continuum of experience
and the acts of understanding of the persons who produce them.
As they appear on paper, tape, or stone, they are not containers of
meaning, although in the process of their production they ordinarily
constitute an essential aspect of the genesis of meaning in the producing subject. They are simply signs of experiences and meanings
that exist and can exist only in a living person.

7. Each Man Possesses a Divisible Experiential Continuum

Seventhly, *man at each moment is composed of a continuum of
experience that can be divided into five basic categories.* First of all,
there is that aspect of his experience which has been explicitly understood. This means ultimately that there are unities within his experiential continuum that have been highlighted in a conscious manner. A man recognizes that his history reveals him to be lazy, inef-
ficient, tender, and observant. Each of these adjectives represents
an abstract conceptualization; each expresses a quality which characterizes a recurring aspect of his multifaceted concrete experiential
continuum. Of course, these conceptualizations may be erroneous
in varying degrees; they may not correspond fully to the actual
characteristics in the experiential continuum because the man has
not adverted to all the pertinent data within that continuum. No
man grasps himself completely in all the depths of his experience;
hence he never possesses all the data that would enable him to posit
with undeniable certitude the specific unities in his own historical
makeup. It would always be possible that advertence to as yet unexplicated aspects would demand a reconceptualization and a re-
finement of what is now posited as a unifying aspect.

In the second place, there is that aspect of a man's experience
which has not as yet been understood, although it could be understood and unified. This means within each man there is an area of
experience that is unifiable, although it has not yet been consciously
unified. It is this area which is manifested in human expressions
that body forth something "more" than the explicitly understood.
Such expressions are exemplified by the arts of painting, music, and
sculpture. They are further exemplified by moral activity, because
such concrete activity can never be fully explained by already

known and explicated principles; by symbolic language like that of
the parable, because such language always suggests further meanings; by conceptual discourse itself, because the words used in such
discourse inevitably connote more than the meaning of the concepts indicated. It is this area which constitutes the matrix out of
which a man makes personal discoveries about himself and the
world in which he lives. Thus, David grasped something of his own
weakness as a result of his conduct in the affair of Uriah the Hittite
(2 Sm. 11:1—12:15); and Archimedes was able to uncover the principle that bears his name as a result of a common experience in a
public bath. Without their personal past histories of unifiable,
though not yet consciously unified, experiences neither one would
have made such a momentous discovery. It is this area, finally,
which makes it possible for the psychologist to enlighten a patient
about his character and for the teacher to inform his student about
the world he lives in; for both the psychologist and the teacher
have as one of their chief functions the bringing to light of what is
already embedded, however concealed, in the experiential continuum of the person they are dealing with. Even when they stimu-
late their client to further activity and experience, the psychologist
and the teacher make use of the basis already existing in his experiential continuum.

In the third place, there is that aspect of a man's experience which
is *ex se* unintelligible. Because a man does not fully grasp himself
and because he never fully lives up to the demands of his actual
self-grasp by appropriate moral expression, the experiential continuum that constitutes his historical uniqueness is always more or less
disunified, unintegrated, and hence unintelligible. Each man is to
some extent a congeries of discrete experiences which possess no
total intrinsic unity. He is, as it were, a jigsaw puzzle ready to be
assembled; but the pieces have been more or less misshapen. No
amount of skill or intelligence on the part of the man charged with
assembling the puzzle can enable him to construct a complete and
perfect puzzle. Similarly, no Solomonic wisdom can empower a
man to understand completely an experiential continuum composed
of elements that are not unifiable; they are by nature un-under-
standable; they constitute a surd—an unintelligible element—that
at best can be grasped by an inverse insight that simply recognizes
that they cannot be understood and why not.[8] Finally, if this aspect of

a man's experiential continuum is expressed, it can only be expressed in fragmentary, suggestive, and mythological terms; and such impoverished expression can be overcome not by refining one's language but by rectifying the surd in one's experience that gives rise to such inadequate language.[9]

In the fourth place, there is that aspect of a man's experience that constitutes the dynamic process unifying the three prior aspects in themselves and in their relationships to one another. This process may be schematized briefly beginning from the third aspect and working back to the first. That which is the unintelligible surd of the third aspect can be rendered more unintelligible by further activity of a disunifying nature. However, by an activity that is more or less painful, one can straighten out the distortions in one's past experiential continuum; one can alter the pattern of one's existence so as to render ontically intelligible—that is to say, intelligible as an actual modification of the constituent objectivity of a person—those aspects in his makeup which had been unintelligible. Thus, what formerly belonged to the third aspect becomes transformed into the material of the second aspect. Finally, that which is of the second aspect because it is only implicitly intelligible can become of the first aspect to the degree that it is explicitly grasped and understood. In other words, there are a series of generic processes which to the degree they are implemented, unify the variegated experiential continuum that is each man.

Let me illustrate this process by a concrete example. A teenager is a congeries of unintegrated and unintegratable experiences. Even if he knew himself completely, he would not be able to see in himself a specific vocational direction. He is vocationally a "surd." This means that he has a potential for a number of vocations, but no one of them is clearly indicated by his present makeup as the one he will most easily fit into. However, because of the influence of others and his own free decisions, he begins to participate in experiences that so complement and develop what he already is that his experiential continuum accords well with what is required for the Christian priesthood. Thus, by his activity he has moved from the condition of being an ontic surd to that of being implicitly intelligible. When he explicitly grasps what he has become and sees that he is called to be a priest, he moves into the area of explicit understanding. This illustration, incidentally, does more than indicate the generic processes by which one moves from the third to the first aspect. It also shows that the term "surd" which I have used by no means refers to something negative. Rather, it refers to those aspects of a man's being that can constitute the starting point for the development of what is good and necessary. Its very unintelligibility produces internal pressure to complement it, and this pressure is one of the greatest forces for growth and change.

In the fifth place, there is that aspect of a man's experience that derives from a conscious recognition of the content of the first three aspects and the recurring processes of the fourth aspect. This fifth aspect is to be sharply distinguished from all prior aspects precisely because it constitutes a further level of abstraction in experience that, unlike the others, can attain the level of invariance and certitude. On the one hand, it is true that what has been explicitly understood may or may not represent a mistake in understanding; it is true that what has not yet been understood may be poorly understood subsequently and that there is no guarantee that it will ever be fully and correctly understood; it is true that man is forever a complex of experiences which always includes a good dose of the surd; it is true that the processes by which each man moves from the condition of being an ontic surd to the condition of a full grasp of possessed intelligibility are never perfectly implemented and results are never perfectly achieved. On the other hand, however, once we recognize that the above statements are, have been, and always will be true of man as we know him, then we simultaneously recognize a host of invariant and certainly grasped elements in recurring relationships and processes that pertain to man's developmental life. This fifth area is thus a precipitate of the other four. It represents the thematization of the recurring relationships and processes of the other four. It becomes more detailed and explicit, not by a conscious attempt to make deductions from general principles, but by long efforts at dealing with substantive issues coupled with subsequent reflection on the recurring elements that were employed or misemployed in those efforts. It is this fifth area that is crucial for the subject matter of infallibility and the development of dogma.

8. Many Conditions Govern Communication

Eighthly, *communication actually takes place between two human beings when a number of concrete conditions are fulfilled.* In the first place—and this is indispensable—there must exist in the receiver of the communication a set of experiences and personal differentiations capable of grounding the acts of understanding the communicator desires to impart. Thus, if I wish to communicate to you that a white bird has flown through the window, I must assume that you have had experiences grounding the notions of "white," "bird," "flying," "through," "window," as well as the notion of "past" implied in the verb "has flown." Similarly, if I wish to convey to you the geometric proof that the square of the hypotenuse of a right-angled triangle equals the sum of the squares of the other two sides, I must presume in you a differentiated continuum of experience and understanding that is acquired by the internalization of the succession of meanings imparted by Euclid in the various axioms and theorems that precede this theorem on the right-angled triangle. It follows from this that when the prior experiences and differentiation of understanding that ground what the communicator wishes to impart are lacking in the recipient, the communicator must first see to it that these necessary sense experiences and the succession of insights that furnish differentiation of understanding are provided. Thus a good catechist knows he must first structure certain sense experiences for the child before attempting to teach doctrine; and a good teacher of physics begins with sensible experiments and only gradually works his way up from lesser and restricted acts of understanding to the most fundamental generalizations that ground his science.[10] We have here one basis for employing real dialogue between master and student in all teaching; for even on the assumption that the teacher completely knows the subject to be imparted, he still cannot know *a priori* the degree to which the necessary experiential background and differentiation of understanding for his level of explanation is actually present in the student. Only the student himself can furnish that in some form of dialogue; past scholastic records are often insufficient to indicate the presence or absence of background needed to appreciate a given explanation.

What emerges from all this is that the ideal communicator is one who (1) understands well what he wishes to impart; (2) grasps the process by which he has arrived at that understanding; (3) knows through some form of dialogue where his audience is at; (4) sees what the audience lacks as prerequisites for what he wishes to impart; (5) is willing and able to work toward providing the audience with those prerequisites by creating a personal rapport with it, structuring requisite experiences, and encouraging reflection and (6) is skillful in articulating his understanding of the matter to be imparted in the receiver's language. Precisely because a communicator must possess these skills, in most cases a living man is ordinarily far more effective in communicating than a written text. This, of course, has significant implications for communication by historical documents.

We have been indicating that the first requisite for communication is the existence in the intended recipient of experiences and differentiated understanding capable of grounding the matter to be imparted. Thus communicator and recipient must possess experiential continua which, though necessarily different, are yet capable of grounding the acts of understanding that are the subject matter of the communication in question. Beyond this, however, there is the second requisite, the possession by both communicator and recipient of a common system of symbolization or expression of meaning. This means more than that both parties use the same sounds, written words, or gestures. It means that they employ these symbols as referents to the same acts of understanding. It means, at least for the matter to be communicated, that both parties possess the same language. By language I mean an existential commingling and association of internal meaning and external symbolization. Thus, to possess the same language as another is to possess both of the first two requisites for communication.

Where such a common language is not possessed by both parties through their upbringing in the same society, then communication demands either that (1) they create a new common language by an interaction that fosters development of a common symbolism and underlying experiential continua capable of grounding the same acts of understanding or that (2) one of the parties undergoes the difficult process of learning the other's symbolic system and developing the experiential continuum that will be capable of grounding the acts of understanding the other wishes to communicate. The present ecumenical endeavor is an example of the implementation of the first alternative; the interpretation of historical documents well illustrates the second. Of course, the schema here advanced is a simplified one. No two people ever possess the same language (in the sense we have defined it) in all particulars. Nor is it practically possible for two human beings to possess totally dissimilar languages. The common dynamic structure of man living in times that are never totally dissimilar precludes this. The process of developing a common language is *in concreto* always a process of moving from a relatively dissimilar to a relatively similar one.

The third requisite for communication is that the communicator actually symbolize and express acts of understanding that can be grounded in the experiences of the recipient. Two men may explicitly understand the same object or process; they may possess the necessary sets of experiences to ground the same as yet unexplicated act of understanding. However, they cannot know of this (and hence no communication between them can exist) until one of them externally manifests in some way that which he understands.

The fourth requisite for communication is that the recipient actually perceive the external expression of the communicator in its precise nature as a referent to a given act of understanding. The words spoken, the tone used, the circumstances surrounding the expression must be of such a nature that the recipient realizes in his own mind that understanding which the communicator intended by his expression.

9. The Process of Communication is Complex

Ninthly, *in the concrete, the process of communication is far more complex than a simple explicit grasp by the recipient of an explicit act of understanding intentionally expressed in external symbolism by the communicator.* This type of communication is attained at times, but accompanying it almost invariably are varying degrees of partial and implicit communication as well as areas in which communication fails. Moreover, there are instances in which real communication takes place without there being an explicit grasp of the communicated understanding by either communicator or recipient. In short, the effectiveness and explicitness of communication vary along a continuum. In the following paragraphs some of the more or less describable positions on that continuum will be set forth.

One possibility is that the communicator explicitly intends to communicate a given act of understanding but that the recipient, although he suspects or trusts that something valid is being expressed, does not fully grasp the meaning. At the same time, however, the recipient is being changed; his experiential continuum is being differentiated; he is becoming a man who can one day grasp what the communicator intends to express. Hence it happens that at some time in the future the recipient "discovers" what the communicator had intended to convey to him. Who has not been chagrined to find a brilliant insight believed to be his own spelled out clearly in a book he had read six months before?

A second possibility is that the communicator unintentionally manifests in his expression an intelligibility which is implicit in his experiential continuum but which he has not yet explicitly grasped. Ordinarily such communication and expression take place simultaneously with explicitly intended communication. Their possibility is grounded on two facts: first, the existence in each of us of areas of experience which have not yet been understood and unified but which can be understood and unified; and second, the fact that we betray much more of what we are than what we explicitly intend when we express ourselves in words and gestures. When such an implicit understanding finds its way into a man's expression, it is possible for an astute observer who possesses a relatively vaster horizon of meaning to make explicit something which the original communicator had not been able to make explicit to himself. It is this phenomenon which accounts for the psychologist's ability to grasp what has gone on in his patient before the patient himself can do so; it is this phenomenon which enables the historian to articulate the causal relationships of a bygone epoch upon the examination of documents written by men who had no express notion of these relationships; it is this phenomenon which enables the exegete to uncover the mind of a Paul or John in matters that never expressly crossed the living minds of these men when they walked this earth. I might add that I believe that this phenomenon partially accounts for the long-standing modern discussion about a *sensus plenior* of Scripture.[11]

A third kind of communication occurs when the communicator (as an aspect of a more comprehensive communicating act) actually expresses in his words and gestures some act of understanding that he has not yet explicitly grasped; and the recipient in turn attains only an implicit grasp of what has been communicated. The raw material of understanding, as it were, passes from one mind to another without being explicitly grasped and formulated by either. Such communication is far more common than we might think. It is a constituent factor in many close relationships of friendship and understanding that apparently have a very poorly articulated basis of union. It depends, of course, like all other communication upon the fact that the recipient has within himself sets of experiences capable of grounding the same implicit acts of understanding that are implied in the different sets of experiences of the communicator.

A fourth kind of communication is the simplest of all. It consists in the explicit grasp by the recipient of that act of understanding which the communicator expressly intended to convey. While this is the ideal of communication and while it is the type that most people assume ordinarily takes place, it is safe to say that it normally constitutes a very small aspect of concrete communication. Supporting this statement are studies which indicate that over ninety percent of the effective communication that takes place between two persons speaking to one another derives from their visual impact on one another and the feeling tone expressed in the sounds of their words.[12] The significance this has for the historical interpretation of documents, which by their very nature exclude the audible and visual aspects of communication, cannot be overestimated.

A fifth element of communication is error. By error I do not mean the failure on the part of the recipient to grasp all that the communicator expressly intends to impart or implicitly manifests in his global expression; for this is inevitable in all communication, and it is better called incomplete, rather than erroneous, communication. Instead, by error in communication I mean that the recipient either (1) assigns to the expression of the communicator an act of understanding not in accord with the act expressly intended by the communicator; or (2) misreads, at least in part, that which is implied in the concrete total expression (the sound of the voice, the facial attitude and gestures, the connotation of individual words and the succession of words) of the communicator, whether that misreading remains implicit in the recipient's being or becomes expressed by him in a concept;[13] or (3) errs by a combination of both (1) and (2).

Error is, therefore, a compounding of imperfect expression on the part of the communicator and a failure to grasp the import of that expression on the part of the recipient. Error in communication can be diminished or removed by the correction of one or both of these two of its sources. Such correction, as well as the filling out of incomplete communication, is best accomplished by the sixth element of concrete communication, dialogue.

Dialogue is really the summary process by which the various elements we have so far mentioned are integrated, complemented, and corrected. Through the interaction of dialogue the communicator can clarify what he intended to say by a variety of expressions; he can respond to the expressed incomprehension of the recipient; he can vary his words and phrases so as to make sense to his listener; he can, in the very process of attempting to articulate his meaning, come explicitly to understand that which was formerly only implicit in his own understanding; he can come to see the inadequacy and error of what he had once thought and expressed and he can correct or supplement his prior meaning. For his part, through the interaction of dialogue the recipient can make known what seems to him incomprehensible; he can suggest further lines of thought that will enable the communicator to modify his views; he can propose explicit meanings that appear only implicitly in the communicator's expression and ask whether his hypothesis is correct; he can point out what appears erroneous in the communicator's views and perhaps bring about a reversal of those views. Finally, both parties by their mutual interaction can come to explicit understanding of what previously had only been implicitly understood by them. In short, dialogue fosters not only the communication of meaning but also the growth in meaning that the parties have to communicate. Conversely, where dialogue is impossible because of subjective unwillingness or objective circumstances, the chances of mistaken communication, continuation in limited viewpoints, and incomplete comprehension are immeasurably increased. When dialogue is impossible, the recipient of a communication is forced to find within himself and his surroundings all the resources necessary to grasp another's meaning. The recipient cannot rely on the communicator to adjust and adapt his original expression to meet the inadequacies of the recipient's stock of meanings and capacities to grapple with expressions. Hence the student in the large lecture hall who hears a clear presentation by the professor invariably learns far less than what he would have learned by a relatively brief but personal dialogue.

The foregoing paragraph has restricted dialogue largely to the realm of explicit meanings and the correction of explicit meanings. However, there is another phase of dialogue that is easy to overlook and yet impossible to overestimate. This is what might be called the ontic-creativity phase. As we indicated in our seventh point, there is an aspect of a man's experience that is *ex se* unintelligible, which represents a congeries of discrete experiences that possess no total intrinsic unity. This surd in a man's experiential continuum, we indicated, cannot be rectified by a reasoning process; rather, it can only be straightened out by a pattern of activity that so fulfills the existing experiential continuum that it becomes intelligible and unifiable. Now it is in this fulfilling process that the ontic-creativity phase of dialogue plays so important a part. The concrete understanding and love of the partner in dialogue can be transforming, curative, creative. The manner in which words are spoken, the attitude expressed in tone and gesture, and the total living context surrounding verbal utterance all can have the effect of ontically changing the basic experiential continuum upon which the recipient's possibility of understanding rests.

Of course, dialogue only has the *possibility* of effecting this enlargement of inherent meanings and capacity for meanings in the partners who are communicating. In the concrete, interaction between persons may do little to foster their mutual comprehension. The sharing process may break down for any of a thousand reasons. What I wish to assert, however, is not the invariable success of so-called dialogues but the fact that without dialogue of some sort—whether directly or through an intermediary—the communicator can do nothing to make his initially expressed communication more understandable to the recipient. The whole burden of understanding is thus thrust upon the recipient and his resources.

10. Interpretation is a form of Nondialogical Communication

Tenthly, *interpretation of historical documents is basically a kind of nondialogical communication.* The communicator's meanings and expressions of those meanings are fixed once for all time. They cannot be developed, corrected, or transformed. Nothing that the recipient, in this case the interpreter, does can in any way alter that meaning or expression. The interpreter's task *qua* interpreter is (1) simply to approximate in his own mind the understanding that once existed in some way in a mind of the past, an understanding that in more or less adequate fashion has found expression in the text now before the living interpreter and (2) to express that understanding in a form that would make it comprehensible to other minds of the interpreter's time and culture. In this task the interpreter gets no living dialogical help from the communicator. Even when the interpreter is confronted by a series of texts that refer to the same events as seen by different authors (e.g., the synoptic Gospels) or when he possesses the whole corpus of a single author, it is a misleading metaphor to speak of the texts as being in dialogue with one another. Texts do not dialogue or confront one another. Rather, they represent meanings that existed in minds of the past or in a single mind at various stages of its development. It is surely an advantage for the interpreter to possess a variety of texts, just as it is an advantage for the detective to possess a variety of clues. However, neither texts nor clues dialogue with one another. Rather, by their multiplicity they permit the intelligent interpreter a better chance of divining the meaning that each clue or text represents in a partial way.

11. Importance of the Interpreter's Experiential Continuum

Eleventhly, *the present experiential continuum of the interpreter and his capacity to grasp meanings on the basis of that continuum constitute the total source of living present meaning and the basic starting point for his interpretation of past texts precisely because such interpretation is a nondialogical form of communication.* On the one hand, understanding and meaning exist only within an experiential continuum and therefore can be present only in a person and not on a piece of paper. The only meanings that at present exist are in the mind of the interpreter; they cannot be in the documents; for these documents are merely clues or indicators or representations of past meaning. On the other hand, the living meaning in the interpreter cannot be augmented, revised, and corrected by the text; for the text is inert and forever the same. If the living interpreter comes to grasp further meanings as a result of reading and rereading the text, it is not that the text has spoken to him but that out of the living source of meanings that stem from his own experiential continuum

he proposes a series of meanings that ever more closely check out as
the probable meanings of the men who authored the text. The text
does not talk back to the interpreter; it does not deny his views; it
does not give him understanding. To speak this way is to speak
metaphorically, and two thousand years of metaphorical speaking
do not make that speaking literal. However valuable and necessary
documents may be for the interpreter, their value and necessity are
not those of a source of meaning.[14]

12. The Interpreter's Experiential Continuum Must be Superior

Twelfthly, *the successful interpreter necessarily possesses in his*
being an experiential continuum and a differentiated understanding
that corresponds to the subject matter of the text to be exegeted; more-
over, his source of meanings as constituted by that experiential con-
tinuum and differentiated understanding must be superior to its
counterpart in the author of the text.

On the one hand, the interpreter's source of meanings must be
adapted to the subject matter of his text. This follows from all that
has gone before. It means that one must be a physicist if one wishes
to interpret a text of Planck or Einstein, and one must possess a philosophical background in order to grasp the meaning of Kant or Hegel.
Similarly, if one is to interpret accurately the life view of medieval
man as expressed in his writings, one must have experienced in
modern life that which can ground an understanding of medieval
man's values; and if one is to comprehend the Gospels, one must be
in contact with a living Christian tradition (whether that tradition is
verbally denominated "Christian" or not); for only this enables one
to possess in modern form the sources of meaning that permit a
reasonably correct exegesis.[15]

On the other hand, the successful interpreter must possess a personal source of meanings which, on the whole, is superior to that of
the author of the text. This apparently shocking statement, which
implies that a successful interpreter of Aquinas must be his superior
in philosophical understanding and that a first-class biblical exegete
must understand more about the Christian message than Paul or
John, follows from the specific tasks the interpreter must perform in
the nondialogical communication he is engaged in. I shall attempt
to illustrate three of these tasks. They correspond to the first three

aspects of the continuum of experience outlined under the seventh point above. A fourth task that does not pertain strictly to interpretation but is essential to the understanding of the function of historical texts will be added.

First of all, the interpreter is called upon to grasp and to express in modern idiom that which the author of the text explicitly understood and intended to express in his text. To do this the interpreter must arrive at the same act of understanding arrived at by the original author. Hence, he must become, at least for the matter in question, the equal of the original author in understanding. However, in order to arrive at this condition of equality, the interpreter must possess far more than the minimum experiential continuum and differentiated understanding necessary to ground the meaning expressed in the text. The interpreter is like a detective who has before him evidence in the form of words on paper. He proposes out of his fund of meanings various hypotheses in order to explain the evidence. If he is to be successful, he must have at his disposal a host of hypotheses, each grounded in his experiential continuum; and he must be so much in tune with the text that he suggests almost automatically those hypotheses that have a possibility of being the meaning of the author. Given the fragmentary nature of all textual expression, given that historical texts are written out of a social context which often differs markedly from that of the interpreter, given that authors frequently fail to take the time to express clearly what they understand clearly, given that the interpreter is not allowed to question his author in order to clear up ambiguities, it becomes evident that the correct interpretation of the explicitly intended meaning of the text requires superior understanding on the part of the interpreter. It is this fact, it seems to me, that at least partially accounts for the myriad interpretations of the great thinkers of the past. Agreement on the meanings directly intended by such a thinker could come only from a group of interpreters who individually had each surpassed him in understanding, at least in the area they were attempting to interpret.[16]

In the second place, the interpreter is called upon to make explicit that understanding which is only implied in the text, that is, that understanding which the author did not explicitly intend to express. It may be that the author did not explicitly ever come to a knowledge of what was implied in his expressed positions; it may be that, although he did come to grasp those implications explicitly, he never arrived

at the stage of putting that grasp in print. In either case, the task of
the interpreter is magnified. He is confronted with the necessity of
unifying by an hypothesis that which the original author either could
not unify, or did not unify textually. In the former alternative, the
interpreter arrives at an explicit meaning that never actually crossed
the mind of his author. In the latter alternative, the interpreter so
masters the actually expressed thought of the author that he is capable of detecting what that author thought but never expressed. When
one considers the difficulties that nondialogical communication
imposes, the feat of accomplishing either alternative is readily seen
as demanding an understanding in the area in question superior to
that of the original author. To be capable of making explicit what
was formerly only implicit always requires superior development
of understanding. Hence, it is only an adult who can clarify expressly
the meaning embedded in childhood; it is only a psychologist or his
equivalent who can lay bare the pattern evidenced by a disturbed
individual's behavior; it is only the trained sociologist who can
make explicit the dynamic relationships that countless ordinary
people live out implicitly each day; it is only the theologian of a later
and more sophisticated age who could hope to articulate the notion
of Church order that was implicit in the mind and activity of St.
Paul.

In the third place, the interpreter is called upon to complement
and correct that aspect of the text which reflects the *ex se* unintelligible aspect of the author's experience. As I indicated in the seventh
point, each imperfect man is to some extent a combination of
experiences that cannot be understood because they possess no intrinsic unity; they constitute a surd. Such a surd may be treated in
one of two ways by the original author. On the one hand, he may
give no explicit interpretation of it. In such a case, however, it will
generally be impossible for him to prevent the attitudes caused by
the surd from being expressed in his concrete action and in his explicit
thought and expression about matters related to the surd.

Thus, St. Paul made no explicit announcement about the permis-
sibility of the institution of slavery, but his actions indicate that he
thought slavery permissible. If the interpreter is to grasp and convey the meaning of the surd and the attitudes and activity that flow
therefrom, he must be able to complement the experiential continuum of the original author; he must be able from his own life and

experience to straighten out, as it were, the life pattern of a man of a prior age so that he can see at a glance why that man could not understand the question at issue and give an intelligible response. In the case of St. Paul and slavery, this means that the subsequent interpreter utilizes the long experience of the race with the institution of slavery to complement the basic Christian drives present in St. Paul. From his superior vantage point the interpreter can grasp why the institution of slavery is evil and at the same time why St. Paul could not see it as such. He can see that St. Paul had only a partial view of the elements of the problem; he can see that it is his own possession of further elements that permits him to come explicitly to a conclusion that St. Paul could not have come to even implicitly. And paradoxically, it is precisely the interpreter's possession of a fuller viewpoint that allows him to see that St. Paul's viewpoint was a partial viewpoint and why. In short, the attitudes and activities that spring from what is *ex se* unintelligible in the experience of another man (or of ourselves in the past) can be seen for what they truly are only by one who has attained an experiential continuum that is not *ex se* unintelligible in the area under discussion.

Up to now we have been speaking of the interpretation of what flows implicitly from the surd in the original author's experience. It is also possible for the author to make an explicit statement on the basis of that surd; and that statement will be in error; it will be an explicit attempt to answer a question when the author does not possess all the elements upon which the answer is founded. As in the prior case, the source of the error can be located only by an interpreter who grasps the elements of the problem that were not grasped by the original author.[17] In both cases of error—implicit and explicit—the successful interpreter can only be a man who possesses a personal source of meanings superior to that of the author of the text.[18] To be able to detect and explain error of any kind is to have transcended it.[19]

There is a fourth reason why the reader of a text must have a source of meanings superior to, or at least different from, that of the author of the text. This reason does not really refer to interpretation at all, although it has frequently been associated with interpretation by writers on the subject. I am referring to what might be called the "stimulative" power of classic and paradigmatic texts.[20]

It is a fact that the reading of the great texts of the past has aroused and stimulated the hearts and minds and hands of living men. These texts have not merely been a factor by which old meanings have been recaptured; they have been a stimulus that has provoked men to find new meanings. Because man is infinitely more complex than explicit grasp can ever attain; because the hidden depths of each man are affected, however unknowingly, by each new experience; because the suggestive power of classic events, even when reduced to ink and paper, is beyond all possible conceptualization; and because men who are aroused by contact with such texts tend to express in word and deed what they have become as a result of that contact: for all these reasons the great texts are an endless source of new acts of understanding and love. However—and this is the point we have been making—such an effect does not take place unless the reader already possesses within himself an experiential continuum that is capable of being stimulated by the text. Thus, to take an extreme case, if a child with minimal experience were to read the Scriptures from cover to cover, he would probably find that few new ideas had occurred to him. Texts, even the texts of the Scriptures, cannot provoke to thought those who have not the internal capacity to be provoked. The broader a man's experience, the more open his heart, and the richer his field of understanding, the more will a great text tend to be for him a catalyst of new thoughts, desires, and actions.[21]

I should note that the fourfold reason given above for the successful interpreter's need of a personal source of meanings superior to that of the author of a text is an obvious attempt to schematize and isolate elements that occur together. Interpretations rarely fit totally into one of the four categories. Normally, the interpreter operates out of a climate of problems that differs from the climate in which the author of the text operated. His questions are not precisely those of his author. Hence some elements of his question may have been explicitly treated by the author; others may have been only implicitly grasped; still others may have been unanswerable for him or incorrectly answered by him because of the surd aspect of his experiential continuum; and finally, it may be that with regard to still other elements the text can only be a stimulus to present thought.

Finally, it is interesting to note that the necessity of an experiential continuum in the interpreter for a proper grasp of the meaning of a text finds oblique support in the Scriptures and in Church tradition. In Acts 16:14, while Lydia is listening to St. Paul, the Lord touches her heart to grasp what he is saying. In 2 Cor. 4:6 we read that "it is the God who said, 'Let light shine out of darkness,' who has shone in our hearts to give the light of the knowledge of the glory of God in the face of Christ."[22] In Mt. 16:17 Peter is told that his recognition of Christ does not come from flesh and blood but from the heavenly Father. In John 7:16–17 Christ declares that the origin of his own teaching from God will be recognized by those who have been doing the Father's will (cf. John 5:38; 6:44; 6:66; 1 John 4:6). Further, there are a few long-existing traditions of the Church that suggest the existence of an internal experiential continuum. The belief that the saints are in some way instructed by God and not merely by human teaching, the notion of the *interior instinctus fidei,* and the continuing assertion of the validity of the *consensus fidelium* are quite pertinent in this regard. Though none of this proves the existence and necessity of what I have called the interpreter's experiential continuum, these indications do seem to point to a reality that in many ways accords with that concept; for they all point to a present transforming activity of God upon the existential person.

2

Implications

Three kinds of implications emerge from the analysis of the interpretative process conducted in the preceding chapter. First, there are implications regarding the basic function of texts of the past in the theological enterprise. Secondly, there are implications that bring to light a number of dangers and mistakes that can occur when one deals with the great texts of the past. Thirdly, there are implications which in practice affect the training of the text interpreter and the very nature of interpretive science.

BASIC FUNCTION OF TEXTS

Texts are not basically sources of meanings; rather, they are multi-purpose catalysts for the development of present meaning and understanding. A catalyst, it will be recalled, is an element that precipitates a process or event without being involved in or changed by the consequences. This notion aptly describes a text of the past. On the one hand, it remains the same yesterday, today, and forever; so does the continuum of meanings existing in the mind of the past which it more or less imperfectly represents. On the other hand, this never changing text continuously precipitates a series of processes in living minds without being involved in the changes worked in those minds. These processes lead to a continuum of results. Three of these are more or less interpretative. They involve the present appropriation of meanings which existed explicitly, implicitly, or marginally and erroneously in a past mind. The fourth result is a new creation stimulated by the text acting upon a mind fertilized by new and enriched present reality. In all four cases, the text functions as an unchanging medium or catalyst by which the experiential continuum and variegated understandings and judgments of the past change, differentiate, develop (and even confuse!) the experience, understanding, judgment, and eventually the action of the present.

DANGERS AND MISTAKES

1. Overestimating the Accuracy of Results

This analysis also reveals the source of some of the dangers involved in working with texts, in particular the Scriptures, when one is not aware of the presuppositions and mechanics of interpretation. The first danger or mistake highlighted is that of over-valuing the accuracy acquired by long and painstaking efforts to find the implicit and subliminal meanings at work in the mind or minds who authored the text. This danger is obviously present in the immense effort now being put forth by modern Scripture scholars. I should add immediately, however, that in calling attention to this danger I am in no way attempting to downgrade scholarly work or to resurrect defunct fundamentalistic and simplistic methods of the past.

This danger appears on the horizon once the directly intended meaning of a past text has been subjected to comprehensive study by the scholarly community. It is true that the meaning of the text has to be re-expressed in each age; meanings exist only in minds, and the ordinary mind of each age inevitably differs from the corresponding ordinary mind of a past age. Further, the present mind can be catalyzed only by a relevant modern expression. Hence there will always be need for exegetes to re-express past meaning in present terms. However, when exegesis is conducted on a large scale by numbers of highly qualified individuals working with relatively immense resources (as is true of the modern biblical enterprise), the directly intended meanings of past texts are soon expressed (though far more imperfectly than men realize) in modern idiom; and it is soon apparent that such directly intended meanings constitute but a small percentage of the total import of the texts. Thereupon scholars, such as modern biblical interpreters, begin to spend more of their time in bringing out the implicit meanings of the text, in ferreting out the subliminal understanding which bound together the thought of a Paul or a John and constructing the synthesis he never constructed. In short, scholars begin to move from working on the first interpretative function indicated above to the second and the third.

This movement to the succeeding interpretative functions can be dangerous in that the exegete can overestimate the accuracy of his results because of the great labors expended in order to attain them. It takes far more effort to construct a Pauline synthesis on the body of Christ or to discover what the great apostle meant by the resurrection of the Lord than it does to restate what he directly intended to say in any given statement. Despite the greater effort, however, the results are inevitably more problematical; in fact, the further removed a given set of meanings or a synthesis is from the direct intention of the author, the more difficult it is to reconstruct and the more doubtful is the accuracy of that reconstruction. There is rarely enough evidence to establish with certitude many of the implicit meanings of a Paul or a John, but there is always the danger that one will think one has reached such certitude because of the importance of the meanings so constituted and the difficulties involved in attaining them. The history of exegesis is eloquent testimony to the truth of this statement.

2. The Danger of Not Realizing
the Existence of Error in Inspired Authors

However, the second danger is even greater than the first because it is less evident. It is a danger that is often present with regard to texts that are considered normative by the exegete; concretely, for the theologian it is a danger that touches him in his work with the inspired Scriptures. I refer to the danger of forgetting, or never realizing, that the greater the extent to which the meanings one tries to uncover were subliminal and only indirectly intended by the ancient biblical author, the more those meanings, *even as they existed in the mind of the inspired author of the text, were subject to error*. This is true not only of geological, astronomical, and other presupposed nontheological meanings but of meanings that refer unquestionably to salvation itself.

Why is this so? Is it not possible that through the charism of inspiration even the implicit and subliminal meanings of Scripture that refer to salvation are all infallibly true? The answer simply is no. Nor is this answer supported only by the fact that we now acknowledge some implicit meanings of the biblical authors to be incorrect. The example previously used, St. Paul's views on slavery as an institution, would be an instance of this. Rather, this negative answer flows from the very nature of human understanding. Once one grasps that understanding and meaning exist only in persons, once one sees that every act of understanding and meaning represents differentiations and unifications of one's own experiential continuum, once one recognizes that the implicit meanings expressed in the totality of one's utterances are mere prolongations of the quality of that experiential continuum, once one acknowledges that by the very nature of his historically conditioned humanity a man is necessarily a bundle of unfinished and at times confused experiences, once one admits with modern incarnational theology that salvation is not concerned with a single aspect of life but is an integral part of every aspect of earthly existence—at that moment, one realizes how utterly impossible it is that the totality of subliminal and implicit meanings of any man, including the authors of the Scriptures, could be infallibly correct.

Of course, I have no intention of denying that there can be so-called infallible statements. I merely wish to indicate here that a *global* infallibility of meaning that would touch on every aspect and implication of a man's thought regarding salvation is impossible from the historical and developmental nature of man. To recognize this is to avoid the danger of thinking that one's painstaking efforts to reconstruct the implicit thought of Matthew or Mark, even supposing that one's reconstruction is correct, necessarily furnish us with unadulterated saving truth. It is to recognize, further, that the decisive confirmation of the validity of the implicit thought of the Scriptures cannot be furnished by the Scriptures themselves, but must come, if it is to come at all, from the subsequent development of meanings in the historical Church. It is to recognize the possibility, therefore, that in a real, if limited, sense tradition is superior to and a judge of Scripture; for it is the superior experiential continuum and the more differentiated understanding required of the successful interpreter (which, after all, is really one of the most significant elements of the living tradition of the Church) that alone can bring to light the incompleteness and the errors in the implicit meanings of Scripture.[1]

3. Believing that Scripture's Role Remains the Same Forever

A third danger, which is related to the second one, is the danger
of thinking that the role of Scripture continues unchanged in quality and degree of significance throughout all of history. In the first
place, the quality or the kind of contribution that Scripture makes
to the understanding and living out of the faith of the Church varies
with the passage of time. In the primitive epoch Scripture was far
more an expression of the concrete nature and understanding of the
Church than a catalyst for renewed and further development of
understanding. In the immediately succeeding years Scripture
tended to be a catalyst which stimulated Christians to arrive at
explicit and implicit meanings that closely approximated the corresponding meanings in Scripture. This followed from the fact that
the level of experiential development of the members of the Church
and the related level of society's cultural complexity and problems
varied very slowly. Even though the Church spread through milieus
and cultures that differed from one another, yet these milieus and
cultures in the early days did not progress to the stage where they
required explicit understanding beyond that articulated in Scripture.
Under such conditions (and, of course, this is only an approximation)
it was possible for the Church to accomplish its mission largely by
preaching the explicit meanings of Scripture; and theology could be
rightly said to be the science of exegesis. However, even by the time
of Nicea the development of Christian man and his culture demanded a shift in the role of Scripture. No longer could the explicit
meanings of the Bible suffice. It became necessary to make explicit
what was only implicit in the text. Hence there followed doctrinal
teachings on the divinity of Christ, on his two natures and one
person, on the presence in him of two wills, on the divinity of the
Spirit. None of these were explicit in Scripture, but they had to be
made explicit for an age that was confronted with the explicit questions they answered. Nor was this all. The slow developments
(and even retrogressions) of the dark ages gave way to rapid
changes in the Church's second millennium. The further complexification of society made it imperative that the Church should articulate not only what was implicit in Scripture but even that which
the men of Scripture did not possess implicitly. Scripture was no
longer simply a catalyst for the recapturing of old meanings,

whether explicit or implicit. It was more and more becoming a catalyst for meanings which were incorrect and incomplete in Scripture; likewise, it was more and more a catalyst which stimulated the discovery of new meanings hardly dreamed of in biblical times. In short, the role of Scripture has changed in the course of history. In the beginning, Scripture was an expression of meanings embedded in the Church's life. Later it served largely as a catalyst for the recovery of past meanings. Finally, it has become to a great extent a stimulator of new meanings. Thus, the passage of time has seen a gradual decline in the relative importance of the directly intended meaning of Scripture and a gradual emergence to importance of other roles for the sacred text. To recognize this is not to denigrate Scripture; rather, it is to recognize that we must avoid the danger of treating Scripture today just as it was treated a millennium and a half ago.

Understanding this change in the kind of role that Scripture plays in the Church helps us to grasp the change in the degree of significance Scripture has had for the life and theology of the people of God. It becomes evident that Scripture necessarily played a proportionately greater role in the theology and mission of the Church of the past than it can be expected to play today. In the beginning Scripture articulated the totality of meanings (practically speaking) present in the life of the Church. It was *the* text and *the* catalyst. It had no need of other textual catalysts. However, with the passage of time and with the development of a more differentiated experiential continuum through the pondering over and implementation of meanings of Scripture, the need arose to articulate newly emergent meanings. Hence there appeared the writings of the Fathers, theologians, and ultimately the proclamations of the magisterium. Moreover, in order that the definitive meanings reflected in these texts might be retained and subsequently developed, it became necessary that they, along with Scripture, function as catalysts for future ages. Thus, Scripture could no longer function as the exclusive textual catalyst but had to take its place in a series of documents that enabled the interpreter to arrive at the explication of the Christian meaning of his time by tracing its development from the beginning.

However, the significance of Scripture in the Church is not lessened simply on the grounds that it has to be complemented by other important texts. The sacred text is now of lesser importance primarily because it has gradually become a creative catalyst of new meanings. In this process Scripture is more a light that enables one to find meanings in the world than an expression of old meanings that continue into the present (though there are such meanings). This means, in turn, that the Church's efforts to understand itself and its mission must include an intense focus on the reality of its time with all its problems and its more differentiated meanings. If Scripture is more and more a light for theology that enables it to create or detect new meanings, then an ever increasing proportion of the Church's theological effort must be spent in coming to grips with the living reality that is the only possible source of those meanings. A source of illumination such as Scripture cannot fulfill its function unless the materials from which these meanings are to emerge have been properly assembled. This means ultimately that the passage of time will see theology becoming more and more empirical,[2] though it will never be cut off from the basic meanings expressed in Scripture.[3] Thus, most of the meanings in this essay come not from an analysis of Scripture or subsequent ecclesial texts but from a study of actually functioning human understanding and communication which emerged with the differentiation of consciousness accompanying man's recognition of his nature as an historically conditioned being. Similarly, principles relating to the exercise of freedom, to the purposes of the state, to the rights of newly developed nations with regard to the world's resources, and to the thorny problem of birth control do not spring out of Scripture but emerge only as the Christian, in the light of Scripture, confronts new and developing empirical reality.

4. Failure to Distinguish Various Functions of Scripture

A fourth danger is that of failing to distinguish an interpretation of a text from a new meaning stimulated by the confrontation of new reality with the text. This failure can lead to unnecessary confusion and to useless conflicts. The fact is that agreement on the directly intended meaning of a text is a distinct possibility because by definition such a meaning is that which the original author directly intended. If subsequent interpreters are diligent, intelligent, and honest, they can be expected to arrive at a more or less similar interpretation. For they are trying to arrive at a meaning that is fixed and determinate. However, as interpretation moves through the explication of meanings implicit in the text to the complementing and correcting of these meanings and ultimately to the use of texts as creative catalysts, it becomes progressively closer to impossible for different interpreters operating out of different experiential continua to utilize the same text in the same way. When a text is used as a light to enable one to interpret reality, then that text will lead to different meanings in accordance with the varying reality it is focused upon. Hence, it is inevitable that men springing out of different religious traditions and engaged in confronting different worlds of reality will see different creative meanings in Scripture. Moreover, it is possible that these different, newly created meanings may be correct; they may be appropriate interpretations of present reality that accord with the basic direction of biblical truth; they will differ, at least in some cases, not because one is true and the other is false but because they reflect different objective realities. However, if interpreters fail to recognize that the source of their disagreement lies not in a mistaken use of Scripture but in a creative use of Scripture which of its nature generates different results, then untold mischief may result. They may accuse one another of dishonesty, incompetency, and prejudice; they may restrict the exegete to uncovering the directly intended meaning of the text and leave the so-called speculation to the systematic (and unbiblical?) theologian. The first alternative represents a misreading of the problem; the second, a divorce of modern theologizing from its biblical roots.

5. Misunderstanding the Role
of the Study of Doctrinal History

A fifth danger is that of misunderstanding the role of the study of the history of doctrine for the modern theological enterprise and a consequent overestimating of the need to know each doctrine through its historical development. Basically, one studies the history of a doctrine in order to come to a present understanding of revealed reality which is in continuity with the understanding of the past. One can understand the past only to the degree that there exists in the present an experiential base capable of grounding past understanding, of making explicit what was implicit in past understanding, of correcting past understanding, and of making creative leaps in the light of past understanding. Thus, history is inevitably present-oriented. One needs to study history precisely because human understanding is cumulative, because one never understands an answer unless one has gone through the process of arriving at it. One does not become a mathematician by memorizing the answers in the back of the book, but by working out real problems; one does not become a physicist by learning the basic formulas to be found in the average physics textbook, but by going through the processes by which these formulas were originated; one does not understand a definition by committing it to memory, but by analyzing all the elements that went into it and their dynamic interrelations. The history of doctrine, therefore, is a manner of telescoping the actual process by which present Christian man has arrived at his present condition; it is the only way in which a modern man can actually retrace how he got where he is. Only in that retracing can he discover the concrete path the Christian Church followed in the development of its understanding of the Faith. Only in that retracing can the Christian attain the existential conviction that what he now believes is in continuity with what Christians of the past believed. The history of doctrine thus provides both present understanding and a realization of continuity with past understanding. It is, therefore, not simply a way to assure orthodoxy; it is also the only way in which modern man can realize in an existential manner his basic unity with the succession of Christians of past ages; it is modern man's way of concretely seeing himself at home in the Church of all ages, the communion of saints.

This analysis of the function and importance of history also reveals possible misunderstandings and overestimations of the role of history. On the one hand, it indicates that it is a mistake to think that history is simply a matter of articulating what another man thought in terms of his own time. Pushed to its extreme, this would mean that any given notion of the past need only be defined in terms of other notions of the past. Thus, if I would wish to understand historically the notion of "blip," I would have to determine that in the era under discussion a "blip" was equivalent to "two blops." While this would relate the notion to its own time, it would make the notion of "blip" and "blop" utterly incomprehensible to the present reader. He would know no more about the matter under discussion than a man who had totally memorized a German-German dictionary would actually know of the German language. One must root what one says about terms of the past in acts of present understanding or one says nothing meaningful at all. It is only because I can root the meanings of some of the words in the German-German dictionary in my own experience that I can actually make sense of the other words and ultimately use the German language. It is only in the measure that I can understand the meanings expressed in Scripture in terms of present experience and understanding that I can say I have interpreted them. In short, if history does not help me understand something of present reality, then it is not history at all. It is simply a word game in which terms like "covenant," "Kingdom of God," and "Messiah" are interchanged with other words.

On the other hand, this analysis indicates that it is possible to overstate the value and necessity of tracing the history of the development of Christian understanding as it unfolds in the succession of texts produced by the past. It is true that one can arrive at the terminal understanding of the historical process only by going through *a* cumulative development leading to that understanding; it is true that it is only by a study of the appropriate chronologically arranged series of texts that one can retrace the single actual process by which modern Christian understanding has emerged and thereby come to an existential sense of a development of understanding in continuity. However, it is not true that the only way a modern man can come to an understanding of Christian meaning today is by history. The very process that makes communication in general and historical understanding in particular possible also makes it possible for the same present understanding to be arrived at by a variety of concrete roads. Just as two men can come to the same understanding of the meaning of the term "generalization" by varied differentiations of dissimilar experiential continua, so too living Christians can come to understand the great faith meanings of today without following the historical path by which they were originally generated. The path to understanding is always a cumulative genetic process; it is not necessarily the actual path by which men (in this case, the Christian Church) historically arrived at a given understanding.

The key point is that the actual historical path to understanding is rarely the quickest and most efficient path. History is character-ized by duplicated efforts, false starts, and wasted endeavors which stem from the fact that at the beginning of an inquiry one tends to ask the wrong questions. Basically, the mode of historical under-standing is the trial-and-error method, and that method is exceed-ingly slow. Yet it is the only method available when one is striving to understand and articulate an unknown goal. However, once un-derstanding is achieved, it is possible to detect the false and useless paths one has followed and to discover more direct roads to that understanding. This is the essence of good teaching. The good teacher knows the terminal understanding to be communicated; he knows the present experiential continuum and understanding of the student; and he is able to set forth creatively the briefest path by which the student can move from where he is to an appropriation of the understanding and meaning that the race may have taken a thousand years to reach.

All this has practical consequences. It becomes clear that it is not necessary that priests and ministers be trained according to a labor-ious historical method in *every* aspect of their formation. They need to be brought to a grasp of the various doctrines by one of the many possible routes of understanding; but they need not reca-pitulate the actual history of the Church's developing thought in their own lives in each case. They have to be made aware of the nature of historical understanding as a necessary phenomenon in the Church's growth; they have to be given an existential sense that their understanding is in continuity with that of the past by a sampling of actual historical development in the case of a few selec-ted doctrines, but that is all. History, even the history of doctrines, is not an end in itself. Present understanding is the end. That end can only be reached through a genetic process; however, that process may be, but need not be, the actual process of history.

6. Mistakes About the Nature of Biblical Theology

A sixth danger is that of falling into mistaken notions about the meaning of biblical theology and biblical theologies. This danger may conveniently be exemplified (1) by exposing the inadequacies of a Christology that simply examines and articulates the meaning of the titles of Christ and (2) by indicating the incoherence of the idea that the normative Scriptures contain various theologies that cannot be reduced to one another or united in a single more complex theology.

A Christology based on titles examines the various designations, such as "prophet," "high priest," "Lord," and "Word," which are applied to Christ.[4] The work of the biblical scholar is "to elucidate the intention of the NT writers and the intention of the tradition behind them at its various levels. . . . The mythological christological titles and patterns of the NT must be translated into propositional form. These propositional statements will then be available for the systematic theologian. His task will be to work out the ontological implications of these statements in a systematic theology which will speak the gospel relevantly to contemporary thought."[5] In other words, the biblical scholar examines the text for what it means with regard to each title of Christ. When this meaning is set down in separate statement form, then the systematic theologian takes over and attempts to uncover the ontic unity that gave rise to the titles in the first place.

What this christological theory fails to realize is that any biblical theologian who really grasps the meanings that lie behind the various titles has necessarily grasped them in terms of the single experiential continuum that constitutes his own concrete existence. If he is not simply playing a word game, he must inevitably reduce meanings that originated in different men having different experiential continua to his own contemporary continuum. Now if this is accomplished and if the various titles thus understood actually refer to correct though limited aspects of the same concrete reality, the Christ, then there must exist in the mind of the biblical theologian a rich and at least partially unified view of the Saviour. In this perspective, it seems obvious that he is the man who should express in contemporary terms the more comprehensive and unified understanding of Christ that emerges from the documents that he has examined. To arrange his findings under various rubrics that were prevalent in the New Testament period and to pass these on to the systematic theologian is to imply that the biblical theologian has not really understood the ancient titles in terms of his modern experiential continuum, and this would mean that he has not understood them at all. If the biblical theologian *has to* rely on ancient categories and ancient modes of expressions in articulating his understanding of biblical reality, he is manifesting that he has not truly understood that reality.

It is true that the biblical theologian must begin with the ancient terminology; he must work out its underlying meaning by every device of historical scholarship. But once he has uncovered that meaning, he will have uncovered it in terms of his own modern experiential continuum. And when he has done that, he should be able to express his understanding in modern terms. Further, he should be able to express in a unified way the content of his total understanding of the single concrete reality the ancient authors grasped partially under their ancient categories. Because the meanings of disparate authors and of the same authors at different times all exist in the single mind of the biblical theologian; because those various understandings correctly if partially refer to the same reality (we assume for the sake of simplicity the inerrancy of Scripture, however much that doctrine needs to be qualified, as will be obvious from all we have said); because the human mind is driven to express the unity of the various understandings it has of any given reality: for all these reasons the biblical theologian who does understand his business will be the one to express that present unified meaning of the ancient texts. Certainly he will be the one best qualified to do it, because he has already done all the work of assembling the biblical meanings in terms of a single experiential continuum.

The same line of reasoning also indicates the fallacy of speaking of various irreducible biblical theologies, those of the Synoptics, Paul, and John. It is true that the various authors operate out of different and overlapping frameworks, that they use different terminology, and that they speak to different audiences. Once more, however, if I say that I can understand their various theologies, I am saying that I can understand them all in terms of my present experiential continuum. I am saying that I have managed to unify in my understanding what had been scattered among various men of the past. And if I postulate that these men actually had a correct though partial grasp of the same reality, then I must admit a potential unity in my own understanding of their theologies and the subsequent compatibility of their theologies. There could be only two possible causes of a discrepancy between different New Testament theologies: either one or more of the New Testament theologians were mistaken; or, I have misunderstood at least one of them.[6]

This does not mean, of course, that if I properly interpret all the New Testament theologies I will be able to construct a synthesis that unifies them all; for it may be that the New Testament information, even if it is assumed to be totally correct, does not furnish adequate materials for such a synthesis. Perhaps the New Testament is like a gigantic puzzle. Each book furnishes a few of the pieces. However, the totality of books do not furnish all the pieces; and without all the pieces the best of puzzle makers will not be able to furnish a complete picture. The conclusion of John's Gospel suggests that this is the actual case (John 21:25).

At this point the question may be raised about the relative functions of biblical, historical, and systematic theologians. If the biblical theologian is the man best equipped to give the current unified meaning of the content of the Scriptures, it would seem that the systematic and the historical theologian have been displaced. While the limits of the purpose of this section preclude an exhaustive treatment of the question, a brief answer can be given in terms of the fourfold aspect of interpretation which I sketched out under the twelfth assertion in chapter 1.[7] The biblical theologian would be, in this perspective, that co-worker in the theological enterprise who articulates in modern terms the explicit and implicit meanings intended by the writers of Scripture. In other words, the biblical theologians are primarily engaged in the first two interpretative functions. On the other hand, systematic theologians are specifically engaged in the work of articulating the enlarged meanings that have arisen in the Church as a result of (1) the correction and complementing of the meanings subliminally expressed in Scripture and (2) the emergence of new meanings through the application of basic biblical understanding to more complex modern reality. In other words, the systematic theologians are primarily engaged in the third and fourth textual functions. Further, the historical theologians are those who articulate the actual processes by which the biblical meaning has been augmented throughout history. They make possible the realization of the continuity of meaning between the biblical era and modern times. What links all functions together is their being anchored in the same presently shared experiential continuum that is the Church, their recognition of the same initial fund of meanings which were expressed in Scripture, and their acceptance of the same living Christian social process that has been the two-thousand-year history of the Church.[8]

SOME PRACTICAL CONCLUSIONS

1. Identifying the Initial Task of the Formation of an Exegete

The import of the preceding view of interpretation can be brought out by indicating the practical conclusions which it dictates. In the first place, this view demonstrates that the initial task of the theological-historical interpreter is not the learning of complicated exegetical techniques or the becoming familiar with the entire background of the period to be studied, however important these activities may be. Rather, the interpreter's initial task is the development of his own present experiential continuum in the area to be studied, his own level of theological understanding, and his own openness to further meaning. This is the fundamental requirement of every interpreter of Christian teaching, no matter in what area he operates. Specialization in the techniques appropriate for the study of documents in a particular area is of little value unless there has been such a prior present development.

2. The Importance of Confronting Present Reality

In the second place, this task of developing the interpreter's own theological horizon is not accomplished principally by working with past texts but by confronting present reality. On the one hand, this confrontation takes place at the scientific level. This means that the theological interpreter must come to grips with the findings of modern anthropology, psychology, and sociology (especially the sociology of knowledge), so that his own openness to possible human meanings reflected in past texts might reach the stage of explicit articulation.[9] On the other hand, this confrontation with present reality takes place at the practical level. This means that the interpreter cannot simply be the proverbial armchair theorist pondering over texts in his room. This may have been possible in a slow-moving age when the actual development and differentiation of human experience were so slight in one man's lifetime that his personal experience prior to becoming a theologian was sufficient to ground the bulk of his theological work from then on. In a dynamic age of personal change, the theologian himself must change and personally become more differentiated if he is to possess and internalize the findings of the modern human sciences which he studies.[10] Otherwise, these findings will become for him mere texts that represent word games and not catalysts for more deeply understanding the more complicated human experience that is his own. This means, however, that the scientific study of theology will require of the theologian that he be deeply involved in individual ascetic and pastoral concerns. In other words, it means that the same factors that once made saintly pastors the chief theologians of the Church have again appeared.

It might be objected that modern scientific studies and the development of a modern, more differentiated personal understanding are not necessary for the study of the science of revelation, a science whose object was fixed and determined in the biblical period. While I shall not reply in detail to this objection, I would suggest a few considerations to help the reader meet it. Once one has grasped that the revelation of God is not a series of statements but a person, God in the flesh, Jesus Christ; once one has admitted that this Christ is in his created nature no other than perfect man; once one sees that perfect manhood involves the realization of the immense possibilities of understanding and freedom that can be grounded in the human experiential continuum; once one grasps that the understanding of such a perfect manhood by another human being requires that this prospective interpreter possess as far as possible an equally comprehensive personal experiential continuum—then one begins to realize that the very notion that one could appreciate the scriptural revelation of Christ simply by exegeting the text without any attempt to develop one's personal fund of meanings is implicitly a denigration of the richness of the revelation that was and is Jesus Christ.[11]

Further, this emphasis on the primacy of the development of the interpreter's personal experiential continuum and fund of meanings through present study of men and present human involvement should not be taken as an assertion that the pondering of texts does not also contribute to the broadening of his theological horizon. Secondarily, but still quite importantly, it obviously does so. In effect, a cycle is set up. From an initial starting point in present ex-

perience the interpreter goes back to a text and discovers in that
process that he now sees further than he saw before; the text has
been a catalyst that has enabled him to see things in a different light.
This new vision now affects his mode of viewing present experience.
It directs him towards aspects he might not otherwise have seen; it
encourages him to make choices in life as well as research that he
might not otherwise have made; it leads, in short, to the development
of new present meanings by catalyzing life and thought. In turn, the
interpreter goes back to his texts with a new capacity to detect further meanings, propose new hypotheses, and complement and correct what is only partially represented there. And he may discover
deficiencies in present views in the light of the text. A grasp of this
continuing cyclical development indicates that even though present
scientific study and present human experience are of great importance
for the theological interpreter, they cannot replace his work with the
text or his exegetical skill derived from a long study of the period
involved.

Hence, in a genuine sense, the text of the past is a present reality
that challenges, judges, and stimulates the present interpreter. It
challenges him to find in his own experience the meanings he has
missed but which the great past saw as important. It judges him in
that it helps him discover the mistakes in thought and action that he
and the present Church are perpetrating. It stimulates him to new
experiences and to new acts of understanding which will enable him
to live out the enduring values of the past into the new context of the
present and the future. The text, then, is a reality that the individual
interpreter and the whole Church must come to terms with. It is the
chief verifiable link with the global understanding of the past; as
such, it facilitates the task of the present Church, especially in its
teachers, to be faithful to the past while going beyond it.

3. Theology's Task is to Propose Hypotheses to Unify
both Textual and Empirical Data

In the third place, theology is now to be viewed as a science whose
initial task is to propose hypotheses to explain data perhaps partly
textual but to a larger extent empirical. Theology thematizes the elements present in the faith reality which exists in the Church owing to

its contact with the living risen Christ across the two thousand years of its history.[12] Because this faith reality exists in the present, present religious experience constitutes the most readily accessible data for theology's hypotheses. Because, and to the extent that, this reality existed in the past and was expressed in texts, it endows the texts which represented it with their license as data that can be understood from the vantage point of the present. Further, there is continuity in the revelational process owing to (1) the enduring presence of the risen Christ and (2) the sameness of the understanding process which enables persons with different experiential continua to make the same act of understanding across the ages. Because of this continuity, it is possible to combine data of past texts and present experience in the construction of a single theological framework. The key element of data is, of course, the present experiential continuum and the present differentiated fund of meanings of the theologian. Without these, the past as represented in texts is forever an indecipherable book.

The foregoing three conclusions might be summed up by saying that theology must now cross a threshold that natural science crossed centuries ago.[13] It must recognize that it derives its basic data from the present and that its primary task is to explain and unify such data. Texts are of significance only insofar as they enable the experience and understanding of the past to be tapped as aids to our understanding of the present. Just as the natural scientist makes use of the reports of the great men of the past as guides to his examination of present natural reality, so too must theology use its treasured texts as catalysts for unlocking the present reality of faith. Once Christians fully realize that God is a living God, that Christ is a living risen Christ, and that theological formulations can only have meaning insofar as they are anchored in a present living faith, the primacy of present faith reality in the theological enterprise will be assured.

Part Two

Infallibility

Introduction

The purpose of this part is to indicate the function in the Church of the (1) existence, (2) explicit understanding, and (3) expression of the universal meanings that constitute its continuing essential nature. An effort will be made to demonstrate that what has been classically called "dogma" and "the infallible pronouncement of dogma" are not simple extrinsic privileges dreamed up by apologists of a triumphalizing tendency but an inner aspect of salvation itself.[1] The discussion falls into two unequal parts: the chapter that follows contains a treatment of (1) universal meanings, (2) infallible understanding of such meanings, and (3) subsequent expression of these meanings as understood at what I shall call "the simple experiential level." All the remaining chapters apply these three notions to the experiential-witness level that constitutes the Christian Church.

The Simple Experiential Level 3

By the existing order I refer to the total network of relationships that *can* unite present flesh-and-blood persons with the surrounding world and the Creator. This existing order is always partially *in actu* and partially *in potentia.* A baby achieves the relationship of gravity to his environment; he does not yet achieve the additional relationship to the world about him that begins to exist when he expressly understands that world. Further, in a primitive civilization the relationships of man to environment are relatively simple. With the passage of several millennia, many more possibilities of the existing order may be achieved—possibilities for both good and evil. Thus, one can say that in general the history of each individual and of the race is marked by an increasing achievement of the possible relationships of the existing order due to the cumulative effects of man's experiences (especially that experience which is understanding) and his creative shaping of his environment. Because man never exhausts the further possibility (1) to experience and shape his environment, (2) to change his experiential continuum by this experiencing and shaping, and hence (3) to change in his total relationship to the environment, there are always further possibilities of achievement in the existing order. Hence the definition of the existing order as the total network of relationships that *can* unite present flesh-and-blood persons with the surrounding world and the Creator points to a never-to-be-achieved goal that can only be approached asymptotically over the whole history of the race.

For the Catholic Christian the risen Christ is part of the existing order. As such, he affects the whole of that order. However, except for those who (1) have received the Christian witness concerning his universal presence and activity and who (2) act upon that witness, his presence is not recognizable as affecting the experiential continua of men in that order.[1] Accordingly, I shall speak of these men who are untouched by the recognition of the existence of the risen Christ as living at the *simple experiential level.*[2] I shall refer to those men who both live in the one existing order and recognize the risen Christ through the Christian Tradition as living at the *experiential-witness level.* Both kinds of individuals, of course, live in the same order; for only one order exists. However, the manner in which they envision that order radically changes their experience within it. It is this difference in respective experiential continua that grounds the distinction I am making between the *simple experiential level* and the *experiential-witness level.* In turn, the difference in experiential continua grounds different possible kinds of understanding and ultimately differences in infallibility.

In the present chapter I will treat of the understanding and infallibility possible to those who live at the *simple experiential level.* In the succeeding chapters I will take up the understanding and infallibility possible to those who are living at the *experiential-witness level.*[3]

UNIVERSAL MEANINGS

1. Notion of a Meaning

What is meant by a universal meaning? First, we must ask what a meaning is. As an initial approximation, let us say that a meaning is a unified differentiation of the experiential continuum that potentially or actually may be consciously understood. A meaning is thus a quality of human experience in the world by which that experience is divided and subdivided, sectioned off as it were into underlying unities, removed from the condition of being a totally disconnected stream of consciousness. As a result of experiences, a man more or less adverts to unities in his awareness, to an interrelationship of aspects of his consciousness, to a sense of direction or integration in his being. That awareness may be reflexive and explicit; or it may lie beneath the surface and exist subliminally, though it can be called to explicitness by the articulation of another or by one's own conscious efforts to understand.

2. Existence of Meanings

The existence of meanings in the sense just described cannot be proved by rational arguments. It is a datum of consciousness that each man can verify simply by looking into his own self. Further, the extent of meanings varies from one man to another in quantity, in quality, and in overall integration. For primitive man meanings are few, comparatively simple, and generally fairly well integrated. For the intelligent and well-educated modern man meanings will be numerous, specialized, and cumulative. They will be numerous because modern man has a far broader fund of experiences, largely due to immensely improved travel and communication and a far greater occasion to reflect on and differentiate his experiences through increased opportunities for formal education and leisurely reflection. They will be specialized because in a complicated and advanced society available meanings are so vast that no man can possess them all; practically, this means that one must limit the field of one's meanings; and since it is both easier and more economically advantageous to concentrate on the interrelated meanings that constitute a specialization, meanings tend to become specialized. Finally, in modern society meanings are cumulative. This follows from the innate drive in man to unify his meanings, to tie them together. The mind cannot hold together more than seven meanings (give or take two) at once. Therefore, when the number of meanings increases, there is a tendency to unify lower-level meanings by upper-level ones. These upper-level meanings can be called "cumulative" because they subsume and unify meanings at lower levels.[4] Such cumulative meanings are exemplified by the great generalizations of the sciences.

It is the existence of numerous, specialized, and cumulative meanings that constitutes the matrix of modern man's possibility of richer meaningfulness or utter absurdity. On the one hand, the richness and complexity of these meanings can lead to a fuller and more meaningful life when they are integrated and seen personally as facets of a single master meaning. On the other hand, that very richness and complexity may be lacking a single unifying thread; in this case, the very superabundance of meanings leads to a consciousness of utter meaninglessness and absurdity.

3. Notion of Universal Meanings

If meanings undoubtedly exist, it is another and further question to ask if there are universal meanings. By a universal meaning I refer to a meaning that exists or can exist as a moment of legitimate and necessary human development in every man of every age and culture. It will be evident to all from this notion that a universal meaning is intimately concerned with human development. In fact, human development is mainly the process of realization of ever more complex and differentiated meanings. What distinguishes the mature adult from the child is not so much the physical growth he shares (though in a human mode) with the plants and animals, as the growth in number, quality, complexity, integration, and explicitness of meanings. Further, not only does this development of meanings characterize the growth of the individual; it also characterizes the progress of the race. It is the fact that man accumulates meanings from one generation to another that has enabled him to develop complex and advanced cultures from primitive ones despite a physical makeup that has remained practically the same for centuries and even millennia.

Thus, to ask if there are universal meanings is to ask if there are aspects of human development that are common to all men. Of course, such a question would not imply that any such universal meaning would be realized *de facto* in all men. It is obvious that infants and primitives and utterly confused people will not realize many meanings proper to a modern adult. When we speak of universal meanings, we refer to *potential* human developments that would be realizable by all men if their root capacities and exigencies were fully developed. Hence the assertion of universal meanings does not entail the assertion that such meanings universally exist; nor does it entail the notion that all meanings are universally realizable or even that all meanings are coherent in themselves or with other meanings. The assertion of universal meanings merely implies that there are some differentiations of consciousness that would constitute a possible and ultimately necessary aspect of the full development of the potentiality of all men.

Such universal meanings would obviously be abstract; for the total meaning of any concrete situation in all its particularity and immediateness could not be of developmental value for all men. Though it may be true that at three in the afternoon on this day in August I am sitting at a typewriter in Burlingame, California; though it will always be true that at this specific time I sat at the typewriter; yet the concrete aspects of my sitting can have no universal value for all men of all times. What can have universal value is some abstract relationship in the given concrete situation which delineates a good and realizable possibility of development of all men. Thus, insofar as my typing represents an effort to communicate myself to other men, it represents an aspect of human existence that has been and always will be (at least, in Christian thought) a good and possible characteristic of the development of all men.

This does not mean that all abstractions are sufficiently broad and significant to merit being called "universal meanings." Many abstractions have applicability only in a given social context or a given culture. Thus, covenant as a global concept had significance in certain Semitic cultures of ancient times; it is doubtful that this concept has universal applicability, as many a modern catechist will attest. (Of course, I do not mean to deny that there may be a more generic notion and meaning true for all cultures that happened to be expressed in biblical times by the particular and culturally conditioned notion of covenant.) There are levels of abstractions and meanings, and only a few of these attain universality. This distinction is brought out by Bernstein, who says:

> Historically, and now, only a tiny proportion of the population has been socialized into knowledge at the level of the metalanguages of control and innovation, whereas the mass of population has been socialized into knowledge at the level of context-tied operations. . . . This suggests that we might be able to distinguish between two orders of meaning. One we would call universalistic, the other particularistic. Universalistic meanings are those in which principles and operations are made linguistically explicit, whereas particularistic orders of meaning are meanings in which principles and operations are relatively linguistically implicit. If orders of meaning are universalistic, then meanings are less tied to a given context. . . . Where the meaning system is particularistic, much of the meaning is imbedded in the context of the social relationship. In this sense the meanings are tied to a context and may be restricted to those who share a similar contextual history. Where meanings are universalistic, they are in principle available to all, because the principles and operations have been made explicit and so public.[5]

4. Existence of Universal Meanings

Are there universal meanings?[6] Are there differentiations of consciousness that are possible to and necessary for the mature development of all men in this concrete world? To establish this directly one would have to examine all the meanings in all the persons who ever lived—an obviously impossible task. However, there is a manner of establishing the existence of such meanings indirectly by indicating that they are a necessary postulate of ordinary human existence and specifically of the communicative process that human existence presupposes and demands. I have already indicated the grounds of this assertion in the first part of this work which treats of interpretation. If man can grasp the meaning of another time and place, then there must be some common underlying meaning that makes this grasp possible. If, in principle, every man can grasp something of the civilization and meaning of every other man of every other culture, then there must be some underlying common and universal meanings or the possibility of developing such meanings. It is only because we implicitly accept universal meanings that we instinctively think history and communication with our fellow men obviously possible. Of course, some erudite scribe may deny the possibility of communication. In this case, however, we would be justified in dismissing his arguments. For how could we have communicated to him our position, and how could he communicate his arguments to us, if communication is impossible? The attempt to communicate that communication is impossible or that the necessary ground of communication is nonexistent does no more than identify the essential incoherence of the person making the attempt.[7]

Yet there is a strong objection to the existence of universal meanings, an objection that would appear to attack the very possibility of history. This objection stems from the developing nature of man. Man, it would appear, is open-ended and unfinished. Nothing he ever is or achieves is fixed and permanent. His experience changes, complexifies, differentiates. To the extent that he lives up to his humanity, he grows and goes beyond all that he was. With the passage of a long period of time we can expect the total sum of man's meanings to be so altered that, practically speaking, no meaning can be called universal.

This argument has an element of truth about it; paradoxically, however, the very truth of the argument provides the key to the kinds of meanings that truly are universal. It is a fact that practically all the truth that is in concrete men and situations *is* provisional. Only a final concrete reality that was absolutely unchangeable could be totally universally true. The more a being changes, the more its intelligibility and its meanings alter, the more its truth must be said to be provisional. However, once one grasps that man is a creature of continuity who builds upon his past, and once one sees that the process of developing his potentialities in contact with the surrounding world is an endless process that flows from man's open-endedness, then one also begins to grasp some of the universal truth that can be stated of every man. For that very changeability and open-endedness is universal; that very relatability to all of creation is universal; that very need to be expressing one's potential is universal. Furthermore, the generic processes by which man's potential for change and relatedness takes place are also universal. Man endlessly experiences, fails to grasp all that he has experienced, provisionally understands, judges, decides, implements his decisions. By these processes he continuously changes. Hence, though concrete meanings change, the meta-meanings and the universally recurring processes that govern these concrete changes do not in themselves change.

INFALLIBLE UNDERSTANDING

1. The Notion of Human Infallibility

A further question is the possibility of infallibility. Can human beings grasp with certitude that certain meanings exist? If such an infallible grasp is possible, then about what objects can it be exercised and under what conditions can it take place?[8]

First of all, it must be clearly understood that the certitude and infallibility about which I am speaking cannot be something absolute. There cannot be a human infallibility that would exist without limitations, that would know, for example, that things could not be otherwise. Infallibility of understanding in an unlimited sense belongs to God alone. Human infallibility, as with all human acts, exists in a human subject and therefore is subject to human limitations. God's infallibility is identical with his nature. He could not communicate his infallibility to any man—even to the most perfect of men—unless he could make that man literally God in nature. All that can be communicated to men is what is receivable by human nature. Hence, if there is a created infallibility, it must be in

accord with the limited finite creature that is man. It must be a finite and limited infallibility.

What this means is that human infallibility in knowledge really
refers to judgments on self and the universe that are coextensive
with one's self-affirmation. No man can be more certain of anything than he is of his own self-awareness. The standard or limit of
human certitude and human infallibility is that consciousness which
one has of himself. Whatever is necessarily implied in that self-
acceptance can therefore be asserted with the same degree of certitude as that self-acceptance. And this is what is meant by being
infallibly certain.

2. What cannot be Infallibly Understood

The difficulty arises when we attempt to pinpoint those implications that necessarily follow from self-affirmation based on self-
awareness. Various candidates for the objects about which man can
be infallible may be advanced: human experience, human judgments on concrete facts, human generalizations about the nature
of the material universe, and human generalizations about the way
man acts as an individual and as a social being living in a concrete
context. I shall examine each of these candidates for the object of
infallible understanding in turn, and I shall attempt to indicate
why none of these can be so grasped as to be infallibly asserted.

Can concrete human experience be infallibly grasped? In the
first place, we cannot make infallible assertions about the objects
of concrete human experience. By experience I refer to an aspect of
all that I do. When I touch, talk, conceptualize, judge, or perform
moral activity, I am experiencing. I am actualizing a potential. In
this sense, experience is nothing other than that which happens to
me and changes me in the process of all activity; it is that aspect
which grounds my self-awareness, which exists even though I am
not explicitly aware of it; it is the realization of self even in those
instances when that realization is unthematized; it is thus a universal aspect of man, something present in all he does; it is coextensive
with life. Experience is thus the actualization of any human potential.

Although I can be certain that I am an experiencing being, I can
never be certain of the quality of the objects of any concrete experience. Error looms inevitably as a possibility not in awareness of

generic experience that is identical with my self-affirmation, but in the more or less explicit understandings that unify the elements of my concrete experience with themselves, with outside sources, and with past experiences. Thus I am aware of myself as one experiencing change. Suppose, however, I judge that the change is *caused* by a well that appears on the horizon. Actually, the well is only a mirage. The point here is that there is no such thing as raw and undifferentiated experience of reality, so-called brute experience. A measure of interpretation is always supplied by the experiencing subject. That interpretation of experience constitutes at once the possibility of diverse concrete experiences by different subjects in the same exterior situation and the occasion for error.[9] It is this type of analysis that leads to the Heideggerian denial that the adequation of the mind to concrete reality is the primary kind of truth. What comes first in this kind of analysis is the existential subject and his openness to being. However, that initial openness falls into error as soon as man begins to dissect and particularize knowledge while moving out of the broad awareness of the mystery of being. All specific knowledge is inevitably shot through with error because it involves a narrowing of the authentic vision of man as open to being as such. The unfolding of being is at once the dissimulation of being. Put in other terms, the nature of man as a creature of total relatability to being necessarily makes any specific kind of knowledge erroneous; it is the error of missing the forest because of the trees. Truth cannot lie in the experience or knowledge of specific beings but only in the undifferentiated openness to being.[10]

If this line of reasoning makes questionable any infallibility with regard to aspects of objects of specific human experiences, its extension would render impossible an infallible judgment about the nature of a concrete object or situation as a whole. Any given object or situation has an untold number of facets. The pencil before me has size, shape, color, a given quantity of lead of a certain quality, and a history. To render an accurate judgment on its place in the scheme of things would require a knowledge without gaps, a veritable omniscience. Even more difficult would be the evaluation of a given human situation. While this does not rule out practical infallibility regarding specific aspects of a given object or situation, it does eliminate the possibility of an infallible global judgment regarding such situations or objects.

Can the objects of natural science be infallibly grasped? The larger generalizations of science about the nature of the material universe and its evolution are no better candidates for infallible pronouncements. These generalizations are based on large amounts of data. They reflect the effort of scientists to grasp the unity of the material universe within a single formula or group of formulas. However, they can be no more accurate than the adequacy of the data upon which they are based. Since no one can ever be sure that all the pertinent data have been acquired, there is always the possibility that new data may overthrow the old generalization. Thus, the master generalization of Newton on gravitation was replaced by the Einsteinian notion of relativity; nor is the end in sight, as the questioning of relativity in this century indicates. In fact, the history of natural science has largely been one in which the master generalization or paradigm of each science has seen a succession of replacements. Hence, all such generalizations are tentative and subject to revision. Even if correct, they could not be known infallibly as such because the possessor of that kind of knowledge would have to know with certitude that he was in control of all the pertinent data, a control that could be had only by an omniscient being.[11]

Can man's individual and social nature be infallibly grasped? Finally, man cannot be infallible in his generalizations about himself and his concrete operation as an individual and as a social being. Psychology and sociology are strangers to infallibility to an even greater extent than the natural sciences. Their unifying explanations of continually recurring human phenomena—e.g., defense mechanisms, group processes, and the reactions of minority groups—face the same difficulty of lack of certain knowledge that all the pertinent data are possessed. Moreover, they are faced with two additional difficulties. The minor difficulty has to do with the complexity of their data. It is relatively simple to isolate and measure factors in the material universe and to propose hypotheses to unify those factors; however, a human person and human society are incredibly complex, and it is much more difficult to isolate a single aspect of that complexity because of the manifold interrelatedness of each human quality with other qualities. The major difficulty has to do with the variability of the data. In the natural sciences the data remain the same, by and large, century after century. Hence the experiment by Archimedes two thousand years ago is still valid. In the human sciences, however, the data change because mankind, in which the data are embedded, changes. The results of an experiment made with groups of people twenty years ago may no longer be applicable to a modern group because people have developed and complexified since that time. Further, the difference in data that can be noticed in people of the same culture over a period of time can also be noticed by comparing the data of different cultures. Man simply is not so homogeneous as the subjects of material science tend to be.

Actually it is the recognition of the increased complexity and variability of human data by scientists that accounts for the later emergence of psychology and sociology as scientific disciplines. (Some would still debate their stature as sciences, of course.) Scientists like to work with manageable data, with what can be precisely weighed, measured, and analyzed. They deal with problems, not in proportion to their intrinsic importance for the human race, but in proportion to their solvability. Hence, astronomy and physics emerged before chemistry; chemistry became a reputable science before biology; and biology antedated psychology and sociology as an acknowledged discipline. The later emergence of the two human sciences is thus a good indicator that they are not apt sources for infallible information.

3. Universal Meanings

The sole possible object of human infallibility. Paradoxically, the above analysis indicating the impossibility of infallible judgments with regard to the concrete universe manifests that there is a sense in which the human mind is infallible. For the difficulty in every case is the impossibility of acquiring certitude that one has all the data pertinent to the question asked. The implication is that should all pertinent data be furnished, then man would be infallible. This explains why man is regularly infallible in mathematics, in which the condition is fulfilled, the data being simply given. This explains, too, why infallibility becomes an ever more distant impossibility as one goes up the scale of being; for the higher the being, the more complex the data and the more unlikely that they will be complete. Finally, this explains the purpose of communal effort and dialogue in the solving of problems. The purpose of such interchange is not to swap conclusions or to vote on a middle-of-the-road position; rather, it is to permit the emergence of all the pertinent data by encouraging a climate in which all views are expressed and all data behind the various views attended to.

Where then can infallibility be operative in the present universe, if at all? Having eliminated other possibilities, I would like to suggest that infallibility can exist only with regard to what I have called universal meanings. It is only these meanings that can be reflexively grasped and identified with certitude; further, it is only these human meanings that can be effectively communicated to everyone in such a way as to be seen to be infallibly true. Such meanings are the sole recurring locus of infallibility possible to man in the present condition.

On the one hand, it is possible in principle for such meanings to be effectively grasped. The very notion of these meanings indicates that they are *universal* and *subjective*. In that they are *universal*, they are present in every instance of knowing; they represent the invariant features of every process of human development, including the knowing process; they refer to the relationships and processes which do not change, although the concrete meanings that emerge from their implementation continually do. In that they are *subjective*, they are not simply present as aspects of the material world, but rather they represent enduring qualities of all subjects who encounter that world. The coexistence of *universality* and *subjectivity* in these meanings makes possible their being grasped infallibly. For one and the same human subject can detect these meanings as present in all his operations as a subject. He can see that they are embedded in all that he does, in all that he experiences.[12] Hence he can be as certain of them as he can be of the experiences whose acceptance constitutes his self-affirmation. Since this kind of certitude is the measure of human infallibility, he can be infallibly sure of them. He can reflexively grasp and identify them with certitude.

On the other hand, these truths can be infallibly communicated to others so as to be seen infallibly to be true. That communication is possible precisely because the very meanings involved already exist in a more or less implicit manner in the universal audience of men. What is required is either a mode of communication that would allow the audience to recognize these meanings if they lie on the surface of its already differentiated experience, or a much longer process of imparted experiences and verbalized understanding permitting the audience to develop potentialities to a level that would enable it to grasp the meanings not immediately accessible to it. In principle, however, such meanings would be communicable to all men. In fact, that very communicability is the final indication that they have been grasped by the subject and that they are not just qualities he possesses as a unique subject, but meanings that pertain to all subjects.

EXPRESSION OF INFALLIBLY UNDERSTOOD MEANINGS

Basically, infallibility has to do with the mind's grasp with certitude of a universal meaning. The expression of such meanings in words, actions, or symbols is an interesting but secondary question. I shall treat this matter of expression more fully in chapter 16, wherein I shall take up the subject of the articulation of Christian doctrine. The same principles that apply to the articulation of doctrine also apply to the articulation of universal meanings at the simple experiential level. To avoid duplication I will postpone discussion of this question until that chapter.

CONCLUDING REMARKS

This notion of what can be infallibly known and communicated goes far towards eliminating the fear of many. According to Antoine Vergote, the modern opposition to infallibility stems largely from the fact that today existence is seen as open-ended, challenging, problematic. Accordingly, a doctrine of infallibility would appear to deprive existence of most of its significant characteristics. Men do desire certitude in their darker moments; but they desire even more to enjoy the possibility to make and to discover and to revise. Hence they prefer the agony of doubt to the closed world of the infallible.[13]

On the present analysis, the dichotomy is false. The true notion of infallibility leaves the meaning of the universe completely open-ended. It allows for limitless expansion of knowledge and for limitless revisions of the theories we now have. It does not close off man. Rather, it establishes with conceptual certitude the relationships and processes that continuously mark the effort of man to grow through self-differentiation in the presence of the universe of being. It is infallible

knowledge itself that permits man to change and develop and become
ever more open-ended. Infallibility does not mark an end to truth;
for it never deals with the judgment of concrete situations. Rather,
it marks the beginning of truth; for it deals with the certitudes that
point out to man where he is to look if he would approach the richness of being that is forever beyond him. To know infallibly that man
is open-ended, that he never can be sure he has exhausted the data in
a concrete situation, that he is forever made for deeper understanding
and love, and that he will be open to each new situation in the measure
that his past history has been cumulatively open is to begin to possess
the truth that makes one free.[14]

Before closing this section on universal meanings, infallible understanding, and expression at the simple experiential level, I would like
to point out the interrelationships that exist between conditions of
the modern world and the recurring universal meanings that ground
infallibility. On the one hand, it is precisely the conditions of the
present world that make possible the articulation of the universal
meanings we have been speaking of. That world is characterized by
greater heterogeneity and diversification of cultures and subgroups,
greater individual and social complexity, more rapid individual and
social change, and more effective communication.[15] The combination
of these conditions facilitates the emergence to consciousness of those
universal meanings that transcend specific places and times. When
men are locked into a given culture or subculture and are hardly aware
of the existence of other groupings, they tend to absolutize the recurring meanings of their own group and to think of these local meanings
as universal. When society is static and men and social conditions
remain relatively the same over many generations, there is little possibility for men to become aware of the recurring processes of change.
However, once there are diversified groupings of great complexity
undergoing rapid change and this diversity is accompanied by a communication system permitting large-scale comparison of these groupings and their varying processes of change, then it becomes possible
for men to see the relational values and the developmental processes
that universally characterize man in his individual and social existence. In short, relational and developmental universal meanings
emerge to consciousness only as precipitates of the sharing of a large
number of temporally conditioned meanings.[16]

On the other hand, the diversity, complexification, and rapid change that characterize the modern scene also necessitate the recognition of the universal meanings that can be infallibly known. When diverse groups exist but are in little contact with one another, they can survive without a common ground that is mutually recognized. Once they enter into a vast array of relationships—social, economic, and political—it becomes necessary that they be able to communicate with one another on some common basis. And that basis can only be the universal meanings that undergird every culture and every civilization. Men will appreciate one another in their diversity only when they grasp that their differences are, by and large, temporally conditioned expressions of meanings that truly are universal, meanings they themselves each express in their own temporally conditioned manner.

Moreover, if man is to maintain his identity in a world of rapid changes, he must have an anchor in the meanings that do not change. In the static worlds of the past it was possible to maintain one's identity by wearing the same garb, engaging in the same social practices, eating the same food, passing through the same life cycle in generation after generation. It was the continuity of concrete modes of operation that enabled a man to think of his life as a unified whole and gave him a sense of "belonging." This is no longer possible. The phenomenon of rapidly increasing social change that affects both the external appearance of society and the internal relationships of men makes impossible an identity and continuity of life based on fixed customs, landmarks, and modes of operation. If men are to maintain a sense of being themselves over a long period of time, if they are to sense a continuity of existence existentially despite rapid change and greater complexification, it will only be because they are consciously anchored in those infallibly known meanings that are universal. The theoretical denial of the existence of such universal meanings and the practical failure to internalize them are, I would suggest, at the root of the modern sense of anomie and despair.

4

The Basic Christian Fact

The function of the remaining chapters of this book is to indicate:

1. the significance of the Christian Experiential-Witness level (to which I shall refer abbreviatedly as the experiential-witness level);
2. the intrinsic connection between this experiential-witness level and the simple experiential level, and;
3. the parallel structures of universal meanings, infallible understandings, and appropriate expressions that characterize these two levels which exist in the one concrete order.

Progressively, I shall move from a consideration of the basic Christian fact, to the notion of Christian faith, to the existence of universal meanings, to a clarification of infallible Christian understanding, to a presentation of the expression of such infallible understanding.

THE PROBLEM TO BE MET

The basic Christian fact is the incarnation, death, and resurrection of the Son of God. Unfortunately, this sentence is merely a series of marks on a piece of paper. It has meaning for the reader only to the extent that he is able to see it as representing certain aspects of the differentiation of his own consciousness. It would have universal meaning only if the various subjects who read it could find it representative of an aspect of their self-differentiation (or an extrapolation from that self-differentiation) which, at least at some ultimate level, could be seen as identical with the self-differentiation reflected in all other readers.

The preceding paragraph is meant to lead into the consideration of a problem that affects every theological affirmation of fact and, *a fortiori*, the most basic affirmation of Christian fact, the incarnation and death and resurrection of the Son of God. The problem is that of the culturally conditioned nature, not just of statements, but of the understanding of doctrines. If there is, as I will assert, a transcultural meaning of the basic Christian fact, it must be admitted that that transcultural meaning was not explicitly grasped and articulated in the past. Men were so immersed in their own cultures and had so little contact with other cultures, and with developments within cultures, that they could not but think that their peculiar way of envisioning the basic Christian fact was *concretely* the only possible way of correctly envisioning it. It is only when they have the opportunity of comparing the various Christian expressions of the basic Christian fact that they can begin to glimpse, embedded in each expression or thought pattern, an underlying meaning that is ever the same.

What I propose to do is to formulate an hypothesis on the transcultural meaning of the incarnation, death, and resurrection of the Son of God. This hypothesis, by the very nature of the case, will not be explicitly present in all particulars in any past epoch or in all the past epochs combined. Nor can it be said that it would have been grasped by most men of the past if it had been proposed to them, though some men undoubtedly would have grasped aspects of it, especially in the light of the fact that some of the ancient doctrine on Christ (at Nicea, for example) was cast in transcultural and heuristic terms. However, it is a generic hypothesis that purports to explain the vast array of practices and formulations of the past in a single unifying view. It is akin to a basic generalization, such as that of Newton, which, though coming very late in the history of science, yet explains data which had been accumulated over the centuries. Such a unifying generalization, precisely because it unifies large quantities of data of diverse kinds, cannot be proposed in the early stages of theology or of any other science. The diverse data, which, in this case, are concrete expressions of belief, must come first; unifying principles always emerge long after the appearance of that which they unify, although they can be said to be implicitly present from the beginning.

WEAKNESSES OF PRIOR TRANSCULTURAL NOTIONS

The Bultmannian effort at demythologizing is the classic modern effort to expound a transcultural notion of the death and resurrection of Christ.[1] Similar efforts have been made in other areas, notably that of original sin, even as far back as Schleiermacher. These efforts have been directed towards finding modern meanings for the ancient expressions, towards uncovering something tangible in the experience of men of today that can interpret the old formulas to our contemporaries. While I believe these efforts are laudable, it seems to me that too often meanings present in modern experience govern all. It is tacitly assumed that the human experience of today, apart from a further assertion of mystery that can be derived only from the witness of the past, contains all that one needs to know about man and his relationship to God. All the Christian message does is clarify what can already be experienced apart from it. Hence one can dismiss the element in the expressions of the past which referred to a real being like ourselves who was God in the flesh as merely the mythological trappings in which the human experience of the past was culturally manifested.

INTRODUCTION TO AN HYPOTHESIS

The view advanced here does attempt to explain the experience of the present, but not simply the present as it is experienced by every man. Rather, it tries to clarify that present which has been modified by a history of meaning, by a Christian tradition whose words and symbols and everyday actions have manifested that there is a continuing universal created reality touching all that is, the risen Christ. In other words, I believe that Christianity has always assumed that it has received from those who lived with the earthly Christ and who became conscious of his continuing presence after the Resurrection an understanding that present creation stands in relationship to One who in his humanity now transcends us and our mode of existence. Hence, by its origin and continuing nature, Christianity cannot be grounded solely upon elements present in ordinary experience. It is true that Christianity accords with such experiences; but it accords with them by pointing beyond them, by indicating One who fulfills what the incompleteness of these experiences points towards. Christ did not come to destroy what went before; nor did he come solely to explicate its meaning; rather, he came to fulfill it. His being present in the world now is the constituent factor that transforms what might have been a universe open only to God as mystery into a universe in which man can relate to God in a personal way. What is meant by "a personal way" will be explicated in the hypothesis to follow.

A proof for the validity of this hypothesis cannot be given in these few pages. Volumes would be needed to show that the theory here advanced represents a transcultural meaning that underlies the various christological and soteriological affirmations of the past. Hence the texts quoted and the practices indicated are meant only to be illustrative of the power of the hypothesis to clarify some of the key expressions of the past. That clarifying power would reach the status of a "proof" only if it were relatively exhaustive in its compass.

THE FIRST THESIS

I shall attempt to express the transcultural meaning of the basic Christian fact of the life, death, and resurrection of God's Son in a series of statements. First of all, *One who is God expressed himself in creation in terms that are fully and exclusively human.* I use the phrase "One who is God" rather than "the Son of God" because I believe that this more generic phrase is groundable in man's present experience, and this is where I would like to begin. God is that Mystery towards whom the whole dynamic open-endedness of man is directed. He is the presupposition of finite man's orientation toward unlimited truth and unlimited love. Though not directly experienced or experienceable, he is the ground of possibility for the ever expanding type of experience that is man's.[2] Man can, therefore, know God—not, it is true, as the direct object of experience, but rather as the Mysterious One ever presupposed as the ground and ultimate term of that experience.

This One who is God *expressed himself in creation.* What he is as mystery infinitely beyond us became expressed, bodied forth, manifested personally in creation. The process by which he personally expresses himself cannot be known to us on the basis of our experience. It can only be pointed at by way of analogy with our modes of expression. The manifestation itself, however, is commensurate with our own kind of existence. It is created like us and can be known univocally as we can know this creation. It is, in fact, a *creation in terms that are fully and exclusively human.* This means, on the one hand, that nothing of the created personal expression of the God of Mystery is beyond the human. It is only human. It means, on the other hand, that that expression is fully human. It lacks nothing proper to the fullness of humanity at the various stages of its existence. He is, therefore, in his humanity like us in all, save sin. Thus, he was in his early existence finite, historically conditioned, marked by finite choices within a given culture, and capable of growth and development. All these characteristics, as far as we can see, belong to the nature of the present human condition on a universal scale; they are transcultural; and to the degree that they are such, they pertain to him who was fully human.

In a certain sense we can know what it is to be fully human; in another sense we cannot. On the one hand, insofar as we ourselves are human and are conscious of ourselves, we can grasp what pertains to defective and partial humanity; we can know the imperfect human beings we are. Further, we can also know some of the generic processes by which our humanity develops. It thus becomes possible for us to know full humanity as the resultant of the unending application of the processes of development to the imperfect humanity we directly know. On the other hand, there is a sense in which it may be said that we cannot know what it is to be fully human. Full humanity is not simply the combination and amplification of elements already existing in partial humanity. The development of a human being is a process in which new and creative aspects are generated, aspects that cannot be grasped and appreciated on the basis of prior developments. Thus, a child cannot really experience what adult understanding and love are, even though these will be resultants of the process of growth as applied to what he now is. He can know these aspects of adulthood in a manner analogous to our knowledge of the term of the infinite series - 2 - 4 - 6 - 8 - etc. That knowledge may rightfully be termed extrapolatory; it cannot be termed experiential. Similarly, it is only in an extrapolatory way that we can grasp what full humanity is.

It should be pointed out that the explanation of the various phrases in this first point has been made in transcultural terms. The notion of God advanced is one founded upon the universal human dynamic process by which men within the context of varying cultures come to varying concepts of God. This dynamic process in a static age led concretely to a concept of God as eternally immutable; in a more dynamic age it has led to a process concept of God. I have opted for neither concept but have remained with the basic human dynamic which generates all the concepts. Similarly, in speaking of full humanity I have not included (except tentatively and by way of example) specific notions of human perfection present in one or other ages. Instead, I have concentrated on the kinds of qualities which characterize the operation of all men of all ages and have indicated that the perfect man would be a concrete development of these qualities in a way that could not be experientially known to us on the basis of our limited humanity. The attempt has been to say what can be said realistically on the basis of our limited experience and to indicate by extrapolatory and heuristic processes what experience cannot make us aware of.

THE SECOND THESIS

The one who expressed himself in creation is the Son of God. This affirmation takes second place, although it might well have been included in the prior thesis, because I believe it is far less experientially groundable than that prior affirmation. The undifferentiated mystery of God can be indicated, if not directly and experientially, at least indirectly as the ground and term presupposed by man's experience of unlimited openness. However, this experience furnishes no basis for the making of any distinct statements about God which are not mere tautologies for the undifferentiated mystery that he is. Hence the trinitarian statements, including the statement that the Son of God became man, are not groundable in our human Christian experience. This is not to deny that there are mystical experiences but to assert that such experiences cannot be directly and immediately of Father, Son, or Spirit; nor, for reasons that I shall attempt to clarify later, can they be immediate and direct experiences of the risen Christ. They are experiences in the depths of the mystic's being which are produced by God but are not directly of God as he is in himself or of the risen Christ as he is in his humanity now, although the mystic is drawn towards one and the other.

Are statements such as "the Son of God became man" meaningless? The answer, of course, is in the negative. However, such statements are not directly groundable in our experience. Rather, they stem from the apostolic experience of the earthly Christ as pondered in the light of the Passion and Resurrection. Because of what Christ said and did when he walked the earth prior to the Resurrection, the men who lived with him were subsequently able to recognize that he had been conscious of being the Son of God who was related in some way to the Father and the Spirit. That awareness of a trinity in the Godhead is proper to him in his humanity. He communicated to his followers by his words and actions only analogously his awareness of who he was and to whom he was related. Of all men who lived, only he was truly conscious of being the Son of God; and whatever

words he used to represent that consciousness could not be understood in a univocal manner by ordinary men; for such men can only
be conscious of their possession of human personalities. They attributed to these words meanings that were groundable in their own
experience; for all one can attribute to the words of others are meanings that already exist, at least implicitly, within oneself.

Hence, right from the outset, the biblical witnesses had simply an
analogous notion of the Trinity and of the Son of God within the
Trinity. Their original affirmations were only attempts to translate
into ordinary human experience what was a unique experience of him
who is God made flesh. The subsequent theological development of
trinitarian relationships on the basis of the analogy of human understanding is but a prolongation of these original analogical affirmations. The Church has always worked off these pointers to the doctrines of the Trinity and the Incarnation given it by the apostolic
forerunners. It does not work off a differentiation of the Trinity that
is a present factor in its consciousness and identifiable as such. It
knows, therefore, that *the one who expressed himself in creation is
the Son of God* only because of the message it has transmitted in an
unbroken fashion from the beginning. It knows, consequently, that
any effort to explain Christianity which relies simply on elucidating
factors in modern experience, no matter how subtle the treatment,
cannot but miss the ultimate mystery of faith.

THE THIRD THESIS

*The expression of the Son of God in creation was a humanly de-
veloping expression from his birth to his death.* On the one hand,
this means that precisely as a personal expression of God, Christ in
his humanity was more complete, more universal, more fully human
at his death than at his birth. If one would wish to say that he was
the perfect baby, one would also have to say that he was the perfect
man at death; but the latter represents a richer human expression.
Christ grew in wisdom and age and grace before God and man. If it
was the same Son of God who expressed himself in Christ at both
beginning and end, the latter expression was immeasurably more
rich and comprehensive on the scale of human expression.

On the other hand, the growth in that expression which was the
humanity of the Son of God was, on the created level, the result of

human activity. The concrete humanity that he possessed at death was the living summary of an ever deepening cycle of experiences, ponderings, judgments, decisions, and actions. That activity was not some playacting made necessary by an arbitrary decree of God. Rather, it was activity by which he became capable of facing in a full and complete way the final moment of life. It was the obedience to the exigencies of every moment that made possible the free obedience to the most demanding moment of death. It was the truth emotionalized, attitudinalized, understood, willed, and expressed throughout his life that made him fully free at death.

We can understand the processes of his growth because they are generically the same processes we undergo. Our own imperfect participation in these processes enables us to ground in our own experience the need of Christ to "merit" by his life to become the concrete human individual who went freely to his death. The activity of that life is not a mystery as is the Second Person who is the source of that activity. Every man of every culture can in varying degrees appreciate why Christ as man had to live in order that he might die in fully human freedom. He had to merit what all men have first to merit, his own becoming.

THE FOURTH THESIS

The freely accepted death of the Son of God enfleshed constituted the supreme moment of his development as man. As a result of that supreme moment, he realized in his humanity the integral and universal relatability that each human nature is intrinsically called to. The first part of this statement situates the death of Christ within the context of his growth. Human growth is the further actualization of human capacities, the orderly development of one's experiential continuum. Such an actualization and development occurs as the result of the conjunction of two factors: (1) the depth and breadth of the capacity to unlock meaning that is implicit in the succession of circumstances an individual is exposed to and (2) the openness and readiness of the individual to respond to and be changed by the factors in those circumstances. The more comprehensive the factors in the succession of situations that face a man, the more those situations can be an occasion of growth; and the more responsive and open a man is to being changed by allowing his own potentialities to be actualized by these situations, the more he changes and grows.

At each moment of his life a man faces God in a limited situation that permits limited growth. However, death appears to be the moment *par excellence* in which he faces his maker as the Creator of the total human condition.[3] At death, all that a man has become as a result of his past history is opened to and challenged by an utterly encompassing situation.[4] To the degree that he responds in openness to the possibilities inherent in that last encounter with the Creator who appears as the author of the total cosmos, to that degree does he grow out to the fullness of his human potential. He is thus challenged by that final situation to leave behind the limitations that characterized his this-worldly existence for the ever expanding existence called forth by an all-encompassing horizon. His readiness to respond totally to that horizon, and thus to actualize and fulfill all the human potential developed in his past, determines the degree of growth that occurs at death.

Christ's death was a fully free and open death. Because of his obedience to his Father throughout his entire life ("I always do what is pleasing to him," Jn. 8:29), through which he responded to the growth possibilities of each moment, he was at death capable of opening himself completely to the possibilities of an all-cosmic horizon. Hence, his death was a completion and a fulfillment (Jn. 19:30). He renounced all the limitations of his past existence and gave himself up fully to the Father. As Philippians 2:5-11 has it:

> Have this in mind among yourselves, which you have in Christ Jesus, who, though he was in the form of God, did not count equality with God a thing to be grasped, but emptied himself, taking the form of a servant, being born in the likeness of men. And being found in human form he humbled himself and became obedient unto death, even death on a cross. Therefore God has highly exalted him and bestowed on him the name which is above every name, that at the name of Jesus every knee should bow, in heaven and on earth and under the earth, and every tongue confess that Jesus Christ is Lord, to the glory of God the Father.

The text just cited does not, of course, directly support the thesis which I have advanced. However, I would suggest that the thesis makes sense of the text by going beyond it. The text indicates that Christ's exalted risen state is one that results from his continuous

obedience until death. The thesis specifies how that free obedience
of each moment of life and ultimately of the moment of death leads
to Christ's exaltation. That constant full and free acceptance of the
Father's will, which appears in the demands of creation, causes or
merits his continuous transcendence of self and the final realization
of his condition of fulfillment—his resurrection, his ascension, and
his glorification. All these biblical concepts express in varying aspects
the completion of Christ's growth in wisdom and grace before God
and man.

The second part of this statement specifies more precisely what
that growth and development of Christ consists in. Man by his nature
is called to dominate the material universe and to make it expressive
of himself; he is called to relate to all his fellow men in a unified way
with every aspect of his being—body, soul, mind, affections, will;
he is called, at an ever deeper level, to give himself totally to his Creator. That call, which is really an intrinsic drive of his being, can be
only partially realized in this mode of existence. No man can actually
love all other men; he cannot physically come into contact with them
all; nor, a fortiori, can he understand them all. Further, he does not
so possess and love himself in an utterly unified way that he can totally and integrally love any other single person with his whole being.
Man is thus inevitably incomplete in his present mode of existence.
Even Christ himself when he walked this earth was restricted in his
humanity. He was able to go out only to the lost sheep of the children
of Israel.

The resurrection and completion that Christ grew into and merited
by his death changed all that. He became the universal man, the
Lord.[5] *He realized in his humanity the integral and universal relatability that each human nature is intrinsically called to.* As man, all
power in heaven and on earth was given him, and he became capable
of being present everywhere to the end of time (Mt. 28:16–20). The
three aspects of the universe in Semitic thought—the earth, the heav-
ens above the earth, and the regions below the earth—became subject
to him (Phil. 2:10–11). As man he entered into the fullest union with
the Father and was glorified with the glory he had possessed eternally
as Son before the world began (Jn. 17:1–5). He achieved and still
achieves in his humanity that full and integral capacity to relate to
all creation and to the Creator which exists in germ in each man.
Hence, it is possible for him to be present in a fuller way whenever

two or three are gathered in his name (Mt. 18:20). Because he is alive and well and universally present in an active fashion, the celebration of his presence and self-giving throughout the world at Mass constitutes a making visible of a true present offering of Christ, and not simply a memorial of an offering made long ago on the cross. Thus, the former attack on the Mass as a true sacrifice by some groups and the modern demythologizing of the resurrection of Jesus Christ are related to one another as implicit to explicit rejections of the continuing life and universal activity of the Son of God in his humanity.

The point I would emphasize here is that Jesus Christ is still true man and, in his created nature, only man. The Resurrection does not lift him to a level of creaturehood that is beyond the human; rather, it places him in possession of full humanity, of full realization of the root powers of man. If now he has entered into a condition that enables him to give himself over wholly to all of creation and to every aspect of it, it is because such a condition of existence belongs to man who is fully alive. By his resurrection he becomes, and hence becomes capable of revealing, what each man ultimately is called to be.

The Resurrection is the central article of faith. It cannot be known simply by analyzing our own experience. Given the apostolic witness that was grounded in the pre-resurrection encounter with Christ and the subsequent reflection on the meaning of the words and deeds of Christ in the light of the Old Testament prophecy, the Church can recognize only in faith the living presence of its master. It cannot identify the risen Christ present in its experience because the risen condition and mode of operation makes Christ inaccessible to present human awareness.

Why is the risen Christ unrecognizable as risen in our experience? This can be answered by setting forth five principles:

1. We never recognize or see another being in itself; we only recognize directly the effects of its activity towards us, activity that occasions the actualization of our experiential continua in a way we can consciously detect and isolate. Hence, for example, we identify the change in us caused by the visible appearance, the barking, and the furry softness of the dog that enters the room.

2. In and through the activity of the other that occasions the recognized actualization of our experiential continua, we infer the existence and nature of the source of the activity.[6] In the example given, we

recognize the dog from what it does to our consciousness. We recognize this "thing" as that kind of being which actualizes a certain spectrum of our capacities.[7]

3. The only kind of activity towards us we can detect is that which tends to actualize *specific* aspects of our human capacities. We recognize only that which affects one or more of our external senses or specified aspects of our internal experiential life. The more profound and all-encompassing an effect is, the more difficult is it to detect and identify. Thus, one notes the effect of the searchlight that brightens a part of the room; one does not so easily note the presence of the sun as illuminating the whole landscape. One recognizes the fact that single objects fall to the earth; one does not so easily recognize the universal law of relativity. One easily identifies a pinprick; one finds it more difficult to identify an all-pervading feeling of uneasiness. Hence, the more a being affects us totally, the more we are apt to be unaware of its activity upon us. A case could be made that we are unaware of God's creativity towards us precisely because that creativity affects every aspect of our existence.

4. Even when we are able to attribute specific actualizations of our capacities to other beings, we do not necessarily understand the nature of those beings. We only understand the other when its mode of operation is encompassed by our own. Thus, an ant can "know" it is being pushed aside by a large black object. It cannot know that the large black object is the instrument or body of a rational being; for the ant's limited self-realization does not permit it to "conceive" a rational being.

5. As one grows in basic humanity towards the fullness of human actualization, one is better able to appreciate the existence and nature of more profound and universal beings. An analogy or two may clarify what I am trying to say here. In a science, the most pervasive and influential principles are the great unifying generalizations. Because these generalizations enter into all specific cases, one might think they would be the first principles to be discovered. Actually, they are the last. Only after one has grown through the detection of a great number of specific instances does one reach the capacity to hypothesize about that which unifies those instances. In like manner, one does not first discover one's predominant fault and only subsequently one's particular faults. Rather, it is the other way around. Only after having detected faults in a variety of circumstances and

having thus expanded one's experiential continuum—only then is one able to grasp indirectly the all-pervasive generator of those faults. Similarly, only by growing does a child begin to appreciate the complexity of the existence of her father and mother.

If we apply these principles to our knowledge of the risen Christ, we can begin to see why, without faith in the apostolic witness, we cannot recognize him as risen Lord in our own experience. On the one hand, the fulfillment of Christ's humanity permits him to act in an all-encompassing way. There is no aspect of any good in the present created order that is not touched by the risen Christ. That very universality makes the effects of his activity difficult to detect. On the other hand, precisely because he is risen, his mode of being and operation is immeasurably superior to our own. That mode is not simply the amplification of our own but a fulfilling mode we cannot conceive or imagine, the risen mode we will one day share, "What no eye has seen, nor ear heard, nor the heart of man conceived, what God has prepared for those who love him" (1 Cor. 2:9; cf. Is. 64:4). Hence, even when we are able to detect a change in our experiential continuum, we are not able by purely experiential means to trace it back to the risen Christ as risen because in our present limited mode of human existence direct awareness of his universal mode of existence and operation is not possible.

However, in the light of the apostolic witness to the abiding presence and activity of the risen Christ, we can look for his activity in our lives; in the light of that witness we can attribute to his risen humanity the religious effects we find there; and finally, as we grow in wisdom and grace through the living out of the two great commandments and expressions of our Christian faith, we can better grasp what that fullness of humanity might be which is possessed by him who is the light of our lives.

On the basis of what has gone before, we can see why the so-called resurrection appearances of the Scriptures, however real they may have been, could not have been of Christ as universal Lord in all his universality. That the Resurrection is an objective reality (though not like the limited objects of our everyday experience) is a truth of faith; that the apostolic Church had a series of experiences by which it realized the continuing living presence of the Christ it had once known in the flesh is the foundation of its faith; that the apostolic Church has passed on its belief to us under the guidance of the Spirit is what grounds our faith. While all this is true, it is not true (nor even possible) that the apostolic Church or we ourselves univocally experience Christ as risen. To make such a claim would be to reduce the Resurrection substantially to a return of Christ to his mode of existence prior to the Resurrection. That he is not now the same as he was when he walked the earth is the burden of the resurrection appearances. The failure of the two disciples to recognize him on the road to Emmaus (Lk. 24:13–35); Mary's mistaking him for the gardner (Jn. 20:14–16); his ability to appear through locked doors (Jn. 20:19) and to disappear (Lk. 24:31,51; Acts 1:9)—all these things indicate that Christ is no longer the limited Christ once known in the flesh but a Christ overflowing with a fuller life.

All this does not mean that we can in no way ground a notion of the meaning of the Resurrection in our own experience. If we cannot have a direct and immediate experience of full and universal humanity such as Christ possesses, yet by extrapolating from the basic condition of present existence and its inner exigence towards universal relationship with creation and the Creator, we can gain an anticipatory notion of what the risen condition of Christ might be once the Faith postulates its existence. To the degree that a man develops his own inner potential and drive towards unity with all creation and the Creator, to the degree that he lives out choices that signify and express his own Christian faith understanding in individual and corporate worship, and to the degree that he becomes aware of the actual development of his potentials—to that degree can he come to a notion of what the risen condition might be; for the risen condition is but the final and most decisive stage of a continuing process of growing inner integration and external relatability that begins even now. The more one participates in the processes of growth which are the earlier stages of that development and the more one becomes aware of the changes in oneself and one's capacity to relate to the other, the more one can effectively envision what the term of that development might be. "By this we may be sure that we know him, if we keep his commandments" (1 Jn. 2:3); "No one who sins has either seen him or known him" (1 Jn. 3:6). It is by fidelity to the demands of the intrinsic nature of his humanity coupled with a conscious striving towards the term who is the risen Christ manifested by the Church's Tradition that the mystic comes to a vision of the Saviour. That vision, however, from the very nature of the limited condition of the mystic can only be a glimpse or foretaste of who the risen Christ is.

THE FIFTH THESIS

The existence of the Son of God in his risen humanity as an integral part of creation establishes the Christian order and consequently the possibility and necessity for man of (1) the Christian experiential-witness level of existence in the present life and of (2) full personal relationship with God in Christ after death.

In the first place, *the existence of the Son of God in his risen humanity as an integral part of creation establishes the Christian order.* As I indicated in chapter 3, an order refers to the total network of relationships that *can* unite persons with the surrounding world and the Creator. Hence, an order depends upon the creation that surrounds persons. Hence, too, the Christian order depends upon the presence in creation of the risen humanity of Christ as an integral part of creation.[8] Consequently, there have been two orders of creation: the pre-Christian, which prepared men for Christ; and the Christian, which is constituted by his presence among men whether they recognize it or not.

In the second place, the establishment of the Christian order makes *possible* for man the Christian experiential-witness level of existence now and full personal relationship with God in Christ after death. The Christian experiential-witness level of existence now and the full relationship to God in Christ after death are to one another as the incipient and the mature stages of a personal relationship. In this context the phrase "personal relationship" refers to a relationship of persons to one another in which the exchange between the persons is at the level of their personhood; it involves communication through the kinds of acts that express or body forth what they are as persons. Thus, two persons sitting in a theater watching a movie have a relationship to one another, but that relationship is merely one of physical juxtaposition; it is not one of a personal nature since there is no communication at the level of understanding and freedom between the two.

In a strict sense, personal relationship requires a fundamental equality of the two parties. There must be a mutual communication at the same level of existence. Hence we recognize that the relationship of two adult friends is a personal relationship in an altogether different sense from the relationship of a mother to a baby; for the baby cannot respond to the mother at the same level of love and understanding as the mother to the baby.

Applying these notions to our relationship to Christ, we note that his incarnation made possible for the first time a strict personal relationship with God. When he walked this earth, the Son of God expressed himself by the same kinds of acts of understanding, of feeling, and of emotion that characterize ourselves; and he received similar acts from his family and friends. The God of the Old Testament who had been totally other now drew near. No matter how much the Old Testament relationship with God had developed, it would have forever remained at a level in which God's activity would have been so utterly beyond man that it could only be known in its effects; it could never have been known as God's unique personal expression at the level of man's operations.

However, Christ now no longer acts at the earthly level of human persons which is localized and particular. Rather, he acts towards us in his humanity at the risen level which is universal. Hence our present relationship to him is an unequal one, for his mode of activity is beyond our own. Whereas he is completely aware of us and our activity, we can reach out to him only in symbol in the light of our acceptance of the apostolic witness. In his present risen condition he constitutes for men who walk the earth the possibility of a dimly-perceived-in-faith personal relationship to God, not the possibility of a strict personal relationship.[9] His risen existence thus makes possible what I have called the Christian experiential-witness level of existence.

After death, however, we shall enjoy once more the possibility of a strict personal relationship to God in Christ such as was enjoyed by the members of Christ's family and the apostles before his death. When we share his risen existence, we shall be able to relate to him with the same kind of human activity that characterizes his relationship to us. As his apostolic followers once enjoyed an equal mutual relationship at the level of flesh-and-blood existence, so too we with them will be able to enjoy an equal and mutual relationship at the risen level of existence.

This analysis indicates the necessity of identifying the present order of salvation with the Incarnation, Death, and Resurrection of the Son of God. This is the only kind of order that would permit the kind of salvation in which man's potential would be fulfilled by a strict personal relationship to the Second Person of the Blessed Trinity. Theoretically, there might have been other orders of salvation (other "supernatural orders" in an older terminology). Of such orders of salvation we know nothing. However, if we are to have the present kind of salvation, then the Incarnation must take place. The Incarnation and its culmination, the Resurrection, are the very conditions of possibility of the present order of salvation. That order can no more exist without the Incarnation-Resurrection than water can exist without hydrogen and oxygen.

In the third place, the establishment of the Christian order imposes on all men the *necessity* of entering the Christian experiential-witness level of existence in the present life and full relationship with God in Christ after death if these men are to attain fulfillment. Man cannot remain indifferent to the Resurrection and be fulfilled. He is confronted with an order of existence, with an ontic reality, that demands a choice. This follows from the fact that man is a creature of total relatability. He is called by his own intrinsic dynamism to reach out to all of creation and to the Creator who is its beginning and end. For a man to deny implicitly or explicitly any aspect of creation or its ultimate ground is for him to deny himself. Under these conditions the nature of *de facto* creation necessarily influences what man is called to if he is to be himself. If creation is merely ordinary creation, then man is called to relate himself to it as it is. However, once the very Son of God enters creation personally in human form, then man is called to accept him as part of creation. Just as man is changed by the acceptance of the ordinary possibilities in creation, now he is changed in a Christian way by the acceptance of the personal presence of God in creation. Because man is called to relate to all of creation, as soon as that creation becomes Christian by the personal presence of God within it, man must make a Christian choice if he is to be faithful to his nature. The Christian order and Christian obligations come into existence, therefore, by reason of the Incarnation and Resurrection.

Simply by being open to all of creation as it now exists man becomes graced. What we have called Christian sanctifying grace is the change brought about in man (always under the creativity of God) by his contact with the living risen Christ. Man can no more detect that change directly than he can detect his ontic relationship to Christ.

However, that change exists and man can know of its Christian nature and origin by the same faith deriving from the apostolic witness that enables him to accept the existence of the risen Christ. To speak of Christian sanctifying grace is only to say that there is a vital relationship between the Son in his risen humanity and the race of men. Because of that vital relationship men are changed, graced. Because the Incarnation and Resurrection which make possible that change are free acts of God, the change that depends on them is also free, is grace. Finally, because that change relates men to the Son, it ultimately relates them to the Father and the Spirit who are one in nature with the Son.[10]

The function of the foregoing presentation of the Christian order is largely to indicate the unity of the Christian view of the present order of existence and the extent to which that view is grounded in aspects of our experience and extrapolations that spring from faith in the ancient message passed on to us from the original apostolic encounter with Christ. The effort throughout has been to present an heuristic view of Christian revelation based on the recurring dynamic processes of human development in general and of human understanding in particular. It is only by an effort of this sort that we can overcome the inevitable tendency to couch the meaning of revelation in the concepts peculiar to a given age. "Covenant," "Lord," "Resurrection," "Ascension," "merit," and similar terms, all bear the limiting characteristics of the epoch that originated them. It is only when one reduces the meaning behind each to its equivalent place in the human dynamic structure[11] that one can convey the kind of meaning that is truly transcultural. And it is only this kind of meaning which can be universal and hence a ground for infallible pronouncement.

CHRISTIAN FAITH AND THEOLOGY

Christian faith is the condition of human acceptance of the Christian order. That acceptance can be incipient or mature; it can exist in varying degrees in the intellect, in the emotions, in the attitudes, in the will, and in the operations of men. Because of the fundamental unity of man, it is impossible that faith should exist solely in the mind or the will or the emotions of man. At the same time, because of the differences of integration in men and the varying components of their makeup, the faith will take diverse emphases. For some the faith will largely be expressed in verbal communication; such are the teachers. For the apostle it will be expressed in action. The basic point is that faith refers ideally to the global response of man. It implies that a man of full faith speaks, decides, acts, understands, and expresses emotions in such a way as to manifest totally his human acceptance of the Christian order. That acceptance tends to lead to an explicit Christian self-understanding; that self-understanding, insofar as it is personally expressed, leads to a personal confession and perhaps to a personal theology; finally, the attempt to generalize about the communal faith understanding of the Church leads to a generic theology and ultimately even to Church dogma.

What I would stress here is the solidarity and developmental continuity that exist between the basic Christian order and faith on the one hand, and between faith and theology on the other hand. In the fifth thesis of this chapter I indicated that because the risen Christ is an ontic fact of creation and because man is the creature whose very nature is to be open to all creation, man is in the concrete universe called to accept Christ if man is to be true to himself. In the present context this means that the very nature of man *in concreto* demands Christian faith. However, there is a further step. Faith demands theology and theology is an integral aspect of faith; in fact, faith without at least an incipient theology is an impossibility. This follows from the fact that Christian faith is an acceptance of the risen Christ by the whole person. Such an acceptance cannot be a mere vague trust; if it is to be by the whole man, it must involve the totality of man's powers. It must affect the attitudes and emotions; it must govern one's free choices; it must lead to an understanding, at least implicit, of the implications of faith for the whole life of man as an individual and social being; finally, because man is an articulate verbal being, faith that is full will be conceptualized and exteriorly promulgated in words. In other terms, by the inherent dynamism that is man's, the faith that possesses him must pass through every aspect of his being if it is to be full faith. In fact, faith cannot exist apart from any aspect of a person's being. If faith does not exist in men's emotions, bodies, intellects, and wills, then it exists nowhere.[12] There is no fleshless, mindless, willless faith floating around. Moreover, because of the at least partial unity of man, that faith which exists in the feelings and the emotions must also, at least implicitly, exist in the intellect. It is for this reason that if one speaks of a certitude of faith, he must also speak of a certitude of meaning and of a theological certitude. It is this certitude of faith which exists in the individual that gives rise eventually to the collective certitude of faith in the Church as a whole and ultimately to the certitude that is expressed in dogma. Anyone who would speak of a certitude of the Church's faith, but of the complete absence of certitude in the Church's understanding and in the prolongation and expression of that understanding which is dogma, is carrying into modern times the ancient notion, long since rendered untenable, of man as composed of disparate parts—the body and the soul. Only one who at least implicitly conceives man as so dichotomized can speak of a Church that is, on the one hand, fundamentally indefectible and, on the other hand, incapable of infallibly understood dogmas.[13] Incidentally, Küng's very formulation appears to hide the vestiges of an infallible belief. Küng appears certain that the Church is indefectible. This, at least, is one of his infallible dogmas.

To conclude, I would point to the obvious fact that in actuality faith is never full and perfect; it never penetrates fully all of man. We all have to proclaim: "Lord, I believe; but help my unbelief." It is this imperfect development that grounds the existence of different charisms; for charisms from this point of view are only different capacities of man that have been permeated with faith to such an extent that the man involved communicates the faith to others by that capacity. Further, it is this imperfect development of faith that makes it possible for men to be men of faith without their explicit recognition of the existence of the risen Christ; for owing to their lack of realistic existential contact with the apostolic message, they lack what would transform their earnest efforts to go out to the whole of creation into a life at the Christian experiential-witness level of existence. Finally, it is the imperfect possession of the faith that grounds the existence of numerous Christian bodies that are so seriously striving today to overcome a cleavage of centuries. To take up these matters in detail would go beyond the scope of this work.

Universal Christian Meanings—
Preliminary Questions

INTRODUCTION

As I indicated when speaking of certitude at the simple experiential level in chapter 3, the fundamental point is the existence of universal meanings. Only such meanings can be infallibly grasped; and this is so precisely because their universality implies that they are present, even when unexplicated, in the recurring relationships and processes that characterize all men. Further, their very universality makes their explication worthwhile for all men because that explication represents the kind of differentiation that is identified with the generic development of man as man.

In the present chapter I intend to relate the notion of universal meanings at the simple experiential level to its counterpart in the Church's life which is lived at the Christian experiential-witness level. This effort to relate universal meanings at two levels will entail two tasks. First of all, the procedure by which one may transpose from the simple experiential level to the Christian experiential-witness level must be justified. Secondly, even if it is granted that this transposition procedure is justified and can lead to universal Christian meanings, one must still clarify the almost insuperable difficulties that are encountered when one treats of the Christian dogmas of the past; for in many cases the meanings dogmatized were evidently confined to a given culture or world view.

TRANSPOSING PROCEDURES

May we transpose to the Christian experiential-witness level what we said about lasting meanings at the simple experiential level? I believe that we may. The basic reason for this is that the presence of the risen Christ which establishes the Christian order is a universal presence that does not destroy the universal meanings perceivable at the simple experiential level but carries them towards a more ultimate perfection. The risen Christ affects every aspect of every relationship and every developmental process in creation. His is an ontic presence that does not destroy the reality that pre-existed him;

rather his presence fulfills it. Hence the man of Christian faith lives and acts and reflects in the recognition of all the universal meanings that pre-existed Christ. In addition, however, he recognizes in dependence on the apostolic witness that these meanings are now fulfilled in the Christ who touches them all.

Universal meanings at the simple experiential level (henceforth I shall call these "natural meanings") are, as I stated in chapter 3, subjective. This means that they are potential human developments that would and should be achieved by all men if their root capacities and exigencies were fully realized. Now such meanings that reside in subjects are not destroyed by the encounter with new objects standing over and against the subject. Thus, the universal natural meaning that man is called to understand all creation is not destroyed when a new object enters creation, even if that object be the humanity of the Son of God. However, that subjective meaning would be transformed and fulfilled if the new object were so all-influencing that it touched the subject at every aspect of his existence. In this case, the universal subjective meanings would possess a further universality that derives from the all-encompassing influence of the new object. Hence one who lives at the Christian experiential-witness level recognizes solely by faith in the apostolic witness that the risen Christ affects every aspect of this universe. He recognizes, further, that this universal influence of Christ necessarily touches and transforms the universal natural meanings that existed prior to Christ; these universal natural meanings are now seen to lead to universal Christian meanings. Thus, a man recognizes that he grows by expressing the capacities he already has; this is a universal natural meaning. Now as a Christian he recognizes that Christ is related to all his capacities; he knows, therefore, that by expressing his capacities in such a way as to reflect his relationship to Christ, he grows in a Christian way. From this emerges the universal Christian meaning of merit.

All universal Christian meanings involve differentiations of experiential continua that derive from the Christian message. That message centers on the proclamation of the universal presence and lordship of the risen Christ. When that basic message differentiates the personality of a Christian who also recognizes the inner need that that differentiation should permeate his whole life of acting and thinking (especially when this takes place within a community), then the dynamic process by which further and derivative Christian universal

meanings are developed is initiated. This process leads to two kinds
of universal meanings.[1] The first kind relates to the manner in which
the Son of God becomes man and the relationship of the Son to the
Father and the Spirit. This kind of meaning is one that totally derives
from the Christian message; it cannot be directly and immediately
grounded in our experience because it refers to relationships, processes, and realities that totally surpass our experience. It can only
be pointed to in faith and described by extrapolations from our experience. Thus, the Christian message indicates that the Son comes
from the Father. We cannot know what ultimate and uncreated
derivation might be, but we can only point to it by derivations in
our own experience such as the derivation of the concept from the
thinker's process of understanding.

The second kind of universal meaning is one that results from the
symbiosis of the differentiation flowing from the acceptance of the
Christian message with the differentiations flowing from the realization of universal natural meanings. Thus, I accept by faith in the
Christian message that the Son of God has now achieved full humanity, and, as fully human, totally relates to all creation as Saviour;
and I further accept that he calls us to the fulfillment that is his own
and makes it possible for us to begin the achievement of that fulfillment now and to complete it after death. I also accept from human experience certain universal characteristics of man and his
development.

When I combine within my own understanding these two kinds
of meaning, I begin to derive universal Christian meanings that are
referred to by the dogmas. For example, since man is a communal
expressive being who grows by bodying forth who he is in community, then as a Christian he must body forth communally Christian meanings; hence the Church. Since man universally has biological, psychological, intellectual, and volitional powers, his fulfillment will entail the fulfillment of those capacities; hence a doctrine of the Assumption with reference to the chief member of the
Church. Assumption refers to the completion of the whole person,
indicated in a long-accepted psychology as body and soul. Since
man can grow only in the society of other men, the perfection in
Christ he is called to will involve a deep relationship with all other
men; hence the doctrines of the Communion of Saints and of the
Last Judgment.

UNIVERSAL MEANINGS IN THE PAST

The second task of this chapter is the explanation of the difficulties encountered when we attempt to understand the dogmas of the past as explications of universal Christian meanings. Much of the old dogmatic teaching seems wedded to a now antiquated framework and a culture long dead. The cry for reinterpretation of dogma has been heard over and over again; and it sometimes seems that reinterpretation is merely a euphemistic term for total revision. The notion of development is stressed, but one does not need to go far to find that many notions of development allow for the total scrapping of old meanings and the emergence of new meanings. The denial of infallibility, I believe, is but the logical outcome of theories of reinterpretation and development that deny a continuance of meanings. These theories, in turn, are the result of a real problem and an almost inevitable shortcoming that concerns almost all of the dogma of the past. That defect has to do with the mode in which universal meanings were grasped, the level of self-differentiation that existed in the Church as a whole and was expressed and promulgated in the dogmas. A failure to pinpoint the limitations of the mode in which former ages grasped universal meanings and a failure to re-express at a deeper level meanings that were once grasped only at a culturally conditioned level have combined to cause modern confusion and disagreement on dogma and infallibility. Thus, an explication of the nature and limitations of the grasp of universal meanings and the enunciations of dogmas by Christians of the past will, at the outset, clear up a basic difficulty.

THE BASIC THESIS

The primary contention I would make is that the Church of the past, at least in its general understanding, not only was culturally conditioned, as is the Church of every age; but it was not explicitly aware of being so conditioned. As a result, the question regarding the distinction between the universal Christian meanings of all ages and the culturally conditioned manifestation of those meanings in the mentality of a given age was not asked at all. Since that question was not asked, there was a tendency to confuse the concrete way in which people understood aspects of the faith within the context of a given culture with the way the faith would have to be understood in all cultures. What was actually universal *in fact* was confused with what had to be universal under all conditions. What was universal under conditions of Western civilization was assumed to be universally applicable to all situations. The distinction between a core meaning that was as universal as man and a peripheral meaning that necessarily accompanied that core meaning within any given cultural setting was not made and could not have been made. Only the rise of historical consciousness that comes with the comparison of different civilizations and cultures makes it possible for man to ask transcultural questions and thus to arrive at explicit transcultural answers. I would suggest that the mistakes made in the missions by the imposition of Western liturgy, Western Church government, and the like are a parallel with the mistake made in imposing on succeeding ages the universal meanings of the past in the culturally conditioned conceptualizations belonging to the past. In both cases, the failure is one of not removing (and replacing) that which pertains to a given epoch from the central core that pertains to all epochs; and the reason is that an earlier age could not make the distinction between the two.

To grasp this line of thought is to grasp the fundamental ambiguity inherent in the classic and oft-quoted phrase of Vincent of Lerins: "We must hold that faith which has been believed everywhere, always, and by all."[2] The danger lurking in these words becomes clear if one applies them to the very beginnings of the Church. At a time when Christians were all of Jewish background, a host of ancient Jewish practices and meanings were universal in the Church. Were these, therefore, to be held and believed by all newcomers? The Acts of the Apostles indicates otherwise. The Gentiles were accepted as full-fledged members, and part of the until then universal heritage was not imposed upon them. The point in all this is that mere universality of acceptance of something by the whole of the past is no guarantee that acceptance must be continued everywhere in the future. It may be that what is universally accepted up to a given time is so accepted because it pertains to a social system and a culture flourishing everywhere in the Church until that time; and yet it does not pertain to the universal dynamic structure of Christian man. Only that which is implied in the recurring relationships and processes of Christian man as such, and not just that which happens to have persisted for purely historically conditioned reasons, can be called a universal meaning in the strict sense. It is only to this kind of meaning that the dictum of Vincent of Lerins applies. He, of course, did not and could not have made this distinction explicit.[3]

AN EXTENDED EXAMPLE

To indicate more clearly this tendency of the past to possess (and then enunciate) as universal some meanings which were not universal in the strict sense, an extended example involving the meaning of the Mass may help. I will not attempt to justify every statement I make here because my purpose is to convey a general principle and not to prove a theory of the Mass.

1. The Eucharistic Doctrine Held by All

It is safe to say that it was universally held in the Church that the Mass was the unbloody sacrifice of the body and blood of Christ under the appearances of bread and wine. By the words of consecration pronounced by the priest over the elements, Christ becomes truly present offering himself to his Church to be eaten in faith. From this long held universal belief I should like to concentrate on two elements. The first is what might be called the meaning element—the Mass as *sacrifice*; the second may be called the symbolic element—the use of bread and wine and the words of consecration. This latter element was designated as the matter and form of the *sacrament*. The Mass was both sacrifice and sacrament.[4]

2. The Mass as Sacrifice

First, let us consider the meaning element, the Mass as sacrifice. Until fairly recent times the basic difference between Catholic and Protestant interpretations of the eucharistic celebration seemed to center on this element. Catholics were united in declaring the Mass a sacrifice (although lately there has been a tendency to stress other elements). Where Catholics were in dispute was in their determination of just what constituted sacrifice. Theory after theory attempted to illustrate that a true offering and sacrifice took place despite the fact that there was no new shedding of blood.[5]

What I would like to suggest here is that the very concept of the Mass as sacrifice was simply a culturally conditioned way of conceiving a transcultural aspect of the universal Christian fact of the resurrection of Jesus Christ. As risen, Jesus Christ is present everywhere in his humanity in power. In the fulfillment of the material body, the emotions, the understanding, and the freedom that were his when he walked the earth, he reaches out to all men and circumstances in their every aspect. It is this universal reaching out of the fulfilled humanity of the risen Christ that is expressed in symbol at Mass. And it is this universal reaching out, which I have purposely attempted to cast in heuristic terms as the fulfillment of the present universal potential of man to relate, that was once expressed under the term "sacrifice." That term took its meaning from the Old Testament Jewish heritage. It was fashioned out of the recollection of the temple sacrifices and of such incidents in the Scriptures as the offering up of Isaac by his father Abraham.[6] However, the term and the very meaning it expressed—that is, the differentiation of consciousness in the men who made use of it—were culturally conditioned. They inevitably carried with them, sometimes only in a connotative way, aspects of their origin in the activities of a given time and culture. And when the doctrine of sacrifice was enunciated, the universal meaning that undergirded this temporally conditioned notion was inevitably inexplicit and concealed. There simply was no distinction of the universal meaning common to every culture and the limited temporal concept in which that meaning was represented. In other words, not only is the word "sacrifice" limited to a given situation, but the actual differentiation of consciousness which that word represents was a temporally conditioned differentiation compounded of a universally possible differentiation and a differentiation of a more limited kind; and the distinction between the two aspects was one that the people of the time could not make. Only we who come later and have the advantage of having lived through a period of comparative cultures have the possibility (and the necessity) of making that distinction.

I would further suggest that the universal transcultural meaning of the Resurrection that undergirds the concept of sacrifice also underpins the notion of communal celebration. Because the Mass represents the uniting of all the faithful to the same universally present risen Christ, it is a communal celebration, a communion of those recognizing the presence and unifying activity of Christ. Sacrifice and celebration conceptualize what is really a basic enduring relationship to Christ risen; both could be altered in a different cultural context so long as they were replaced by another temporally conditioned concept that enfleshed the enduring dynamic relationship to the risen Christ.

3. The Symbols Used in the Mass

The second element of the Eucharist that I mentioned was the symbolic element—the use of bread and wine and the words of consecration. Do these constitute dogmatic elements that the Church cannot revise? In other words, are they representative of lasting meanings? Are they, in an older framework, elements expressly instituted by Christ or the apostolic Church in such a way that they are to be observed until the end of time unaltered.?[7]

The basic theory. I would suggest that the very notion of Christ's instituting a fixed and enduring rite is in itself a possiblity only to a mind that is temporally conditioned but is not aware of the phenomenon of temporal conditioning. When one becomes aware of the fact that rites and symbols as concrete expressions are inevitably tied to the cultural context in which they originate, and when one further realizes that cultural contexts inevitably change, the notion that Christ could have explicitly or implicitly intended that a given fixed rite be perpetuated as such even until the end of time becomes unthinkable. What is primary is meaning and not expression, whether that expression be verbal or symbolic. To insist on maintaining expressions at all costs is to risk destroying meaning. No one would maintain that Christ demanded that we repeat the same Aramaic sounds he enunciated until the end of time; for we all instinctively recognize the primacy of meaning in this regard. Hence, we are endlessly engaged in retranslating the biblical text into the modern vernacular. However, what is true of the verbal sounds is also true of the action symbols. They are expressors of meaning; and if they no longer express the same lasting meaning, then they too must be translated.

I am not saying, of course, that Christ did make or could have made these distinctions. As man he was limited by the culture of his time and by that culture's incapacity to come to transcultural meanings and to distinguish what was lasting from what was temporally conditioned. Assuming that he said, "Do this in commemoration of me," or its equivalent, he certainly did not explicitly mean, "Perpetuate the enduring universal meaning of what I am expressing here, but do it in forms that will be meaningful to the context in which you operate." He could have had only a general notion that the Church should celebrate what he was about to consummate in his whole being on the morrow and which he was anticipating symbolically at the Last Supper.

There is but one thing that is universal in the symbolic aspect of the Eucharist. It is not the formula of institution; nor is it the use of bread and wine. Rather, it is the very necessity to symbolize and express in a present significant manner that which I have called the universal meaning of the Eucharist. Man is by his nature a symbolic being; in fact, being is *ex se* symbolic.[8] As a man grows and develops, he implements the drive towards total relatability enunciated in the two great commandments by expressing himself, that is, by projecting forward the capacities already realized. He must express the relational being that he is in order to grow from his present unfinished and limited potential towards the fullness of knowledge and love of all creation, of Christ, and through Christ of the triune God. Moral activity is one kind of such expression; conceptualizing the faith is another; symbolic activity, such as is found in the Eucharist, is a third. This latter is most apt to express the ineffable, the mysterious, the straining towards the infinite. Symbols are not tight and neat as are concepts; they have a connotative force that concepts often lack; and they have a capacity to body forth the murky and not yet explicitly grasped depths of a person. More than specific concepts, they engage the whole individual. Hence, they tend to promote the growth of a person as a whole when they are fully entered into.

The Church must continue to celebrate the death of the Lord until he comes. It must, by the universal and lasting symbolic nature of man, express its faith in the enduring fact of the universal active presence of Christ; and it must do so in words and symbols that truly mean for its celebrating members that the risen Christ is living and acting in their midst calling them to unity with one another, with himself, and through him with the Father. That enduring meaning of the risen Christ and that enduring need of man to express his meanings are what ground the Mass as sacrifice and sacrament. These traditional ways of referring to the Mass are temporally conditioned ways of pointing to a much more enduring and universal relationship and dynamic.

The universal presence and activity of the risen Christ must, of course, be expressed and celebrated by the individual as an individual. For each man is unique; all his uniqueness is related to the risen Christ; and all that uniqueness ought to be expressed, that it might grow and develop. Hence, there is need of individually chosen moral actions, individually made reflections and personal prayer, and even individual symbolic activity. All of these have to be done more or less consciously in the name of Christ, that is, in recognition of his abiding presence and activity.

The Mass extends this kind of dynamic to the social realm. Man is not simply a unique individual. He is an individual who achieves his humanity in a social context and who receives Christ not just uniquely in the depths of his own being but also as reflected in his fellow men, especially those who are of the household of the faith. The mass is necessitated as the expression of this enduring social Christian dynamic.

A qualification. One qualification must be made about the use of bread and wine and the words of institution. To say that these are culturally conditioned elements that Christ could not have willed as such to be used by the Church until the end of time is not to say that the Church or one of its priests can by mere *fiat* change these symbols. It may be that *de facto* these symbols will be for all of time the best ways of expressing the universal meaning of the Resurrection as celebrated in community. If this is the case, it will be so for two reasons. On the one hand, these words and the use of bread and wine may *de facto* in all cultures continue to possess a natural symbolic capacity to express the union of men with one another and with Christ present in their midst. On the other hand, man is an historical being and the Church is by nature historical. It lives necessarily out of a past; its words and symbols are forged in that past and it cannot by a simple legal maneuver abrogate them. Great words and symbols can so pass into the very texture of a society that a legislator or priest can no more legislate them out of existence than he can by decree decide that man shall no longer be a symbolic being. Thus, the word "home" in English has an existential meaning that is ground into the fiber of those brought up in the English-speaking world; no head of state would be able to decree that henceforth it would be replaced by "domicile" in the hearts of men. How much more has the long history of the Church and the recollection of the initial usage by Christ hallowed, if not eternalized, the symbols of bread and wine and the words "This is my body; this is my blood."

I should note that the dynamic process relating to these symbols is one of the lasting processes of man. It is based on man's fundamental historicity. A man and a society in which he lives are inevitably marked by all they say and do. All other things being equal, the more they are significantly influenced by certain acts, by certain words, and by the use of certain symbols, the more these acts, words, and symbols leave their mark on them. While one cannot make any certain statements about any single word or symbol, one can indicate with certitude the lasting and universal dynamic that is at work with each word and symbol. This dynamic grounds one of the lasting natural meanings that also enter into what we have called the Christian order.

4. Testing the Validity of the Theory

The reader can test the validity of the universal risen Christ *meaning* and the correlative varying relevant *expression* context that I have set up for the Eucharist by noting its explanatory power with regard to many of the classic conceptions applied to the Mass and Communion. Thus, the Mass is said to "proclaim the death of the Lord until he comes." Once one grasps that the Resurrection is but the continuance and fulfillment of Christ's total drive towards unity with all men, which led to the Passion, then one has no difficulty in seeing that behind the Passion and Resurrection lies the same dynamic that we have indicated as the universal lasting meaning expressed at Mass. Similarly, a careful application of the dynamics of meaning and expression to the notion of presence will reveal what lies behind that which we formerly expressed by "transubstantiation" and are now beginning tentatively to express by such concepts as "transsignification" and "transfinalization."

Actually, it is the explanatory power of the theory I have advanced, and this alone, that can constitute its historical justification. *A priori* one can admit that one will not find direct evidence for the theory in the texts that carry forward for us the Church's Tradition. The theory is not, and could not have been, explicitly present in the past; for a transcultural theory would be possible only to a generation which had arrived at a consciousness of the succession of historical contexts and which, from that consciousness, moves to the need of a theory which would transcend whatever pertains specifically to any given context. Past generations, as we have seen, did not have this consciousness. However, we can propose as a transcultural hypothesis a theory drawn from the recurring relationships and processes of the faith life as observed; and that theory can be checked in the same way a scientific generalization is checked, that is, by its power to unify and clarify all the data. The various culturally conditioned concepts, activities, and verbalizations are thus seen not as lasting universal meanings but as so many diversely situated points plotted on lined paper whose overall unity is indicated in a single equation arrived at *after* all the points have been noted.

THE GENERIC PROBLEM THIS EXAMPLE ILLUSTRATES

The foregoing lengthy example on the Mass was not furnished for its own sake but to illustrate the kind of difficulty encountered when we attempt to regard the dogmas of the past as explications of universal Christian meanings. The fact is that much of the dogma of the past, even as enunciated by general councils, was not representative of universal meanings, which are by nature transcultural; rather, it was representative of a limited and culturally conditioned understanding of these universal meanings in which the universal element was not explicitly distinguished from the temporally conditioned trappings in which it was necessarily packed. There were exceptions, of course. The two great commandments (Mt. 22:36–40) seem to be a classic example.

The non-universal character of many past official pronouncements has caused, I believe, untold mischief in interpretation; for even if one succeeds in grasping the context of a council, or a papal statement, or a passage of Scripture, one still finds oneself in possession of nothing more than a meaning which, *taken as a whole*, pertains only to a given place and time. Thus, there have been long controversies on the enduring matter and form of the sacraments. There have been attempts to absolutize the charismatic gifts as these appear in a scriptural context. Who has not heard, for example, that a modern prophet should act as the biblical prophets did? Finally, there have been efforts to set up the biblical form of government as the model for all future ages, and these efforts have produced tendencies to read back into the Scriptures all subsequent developments. All these are as much products of a failure to realize that the ancient texts represent temporally conditioned understandings as they are products of an antiquated exegesis. Nor is the problem confined to the text of the Bible. Conciliar and papal definitions labor under the same kind of unrecognized difficulty. That difficulty, in its turn, has produced confusion and the questioning of universal meanings and the infallibility which rests on those meanings.

A PROPOSED ANSWER TO THE PROBLEM

How does one go about sifting out what is universal and lasting from what is temporally conditioned and ephemeral? The prevalent answer is by an analysis of texts. I would suggest, however that this method cannot succeed; for it rests upon the highly dubious assumption that the men who wrote the texts actually made in some fashion or another the distinction I have been making between the transcultural and the temporally conditioned within which it is embedded. Instead, I would frankly admit that the writers of the texts, including the biblical writers, simply did not make this distinction at all. I would further assert that the modern interpreter alone can make that distinction, and that only he can hypothesize as to the transcultural meaning embedded in the understanding and activity of another age. These transcultural meanings, precisely because they are transcultural, will exist in the present age and in the many faith contexts of this age. The alert interpreter, if he is also a deep-living and reflective Christian who is on the lookout for transcultural universal meanings, should be able occasionally and tentatively to spot them and to propose them as hypotheses. It is then his task to check the proposed universal Christian meanings against the past by showing that time and again they appear in an implicit way as underlying and unifying the varying culturally conditioned meanings that are reflected in the texts representing the past. Here his knowledge of the contexts of past texts will be of service; for it will enable him to uncover the temporally conditoned meaning of the past that constitutes an element of all the data his hypothesis must unify. Should the texts not support the hypothesis, then he must either revise the hypothesis or demonstrate that one and all non-supporting texts represent understandable and provable distortions. This is the method I attempted to follow with regard to the example of the Eucharist, although, of course, the analysis of texts and contexts was necessarily almost nonexistent.

The proposed method would make possible a kind of restatement of many dogmas without a destruction of the core of the ancient meaning and without the imputation of error to the collective wisdom of the past. It would expose the serious limitation of our theology of the sacraments, of our notions of the generic Christian vocation and the various specific vocations, such as priesthood, marriage, and religious life, by defining these in terms of transcultural values instead of in terms of the way these values were expressed in one or more limited contexts of the past.[9] It would also facilitate the task of determining authentic developments and distinguishing these from unprincipled change. All this, I believe, could be done without calling into question the truth of many past formulations; for the method I propose would recognize that these formulations represented universal meanings as those meanings were clothed in a temporally conditioned dress. Those meanings were basically correct and appropriate for the given context. They cannot be called incorrect on the grounds that they do not have validity for other contexts; for the framers of those meanings never purported to give answers for other cultural contexts since they were not aware there was such a thing as another cultural context. They simply worked on the assumption that all contexts were the same; or, more precisely, they acted without any knowledge that they were making such an assumption.

I do not believe that this is simply an expedient to save the truth of past dogmas. Rather, I would save the truth because I believe that this is the only intelligent procedure. Every answer which a person gives is a limited answer to a limited question. It is an answer that necessarily implies numerous assumptions, many unknown, because it reflects only a small portion of the single universe of reality. Ask a man if he will come to visit you tomorrow and listen to his affirmative answer. Do you say he spoke untruth if he does not come because of serious illness? Obviously not. You would reason that the assumed condition of his answer was that he would be in good health, although he did not state that condition and it did not even cross his mind. Only if he had expressly considered the possibility of ill health and had promised to come anyway—only then would his failure to come be evidence in this case that he had lied. This does not mean, of course, that all past ecclesial statements are true or that all so-called dogmas are true, even in the limited cultural sense I have just indicated. Textbooks have demonstrated this by admitting in later editions that what had been called dogma in earlier editions was now an open question. Moreover, the notion that the Church moves erect throughout time, never making mistakes, is manifestly unhistorical. However, under the conditions I will indicate in the following pages, I believe that the Church today can come to consciously recognized transcultural meanings; and I believe that under analogous conditions in the past it was able to come to culturally conditioned meanings and even at times to universal ones.

Universal Christian Meanings—
Nature and Significance

SUMMARY AND PROSPECTUS

In chapter 3 I treated the simple experiential level and indicated a basic division at that level of (1) universal meanings, (2) infallible grasp of such meanings, and (3) the expression of those infallibly grasped meanings. In chapter 4 I began the treatment of the Christian experiential-witness level by attempting to clarify the meaning in transcultural terms of the Christian order which grounds that level. In chapter 5 I initiated discussion of the universal Christian meanings that are present at the Christian experiential-witness level by taking up two preliminary questions: the justification of the procedure by which we transpose what was said about universal meanings at the simple experiential level to the Christian experiential-witness level; the explanation of the difficulties encountered when we attempt to understand the dogmas of the past as explications of universal Christian meanings. The present chapter takes up the nature and significance of universal Christian meanings; chapter 7 treats of the historical genesis of such meanings; chapter 8 concludes the discussion on these meanings by taking up their characteristics. Chapters 9–15 move into the question of infallible understanding of universal Christian meanings. Chapter 16 takes up the expression of those infallibly grasped meanings. Thus, chapters 4 through 16 parallel at the level of the Christian order and the Christian experiential-witness level of existence the three basic divisions of universal meaning, infallible understanding of such meaning, and consequent expression of that meaning and understanding which were set forth in the chapter on the natural order and the simple experiential level of existence. These three divisions can be more simply called (1) "dogmatic meanings," (2) "dogmatic understanding," and (3) "dogmatic statements."

I believe this division is valid because meanings exist in subjects before they are grasped; and they are grasped before they are articulated. Of course, meanings, understanding of meanings, and statements represent elements of a continuous process and shade off into one another. Yet for conceptual purposes the division given seems valid and profitable.

NATURE OF A DOGMATIC MEANING

A dogmatic meaning in the strict sense refers to an actual or potential differentiation of the human experiential continuum which (1) has been achieved in Christ as the universal perfect man and (2) is demanded, at least as a goal, as an achievement of all men in this life by their very nature as creatures made to reach out to and encompass all creation and the Creator. Dogmatic meanings, therefore, exist in subjects. First of all, they exist in Christ; then, in the measure that men grow up to his universal stature, they progressively appear in others who are thereby constituted his brethren. Not everything that existed and exists in Christ falls under the heading of dogmatic meaning. Only those aspects of his experiential continuum that constitute what is now universally shareable with others can be thus described. Hence, his birth at Bethlehem, the time and place of his death, and the like, cannot, as they concretely occurred in a local context, be considered as dogmatic meanings. One might by some happenstance know the exact time and spot of Christ's birth with complete certitude; but that knowledge would not constitute a dogmatic meaning, for it would not constitute a differentiation of consciousness that in principle could be demanded as a goal of the self realization of all men in this life. Such knowledge simply could not now be seen by all men as pertaining to their necessary personal development and self-differentiation; and it could never be certainly affirmed, as our discussion on natural infallible meanings indicated.[1]

It may be objected that this notion of a dogmatic meaning renders that meaning subjective and not objective, as the tradition would demand. It is true that in the past the emphasis was placed directly on the so-called objective truth, which appeared to be conceived as being out there in the nature of the universe as created by God and redeemed by Christ.[2] However, I would suggest that this was so because men as a whole were not sufficiently aware of the enormous problems of self-appropriation of truth and the fact that truth saves only when it is so appropriated. They spoke as if the central point were objective truth because of the largely prevalent assumption that such truth could be easily appropriated by any man with a modicum of intelligence and good will. The greater ease with which bad will was attributed to adversaries, the cruelty with which heretics were treated, and the manner in which those who did not see the majority view on doctrine were coerced are all evidence of the fact that men of the past underestimated the difficulties entailed in subjective appropriation. If I define a dogmatic meaning as a quality inherent in subjects, it is not that I wish to deny the objective existence of Christian reality, fundamentally the risen Christ, apart from the subject. Rather, I wish to stress that (1) it is the subjective appropriation of objective reality that is the locus of the problem and that (2) this subjective appropriation of universal dogmatic meanings can and must be a quality of all subjects if they are to be saved. Thus, the view I have proposed stresses not only that there is objective reality in the world apart from the subject but that all subjects are so constituted that they can and must grow by the same basic generic differentiations of consciousness.

I might note that in this view not only is non-personal reality objective; even the self-differentiation of the person is objective. In fact, I would hold that nothing in this visible universe of men is more objective than the self-differentiation of a person which takes place when he or she understands, decides, and acts on decisions. The adult is objectively "more" than the infant not primarily because he is bigger and stronger but because he is constituted by meanings that have not yet entered into the makeup of the infant. Dogmatic meanings, therefore, precisely as existing in subjects, are objective. In fact, a world in which Christ lived, died, and rose, but within which no visible person had subjectively appropriated the significance of his activity, would be an objectively poorer world by that fact alone. Dogmatic meanings in subjects, therefore, are not simply a reduplication of already existing objective meanings in the exterior world. They are rather a significant new objective reality within the makeup of the subject whose self-differentiation they constitute.

THE NECESSITY OF DOGMATIC MEANINGS FOR THE CHURCH

Are such universal Christian meanings or dogmatic meanings

necessary for the Church? The answer is in the affirmative on a number of counts, although an important initial qualification must be made. That qualification has to do with the stage of consciousness which happens to characterize the rank-and-file membership of the Church of any given age. When Church members live in a single relatively stable culture and are comparatively isolated from other cultures, they can identify themselves and their relationships to their peers and to the Christ living and dwelling within the community by concepts, verbal expressions, symbols, and acts that have universal meaning only within the context of the shared culture. In such conditions the meanings that must exist in order for the Church to operate effectively as the Church are not what I have called dogmatic meanings but rather meanings of somewhat lesser universality, that is, meanings which are realizable within the whole of the given culture though not necessarily within the whole of all cultures. This, I believe, was largely the condition of the Church of the Scriptures; and it has been largely, if not exclusively, the condition of the Church of subsequent ages. It is true that the limited universality of meanings which often characterized the scriptural period was successively broadened; however, as the extended example of the Mass given in chapter 5 has demonstrated, that relative universality did not always reach out to the complete universality of the human condition. The Church, as it were, subsisted on meanings that were as universal as the kinds of cultures and subcultures she embraced. Her meanings were *de facto* universal for the people who constituted her; they were not, at least in many cases, what I have called dogmatic meanings, that is, meanings *ex se* universal. However, these limited universal meanings were sufficient to identify and unify the Church under the conditions of limited self-consciousness prevailing in the culture of the primitive Church and in the several kinds of culturally conditioned people operating within the narrow world spectrum of Western European civilization. For most of the past, therefore, a multiplicity of dogmatic meanings (in the sense I have defined them) were not a necessary constituent of the Church. In fact, given the limited outlook of most Church members, the very notion of a dogmatic meaning of a transcultural nature would not have been intelligible at all.

It is for this reason that there were few dogmatic statements in Scripture and the early patristic period. Dogmatic statements of the strictest type are formulas that represent dogmatic meanings. Since such meanings were not common coin in the early ages of the Church, it was neither necessary nor possible that formulas representing them should be frequently found in the classic texts enunciating the Church's then current understanding. To argue that the paucity of dogmatic statements in Scripture means that the Church has no subsequent right to make dogmas in later ages is to absolutize what flowed from a contingent and limiting quality of the New Testament period.

THREE REASONS INDICATING THE NECESSITY
OF DOGMATIC MEANINGS

Under modern conditions dogmatic meanings are a necessary constituent of the Church for three reasons: (1) they are the essence of its unity; (2) they ground the possibility of its internal communication; (3) they are the foundation of its enduring identity.

1. The Essence of the Church's Unity

First of all, dogmatic meanings constitute the essence of the Church's unity. That unity is said to be "in Christ." What precisely does this mean? Does being united in Christ merely refer to the fact that somehow Christ reaches out to us and that all of us reach out to him? Or does it mean that there is something ontically within all of us which we share in common, something about our relationship to Christ that is the common possession of all? I would suggest that what I have called dogmatic meanings do not simply promote the unity of Christians; rather, they are by their very nature the heart and manifestation of that unity.

For two entities to be united to one another a prerequisite is the existence of something in common in their makeup. Thus, the sun and moon attract one another by the force of gravitation which is grounded in their common existence as physical beings. For two persons to be united to one another as persons there must be a common *personal* possession which can furnish the basis of that personal union. For Christians to be united to one another as Christians there must be a common *Christian* possession to ground the union. Finally, if all Christians of all cultures are to be united as *Christian personal beings*, they must possess *universally* something that is *ontic*, *personal*, and *Christian*.

Dogmatic meanings constitute the sole possible source of Christian unity because they are *universal*, *ontic*, *personal*, and *Christian*. They are *universal* because their very nature is to be a good and possible self-differentiation of all persons of all cultures. They are *ontic* because, as I have already shown, they are actual modifications of the constituent objectivity of persons. They are *personal* because the modification of the individual which they represent is a modification of him as a person; for they are directly a differentiation of the understanding and subsequently a differentiation of the whole man. Finally, they are *Christian* because they all reflect some aspect of the relationship to the risen universal Christ. As *universal*, *ontic*, *personal*, and *Christian*, these dogmatic meanings ground the possibility of a genuine conscious Christian sharing. As such, they are the immanent created source of Church unity, the change in men created by God and effected on the created level by the humanity of Christ which, when publicly recognized and expressed, founds the visible Church.[3] There is no other candidate for the role of source and essence of the Church's unity that possesses these qualities.

2. The Ground of Communication

Secondly, dogmatic meanings constitute the ground of possibility of communication within the Church. Communication is primarily not a matter of using the right words but one of having a common stock of meanings. If by some incredible procedure it were possible to produce two men who possessed within themselves the same stock of meanings but who used a different sound for each of those meanings, it would be discovered that these two men would soon be able to communicate with one another on the most difficult topics. The real difference in cultures and the real difficulties in their possibilities of communication stem not from a diversity of sounds but from a much greater diversity in the underlying sets of meanings. What enables the Church to communicate the world over, despite diversities of languages, customs, symbols, and the rest is primarily the universality of the dogmatic meanings that constitute the heart of her life and unity. There are undoubted difficulties involved in arriving at commonly agreed-on expressions; and those difficulties have multiplied in the modern world. However, the underlying universal dogmatic meanings that characterize the Church constitute the grounds of a genuine possibility of communication at a Christian level. When these dogmatic meanings are expressly grasped by all—that is, when the Church moves from dogmatic meanings to dogmatic understanding (in accordance with the terminology utilized at the beginning of this chapter)—then the possibility of Christian communication becomes a probability. The ecumenical movement among Christians, I suggest, will benefit enormously by the conscious grasp and articulation of these dogmatic meanings; similarly, the communication among all who believe in God will be facilitated by the conscious grasp and expression of universal natural meanings. This, however, is to anticipate our treatment of dogmatic understanding.

3. The Foundation of the Church's Enduring Identity

Thirdly, dogmatic meanings are the foundation of the enduring identity of the Church. Dogmatic meanings, considered in both their potential and actual realization, alone constitute the created ecclesial reality belonging to our present mode of existence that makes the Church of all ages to be one identifiable Church. This statement has three implications which must be clarified.

Need of an enduring ecclesial Reality. In the first place, the statement implies that if the Church can be said to be one identifiable Church throughout time, there must be within it some created ecclesial reality belonging to the present mode of existence which has persisted throughout all past ages and which will endure until the end. I do not think it sufficient to say that there is one Church because God continues in his love for men throughout time. This assertion resembles the fallacy of those who claimed that men remained intrinsically sinners after justification, although God now looked upon them as if they were justified. This propostion has been almost universally rejected; because if there is no change in the sinner, and if we are incapable of making meaningful statements about changes in God's attitudes, then talk of God looking upon the sinner as if he were justified is nothing but a word game. It has no reference in reality. Similarly, to state that the Church is constituted in continuous being by God's fidelity without in any way indicating what continues in created reality is to play with words. No talk about God has any meaning unless it can in some way be grounded—whether by analogy, projection, extrapolation, or the like—in human experience. By its very nature, meaning, as a differentiation of man's experiential continuum, is grounded in experience.

Moreover, it will not do to say that the Church is constituted by the fidelity of the risen Christ to it. This is to reduce the Church to the universal unfailingness of the risen Christ. This method would make it impossible to distinguish the Church from any other social reality, because all of reality is under the dominion of the risen Christ. The fact is that no created reality of the present mode of existence can be distinguished from any other created reality except by some quality that belongs to this mode of existence. Hence, if the Church is said to persist in being as an entity distinct from other beings, it must possess some quality of the present mode of existence that distinguishes it. If one places all the difference in the risen Christ, then one is saying that the unfailing influence of the risen Christ upon the Church has absolutely no effect upon it which is distinguishable by us and which constitutes it perennially as his Church. If there is a Church, it is identifiable only by Christ and his Father.

The enduring ecclesial reality cannot be concrete. In the second place, the ecclesial reality which is said to identify the Church and to endure over the ages cannot be some external visible concrete reality. No persons persist over the life of the Church; no concrete operational structures have eternal validity; and despite what certain older apologists may have thought, no concrete organizational constitution has distinguished and will distinguish the universal Church of all the ages.[4] The attempts to identify the Church by exterior visible marks supposedly noticeable by all has failed remarkably to convince any but those who already had identified the Church.

Dogmatic meanings identify the Church of all ages. In the third place, that which does identify the Church of all ages is what we have called dogmatic meanings. The Church consists of people who are distinguished by their relationship to the risen Christ and the change that relationship works in them as persons. What identifies these people and separates them from others is *primarily* that set of universally present differentiations of experiential continua that are constituted by these dogmatic meanings. This is not to deny that because of the expressive nature of man there will necessarily be external expressions of those meanings; hence these expressions have perennially been in evidence in the Scriptures and subsequent ecclesiastical writings, in liturgical symbols, and in a visible chain of Church leaders. However, these expressions, though necessary, are secondary. Ontically, meaning always precedes external expression, even if in the concrete they mutually affect one another.

Finally, a distinction needs to be made between potentially achievable dogmatic meanings and actually achieved ones. At no stage of its existence before the end of this eon will the Church actually achieve all the universal differentiations of experiential continua possible to this mode of being. These possibilities will be achieved more and more, however, as the ages go by; and this progressive achievement constitutes the inner ground of the phenomenon we have come to denominate as the development of dogma. Moreover, as we have seen, in the early ages and even up to the present time, much of the Church's understanding has not been explicitly at the level of universal dogmatic meanings. Rather, that understanding has tended to remain at the level of temporally conditioned meanings in which were embedded, in a manner not distinguished or distinguishable for the most part, these universal meanings. Hence the Church of prior ages cannot be said to be identified with the Church of subsequent time by the possession of the same set of achieved universal meanings.

However, we can say that the universal meanings achieved in subsequent ages have been present *in potentia* in prior ages in that (1) earlier concrete activities, symbolic acts, and temporally conditioned concepts and verbalizations actually represent later dogmatic meanings, although in a form in which these universal meanings were not distinguished from the culturally conditioned accidents in which they were embedded, or (2) the later universal meanings emerged from the concrete application of prior universal meanings to the various new situations in which the Church successively found itself.[5] The explicitly grasped dogmatic meanings of later ages were present in former ages only as the generating equation is present in each point of the curve or line which it generates. It is this continuity of generating meaning which constitutes the enduring identity of the Church.

In this context one can begin to discuss the question dealing with the relative priority of infallibility and indefectibility. It has been claimed that indefectibility is the more basic attribute.[6] I would claim it is more precise to say that what is basic is the persistence of dogmatic meanings. These dogmatic meanings, because of their universality, are present in the Church throughout its history. As such, they constitute the specific essential element whose continuing existence in the makeup of the Christian people enables us to speak of the one Church as being indefectible. At the same time, because this enduring element is not some concrete thing but a set of meanings, it is also what grounds the possibility of infallibility, as I shall attempt to show in greater detail.

AN OBJECTION

It would be understandable if at this point someone would raise an objection against the centrality we have assigned to dogmatic meanings. If these meanings are so universal and significant, then why were they not stressed in the great tradition of the Church's past? Can it be that such a basic category was totally unknown or only half-glimpsed for centuries? The answer to this objection is twofold. On the one hand, the reality I have designated as a "dogmatic meaning" was not unknown in the past; it was referred to in more or less general terms, and its existence was implied in the theological operations of the centuries. On the other hand, the fact that this reality was not precisely designated and its importance not strongly emphasized is completely comprehensible in the light of the dynamics of human understanding and articulation.

On the one hand, dogmatic meanings were acknowledged in a general way in the past. They were acknowledged, first of all, in the stress placed upon truth and orthodoxy. One has to do a great deal of dubious interpreting to establish that the early texts treat directly of infallibility in the Church. However, there is no doubt that the truth is stressed both in Scripture (Jn. 8:32; 1 Tim. 3:14–15) and in the activity of the early Church. This central importance of the truth appears in the tendency to distinguish what must be held by all from the culturally conditioned practices of a few (e.g., at the so-called Council of Jerusalem). It also appears in the condemnations of those who were believed in error which fill much of the history of the early Church. Nicolas Afanassieff, speaking for a modern Orthodox view on the subject of truth, expresses what I believe is essentially in accord with the early mentality of the Church:[7]

Orthodox thought does not move in the category of infallibility but in that of Truth. If one thinks in the category of Truth, then one sees that infallibility is the result of the Truth. The Church has in itself the truth; for it possesses the Spirit of Truth, who was given to it at the moment when the Church came into visible existence." And I will pray the Father, and he will give you another Counselor, to be with you for ever, even the Spirit of truth, whom the world cannot receive" (Jn. 14:16–17). Revelation, under the form of Sacred Scripture and Tradition, is confided to the Church, which is its guardian and consequently "the pillar and ground of truth." The gift of guarding revealed truth implies that of judging doctrines which arise in the milieu of the Church and which claim to be true. The Church judges these doctrines on the basis of the doctrine that she herself possesses. In the history of the condemnation of Noëtus, one finds a classic example of the position of the Church with regard to heretical doctrines. Hippolytus of Rome recounts that when the content of the teaching of *Noëtus* had been divulged, the presbyters summoned him, probably before an ecclesiastical assembly. Having listened to an exposé by Noëtus of his doctrine, the presbyters read the profession of faith which was at one and the same time the condemnation of this doctrine. Noëtus was then expelled. We do not know exactly who Noëtus was or where the assembly took place; that is unimportant. The essential point is that from the beginning the truth contained in the Church condemned the heretical doctrines, thus manifesting the truth. All the dogmatic decisions of the Church are manifestations of the Spirit of Truth, who inhabits the Church and acts in her. "He will glorify me, and he will take what is mine and declare it to you" (Jn. 16:14). Here we see why Truth and Church are identical. The notion of truth includes that of infallibility. The Church is infallible because it is Truth. Only the true may be infallible. It follows from this that in the consciousness of the Orthodox Church it is the truth and not infallibility which occupies the first place. Of itself and without any relationship to the truth, infallibility is a concept without content.

This presence of Truth within the Church, by reason of which error stands condemned, is also implied in the standard theological operating procedure of the centuries that we still implement when we appeal to past texts. How can texts be said to be normative if there is no enduring truth that they refer to? To accept a text as normative and to appeal to it against a present meaning over and over again is to assume, whether one realizes it or not, that there is a lasting meaning that men are capable of grasping. The more one refers to a given text such as the Scriptures in an ever growing number of epochs and civilizations, the more one is implicitly admitting that there are transcultural meanings.

On the other hand, it must be admitted that what I have called dogmatic meanings were never articulated precisely as such in the early Church; nor is there evidence that such a concept existed in the minds of early Churchmen in an implicit fashion. However, this is quite normal, given the ordinary dynamics of human understanding and articulation. The concept of dogmatic meanings is a second-order concept that by the nature of things can only spring into men's minds after a long series of prior first-order concepts. First-order concepts are those which reflect individual dogmatic meanings generated in the Church. As I shall attempt to show in the following chapter in some detail, the Church first lives out its life. Only subsequently, and sometimes long afterwards, does it detect the recurring meanings embedded in its life, the meanings I have called dogmatic meanings. Further, it takes even longer before the Church is able to enunciate and proclaim these individual meanings. All of this, however, is still at the level of *first-order* dogmatic meanings, that is, meanings that *immediately* reflect aspects of concrete Church life. What takes far longer is the understanding and articulation of the generic relationships, processes, and implications that characterize all individual dogmatic meanings and their emergence. These *second-order* meanings constitute the lasting structure within which all first-order meanings are generated. By their very nature these second-order meanings can exist only in a mind already differentiated by a series of first-order meanings that constitute the experiential matrix out of which it can grasp and subsequently articulate meanings of the second order. The concept of dogmatic meanings is such a second-order concept. Therefore, it is to be expected that it was not grasped in the early Church.

Let me be more specific. In the beginning the Church lived out its belief that Christ was true God and true man; and it reflected in its activity that it was related to Father, Son, and Spirit in its worship.

Only after the passage of centuries was it able explicitly and definitively to grasp and enunciate what had been embedded in its practice
from the outset. Thus, we had the doctrines of the Incarnation and
the Trinity. In a similar manner there emerged doctrines about the
Eucharist, the saints, and the Church. All this is, of course, purposely
oversimplified. I wish only to point out that what came first is what
I have called *first-order* doctrines. However, after a large number of
such doctrines had emerged, the Church became capable of examining
the process by which they emerged. It could then detect elements
that appeared in the emergence of all doctrines. It could then, and
only then, begin to grasp *second-order* meanings. Now one of these
elements that could only be detected as being common in the emergence of all doctrines is that of universal meanings. Therefore, it is
not surprising that there was no explicit understanding of the phenomenon of these meanings in the early Church.

7 The Emergence of Universal Meanings

How do individual dogmatic meanings actually emerge? How can there begin to exist in living members of the Church a differentiation of experiential continua which has been achieved in Christ as the universal and perfect man? Do dogmatic meanings spring immediately from God through Christ to the members of the Church? Or is there a process by which such meanings eventually become embedded in men's minds and hearts? The contention here is that there is such a process and that this process by which dogmatic meanings emerge is merely the natural process of human understanding as it takes place in men grasped by faith in the risen Christ. I shall attempt to present the steps of this process in more or less schematic fashion. These steps are not meant to be taken as following in precise chronological order. Rather, I have simply tried to gather in one place the various dynamic factors which regularly occur in the Christian process that leads to the emergence of dogmatic meanings.

TEN ELEMENTS

1. The Apostolic Experience

The first and most important element was the experience of the earthly Saviour by the men who accompanied him during his public ministry. These men were steeped in an Old Testament background, and their experience of Christ was necessarily modified by that background. It was that experience of Christ and that Old Testament background which subsequently enabled them to recognize in faith the universal presence of the risen Lord. The grasp of this basic faith truth and its gradual penetration into the whole of their emotions, attitudes, modes of acting, and conceptual understanding enabled the apostles to become the primary witnesses of the faith. That is why the New Testament speaks of them so often as "witnesses to his resurrection" (cf. Acts 1:22; 2:32; 3:15; 4:33; 10:41). Through them, all subsequent Christians have come to believe in the risen Christ.

2. *The Personal Response to the Risen Christ*

A second element in the process leading to the emergence of dogmatic meanings is the personal response of each Christian to the risen
Christ present in his life. This response, which is a carrying out of
the implications of the universal saving presence of Christ, leads inevitably to the modification of each individual's experiential continuum in varying degrees. When a master idea grips a man and is by
its very nature present, at least implicitly, in all that he does, it soon
leads to the modification of the whole context of his life and the
quality of all his experiences. This follows not so much from thought
as from actions, emotions, and attitudes which prolong thought and
make its meaning penetrate the various levels of a man's personality.

3. *Individual Understanding of Christian Experience*

A third element is the individual's understanding of his own Christian experience. That understanding necessarily presupposes a prior
experience impregnated with the recognition in faith of the saving
presence of the risen Christ. Because nothing is understood unless
there has already been an appropriate modification of one's experiential continuum, it is impossible for a person to have that differentiation of consciousness which we call faith understanding unless there
is present within him in some way the kind of faith experience which
can ground that understanding. A man who has been born blind cannot understand the specific meaning of sight (though he can grasp
that it is another sense because he has experienced the meanings
underlying "sense" and "another"). Certain groups of individuals in
the ghetto cannot understand existentially the notion of justice because
they have no extended experience of just treatment. Similarly, no
one can understand the personal implications of the faith acceptance
of the risen Christ in the absence of an experiential continuum in
which the initial notion of that doctrine has been lived out. Understanding the implications of a universal influence flows not so much
from deductions made abstractly from the principle, as from having
the principle permeate one's life and guide one's choices. It is the subsequent reflection upon the changes that have occurred in oneself as
a result of this permeation and guidance that enables one to grasp
the further implications of the principle. It is this latter kind of under-

standing that is akin to what Newman called "real", as opposed to
the former kind of understanding, which is approximately what he
called "notional." Only real understanding unifies the person as a
whole, and it alone can be the mark and presence of salvation; for
it sums up and unifies what has been present in the whole of the
person's being and life.

I might add that such real understanding is not distinguished from
notional understanding simply by the degree to which it permeates
the person. By its very origin in the context of a fluid experiential
continuum, real understanding differs from deductional notional
understanding. This follows from the fact that the implementation
of a principle by free activity changes a person in ways not previously
foreseen, and this unforeseen change leads to an understanding that
is not simply deducible from the original generating principle. Finally,
this conscious grasp of the self-differentiation brought about by the
carrying out into life of the import of the universal presence of the
risen Christ can be said to be a necessary consequence of man's
dynamic nature; for no one in reasonably full possession of his humanity can experience anything significant without also experiencing
the desire to understand and integrate that experience into the whole
of his self-image; *a fortiori*, this is applicable to the most basic of
Christian experiences.

4. Conceptualization of Individual Religious Understanding

A fourth element is conceptualization by each individual of his
religious understanding. The concept in this and other cases is merely
the human product that expresses the results of the act of understanding. When the mind grasps and understands—even before it
speaks a word or writes a sentence, or even without its becoming
reflexively aware of its understanding—it sums up and expresses that
understanding in some kind of concept. Religious concepts are, therefore, the fruit of religious understanding.[1]

5. Judging the Validity of Individual Religious Understanding

A fifth element is the judgment of the validity of the individual's
understanding of his experience as viewed in the light of the universality of the risen Christ's influence. Has one correctly understood?

Has one correctly identified elements in one's religious experience? Have the choices that generated the experiences been in accord with the implications of the universal reaching out of Christ already grasped by the Christian community? These and similar questions are not explicitly asked in most cases, but they are more or less present in the Christian's mind and operation. Unreflexively, the average individual usually attempts to verify the validity of his understanding and the subsequent conceptualization of his Christian experience by checking it with his prior experience and the articulations of the experiences of others who share his basic religious inclinations. This process of verification is, in the concrete, practically identical with the process of further understanding and deepening of the experience (assuming the validity of the experience and its understanding). For the more one verifies the validity of an understanding of a religious experience by checking its conformity with the totality of one's religious life, the more one actually differentiates that experience and understanding. The process is analogous to that of checking the validity of a general principle. The more one sees that the proposed general principle actually explains a great number and variety of concrete facts, the more that principle becomes established. At the same time, however, the person who actually establishes the principle by this mode of verification existentially grasps the full meaning and range of the principle ever more deeply. In short, to check a meaning is concretely to grasp it more fully. Therefore, to verify the meaning of the Resurrection with regard to its implications for life in the context of a life lived in its conscious acceptance is to grasp more fully what the Resurrection means.

6. Articulation and Communication of Individual Understanding

A sixth element is the articulation and communication of conceptualized religious understanding by the individual Christian. By its own inner dynamic, understanding leads to articulation. The grasp of a new relationship to another or of a new understanding of self, when coupled with man's need to grow by expressing himself, induces him by inner necessity to express that understanding in word, in action, and sometimes in ritual. Such expressions are really the means by which the individual concretizes an acquired understanding and makes it pass into the whole fiber of his being. In a religious context such articulation is the source of prophetic preaching, concrete moral activity, and personalized prayer. All of these activities are really so many personal professions of faith, external manifestations of the basic inner principle of the faith acceptance of the risen Christ. They are not the faith expressed in some abstract and general sense but unique manifestations of the dynamism of faith in the concrete individual. They are to the average individual what the more widely known professions of the *Confessions* are to Augustine. They contain aspects of the unique faith of the individual. Finally, these individual professions of faith precede rather than follow the generic universal understanding of the Church's faith. The picture of an initial generic faith understanding that is gradually appropriated in a unique way by individuals is not consistent with the developmental nature of understanding. The faith exists originally in unique persons in a unique way. This was true even of the primitive witnesses. Only subsequently, as I shall indicate, could there arise those dogmatic meanings that constitute the universal heritage of faith.

Allied to articulation is communication. If articulation follows understanding because a man needs to express himself as an individual, communication is necessary because a man also needs to express himself as a social being. In the concrete, the very acts by which a man articulates his understanding may also be acts in which that understanding is communicated. The actions one performs, the emotions one expresses, the words one utters to articulate and deepen one's own understanding are often also the means by which one communicates to others the experiential basis of one's own religious understanding as well as that understanding in verbal form.

Thus, religious understanding is constantly being articulated and communicated. In fact, one may say that the Church is most deeply constituted by an unending series of such articulations and communications. Day in and day out, those who call themselves Christians keep alive, deepen, and share their living experience of the risen Christ in and through these activities. Each such activity either brings into visibility, into consciousness, or into implicit and unreflexive existence a new aspect of the risen Christ or reaffirms an old one (cf. Mt. 13:52). It is these activities that carry the faith across the ages, constituting the irreplaceable matrix of individual traditions that makes possible the great Tradition of the Church.

7. Emergence of Common Understanding

A seventh element is the gradual emergence of a *common* understanding of the varied shared Christian experiences and expressions
of the risen Christ. Beyond the uniqueness that characterizes every
experience and understanding of the individual there are common
elements which are gradually seen to be present in large numbers of
experiences. This common element first emerges in a local group
and reflects what is common to the faith of that group. Thus, a local
Church comes into being that possesses a shared Christian understanding and a shared series of expressions which manifest that
understanding.

8. Formulation by the Local Community

An eighth element is the formulation by the local community of
its understanding in words. Generally, through some representative
or representatives the group articulates, first orally and then on paper,
the meanings common to the faith that lives within its members.
Thus, we have a Gospel according to St. Matthew, a book that
articulates the faith as it existed in a given local community of Jewish
Christians. Thus, too, we have the corpus of epistles attributed to
St. Paul, most of which reflect the needs of local Churches. This does
not mean that there were not aspects of the Christian faith that were
universal by nature from the outset; it means, rather, that these
universal aspects were first grasped within a local community; it
means, further, that they were first articulated without explicit differentiation as to degree of universality within a constellation of
numerous culturally conditioned meanings of the local community.
As a result, the Scriptures, on the whole, are repositories of dogmatic
meanings only insofar as these meanings are surrounded by many
limited culturally conditioned understandings and expressions. Thus,
"Jesus is Lord" represents a universal Christian meaning in Scripture.
Yet it appears with other assertions of non-universal significance
(e.g. assertions regarding the eucharistic symbols as I explained them
in the extended example of chapter 5); and the distinction as to
universality or non-universality is not explicitly grasped.

9. *Emergence of Universal Understandings*

A ninth element is the emergence of a relatively *universal* understanding of the faith understood and expressed in local communities.
The personal relationships of men of various communities (recall
the visit of Polycarp to Rome), the interchanges of letters, the holding
of assemblies of bishops, the very establishment of a *universally* recognized New Testament (not at the outset but after a few centuries)—
each of these contributed to the gradual explicit realization of what
was common to all the local Churches and their faith expressions. It
was only at this moment that a need could arise to grasp an abstract
dogma which could somehow unify the Church of various localities
and customs within the Empire.

10. *Articulation and Communication of*
Universal Understanding

A tenth element is the articulation and communication of this
relatively universal understanding. In the main, this took place at
what we have called general councils. The process involved was
analogous to the one I described for the emergence of a local community formulation in element 8. What I would like to stress here is,
on the one hand, that such conciliar teaching necessarily came later;
and, on the other hand, that such teaching is still only relatively
universal and does not yet, for the most part, constitute the expression of dogmatic meanings in the sense that I have defined these
meanings.

On the one hand, such conciliar teaching understandably came
later. In general, there could not have been a universal teaching before
there had been many local teachings; nor could there have been a
universal council before there had been local sharings. We have to
overcome our tendency to think that meanings usually moved from
universal to particular; instead they tended to move, at least in the
period when they first emerged, from the particular to the universal.
If there are universal tendencies and dynamics expressed in local
situations, the explicit recognition of these tendencies and dynamics
in the understanding of men and their subsequent expression by
appropriate formulas and structures ordinarily follow long after

many concrete specific expressions of these tendencies and dynamics. The same kind of movement is manifested in the *emergence* of a hierarchy of leadership. Catholics have sometimes spoken as if the universal Petrine office was instituted with its present main features at the beginning. They were embarrassed by findings which indicated that the early local Churches appear to have had no recognizable episcopal leadership (e.g., at Corinth) and that subsequently and for centuries there is little evidence for an acceptance of a role for the See of Peter which matches in importance the role now exercised by the papacy. Non-Catholics sometimes used this evidence to show that the papacy represented a usurpation of power because it was not biblically based. Consonant with the view here advocated of the inevitable *initial* generic movement of meanings and structures from the specific to the general, I would say that the early appearance of a universal papacy would have been utterly impossible; that relatively charismatic and acephalous Churches were to be expected at first, until a community of meanings emerged and a need to unify appeared; that only long afterward would the necessity arise for the universal leader and unifier we know as the pope. The hierarchy is the parallel in the order of concrete leadership to meanings in the order of understanding. In both cases the movement is *initially* from the particular to the universal, and *it could not be otherwise if man is to remain man.* No universal truth can be effectively understood unless one previously grasps the particulars which it unifies; no universal leadership built upon understanding and freedom can effectively appear unless a common basis for that leadership has first been manifested.[2]

On the other hand, even the conciliar teaching that we now have is on the whole only relatively universal. The point was made before, but it can be profitably reiterated in the present context. The bulk of the Church's universal understanding of the past two thousand years sprang from a culturally conditioned Church which was not reflexively aware of its cultural conditioning. Hence its teaching inevitably contained elements which were universal in that culture but were not universal *tout court.* It thus becomes a task for the present to realize on a large scale those dogmatic meanings that are truly universal; and it is these meanings alone that can ground infallible proclamations.

PROOF OF THIS MOVEMENT OF DEVELOPMENT

Of course, this whole movement of development from an initial local experience towards universal meanings has not been proved from an exhaustive analysis of early texts. Such a proof is neither practically possible nor necessary. It is not practically possible because of the scantiness of the evidence and the level of reflective consciousness of biblical man. All we have are scattered texts that manifest in a fragmentary way the articulation of the understanding of the primitive communities. By painstaking dissection of these texts we can with some probability arrive at the subsidiary documents which they are derived from, and even at some of the overall community concerns which led to their production. However, the paucity of the documents makes impossible a tracing of the kind of processes I sketched out in ten elements; moreover, even if we had a great many more texts, it is doubtful that we could find evidence for these processes; biblical man was not interested in them, was hardly aware of them, and certainly did not write them down in detail.

Nor is a proof from the texts necessary. The basis of all historical interpretation is the fundamental assumption that the interpreter is the same kind of being as the men whose thoughts and movements he is interpreting. As I tried to show in the section on interpretation, the interpreter must have a fund of meanings that he hypothesizes as being the meanings that explicitly or implicitly were the meanings of the age gone by. However, meanings exist in the modern interpreter only by a process by which lower meanings are combined and integrated into higher meanings. To grasp another's meanings one has to share in one's own way the process by which they were generated. Thus, to understand what you mean by "definition" I must undergo a mental process in which the appropriate experiential elements in my background enable me to grasp what is generic in the process of coming to the notion of definition. In the simplest terms, I must have in my background the experience of coming to a definition a number of times, so that I can appreciate what is generic to definition. The point here is that historical interpretation presupposes similar processes in the interpreter and the people being interpreted. Therefore, one need only investigate the generic processes now visible to the interpreter. Owing to a variety of factors: our far greater self-consciousness and self-differentiation; our far more developed sciences of psychology, sociology, epistemology, learning theory, and group dynamics; our far greater opportunities for examining the relevant data—since such data now exist in living men and not in faded texts—these processes are more open to being verified by present empirical investigation, rather than being wrested from ancient documents. In any and all ages, historical investigation presupposes a similarity in the understanding processes of all ages. Hence, if the method I propose is declared invalid, then the historical method itself, which is to replace it, is thereby declared to be invalid. This does not mean that an analysis of the present can enable us to state what concretely happened in the past. It only means that whatever specifically happened in the past must be presumed to have happened in accordance with the recurring processes of development of understanding now taking place. Knowing these processes enables us to put into a human context the data available only in the texts; it enables us to hypothesize with great probability when data are scarce; above all, it enables us in a number of cases to arrive at dogmatic meanings never before grasped in all their universality.

SUMMARY

In summary of the processes by which dogmatic meanings emerge, we can say that the whole life of the Church is the living matrix of such meanings. The persons involved are individuals as such, local communities and their leaders, the members of the universal Church of varying cultures and those who represent them. The acts involved are basic faith, decisions made in the light of that faith, moral activities carried out, understanding and conceptualization and articulation, liturgical expression, and decisions of leadership. Thus, dogmatic meanings are not simply the product of the work of the magisterium and the theologian. The work of these two groups is properly that of generic understanding and articulation. However, they are enabled to function because long before they arrived on the scene, the living out of the faith had set in motion a dynamic process that eventually called for their emergence.[3]

To some it may seem that on this theory the emergence of doctrine is reduced to a purely natural process. To such objectors I would point out that the development I speak of takes place concretely in those who have the faith; it presupposes a faith experience that is logically unprovable to those who lack it; each step of the process is thus compounded of what derives from faith and what is knowable from an examination of human development everywhere; it is thus, from beginning to end, a faith-emergence process.[4]

Characteristics of Dogmatic Meanings

One of the marks of a good explanation is its capacity to clarify all the data under discussion. In the present chapter I shall set forth some of the characteristics and relationships traditionally associated with dogma, and I shall attempt to show how the explanation I have given clarifies and explains this notion. I shall take up the following topics: the hierarchy of dogmatic meanings; the relationship of dogmatic meanings to theology; the stability or irreformability of dogma; the mysterious and eschatological nature of dogma.

THE HIERARCHY OF DOGMATIC MEANINGS

The process by which dogmatic meanings emerge sheds light on the hierarchy of doctrines.[1] It is a commonplace that some doctrines are central and significant; others are said to be more peripheral and of secondary importance. For the uninitiated it might seem that what counts is unity in the central meanings, whereas there is lesser need for agreement on peripheral ones. We must be united in our acceptance of the risen Lord; it may not be necessary for us to agree on the Immaculate Conception, the Assumption, or Papal Infallibility.

On the basis of what has been stated on dogmatic meanings and their origin, I believe that the concept of the hierarchy of dogmatic truths is an undifferentiated manner of viewing a complex reality. A more nuanced procedure would be to classify dogmatic meanings into the first-and second-order meanings mentioned in the last chapter; in addition, first-order meanings would be subdivided into immediate and mediate implications of the basic acceptance of the resurrection of Christ.

The basic first-order dogmatic meaning is the acceptance of the universal presence and activity of the risen Christ. In its immediate implications this refers to the fact that Christ was and is true man; that he is present as fulfilled man, reaching out to all creation with the totality of his perfected human powers; that his presence makes possible the world-wide celebration of the Mass; that all activity which brings men into unity with creation thereby unites them to

Christ present in creation; that in and through Christ, and through him alone, the Son of God enfleshed, we have access to the Father and the Spirit. Thus, immediate implications have to do with the condition of Christ himself and what is accepted when we accept him as risen.

Mediate implications refer to what the resurrection of Christ reveals about man. If Christ's resurrection is but the prolongation and fulfillment of his earthly condition, if he is as a creature still only man, then he reveals the possibilities and ultimate destiny of man. Because he is risen and perfected in his whole humanity, body and soul, all men are called to that destiny with him. Hence the dogmatic meanings of the Resurrection of the Body, the Assumption, and Heaven speak of the perfected condition of the followers of Christ. The Communion of Saints refers to the total relatability of the perfected Christian that parallels the universality of the risen Christ; and the General Judgment is but another way of speaking of the achievement of (or utter falling away from) that total communion. The doctrine of Merit speaks of the intrinsic development of the Christian insofar as he follows the growth pattern of Christ; whereas Original Sin, Personal Sin, and Hell indicate respectively the collective, individual, and definitive falling away, in act and in subsequent ontic development, on the part of men who do not live up to the fully intelligent and free performance of Christ.

Second-order dogmatic meanings would be those which thematize the process by which first-order meanings or doctrines emerge. They represent the further differentiation of consciousness possible to men who have realized over a long period of time the immediate and mediate implications of the resurrection of Christ. They are to the Church's teaching enterprise what method is to the sciences; they are achieved last of all because they thematize the recurring features of first-order performance; and performance must precede thematization. The realization of the phenomenon of dogmatic meanings, the grasp of the genesis of such meanings, the teaching on Infallibility, and the notion of development of doctrine are all second-order meanings.

What this classification and the ordering of the various dogmatic meanings in each class to one another reveal is the danger of referring to central and peripheral meanings in such a way as to make it seem as if the peripheral meanings might be more easily dispensable.

No dogmatic meaning is in any way dispensable; for all meanings are either first- or second-order derivations from the resurrection of Jesus Christ. They are merely the differentiations of experiential continua which occur at various stages in the lives of individuals and communities who accept the implications of a view of reality which is seen as everywhere touched by the risen Christ. To deny any of these differentiations is ultimately to deny the universality of the influence of Christ. Only those who think of doctrines as simply being truths of various kinds gathered by God for our belief, but having no intrinsic ontic relationship to a single reality, can think in categories of peripheral and central. Christian meanings can be dispensed with only if they are untrue; all true meanings of universal import are significant because all in some way are expressive of the absolutely core doctrine of the Resurrection. They are reflective of the ultimate meaning of the Christian life from which they emerge.

RELATIONSHIP OF DOGMATIC MEANINGS TO THEOLOGY

For similar reasons the tendency to separate dogma and theology can be overdone. Dogma (more properly what I have termed "dogmatic meanings") can be looked on as pertaining to God's revelation itself, whereas theology is considered as further speculation about that revelation. In the terms of one author

[Dogmas are] . . . judgments . . . proposed to us by the teaching authority of the Church. . . . They are not, however, *mere* intellectual judgments. . . . They are like the face through which we come in contact with the person. They are the visible or intellectual face of the mystery of communion with Christ. They are the intellectual contour of the mystery itself. They have an *immediate* relationship with the mystery of Christ and God. Theology is thinking *about* the mystery, whereas those judgments which express the content of the mystery are not simply judgments *about* the mystery. They share in the life of the mystery, while they throw into bold relief the development of that mystery in the judgmental power of the human mind.[2]

I believe that the relationship between dogma and theology can be set forth more precisely. First of all, both theology and dogma have to do with meanings regarding the mystery of faith. Secondly, theological meanings are more or less limited ecclesial meanings whereas dogmas are universal meanings. Thirdly, theological meanings are united to dogmatic meanings by a process of development. Fourthly, in that developmental process, some theological meanings perish; others singly or collectively constitute with the old dogmatic meanings the matrix from which new dogmatic meanings emerge.

The points made above should be clarified. Faith involves the total acceptance by the person of the resurrection of Jesus Christ in all its implications. Reflection or thinking on faith means thematizing aspects that unify faith as actually lived in Christian persons. What theology does is to initiate the process of thematization at various levels. At the prophetic level, theology draws out the implications of the resurrection for a *hic et nunc* situation. At the level of practical living in a given cultural situation, theology (again in a loose sense of the word) articulates rules of thumb such as the well-known injunction of St. Paul that women should cover their heads while praying (1 Cor. 11:4–6) or the apparently contradictory sayings attributed to the Lord: "He who is not against you is for you" (Mk. 9:39) and "He who is not with me is against me" (Mt. 12:30). At the level of the whole of a culture or civilization, theology attempts to express the common elements in the faith as truly lived out in the Church. At every level, theology is subject to modification and correction, and ultimately expansion to a higher level. At no level is theology divorced from faith, nor is it simply an extrinsic product of faith; rather, it is a tentative expression of faith that has a more or less intrinsic unity with that faith in being its intellectual projection and extension. Dogmatic meanings, as contrasted with theological meanings, are universal and not particular, certain and not tentative. They represent those meanings which are explicit or implicit, or whose development is demanded in every Christian of every age as a necessary concomitant of the universal acceptance of the risen Christ. They are the intellectual aspect of the full flowering of Christian faith, and in concrete persons (the only focus of faith) they are identified with that faith.

The basic point is that theology and dogma are not to be considered as distinct from one another, on the one hand; nor should either or both together be considered as separate from faith, on the other hand. They are really the successive intellectual steps of a dynamic process (which includes moral acts and liturgy) by which faith becomes more deeply and universally rooted in the lives of persons who become more complex and differentiated. If the Church and its faith can be compared to a tree that keeps developing over the centuries, then theology may be compared to the leaves that express the tree's life each year and then perish; whereas dogma may be compared to the rings on the trunk that emerge year by year and yet remain for the rest of the life of the tree as a part of that life.

What primarily distinguishes dogma from theology is not that dogma is true and theology is not; for prophetic actions and judgments based thereon can be true, as theological understanding in a given context can be true for that context. Nor is it that dogma is identified with faith and mystery whereas theology is not; for good theology springs from faith and mystery and thematizes them. Rather, the difference is that dogma refers to universal meanings whereas theology (at least theology that is not incipiently dogma) refers to more limited meanings. It is this fundamental distinction that ultimately grounds the other distinctions we make between the two.

THE STABILITY OF DOGMA

It is in this light that we can grasp what has traditionally been called the "stability of dogma." This stability or irreformability of dogmatic meanings is a consequence of their universality. To grasp (1) that a meaning is a differentiation of the experiential continuum of the subject which constitutes an aspect of his development and (2) that a dogmatic meaning is one that all men are held to achieve as an aspect of their full development towards union to the risen Christ is to grasp that dogmatic meanings are irreformable. It remains to clarify the foundations for this irreformability in the realities of faith and reason.

Let us begin by posing a plausible objection. Historically, there have been meanings that seemed to be totally universal. Thus, beliefs forbidding usury and birth control persisted unhindered in the Church for centuries and even for a millennium. Yet such beliefs have come to be questioned and even discarded as universal truths. What is to assure that any other truth or differentiation of consciousness has guaranteed validity for all time? Now we can see reasons why interest-taking is not always immoral. In a similar manner, we may be able to see in the future that what appears universal today possessed a universality based on historical circumstances which happened to persist from the beginning up to the present. In principle, may it not

be that *every* self-differentiation or meaning is ultimately revisable
and that there are no universal meanings in the sense in which I have
defined them?

The objection can be met with a distinction between factual universality and presuppositional universality. Factual universality refers
to any condition of the concrete universe of creation and its relationship to the Creator which will persist *de facto* throughout this present
mode of existence before the Parousia. Such factual universality, if
it exists, can exist either in personal subjects or in the world of things.
Thus, assuming that Einstein's theory of general relativity thematizes
conditions which will always exist, we have an instance of factual
universality in the world of things. Further, assuming that the Skinnerian rules for the conditioning of persons will always be operative,
we have an instance of factual universality in the world of persons.
Now such universality, whether of persons or things, can ground
self-differentiations of all subjects of all ages who grasp them. Given
the assumption that both general relativity and Skinnerian rules will
always be operative, and recognizing that man develops and self-
differentiates by his experience, understanding, decision, and activity
in the concrete world, it would follow that all fully developed men
would have to possess the common self-differentiation stemming from
a grasp of Skinner and Einstein.

Presuppositional universality is a specific aspect of factual universality. It is called presuppositional because it rests solely upon the
basis of what must be present when any person accepts the Christian
faith. These necessary presuppositions are, first of all, the presupposition in faith of the all-pervading presence and activity of the risen
Christ. This presupposition cannot be proved or disproved by empirical means; it is, however, that which must be accepted from the witness of the past as the distinguishing badge of the Christian tradition.
The second necessary presupposition is the presupposition of reason.
This presupposition involves all that is contained in the generic processes by which the human person through experience, understanding,
judgment, decision, and implementation develops from simplicity
and undifferentiation to complexity and differentiation. It will thus
be seen that presuppositional universality refers not to a universality present in objects but only to a universality present in subjects—
the risen Christ and the Christian subject. These two subjects and
their processes are present whenever faith exists; for faith is always

of the universal risen Christ, and faith always exists only in a subject, and in him always as a result of generic processes common to all subjects. The common nature of these processes, as I have indicated, is implied in all communication and in the possibility of history.

Now factual universality apart from presuppositional universality, which is a part of it, cannot be the grounds of dogmatic meanings. Men change and develop, and as they do their grasp of the data of the universe becomes more complex and complete. The generalizations they made that unified the data possessed at a prior stage may eventually be seen to be unwarranted by new data; a broader generalization may be required. Moreover, there is no way of telling when one has arrived at all the data. As Einstein clearly saw, no amount of positive evidence could prove his theory; but one single piece of contradictory data could disprove it. Whether such data exist or not can be known only by one who is omniscient.

Presuppositional universality can and must ground dogmatic meanings for all time. This universality is coterminous with the qualities embedded in the very effort to come to grips with the universal presence and activity of the risen Christ. To postulate that the meanings which unify presuppositional universality are not in themselves universal is to postulate the disappearance of the risen Christ or of the human subject as we now know him. It is to postulate a Christless Christianity or an imaginary subject of the future who will transcend the processes of historical man till now. Such a postulation is possible. In either case, however, it would be the end of the Christian faith in any sense that would be meaningful to present man; for it would be the destruction of at least one of the two subjects necessary for the existence of faith—the risen Christ or the human knower and lover. Thus, the stability of dogmatic meanings based on presuppositional universality is a stability which is coextensive with the existence of the risen Christ and the human subject. Such a stability, while not absolute as is the stability of God, is the supreme kind of creatural stability;hence dogmatic meanings can rightly be denominated as possessing stability and irreformability.

It might be thought, however, that with the advance of understanding some prior dogmatic meanings, while not undergoing modification, would be relegated to a collection of doctrines that are no longer relevant. Men can pass a stage in which some meanings were important; and in a subsequent stage they may discover that this group of dogmatic meanings no longer existentially has significance for vital Christians. While such an objection seems plausible, I find that it fails to take into account the dynamics of human development, and in particular of human understanding, as these pertain to dogmatic meanings.

A dogmatic meaning represents a self-differentiation of each Christian subject in his contact with the universal object of faith, the risen Christ. The most immediate self-differentiations emerge first; the more complex and mediate self-differentiations emerge later. However, subsequent differentiations are always dependent upon the realization of prior differentiations, at least as habitually possessed. This follows from the cumulative nature of understanding and development. Just as one cannot really understand (and hence be differentiated by) the Pythagorean theorem unless one has understood and assimilated the meanings of the prior theorems upon which it rests, so too one cannot really grasp and be self-differentiated by later dogmatic meanings unless one has in some way recapitulated in oneself the self-differentiations of prior dogmatic meanings. This does not mean that one must consciously and separately acknowledge the formulas under which prior dogmatic meanings were expressed; nor does it even mean that one must consciously and reflexively grasp that he possesses these prior meanings. What is required is that the prior meanings should actually affect his life by being at least implicitly embedded in his makeup; for one can advance to a further explicit meaning on the basis of a prior implicit meaning. Thus, it is possible for a man to grasp the meaning of the Eucharist in an explicit way without having previously thematized the meaning of the Resurrection upon which it rests, provided that he does acknowledge the Resurrection meaning implicitly in some fashion. However, if he has in no way internalized the Resurrection doctrine, than eucharistic explanations such as transubstantiation will remain meaningless formulas. Thus, dogmatic meanings never become irrelevant, although their conscious and reflexive understanding and their articulation in traditional formulas may in certain circumstances be omitted.

THE MYSTERIOUS AND ESCHATOLOGICAL NATURE OF DOGMATIC MEANINGS

The mysterious and eschatological nature of dogmatic meanings should now be evident. All dogmatic meanings are "reasonable" in that they explicate and thematize the elements of the lasting dynamic process by which Christian man grows. However, all dogmatic meanings are necessarily "mysterious" and have an eschatological reference because they all flow from that growth process as it is carried out in the faith contact with the universally present risen Christ. Because the present mode of existence of the risen Christ is beyond our powers of experiencing and understanding, we can only point to it as the final extrapolation and fulfillment of what we imperfectly are and Christ (when he walked this earth) incipiently was.[3] We cannot know that condition univocally, but only in faith and mystery; and since that condition of existence touches all our activity and is explicated in some way in every Christian dogmatic meaning, every dogmatic meaning necessarily participates in the mystery. There are not, therefore, many mysteries of Christianity, but the one mystery of the Resurrection refracted through the various aspects of the universally recurring features of human growth and development. That which makes dogmatic meanings ultimately one, so that they all stand and fall together, also makes them all mysterious.

At the same time, the Resurrection element makes all dogmas eschatological. The eschaton is that condition that is characterized by the universality of risen existence. Dogmatic meanings thematize for ourselves a condition in which Christ possesses risen existence while we are still *in via* towards such a condition. Their inadequacy and mystery are reminders that this is not a lasting city. On the one hand, they are inadequate in that they only thematize a number of generic processes; for much that we now know, or believe we know, is provisional. As inadequate, they point towards the condition of risen existence, when not only generic processes but also every intelligible aspect of each individual nature will be shared in a total communion of saints. On the other hand, they are mysterious in that they point to a not yet experienced state in which we shall know Christ as he knows us. Then the mystery of risen existence and the other mysteries which express the facets of that primary Christian mystery will be dissolved by our achievement of resurrection; for that achievement will enable us to know on the basis of our own experience what is now the lot of Christ. Only then will it become evident that the infinite mystery which grounds all creation and its unending call to development is that of the life of Father, Son, and Holy Spirit. Heaven is not the dissolution of that final mystery but the supreme realization that life begins and ends with it.[4] Just as in this life we find that the clearing up of more immediate mysteries leads to the uncovering of greater mysteries, so that awe and wonder characterize the real expert in a field more than the tyro, so too the resolving of what is now mysterious to us will lead in the eschaton to the deepest existential realization that all we are tends towards infinite mystery.[5]

SUMMARY OF CHAPTERS 3 TO 8 ON UNIVERSAL MEANINGS

A meaning is a condition of a human person by which his experiential continuum is differentiated in a unified way. A meaning is, therefore, an objective change in a subject; and if that change is in accord with the deepest nature of the subject and his relationship to the world about him, it is identical with what we call the development of the subject. A universal meaning refers to that kind of meaning which exists or can exist as a moment of legitimate and necessary development in every man of every age and culture. A dogmatic meaning refers to a universal meaning which has been achieved in Christ and which is demanded, at least as a goal, as an achievement of all men in this life. Dogmatic meanings make sense only to those who accept the basic apostolic witness about the risen Christ.

Dogmatic meanings are the abstract generic meanings which are present or implied in any person in whom there exists a twofold acceptance: (1) an acceptance of the universal presence and activity of the risen Christ, who now fulfills the incipient exigency for total relatability that was his when he walked this earth, and (2) an acceptance of the recurring exigencies of all human subjects. These are (a) the exigency to relate to everything in creation (above all to the risen humanity of Christ as known by the witness of the Church) with the whole of one's powers in an integrated way, (b) the exigency to relate ever more deeply with the Creator, and (c) the exigency to utilize the recurring processes of development which enable all subjects to move towards their goal of total relatability. Whoever accepts the risen Christ and all that is implied in self-acceptance thereby accepts dogmatic meanings which are embedded in that twofold acceptance. Dogmatic meanings are based, therefore, not on the factual universality of laws inherent in the universe of objects but on the recurring relationships and processes characterizing the operations of subjects—the risen Christ and ourselves.

The existence of dogmatic meanings is implied in the acceptance of Christian communication, in the belief that we can learn from tradition and traditional books wisdom for our own day, and in the acknowledgment of a Christian community and an ultimate communion of saints. However, dogmatic meanings do not come ready-made; they are not achieved at the outset of the Christian quest. Instead, they are the precipitate of a long process involving the whole life of the Church in its faith acceptance of the risen Christ. The Church needs to express itself and its initial understanding of what its acceptance of Christ entails. That expression occurs internally in acts of understanding and conceptualization; it occurs externally in words that represent and simultaneously deepen understanding, in moral actions, and in symbolic manifestations such as liturgy. These expressions are necessarily temporally conditioned and reflect not only what is generic to man but also what pertains to the varying cultural settings in which they occur. Their performance, however, eventually makes it possible for individuals and ultimately the whole Church to recognize certain common relationships and processes that underlie all Christian performance. Within the context of a Church of one culture or one civilization, there emerge what might be called "limited universal meanings." These are meanings which are universal within that culture, although they might not be universal in all cultures. They are true within that culture and are not to be despised. Much of the doctrine understood in the past, such as the doctrine about the matter and form of the sacraments, consisted of these limited universal meanings. However, such limited universal meanings no longer suffice. The spread of the Church to many cultures and the rapid rate of change which effectively compels individuals to change cultures in the course of a generation make it both possible and necessary to achieve truly universal meanings, dogmatic meanings in the strict sense we have defined. These meanings could emerge only after the Church had become conscious of the historical conditioning of all concrete cultures and thus enabled to compare its life in many cultures and see what truly transcended any specific culture because it was rooted in the very acceptance of humanity *per se* and the risen Christ.

Such dogmatic meanings are by their very nature irreformable. They cannot change because they are grounded on what is presupposed in the continuing life of the Church at every instant of growth. Even though a subsequent age can achieve further and more profound dogmatic meanings, it can do so only by a cumulative process of understanding which realizes prior dogmatic meanings at least in an implicit way. It is the cumulative process of understanding in conjunction with the basis of dogmatic meanings in the risen Christ and the recurring universal processes of human development that grounds the unity of all dogmatic meanings. These dogmatic meanings are not so many isolated differentiations; rather, they are the set of differentiations which proceed from the developing interaction of two subjects—the risen Christ and the earthly society of the Church. Because all dogmatic meanings arise from the shared life of Christ and the Church, they possess a profound unity which the Church must continuously strive to grasp, lest it be fragmented. It is this unity which demands that the question of the hierarchy of doctrines be treated with great care; for all doctrines (like the dogmatic meanings they refer to and express) manifest some facet of the basic faith affirmation of the Resurrection; and neglect of any dogmatic meaning can lead existentially to the slighting of the Resurrection itself. Thus, the denial of the living present efficacy of the Mass can be but a step away from the denial of the continuing existence of the risen Christ.

Dogmatic Understanding—The Official Teaching

INTRODUCTION

Chapters 3 to 8 treated dogmatic meanings in themselves and isolated for conceptual purposes from the certain explicit grasp of such meanings by persons. In this chapter and in the six chapters that follow (9 to 15 inclusive), I shall take up dogmatic understanding, that is, the Church's explicit, assured awareness of its possession of dogmatic or universal Christian meanings. Thus, this dogmatic understanding is to be distinguished from its partial component, the dogmatic meaning treated in prior chapters. Further, dogmatic understanding is also to be distinguished from a dogmatic statement. This last represents by sounds or marks on a piece of paper the more fundamental dogmatic understanding of dogmatic meaning.[1] We thus have three interrelated realities.

While a dogmatic statement is necessary for the communication of dogmatic meaning, it is by no means as important as the dogmatic understanding which it reflects and which gives it life. It is a mistake, I believe, to treat infallibility basically as a problem of infallible statements. It is far more, in my view, a problem of the recognition of dogmatic meanings.[2] That recognition is an achievement of a mind or minds above all; it is, as I shall show, only subsequently and secondarily a problem of verbal expression. In this chapter and those that follow I shall treat, therefore, the question of dogmatic or infallible understanding.

PROLEGOMENA TO A TREATMENT OF DOGMATIC UNDERSTANDING IN THE CHURCH'S TEACHING

We are immediately confronted with a problem when we attempt to uncover the Church's official teaching on dogmatic or infallible understanding. Here the Church in its official pronouncements has not conceptualized or expressed its teaching in the categories which

I have been employing. In fact, the teaching with which we have to deal has, in the main, failed to differentiate dogmatic understanding from dogmatic statements. This, of course, is to be expected. Teaching popes and general councils are basically interested in communicating understanding, in expressing it in words. When they reflect upon their teaching function, they invariably concentrate on the communicating aspect of that function. They are primarily interested not in making distinctions having to do with the processes of understanding and expression, but in conveying in as simple a way as possible the external signs of concrete infallible communication.

Hence a presentation of the doctrine of the Church, especially as that doctrine was expressed at Vatican I, cannot be expected to be a direct and immediate explanation of dogmatic understanding. However, I believe that if we carefully present what Vatican I meant in the context in which it operated, we shall be able to glimpse a temporally conditioned and limited presentation of a much more fundamental dynamic that is grounded in the nature of Christian man. In other words, I believe that the doctrine of Vatican I is a very limited and undifferentiated doctrine. It presents in a somewhat legalistic manner (but by no means in as legalistic a manner as some commentators would have it) the conditions under which the Church, and in particular the pope within the Church, attains to the level of infallibility. That presentation, I believe, is inadequate for meeting the questions and needs of the present time; it lacks certain qualifications and distinctions and a grounding in the very nature of Christian man, all of which are imperative if the doctrine of infallibility is to be meaningful today. However, I believe that the hypothesis I shall propose is compatible with the meaning of Vatican I, in much the same way as I believed that the theory of the Eucharist presented in chapter 5 was compatible with the teaching of the Council of Trent. This compatibility is not the compatibility of a meaning in one historically conditioned context with that of the same meaning differently expressed in a different historically conditioned context; rather, it is the compatibility of what claims to be a basic transcultural understanding of a universal Christian dynamic with a limited concrete grasp of that dynamic as it existed within a given cultural framework. Hence I make no claim that the summary of Vatican I presented here directly supports what I shall subsequently hypothesize. Reading such an hypothesis into the century-old text would simply be dishonest. Instead, I would claim that the understanding of Vatican I constitutes one datum that can be pointed to as support for a more basic theory; I would claim further that the ultimate justification for the theory cannot be had by examining the teaching of the past alone, but only by examining that teaching in the light of what we now know about culturally conditioned understanding. I realize, of course, that some of my readers will say that all this has to be supported by past texts, especially the texts of Scripture. That demand, I would say, is unreasonable because of the whole dynamics of understanding that I have stressed from varying points of view in these pages.

However, to one whose basic presupposition is that everything essential must be in Scripture, such an appeal to the dynamics of understanding may seem unfaithful to the Tradition. That the very effort to come to grips with the Tradition involves the acceptance of a whole series of presuppositions about human understanding and communication which are not contained explicitly in Scripture goes unnoticed. Of course, I would argue that these presuppositions are implicitly accepted by those who wrote Scripture; but the recognition of this implicit acceptance by the modern interpreter demands that he should explicitly come to grips with the dynamics of his own understanding, since no one can see what is implicit in the mind of another unless he first makes it explicit in his own. The very nature of the appeal to traditional texts demands that the present interpreter be a person who has gone beyond the writers of the traditional texts in his grasp of the process of understanding. To demand that the texts justify what one explicates about the nature of understanding from a more differentiated modern experience is to deny *a priori* the whole idea of human development.

In the following paragraphs, I shall attempt to sketch briefly the more or less official teaching of the Church on infallibility as that teaching was articulated at Vatican I and interpreted subsequently. The teaching of Vatican I was admittedly one-sided. For one thing, it concentrated on the infallibility of the pope; for another, even in its treatment of papal infallibility, it limited itself to emphasizing certain aspects that corresponded to what were conceived to be the pressing needs of the day. This should not surprise us. General councils invariably deal with what are thought to be pastoral needs by the prelates involved, even if outside observers at times have great difficulties in finding the Christian value of such pastoral concerns. A council speaks to a given concrete situation as that situation is judged by the participants. No council ever made timeless statements, even if the bishops thought this is what they were doing. In the light of this state of affairs, the following summary must be seen as an attempt to approximate the teaching intent of the council. An effort will be made to give the contextual intent that animated the Fathers. Some of this intent is reflected in the final statements issued; other aspects of this intent appear only in the debates at the council. Hence, what I say here cannot be fitted into neat categories of the old theological notes. To isolate what is *de fide* from what is theologically certain is not the comparatively easy venture which some former theologians thought it to be. Human understanding is a process, and human intent springs out of that process. What a group certainly grasped and what they intended to teach as certainly grasped cannot be separated from the context of that thinking and explicating process. This is especially true of a group that had not yet reached a conscious grasp of the dynamics of group understanding and hence was incapable of pinpointing certain aspects of that process.

THE OFFICIAL TEACHING ON INFALLIBILITY

1. The Term "Infallibility" Was Not Defined

The official Church teaching enunciated at Vatican I and prolonged with little amplification at Vatican II may be summed up under six headings. First, the term "infallibility" was never precisely defined. On the negative side, infallibility was distinguished from sinlessness by Bishop Gasser, the official expositor of the definition of papal infallibility at Vatican I (*Mansi*, LII, 1219). On the positive side, infallibility was said to deal with truth, more exactly with the proclamation and acceptance of truth. However, the larger question of the nature of truth itself was hardly discussed. The teaching Church proclaimed truth without error; the faithful grasped truth without error. In scholastic terms, truth is the adequation of the intellect and reality. Infallibility is the recognition and proclamation of that adequation without fear of error.

2. *The Spirit is the Fount and Source of Infallibility*

Secondly, the fount and source of the gift of infallibility in the Church is the Holy Spirit.[3] This gift of the Spirit is given to persons in the Church, such as the pope, not habitually but in the exercise of certain qualified functions in certain limited circumstances. It is not an active gift to proclaim new truths but a divine assistance given to recognize and proclaim the deposit of revelation.

3. *The Goal of Infallibility*

Thirdly, the goal of infallibility is to insure the integrity of truth in matters of faith and morals for the society of the faithful. It is to maintain and promote the unity of faith and the community of the faithful. By preserving the truth umblemished in the Church the gift of infallibility enables the Church to unite its members in a given age with one another and with the members of other ages and conditions.[4]

4. *The Object of Infallibility*

Fourthly, the object about which the Church can be infallible is the content of revelation. Primarily, this refers to truths *per se* revealed. Vatican I tended to speak of revelation in propositional terms, that is, in terms of verbal proclamations of truth. Within the context of this problematic, it *defined* that the infallibility of the Church as a whole and of the pope acting either *ex cathedra* or in concert with all the other bishops extends to all truths of faith and morals which have been directly or *per se* revealed. Such truths are called the primary object of infallibility. It was generally agreed, though *not defined*, that the Church can also teach infallibly those matters necessarily connected with the safeguarding of directly revealed truths (e.g., it can infallibly indicate which councils are ecumenical). Such matters are known as the secondary objects of infallibility. L. Choupin sums up the teaching on the object of infallibility with regard to the pope as follows:

> When the pope defines *ex cathedra* a revealed truth concerning faith and morals, or when he condemns *ex cathedra* as *heretical* a teaching regarding faith and morals, his infallibility is not only a revealed truth

but a truth defined by the Vatican Council. It is a truth of the Catholic Faith.

On the contrary, when the pope, employing the fullness of his authority in an infallible pronouncement, defines *ex cathedra* a truth connected with revelation, or condemns *ex cathedra* a doctrine or proposition with a note inferior to that of heresy, or pronounces definitively upon a dogmatic fact, his infallibility is *certain*, but it is not a *defined* truth of faith.

To deny this (latter) infallibility would be to commit a very grave sin, but it would not be heresy.[5]

It should be noted that the extent of the secondary object never has been precisely indicated and that in recent years there has been a tendency to downgrade, and even eliminate, its content in some quarters. What was agreed on and is still agreed on by most is that the object of infallibility is the same for the Church as a whole as for the pope.[6]

5. Infallibility is Shared by All Members of the Church

Fifthly, infallibility is a quality shared in varying degrees by all the members of the Church. On the one hand, the whole body of the faithful (and this includes the pope and the bishops) possesses what has sometimes been called "infallibility in believing." This "passive infallibility" means that the whole Church, in the depth of its collective understanding, always remains in the truth upon those matters of revelation about which there is agreement. While this notion of infallibility in believing should be more precisely explained, the fact is that the official teaching of the Church has given it but rare, and then indirect, treatment.[7]

On the other hand, there is an active or articulatory infallibility which resides in the pope and the body of the bishops. Under certain conditions the pope acting alone, but in the name of the whole Church, can pronounce infallibly. The body of bishops with the pope at their head may also so pronounce.[8] What has not been determined is the precise relationship between these two articulators of infallible utterances. After Vatican I, some theologians held that in the final analysis only the pope was the real subject of infallibility and that the episcopal college exercised this power only by participating in a dependent way in the power that was basically his. Others, however, would side with Karl Rahner in asserting that there is but one subject of infallibility, the college of bishops united under the pope as its head. Sometimes the pope alone can articulate infallibly for this college; he represents the college and its infallible power although the other bishops may not physically be present with him. At other times the whole body together pronounces infallibly.[9] This latter view accords with the judgment of Thils, who believes that any view which would make the infallibility of the body of bishops dependent on that of the pope would not be in harmony with the intention of the Fathers at Vatican I.[10]

6. Five Limiting Conditions on Infallibility's Exercise

Sixthly, infallibility is not an habitual and omnipresent condition of existence in the Church but an actualization that can take place only at certain times and under certain limiting conditions. These conditions have been elaborated to some extent for the pope but to a much lesser extent, if at all, for the bishops and for the faithful with their passive infallibility. Accordingly, it is to the conditions of the exercise of papal infallibility that we first turn.

The Pope must act as universal pastor and teacher. The pope is infallible in proclaiming the content of revelation when at least five conditions are met. In the first place, he must be acting in his capacity as the pastor and teacher of all the faithful. (The pope is always the pope, but he can act at times in his capacity as the ordinary of the diocese of Rome or even as a private Christian.) This first condition of papal infallibility was expressly defined at Vatican I.[11]

The pope must employ his supreme apostolic authority. In the second place, the pope must act in virtue of his supreme apostolic authority. It is not enough that he act as pastor and teacher of all the faithful. He does this in his Christmas addresses, in many encyclicals, and in decrees issued under his name. What is further required is that in an infallible statement he must employ his supreme apostolic authority. He must put the whole force of his doctrinal authority behind what he says. This requirement was also expressly defined at Vatican I.[12]

Papal infallibility refers to a personal act of one pope. In the third place, papal infallibility refers to a personal act of a single pope. It deals with the free utterance of the understanding of one man. This third condition can be broken down into three subconditions. According to the first subcondition, it is a single pope who is infallible in his own right. By this are excluded the views (1) that it is only the series of popes that possesses infallibility and (2) that infallibility is an attribute not of the pope as a person, but of the Roman See. Hence it is opposed to the mind of Vatican I to hold that all infallibility means is that the chain of popes or the Holy See itself eventually remains in the truth even though no single pope is without error.[13] Moreover, this subcondition excludes the necessity of explicit approval by the whole Church or by the whole episcopate of a papal definition at any time, either before or after its proclamation. Hence the proclamation of papal infallibility states in its concluding phrase that "definitions of the Roman Pontiff are irreformable because of their very nature and not because of the consent of the Church" (ex sese, non autem ex consensu ecclesiae—D.S. 3074).

This famous phrase intends to convey that there is no set legal form of consultation or voting that the pope must follow in order to arrive at the condition of infallibility. In other words, the Church cannot demand that given external procedures be followed before the pope's utterances become infallible. He is under a serious moral obligation to inform himself by all reasonable means with regard to the subject upon which he pronounces. Further, he can pronounce infallibly only upon those matters that are contained in the universal tradition of the Church. However, the means by which he arrives at an infallible grasp of the Church's position cannot be set out beforehand by some legal code that would demand prior consultation of the episcopacy or its subsequent approval.[14] What is being said here is that in pronouncing infallibly the pope, though acting externally apart from any predetermined legal connection with the rest of the Church, is yet not separated from the living tradition residing in the whole of the Church.[15]

According to the second subcondition, the infallible proclamation of the pope must be a free act. Although this condition was not defined at Vatican I, it was discussed and accepted by all. It is meant to rule out the situation in which the pope would be coerced by fear to issue a statement he did not really believe in. In essence, then, this condition makes more explicit the notion that papal infallibility refers to a personal act of the Bishop of Rome and not to some purely juridical formulation.

According to the third subcondition, an infallible papal proclamation must flow from the pope's understanding. This condition
was more assumed than explicated at Vatican I. It means that one
cannot, as it were, slide an infallible proclamation past the pope's
desk. One cannot get the pope to approve infallibly a statement
that he has not understood and assimilated. One cannot, in other
words, get the pope to agree freely that whatever some commission
holds will now be infallibly proclaimed even though the pope does
not understand what the commission holds. Because of this assumption, the basic rule of the interpretation of infallible papal
statements is to discover the "mind of the pontiff." If he has no
mind on the question, then the statement is not his personally; and
it is not, therefore, an infallible papal statement.

The pope must intend to define for the whole church. In the fourth
place, the pope must have the intention to define in a universally
binding way. This fourth condition can also be broken down into
three subconditions. According to the first subcondition, there
must be a genuine *intention* on the part of the pope. Just what constitutes such an intention was not made precise at Vatican I and has
not been the subject of any lengthy examination since, at least to
my knowledge. Some men write as if all that is required is the explicit notion in the pope's mind that he wants to define. Hans Küng
assumes that this is so. Here I would only suggest that intention is
a far more complicated affair than a simple verbalization that one
wishes to do something. Thus, two teenagers may announce their
intention to marry; but if they lack inner comprehension of the
meanings of marriage and if their present stage of existence is such
that they do not possess the basic realized human capacity necessary to give themselves to one another for the rest of their lives,
then they cannot be said to have a genuine intention to marry. The
intention to perform an act that involves the commitment of some
aspect of one's own personal being requires that one has actually
realized that aspect in himself. It is on this basis that a number of
theologians are beginning to realize that many marriages were
simply invalid. Analogously, one may say that a so-called papal
definition would lack the proper intention if the pope's "intention"
were simply a verbal notion, a kind of announced intention bereft
of a requisite underlying intellectual and personal realization.

According to the second subcondition, the intention of the pope

must be to *define*. It is not sufficient that he should desire to teach;
he must desire to teach in such a way as to settle a dispute in a judgment without appeal. He must intend to say that a certain view is
conformable to reality and is as irreformable as reality itself.[16] Nega-
tively, the irreformability that follows on a definition means that a
view expressly excluded can never be true. Positively, however, it
can only indicate at most that certain aspects (very difficult to determine precisely) are guaranteed to belong irrevocably to the subject of the definition. This does not mean that all that can be said on
the subject has been included in the definition. There is always
room for expansion, addition, and amplification.[17] Dogmas always
treat of realities infinitely more vast than the single aspect they express. The very existence of the phenomenon of the development of
dogma, sanctioned at Vatican I (D.S. 3020), strengthens the view
that what is defined is not the whole truth. Further, a more profound recognition of the ultimate unity of the revealed reality expressed in any single dogma and the whole ensemble of dogmas
would indicate that the notion that a single dogma could exhaust an
aspect of revelation is preposterous. Because the reality pointed at
in a dogmatic statement is related to all other aspects of revelation,
it is impossible that one statement should reflect that reality in its
totality.

According to the third subcondtion, the intention of the pope
must be to define *in a universally binding way*. Two factors are
included here: universality and obligation. On the one hand, the
matter of the definition is proclaimed not just to a small group,
but to the whole of the Church spread throughout the world. On
the other hand, the intention of the pope is to indicate that the
whole of the Church is morally obliged to accept what has been defined as a constituent of its acceptance of the Catholic faith.[18] Unfortunately, the meaning of this obligation to accept what has been
defined was not much clarified. Is it sufficient to accept the formula
of a pope or council? What kind of acceptance is required of the
classical *rudes* who cannot grasp the meaning of a doctrine?[19]

The pope's intention to define must be manifest. In the fifth place,
the intention of the pope to proclaim infallibly must be clearly
manifested to the Church. As the Code of Canon Law puts it:
"Nothing is to be considered as dogmatically declared or defined
unless that intention is manifest."[20] What this fifth condition does is

to establish that the other conditions must be clearly indicated to the Church if its members are to be bound by an infallible definition. In the light of some of the questions I have raised regarding these conditions (e.g., in the matter of the pope's intention to define or with regard to the moral obligation that he has to be informed), the verification of this *manifest* intention to define is not as simple as it was once thought to be.

In the past few pages, I have treated the conditions of papal infallibility. These conditions have been fairly well set out in the Church's tradition. When we come to the infallibility of the bishops of the Church and, even more so, to what is called the "passive infallibility of the faithful," we find that the conditions for their exercise are quite vague. What is clear is that the primary and secondary objects of infallibility are the same for pope, bishops, and faithful. It is also clear that there are differences in the mode of exercise of infallibility between the pope on the one hand and the whole Church on the other. Vatican I defined that the pope was infallible only under the very limited conditions indicated above. It did not define that the ordinary teaching of the pope—his teaching in addresses and encyclicals—is infallible. However, it did state that "by divine and Catholic faith everything must be believed that is contained in the written word of God or in tradition, and that is proposed by the Church as a divinely revealed object of belief either in a solemn decree or in her ordinary, universal teaching."[21] Hence the infallibility of the ordinary magisterium of the bishops spread throughout the world was asserted by Vatican I, although it made no such assertion about the ordinary magisterium of the pope.[22]

Unfortunately, the conditions under which the bishops are infallible, whether they are gathered in a general council or scattered throughout the world, have not been officially spelled out. No pope or general council has pronounced on the question, and the theological manuals usually do not offer much clarification. It is generally assumed that the conditions for the infallible issuance of a solemn decree by a council parallel the conditions for papal infallibility.[23] With regard to the infallibility of the ordinary magisterium scattered throughout the world, little is said. Just what is necessary in order that a teaching should belong to that ordinary magisterium which is infallible? It seems, for example, that the teachings on limbo and on birth control were universally proclaimed with the active assistance or, at the very least, the tacit consent of the vast majority of the bishops of the world. Does this make these doctrines part of the infallible teaching of the Church? Few would say so. But on what grounds does this denial rest?

Similarly, the doctrine of the so-called passive infallibility of the faithful has remained undifferentiated. Just what is meant by the *consensus fidelium*? Does it refer to the results that would be obtained by taking a poll on this or that doctrine? Is it sufficient that the laity throughout the world take for granted that a given doctrine is true without that doctrine having been seriously examined by them? Even these elementary questions have not yet been answered. Finally, just how the infallibility of the faithful in believing and the infallibility of the pope and bishops in teaching constitute one infallibility in the Church remains to be explained.

LACUNAE IN THE CHURCH'S OFFICIAL TEACHING

This brief summary of the generally accepted teaching on infallibility reveals three serious kinds of omissions in the Church's teaching. First of all, there are omissions of key elements necessary for an integral doctrine of infallibility. In addition to the many such elements which I have pointed out in the course of my summary of the official teaching, there is the understandable omission of the key distinction regarding dogmatic meanings, dogmatic understanding, and dogmatic statements.

Secondly, there is a failure, again understandable, to integrate the various elements regarding infallibility into a single comprehensive teaching which would show why and how infallibility and the dogmas flowing from it are inextricably bound up with the very nature of Christian salvation. It is true, as I have indicated, that the discussions of Vatican I brought out that the function of the gift of infallibility is to maintain and promote the unity of faith and the community of the faithful. However, little more was done than to state this principle. One could conclude that unity was promoted simply by an *ad hoc* gift accorded to the Church by which truth would be proclaimed in a formula that brought about unity among the faithful by their adherence to it and its meaning. It does not appear that infallibility is an *ontic* element of the single saving process by which men are constituted as a redeemed community. In other words, it does not appear that without the presence of infallibility in the Church it would be impossible for man to be the kind of saved being he now can be. It is precisely because of this failure to demonstrate that infallibility is intrinsic to salvation that it has been possible for some men to conclude that one can dismiss the doctrine enunciating it or, at least, relegate that doctrine to a kind of secondary status which need not be a bar to ecumenical reunion.

Thirdly, there is a failure to make explicit the method by which the elements actually defined as pertaining to the infallibility doctrine were uncovered. How does one justify as prerequisites of infallibility the many conditions imposed on the pope, and how does one prove that when these conditions are fulfilled the pope is infallible? Does one appeal to Scripture? It is obvious that Vatican I made no such appeal for its detailed conditions. Does one appeal to the now almost discredited notion of unwritten apostolic traditions? Vatican I did not do so. The discussions indicate that the qualifications were worked out by a process of reasoning among the delegates in the light of prior doctrinal formulas. The Fathers at the council reflected on the general tenor of the earlier tradition and in the course of discussion refined certain principles pertaining to the exercise of papal infallibility. Just what methodology for the enunciation of dogma was at work here and what was its justification? Vatican I did not say. It performed, but it did not give the rationale for its performance. And because it did not explicate and justify that rationale, it has been a natural target for those whose explicit methodology is to find everything, at least in some way, in Scripture.[24]

Transcultural Interpretation of the Church's Teaching on Infallibility

THE NATURE OF INFALLIBILITY

The purpose of chapters 10 through 15 is to propose a transcultural theory of infallible understanding that (1) will be reconcilable with the fragmentary and not fully unified assertions of Vatican I and of the Church that followed it and (2) will fill in gaps between those fragmentary assertions in such a way as to manifest that the doctrine of infallibility is unified in itself and is integrally related to the whole corpus of Christian self-understanding. The exposition will follow, though not in the same order, the aspects of the official teaching presented in chapter 9, but it will flesh out those aspects with the details of a unifying theory. To use an analogy, the official teaching may be compared to the series of dots on paper in books designed to help children draw. The theory I am about to present is one possible finished drawing that results from connecting all the dots and painting in appropriate colors. The present chapter treats the nature of infallibility. The succeeding chapters will treat (1) the object of infallibility, (2) the source and goal of infallibility, (3) generalities regarding the bearers of infallibility, (4) papal infallibility, and (5) episcopal infallibility.

INFALLIBILITY AND SELF-AWARENESS

In line with what I have already stated in treating the simple experiential level,[1] it can now be asserted that Christian infallibility is a concomitant quality of Christian subjective awareness. That prior awareness of the subject cannot be proved; in fact, it is the ground and presupposition of all so-called proofs. It is simply given, accepted, self-evident. To prove that I am aware of myself would require that I possess a condition of self prior to myself from which I prove that I am aware of myself. Merely to state these conditions of proof of self-awareness is to reveal the inherent contradiction involved in trying to prove one is self-aware. On the other hand, any attempt to prove that I am not aware of myself is intrinsically incoherent; for it presupposes that there is a self-aware "I" who is articulating the proof.

The self-awareness which fixes one's identity is not a specific and discrete act apart from the other acts of the subject. Rather, it is an aspect and an accompaniment of all acts of the subject. He is self-aware as a talker, eater, writer, maker, lover. That self-awareness exists even when he is not consciously thinking reflexively about what he is doing. It exists in eating even when the subject does not say to himself, "I am eating." It exists in thinking even when he does not explicitate to himself that he is thinking. It exists in each act and human process which, however vaguely, enters into the self-definition of the "I" in some conscious way. In fact, one can define the conscious subject as that which is constituted by a given continuum of self-awareness.[2]

Infallibility is a quality of a subject; it is defined and limited by that subject's self-awareness. It is that subjective certitude which accompanies self-awareness. The subject can never be more certain than he is of his own self-awareness. That self-awareness is the standard and limit of his certitude. It is the standard and limit of infallibility for this kind of subject. An infinite subject who is infinitely aware of himself and all else as projections of his self-awareness would possess, by that fact, unlimited and total infallibility. By immediate and direct vision, he would know in a single glance all that could be known. His infallibility would be global and absolute because his self-awareness is global and absolute. In contrast, a limited finite subject possessing limited finite self-awareness could have only a correspondingly limited infallibility. Such a subject would be said to be limitedly infallible about those aspects of experience whose denial would be utterly incompatible with the acceptance of his own identity, which is established in his global self-awareness.

Thus, it is possible for me to be mistaken about the existence of the oasis that I see; for the oasis may be a mirage. It is possible for me to be mistaken about the tracks that come together; for they only appear to do so, as subsequent observation establishes. There is nothing incompatible in simultaneous assertions (1) that I am aware of experiencing an oasis and approaching tracks and (2) that in reality neither exists. My self-awareness relates immediately to my own conscious experience and not immediately to the oasis and the tracks that meet. That self-awareness is constituted by acts such as my experiencing the oasis and tracks; it is not constituted by the existence of the oasis and the tracks as such. What I cannot deny without denying my own identity and self-awareness is that I experience within myself a condition of awareness which is reflected in my speaking about the oasis and the tracks. That awareness as well as the awareness which accompanies all other conscious acts can be said to be infallibly known precisely because to deny it would be to deny what gives me identity as a subject. I am, consequently, as certain of that awareness as I am of my own existence. And this is the standard of infallibility.

What this brings out is that infallibility is inexorably a quality of the experiencing subject. Whatever is so associated with the identity and self-awareness of the subject that its denial means the denial of the subject is infallibly known by that subject. Because in God that self-awareness involves the awareness of all else, his infallibility is universal. Because in man that self-awareness is limited, his infallibility is necessarily restricted.

INFALLIBILITY AND PRECONCEPTUAL OBJECTIVITY

At this point it would seem that there can be no human infallibility about reality outside the subject. This, however, is not the case. A few refinements and distinctions will make this clear. These will involve the relative nature of objectivity and the corresponding relativity of the infallibility possible to each nature.

First of all, objectivity is an attribute which is relative to a specific kind of subject. It is a vast oversimplification of the issue to speak of objective knowledge as if there were some absolute standard of objectivity independent of any subject. Objectivity always refers to a subject and the subject's capacity to know. What would be objective knowledge for man would not be objective knowledge for an angel and certainly would not be objective knowledge for God. Objective knowledge actually refers to the kind of knowledge which would exist in a perfectly functioning member of a given species. Normally, we speak of human objectivity because we belong to the sons of Adam. We hardly advert to the relative notion of objectivity we are using. However, if we were to imagine for a moment a race of creatures somewhat like men but deprived of the sense of sight, we would begin to realize that for that race color would be unknown. (I abstract from the possibility that color could be transformed into sound waves by instruments. After all, even in such a case color would not be known as color but under the guise of sound.) Color would not be part of objective reality as subjectively perceivable. Moving in the other direction, we can conceive of a knower who could detect innumerable aspects of reality which are now totally unknown to us with our limited powers. For such a knower the standard of objectivity would be far more comprehensive than it is for us. Finally, in the limit we would have an infinite knower before whom every possible aspect of everything would be known. Relative to him alone would the standard of objectivity be absolute.[3]

This line of reasoning indicates why the attempt to speak of "reality as it is in itself" is misplaced. Man cannot know "reality as it is in itself." He can know reality only as reality is knowable by man. He can know himself and what is other than himself only to the degree that man's capacities permit knowledge. For a man the standard of objectivity in the fullest sense is human nature fully developed as knower.

Secondly, the existence of extra-human reality must be postulated with the same degree of certitude that man has of his own existence. As existentialists assert, man exists in a world. That existence in juxtaposition with the surrounding world is not something to be explained after one has asserted self-awareness but is the initial condition in which self-awareness comes to be. It is a given that can no more be proved than can one's self-awareness. Man comes to recognize that he is a knower and one who is self-aware only at the very moment that he becomes aware of knowing what is other than himself. He becomes aware of his individuality and uniqueness only when he concomitantly becomes aware that there are things that are not himself. He accepts his identity as one who sees, hears, touches, tastes, and thinks about a surrounding world only to the degree that he accepts the existence of that world. Practically speaking, then, he becomes aware of himself as an "I" only to the degree that he becomes aware of the "not-I." Hence he postulates the existence of the "not-I" with the same degree of certitude that he postulates the existence of the "I." Consequently, he can be said to be as infallibly sure of the existence of external reality as he is of his own existence. The standard of infallibility for any subject is the degree of existence and self-awareness of the subject. No one can be more sure of anything than he is of his own existence. Whatever is presupposed by and is concomitant with a being's acceptance of his own existence in his self-awareness meets the only possible standard of infallibility for that creature. What can be objectively known are the self and the non-self. Both are known infallibly in the measure that they are concomitant with the self-awareness that constitutes one's own personal identity.

What we hope to have established thus far is that there is a preconceptual infallibility possible to man, a certitude about his own existence and the existence of other reality that is the accompaniment of his self-awareness as a person. Such an infallibility, however, is in a certain sense tautological. We equate infallibility with self-awareness; then, having postulated self-awareness, we necessarily assert infallibility. What appears more to the point is the possibility of making infallible judgments of a conceptual nature. Is it possible for man to understand himself and his relationship to the world in an infallible way? If so, to what degree and under what conditions?

HYPOTHETICAL UNDERSTANDING AND INFALLIBLE JUDGMENTS

First of all, I would like to clarify two terms: human hypothetical understanding and human infallible judgments. By human hypothetical understanding I refer to the actualizing of man's capacity to grasp the unities inherent within man's self and activity, or within the world external to man, or within man's relationships to that external world. The innate tendency of man is to be dissatisfied with an undifferentiated self-awareness and awareness of the world. Man constantly seeks to unify, to tie together, to grasp the connections between himself and the world, between his past and his present, between one aspect of the world and all other aspects. He is continually theorizing about the relationship of each part to each other part; and that theorizing has produced a whole gamut of sciences of varying degrees of practicality and abstractness. This innate tendency presupposes that the universe is a universe of intelligibility to be grasped. This presupposition is at work whenever one experiments and whenever one attempts to explain. It is even at work whenever one attempts to explain that there is no intelligibility and no explanation; for even such an effort to explain presupposes some unifying thread in the explanation given.

All such efforts to grasp the unities that are supposed to exist in the universe by all who attempt to understand are initially hypothetical. This means that they may or may not reflect the actual unities in the universe which are graspable by a man fully aware of the pertinent facts. They are suppositions that must pass the test of evidence. They are acts of hypothetical understanding. They become judgments when the subject, having duly tested them by appropriate experiments, becomes convinced of their reliability. Finally, such judgments become infallible judgments when they are so grasped by the subject that their denial would be tantamount to the denial of the subject's awareness of himself.

The standard of infallibility of judgment, like that of infallibility for preconceptual acceptance of self and the other, is one's own self-awareness. Hence the standard of infallibility of judgment is also not an absolute standard but one relative to the kind of subject who judges. In the present case, we are dealing with the human subject. Our question then becomes one of determining under what conditions a human subject can make judgments of such a nature that he can be as certain of them as he is of his own self-awareness.

THE UNRESTRICTED HUMAN SUBJECT

Three kinds of human subjects can be envisaged. The first would be an unrestricted human person. This would be a subject whose capacities as human would be developed to the fullest extent possible to man. Such a subject could be viewed abstractly as static or dynamic. A static unrestricted subject would be one whose self-differentiation would be conceived as totally developed in regard to the world in which he lived. Every capacity of this subject within that world would be developed to its fullest extent so that no further development would be possible. This would mean that every conceivable unity in the world of self, in the exterior world, and the relationship of self to world would be realized in the consciousness of the subject. The human self would truly be at one with the world; and the consciousness of self as well as the concomitant consciousness of the world would be total. No further self-awareness or awareness of the world, whether preconceptual or conceptual, would be possible. The static fully developed subject would live in a static world and would fully grasp himself and the world. He would realize the possibilities of man in being fully open to the world. He could not err because he could not possibly know anything further about the world with which to correct his present understanding. He would, therefore, be universally infallible. By reason of a self-awareness which had reached the limit of comprehensiveness and unity possible to man, he would have personally achieved the standard of human infallibility. If more could be known, that more could be known only by a subject that was more than human.

However, this static view of the unrestricted human person appears to be a mere construct which could have only hypothetical existence. If there is or can be an unrestricted human person, he cannot be a static individual living in a static world. It appears that man is a creature of unlimited self-awareness and self-differentiation within the world. He can never reach a term of development; for he is open to the infinite. Operationally, this means that each act of self-awareness and self-differentiation within the world constitutes man as a more comprehensive subject. In turn, he (1) can be known as more comprehensive and (2) can utilize his increased being for further changing the world in which he lives and himself as living in the world.

This means that the unrestricted human person would be utterly dynamic. He would constantly be expanding his consciousness within a constantly expanding world, a world whose intelligibility would be ceaselessly increasing. At every moment he would be completely aware of every aspect of his self-differentiation within the world of that moment. Further, he would completely express that self-awareness out into the world. This would mean, on the one hand, that he would fully grasp the intelligibility immanent in himself from every conceivable angle as well as the intelligibility in the world about him that corresponds to that immanent grasp. He would, therefore, infallibly know who he is at that particular moment with an infallible set of judgments that would reflect all the unities then present in himself and in the world and his relationships to it. It would mean, on the other hand, that he would infallibly express by appropriate action the potentialities inherent in his being at that moment. He would be utterly free to be himself.

The unrestricted human person would thus be the subject of a continuing infallibility; yet this infallibility would be continuously exercised with regard to a ceaselessly expanding object. At every moment, he would know and express his world to the degree that he and his world had developed in relationship with one another. Because of his total and immediate human self-awareness at each moment, he would always be able to thematize correctly the intelligibility immanent in his field of relationships. Hence he would be infallible to the limited degree that man can be infallible. At the same time, since his own intelligibility would be constantly increasing (and with that increase an increase of self-awareness), the field of exercise of that infallibility would be ever widening. Paradoxically, he would always judge infallibly; and yet he would always be revising or expanding his judgments. However, the cause of the revision or expansion of the judgments would not be the detection of error but the expansion of the intelligibility immanent in him as he exists in the whole of the world.

It is evident that none of us is an unrestricted human individual. Moreover, within the present mode of existence, an unrestricted human being would appear to be an impossibility. Such an existence would demand an openness to the whole of creation that is impossible to creatures who are limited by temporal and spatial qualities to a very restricted presence to the world. Even the Christ who walked this earth two thousand years ago was limited to a small area of the world within which he was able to develop his self-awareness and self-differentiation. His was not an unrestricted humanity; hence he could not then have possessed the global infallibility possible to such a human nature. That he is now unrestricted in his risen state is, I believe, the truth of the matter. However, the establishment of this assertion would carry us beyond the subject at hand. I might indicate that such an understanding of the risen Christ would help clarify how he can be considered "the way, and the truth, and the life" (Jn. 14:6) for his followers. This will be of importance when I consider the notion of dogma as saving in chapter 11.

THE TOTALLY AWARE BUT LIMITED HUMAN BEING

We can envisage a second type of human being—the totally

aware but limited individual. He would be a person who finds himself in a limited situation in the world but who is fully aware of his limited experience in that world. At every moment he is conscious of his whole historical past and how that past has affected him; and he is conscious of his present experiences as they are colored by that past and grasped within the limited framework achieved in that past. He is aware of all the differentiations of his own concrete personality as they have occurred in his history. Thus, he is fully and immediately in touch with himself in the limited way in which that self has been realized in the world. Such a human being would possess not only the preconceptual infallibility concomitant with self-awareness but also a global conceptual and judgmental infallibility whose limits must now be established.

Every judgment about the unities within oneself, within the world, or within one's relationships to the world is a judgment on prior data that have appeared in awareness. It is a thematization of the unities in that prior awareness. Thus, I may have become aware of certain sense reactions in response to the presence of a face. Subsequently I become aware of the presence of the same sense reactions in the presence of another face. On the supposition that I have been continuously fully aware of myself and objects about myself, I am able to make infallibly the judgment that I have experienced the same self-differentiation in the presence of the first object as in the presence of the second. I can make the further infallible judgment that the two objects as presented to me have manifested the same intelligibility. Precisely because of my full awareness of myself and of my reactions both past and present, I am able to make the infallible judgments about the intelligibility of the two faces to me.

It should be noted, however, that this infallibility is quite limited. It does not allow me to assert that the two faces are one and the same. It may be that two different persons present the same sensible appearance to one of my present self-differentiation. The two faces could be different, but no differences would have appeared in my awareness. It would be stretching the evidence for me to assert that the fact that I have become aware of no differences implies *tout court* that there is no difference. I could infallibly state that the two faces are the same only on the supposition that (1) my awareness of both faces is exhaustive and (2) no two faces ever present exactly the same sensible appearance.

What this analysis indicates is that the human mind is regularly infallible with regard to its judgments on data of which it is aware. Its infallibility is measured by the degree of that awareness. When a person is fully aware of all the data brought to his cognizance, then he can make infallible judgments as to such data. However, because the data of exterior reality may be far more vast than what he is aware of, his infallibility about the data of awareness does not necessarily imply an infallibility in judgment about relationships which exist between objects in the exterior world. Only when the data of awareness are exhaustive for the question at hand can there be infallibility of judgment with regard to relationships outside oneself. This regularly happens in mathematics when all the data are given. I am told that there are three, and only three, points on a graph. I am asked to provide the simplest equation defining the three points. Having grasped the data as exhaustive, I come to an infallible judgment about the required equation. In a similar manner, a person can come to a limitedly infallible judgment about concrete exterior reality by bracketing out factors of which he is unaware. He says, in effect, that a given judgment sums up and unifies all the data thus far presented. Because he is fully self-aware, he has no fear of overlooking any aspect of the data experienced. However, he has no assurance that his infallible judgment on his personal data of experience necessarily implies a corresponding judgment about the relationships actually existing in reality outside himself.

It may be of help to note the difference between the judgments of the totally aware but limited individual of whom we have been speaking (whose classic model is the earthly Christ) and those of the partially aware individuals whom we all exemplify. That difference is basically one of a degree of self-awareness. The ordinary individual has been differentiated in his history by a host of experiences, acts of understanding, judgments, and decisions. However, he is only partially aware of these differentiations that have been grooved in his original *tabula rasa*. Some have receded to the level of the unconscious; others have been largely forgotten, although they may be recalled by the proper stimuli. Moreover, in his make-up reside a large number of assumptions that have never been made explicit but have been taken into his being unknowingly from the surrounding environment. As a result of this, when he comes to make a judgment regarding a given question, he invariably is unable to call up every differentiation of his being that could bear on the question. He can err, therefore, not only because he has not been exposed to all the data in the external world that bear upon the matter, but also because the data embedded in his own person are not fully retrievable. He cannot recall them all; nor can he combine them in the new ways that may be necessary to meet the question being asked. Thus, the detective may have seen all the evidence necessary to establish the identity of the murderer, but he may have forgotten some of it and be incapable of recombining all the data of which he is aware in such a way as to see their bearing on the criminal's identity. Because the information possessed by the ordinary person is not fully retrievable as a consequence of his incomplete self-awareness, he can err not only with regard to the relationships existing between aspects of the external world but also with regard to aspects of his own inner history and his relationships to the external world. He can make the kind of error which can be corrected by another who reminds him of pertinent data. The totally aware but limited individual, however, can only err with regard to relationships which exist between aspects of the external world. He may be mistaken because of a lack of data; but he knows this and makes his judgments provisional. However, his full self-awareness makes impossible erroneous judgments about the data which have differentiated his person. He can make infallible judgments about his own inner self-differentiation and about the limited significance of the data of the external world that have produced that differentiation.

Finally, we note the restriction on the capacity of the totally aware but limited person to share what he has infallibly understood. Precisely because his infallibility relates to the inner differentiation of his person and to the judgments made on the limited data he has personally encountered, it has value only to another who shares that inner differentiation and the data which produced it. If the world were made up of men who possessed total awareness of their own limited but different experience, there would not be automatically shared infallibility; rather, the possibility would exist of encounters in which each would challenge the others to broaden their experiential continua. This would promote the condition of growth toward (1) the mutual possession of all data and (2) the infallibility which depends upon the possession of such data.

What the above tends to make evident is the enormous problem involved with making infallible judgments about concrete human situations. Here the data are so vast and so complex that even a totally aware subject would never be capable of making infallible judgments. The earthly Christ himself was thus incapable of infallibly determining the total conditions of the environment about him. How much less would be the capacity of the less than totally aware Christian leaders who have followed him. Hence the idea that the Church could make infallible moral judgments about the global goodness or sinfulness of a concrete act—e.g., a given act involving birth control—was and is and always will be misplaced. I believe that the Church can exercise infallibility in moral matters. However, that infallibility, as I shall attempt to clarify it in the following chapter, is an infallibility regarding universal and abstract moral principle. It is not an infallibility regarding value judgments on concrete moral acts.

THE ORDINARY LIMITED AND NOT FULLY AWARE SUBJECT

The third type of individual to be considered is the ordinary limited and not fully aware person who populates our globe. This individual, as I indicated in the section on Infallible Understanding at the simple experiential level (chapter 3), can be infallible only with regard to universal meanings. These are differentiations of the human experiential continuum that are possible and necessary for the development of all living men. On the one hand, these meanings are enduringly relational; they are the differentiations deriving from the total potential relatability of man. By his inner nature man is related to the whole of the finite and to the infinite within the finite. Hence, to be himself he has to relate to himself, to all other persons, to the whole of visible creation, to the risen Christ (when he lives at the experiential-witness level), and ultimately to the Trinity. All these relational meanings endure, although their complexity and man's awareness of them increases with time. On the other hand, these enduring relational meanings are dynamic. There is a pattern of development, a cyclical or spiral process of growth, which can be detected in the integral development of man in whatever time and culture. This is the dynamic pattern which gradually emerges to consciousness as the result of a long reflection on an individual and social past dedicated to an openness to creation. Both the relational and the dynamic aspects can be grasped in the measure that a man possesses past tradition and present reality. The possession of present reality in its breadth safeguards him against the possibility of mistaking what is true of his own specific cultural development for what is true of man in general at his epoch in history. The possession of past tradition safeguards him against the possibility of mistaking what is true of his present level of development for what is true of all levels of development. In short, it is man's contact with the varying conditions of concrete realization in a more or less universal way that permits him to attain the infallible grasp of universal meanings. For a Christian this means that it is a churchman's grasp of the long living tradition of the Church in its history plus his contact with that tradition as lived in its varying forms in the present which permits him to approach the condition of infallible awareness of Christian universal meanings.

SUMMARY

Infallibility is an attribute of a subject who grasps with the immediacy and certitude of his self-awareness (1) all the data pertinent to a given question which are perceivable by an individual of his nature and (2) one or more unities in those data. All human infallibility is thus relative to the human condition and cannot be the absolute infallibility possible to God alone. The extent of human infallibility depends upon the degree of universality and integration of the subject, that is, upon the quality of his self-awareness. For the unrestricted human subject open to and self-differentiated by the totality of the world at any given moment, all judgments would necessarily be infallible; total awareness of the totality of humanly knowable data would make every judgment a judgment of immediate awareness and hence invest it with the same infallibility as immediate awareness. For the totally aware but limited individual, the person who is immediately aware of his whole self-differentiation but whose whole self-differentiation does not reach out to the whole of the data of the created universe then available, infallibility regarding relationships between aspects of the world exterior to the subject are regularly excluded. However, there will be an infallibility of judgment regarding the unities existing in the totality of one's own experience of the world as well as about the relationships inherent in the substance of one's inner self-differentiation. Finally, for the ordinary individual who has inhabited this planet from the beginning, the only possible infallibility of any consequence has to do with universal meanings. After an individual and collective life spent in reaching out to the universality of the tradition within which one lives and out of which one has grown, it is possible to become aware of continuing relational and dynamic aspects which permeate all experience in that tradition. This last is an infallibility of abstract principle, and it can never be simply and infallibly applied to concrete cases even for the saint and mystic. Such infallibility implies the unrestricted mode of the human subject; and that mode is the property of the next life alone. Within the Church this means that the sole object of infallibility is universal Christian meaning.

COMPARISON WITH OFFICIAL CHURCH TEACHING

How does this notion of infallibility accord with the teaching of the Church? As I indicated, Vatican I never precisely defined the meaning of infallibility. It did distinguish infallibility from sinlessness and proclaimed that this gift of infallibility had to do with the proclamation and acceptance of truth. In the scholastic frame of thought out of which Vatican I operated, truth was the adequation of the intellect to reality and infallibility was the recognition and proclamation of that adequation without fear of error. What is interesting to note, however, is the aspect of universality that permeates all of the treatment Vatican I accorded to infallibility. Only the universality of a pope, or of the bishops operating under conditions in which their universality is maximized, ever attains this condition, and then only in regard to the universal belief of Christians.

While it would be rash to argue that the doctrine of Vatican I is identical with our theoretical exposition, it seems permissible to state that our theory is in full accord with Vatican I, although going beyond it in detail. Further, this theory accords with the long held notion that no one can be certain of the condition of his own conscience before God with the certitude of faith (see D.S. 1534 and 1563). Finally, it evidences great possibilities of explaining the pre-

cise sense in which the earthly Christ could be without error, despite
his manifest limitations in knowledge; it can also helpfully explain
in what sense we may speak (and here we are obviously only speaking analogously) of the total knowledge of the risen Christ.

Does not this theory reduce the doctrine of infallibility to a strictly
human construct? Must we not hold that infallibility is a gift of
God to his Church and that, consequently, it cannot be explained in
terms of purely human understanding? Is there not added some special charism beyond the human by which Church leaders at certain
key moments speak beyond their normal powers with a participation in the uncreated infallibility of God himself?[4] I must admit that
this is the assumption of much of the theological tradition of the
past; but just as honestly I must state that I believe that this theological tradition is as mistaken as it was about the human knowledge of Christ. The textbooks once largely held that Christ was in a
true sense omniscient. "From the beginning he knew in the Word all
things—past, present, and future—that is, all that God knows by
the knowledge of vision."[5] I believe that this view would now be
severely qualified by the majority of theologians because it is difficult to see how Christ could have possessed a true humanity if, from
the beginning and apart from any historical experience and historical processes, he knew all that God knows by the knowledge of
vision. Human knowledge is integrally wrapped up with human experience and is a dynamic aspect of that experience. To think of it
as infused by some divine process is possible only if one divorces
knowledge from every other aspect of man; and then one may legitimately question if that knowledge is truly human.[6]

For similar reasons it now becomes difficult to think of infallibility as some supernatural non-human charism that Christ has left to
his Church. Infallibility pertains to revelation and revealed truth,
and that revelation is conveyed to us in creation by the humanity of
Christ. In and through that humanity alone do we glimpse the infinite mystery that is Father, Son, and Holy Spirit. However, that
humanity is like ours in all but sin. It possesses the limit of powers
possible to men like ourselves, including the power of infallibility.
It possesses no power that is beyond the human and it conveys
upon us no power that is beyond the human. If there are mysteries
of the supernatural order—and there certainly are—these mysteries
pertain not to the powers of human comprehension but to the divine

that the human strives to comprehend and to the relationships between the divine and the human. There is a mystery of the Trinity; there is a mystery of the relationship of the divine and human in Christ; these are absolute mysteries that human knowledge can never fathom because they represent a condition of existence that forever transcends creaturely experience and consciousness. Further, there are mysteries of the created condition that transcend our present experience and direct understanding but one day will be understood when we attain them; such would be the assumed condition of the Virgin Mary and the intimacy of the Communion of Saints. However, there is no proper mystery of infallibility that relates to the divine or to a creaturely condition that transcends our present condition. Infallibility refers to a present mode of knowing the mysteries by human beings who, like the Christ as creature, have nothing but human powers of knowing. Mysteries refer to objects of faith, to the divine and to the created conditions affected by the divine.

I am not saying that the concrete exercise of infallibility within the Church is a merely natural act. Such a concrete exercise of infallibility is no more a purely natural act than is the concrete virtuous act by which a man lays down his life for his friend for the sake of Christ. However, just as the physical aspect of the act of laying down one's life follows the natural physical laws of the universe, so too does the cognitive aspect of the act of infallible understanding follow the natural cognitive laws. What makes both acts supernatural is not that in some way the physical or cognitional laws of nature are superseded, nor that the actor has some implicit or explicit Christian intention in mind, but that both acts are performed in a mysterious union (explicitly recognized only in dependence upon the apostolic witnesses) of faith with Jesus Christ risen from the dead. That acting with Christ and his Spirit to whom he is united renders the concrete act entitatively saving. It does this, however, not by destroying or transforming the physical or cognitional laws that enter into the act but by making these laws operative in a context of faith.

The Object of Infallibility in the Church

SUMMARY OF VATICAN I

According to Vatican I, the primary object of infallibility is the content of revelation regarding faith and morals made known to the whole Church. About this primary object the Church definitely can be infallible. With regard to the secondary objects of infallibility—the truths necessarily connected with safeguarding the primary object—Vatican I made no definition. Here I will take up only the primary object of infallibility; I will leave the treatment of the secondary object to chapter 16.

The primary object of infallibility refers to truths of faith and morals which are *per se* revealed for the whole Church. These truths were revealed by Christ to us through the apostles. How this was done and in what form it was carried out was not made specific by Vatican I. At the time revelation was considered in terms of verbal proclamations of truth. These proclamations were made prior to the death of the last apostle; henceforth the period of revelation would be closed and the Church could only go on continuing to proclaim the traditional revelation, developing its implications, and expounding its meaning in new contexts. The anthropological and epistemological problems connected with this rather simplified notion of revealed truth did not occur to any great extent to the assembled Fathers. They were content to enunciate that only truths *per se* revealed constituted the primary object of infallibility. Further questions and nuances were left to the discussions of the theologians.

THE RISEN CHRIST AS LOCUS OF REVELATION

In line with our past exposition, however, we must give a more nuanced notion of the meaning of *per se* revealed truth of faith and morals for the whole Church. The basic contention here is that the concrete risen Christ is the total locus of the Christian revelation. In his humanity and its activity in the risen state, all that God has revealed of himself or ever will reveal of himself is expressed definitively. By the resurrection, Christ is constituted as the supreme and all-encompassing object of faith. When the Christian expresses belief in the resurrection of Christ, he is accepting the risen condition of Christ as the central reality of faith; and implicitly he is saying yes to all that is implied in that primary acceptance.

God can reveal himself to man only insofar as he acts in the world of man. On the one hand, his activity reveals himself because every activity in some way expresses the one who performs it; consequently, God's activity in creation expresses him in the medium of creation. On the other hand, this expression of God is revealing to man only insofar as it appears in the world man can grasp. Thus, if there is some aspect of creation that is forever unknowable to man, that aspect cannot be a source of revelation to man. If man had not the power of sight and if the visibility of created beings were in no way translatable into a medium that could be grasped directly by man, then visibility would not be for man a carrier of the revelation of God.

The medium of revelation limits what God can reveal of himself. He can reveal comparatively little of what he is through inanimate creation; much more can be manifested by living things. However, it is in and through the supreme creature of visible creation, man, that God can most fully reveal himself. Man sums up and encompasses all of visible reality in his own makeup. He is by nature open to all of creation and to the infinite. In his consciousness there can be recapitulated the whole of creation. The more full and perfect a man is, the more he can serve as a medium for the revelation of God to his fellow men.

In the Incarnation the Son of God enters creation in the most profound way. He takes on a humanity which becomes his self-expression to the race of men. With Karl Rahner we may theorize that man is the creature "which ensues when God's self-utterance, his Word, is given out lovingly into the void of god-less nothing . . . . If God wills to become non-God, man comes to be, that and nothing else."[1] In this theory man would be by his very nature the expression of God in creation. Even if we reject it, however, man does remain the highest possible medium God can use to make himself known to men.

The life, death, and resurrection of Jesus Christ are stages in the development to created fullness of that humanity by which God reveals himself in creation. While he walked the earth, Christ in his humanity grew in wisdom and age and grace before God and man; consequently, he grew as the revelation of God to man. In every challenge of life he grew because he faced up fully to the demands of the moment; he always followed the will of his Father; he was obedient until the last moment of life. For him no moment was final and to be clung to; it had to be relinquished for the sake of the future coming towards him from his Father. He died to each moment of the past that he might be open to an ever more demanding future. In this light his death is simply the crowning moment of his life. It is the moment when he freely relinquishes all that he had previously been in order to open himself fully to the mystery of God in his humanity. It is the moment of greatest growth of that humanity when Christ becomes the supreme Lord of creation who is present to all men of all days even to the consummation of the world (Mt. 28:20). The resurrection thus becomes not the removal of Christ from the human scene but the fullest realization of the universal relatability to creation that belongs to man. By the resurrection Christ becomes utterly and universally human; and by that same fact he also becomes *the* revelation of God for man. At one stroke he becomes Lord, Redeemer, and Revealer.

On the one hand, by the resurrection Christ becomes utterly and completely human. Man is that creature who is intrinsically called by his inner dynamism to go out to and to possess all creation with heart, soul, mind, and will. He is called to reach out to God present in every aspect of his own existence and the existence of every creature. To be fully human is to possess oneself totally in utter unity, to relate totally to all of creation apart from oneself, and to reach out to the infinite God present in every aspect of creation. This fullness of humanity was attained by Christ at his resurrection. He relinquished freely all the partial realizations of humanity that had been his at various stages of his life upon earth and thereby attained to that fullness of humanity which we call resurrection.

On the other hand, it is the fullness of humanity attained in resurrection that makes Christ the fullness of revelation for us. Because in him all the capacities of humanity are realized, he is capable of expressing his unique divine sonship to every aspect of creation. He sums up, interrelates, and unifies all of creation in himself. In and through his humanity which recapitulates all, he images forth the divine personality he is. In him every aspect of creation becomes the vehicle of divine revelation. Further, there is nothing expressed by his risen humanity which is not in principle attainable by us; for he expresses and reveals himself in creation only by means of a humanity in whose fullness we participate in varying degrees now and according to our totally achieved capacity after our deaths.

MAN'S SUBJECTIVE APPROPRIATION OF REVELATION IN CHRIST

I have stated that the concrete risen Christ is the total locus of the revelation of God to man. Now I would stress that *de facto* Christ becomes that saving revelation to man only insofar as he actually becomes accessible to man, that is, graspable by the powers of man. The most beautiful painting in the world will not be a gift of beauty to man who cannot or will not see; the most delicious food will be insipid to the man whose taste buds and sense of smell have never developed; and the total revelation of God in the risen Christ will have meaning and saving power only for those who are able to appreciate it.

How does a man become capable of grasping the revelation of God that is in the risen Christ? The answer is that he has to grow up to the fullness of Christ's humanity, that he must follow the same path that Christ followed of dying to the present in which he stands and obeying the exigencies of God's future coming to meet him. Accompanied by the living but invisible risen Christ, man must live fully by faith. He has to speak and act as if the present and its good are inadequate. He has to recognize that he himself is not a fully relating creature, one open to all men and things with his whole being. He has to be willing to forsake the tried and the true and the known in his relationships in order to find God in the new that comes to meet him in every event. He has to build constantly on his past by going beyond it. He has to be forever dissatisfied with the present limitations of his understanding, his emotions and attitudes, and his loves. Like Abraham he has to be ever willing to leave his present city for that eternal city which is God's. Never must he rest short of the goal of total relatability which is the property of the risen mode of existence achieved first of all by Jesus Christ. Forever he must push on, knowing that he will never attain that goal while in the flesh but confident that in death he will find God in Christ and hence his own deepest self.

The point here is that a man can appreciate the revelation of God which is expressed in the risen Christ only to the degree that he becomes like Christ's humanity. A man can understand and love only to the degree that he is. He can love only to the degree that he understands; he can understand only on the basis of his experience; and his experience is limited by the degree of his self-realization. An illiterate savage could never understand and love the intricacies of a modern airplane because his total life development has not prepared him to grasp the intelligibility of the machine before him. A child cannot grasp and appreciate the splendors of adult love and concern because his degree of personal self-realization does not furnish him with the differentiated personal background against which he might interpret the activity of his parents. In short, a man can appreciate intelligibility and values outside of himself only to the degree that his own self-realization furnishes him with the experiential basis upon which to interpret that reality. This means that the only person capable of appreciating the revelation of God in the risen Christ in all its fullness would be a person who already shared the risen mode of existence. One has to die and be with Christ before one can really see him as he is.[2]

This means, of course, that revelation is eschatological. It can be possessed by us in its fullness only when we share the risen existence of Christ. Before that moment we can see only as in a cloudy mirror. We do possess it in part, however; for though we are not fully human, we are a beginning of humanity. To the degree that we are achieving that fullness of humanity even now, to that degree are we capable (all other things being equal) of grasping *the* revelation of God that shines on the face of the risen Christ.

In this perspective, fully to accept revelation in faith is concretely identical with the willingness to grow in faith as a human being united to Christ and with the gradual realization of the condition of salvation. On the one hand, to accept revelation is to accept it not simply as a theoretical construct or a series of propositions but as it comes to us in the full humanity of Christ. This means to accept it as one accepts a person. With one's whole being one goes out to the wholeness of another, in this case Christ. However, such full acceptance is impossible now. What is possible is to accept in the measure that we can, with the realization that this acceptance is only the beginning of full acceptance. By our willingness to develop in understanding and love of all creation so as to become more fully human, we manifest our real desire to accept one day the fullness of revelation in Christ. In the measure that we are achieving a growth to full humanity in and with Christ in faith, we are simultaneously manifesting our willingness to achieve the condition of self-realization necessary to accept the revelation of God in Christ fully. To accept the revelation of God in the risen Christ *is* to become like him; it is to be growing up to the full stature of the humanity of Christ.

On the other hand, this acceptance of revelation is identical with the condition of salvation. Salvation is not some extrinsic reward that is accorded by God on the condition that we accept his revelation as true. Rather, it is the intrinsic result of a life lived out in the acceptance of revelation and culminated by the achievement of the risen condition of Christ in union with him. To be saved is not so much to be redeemed from sin (which it is, of course) as it is to be fulfilled. To be saved is to have achieved the fullness of humanity; it is to have developed all of one's potentialities for inner integration and outer relatability to all of creation, to Christ as the summary of creation, and in and through Christ to God. To be saved is thus to have achieved the condition of the Communion of Saints around Christ as the saint of saints, and in and through him to have won access to the Father. Salvation is, therefore, but another way of looking at the same reality that I have called the acceptance of revelation in Christ.[3]

REVELATION IN CHRIST AND ITS RELATIONSHIP TO INFALLIBILITY

It should now be apparent that the grasp of anything truly human is the grasp of something summed up in Christ; hence it is capable of revealing God.[4] It would seem as if the Church could teach anything truly human and humanizing infallibly, since the object of infallibility is that which is *per se* revealed. On the notion of revelation I have advanced, every meaning incarnated in the humanity of the risen Christ would be *per se* revealed. Hence all should be capable of being taught infallibly, at least in principle.

This would be a mistake. Its cause would be the popular tendency to view infallibility as an extrinsic supernatural gift bestowed upon the Church by God's bounty. This gift is seen as independent of the

nature of revelation and of human knowing. It is an interpolated
factor in the universe, an unexpected bonus granted to man out of
God's goodness. It has no intrinsic connection with God's other
gifts to man. The view I wish to advance considers infallibility as
an intrinsic part of the human and Christian view of revelation.
When taken as such, this view explains why it is impossible for the
Church to be infallible about all aspects of revelation. To clarify
further why this is so, a few distinctions will be helpful.

PARTICULAR ASPECTS OF REVELATION

Under the condition of limited earthly humanity prior to eschatological realization, revelation must be considered as being particular or universal. By a particular aspect of revelation I refer to an
aspect of the realization of the full humanity of Christ that is presently achievable by one man or a limited number of men only.
Each man now achieves to some extent that full humanity which
exists in the risen Christ. When any man truly understands any
aspect of the world about him, when he expresses love for the persons he encounters, and when he develops a greater personal integration of his various powers, that man is acting out of faith, whether
he recognizes this explicitly or not.[5] As a consequence, he thereby
becomes capable of appreciating corresponding aspects of the revelation of God that is summed up in Christ. His growth, however,
is particular to him; the path he follows to that growth is, in its
concreteness, also particular to him. It is his unique way of living
out the exigency now placed on all men to achieve full humanity in
Christ. Because he is a unique individual with unique capacities and
in a unique historical situation, his concrete development—even if
it has been practically perfect—will be particular to him. Consequently, his present capacity to grasp the revelation achieved in the
risen Christ will also be particular to him. Any thematization of his
overall grasp of that revelation would be fully appreciated by him
alone. It could not as a totality be accorded universal validity; nor
could it become the subject of an infallible pronouncement of the
Church. Furthermore, any thematization of the concrete processes
by which he arrived at his present stage of growth in Christ—even
presupposing that his arrival were in a perfect manner—could not
be universalized and dogmatized. Because of his uniqueness at each

moment and because that uniqueness constitutes the starting point for his further development, the concrete processes of his march toward total integration and total relatability to the rest of creation must be unique. Hence these processes, too, cannot be generalized and thematized for all. Therefore they cannot be the object of ecclesial infallibility.

UNIVERSAL ASPECTS OF REVELATION

By a universal aspect of revelation, I refer to an enduring aspect of the risen Christ which is in some way graspable by all Christians in the present condition of existence. I say "in some way" because no man in the present mode of existence can grasp fully any aspect which pertains to the risen mode of existence. It is only because of the continuity between this life and the next that an analogous understanding of what is fully realized by Christ can be attained by us.

1. Relational Aspects

These universal aspects of revelation are either relational, ontic, or dynamic. The dynamic is but the forward thrust of the relational and the ontic. First of all, they are relational. These relational aspects are twofold. On the one hand, the risen Christ sums up and perfectly manifests the human relatability which was already manifested in the epoch before his coming on earth. In his humanity he is totally dependent upon God by being created in every aspect at every moment; he is totally related to all his fellow men on the creatural level with all that he is—this accounts for his being *universal* Saviour; he is completely related to the whole of the material universe and hence is its Lord. He is thus the living summary of the two great commandments of love of God and love of neighbor and of the injunction of Genesis requiring that man have dominion over material things (Gen. 1:26; 2:15).

On the other hand, he introduces into the world a new set of relationships that profoundly alter the conditions of human existence and initiate the lasting Christian dispensation. His humanity from the very beginning and throughout every development is related to the Son of God as the creatural expression of his own personality. Further, in and through the personality of the Son, that humanity becomes uniquely related to the Father and the Spirit. That relationship is not simply one of creature to Creator but also one of personal expression to a person who is intimately related to two other persons. As a result of this relationship of the risen humanity to the person of the Son, a new possibility arises for all mankind. Since the humanity of the risen Christ is united to all of creation, it makes possible for the first time a personal relationship of all men to God. Before the Incarnation the relationship of men to God could never be that of equals. That is, God was always the totally other in nature, no matter how much he showed his love for man. After the Incarnation, however, all men are capable—in an incipient way now and in a full way when they attain risen existence—of relating to God, God as expressed in the humanity of the risen Christ, at a level that is equal to man's nature. This relationship at the level of an equality is a relationship of friendship (cf. John 15:15), resulting from the mutual self-giving of our humanities and the humanity of Christ. Because of the universal reaching out of the risen humanity of Christ, this personal relationship is made accessible to all men, and it too is thus universal.

These relational aspects of universal revelation are the aspects that come through most clearly in Scripture. The men of the Old and the New Testaments were not primarily interested in God as he exists in himself or in the nature of man but in the relational aspects of God and man. The God of the Bible is a God concerned about man. In the Old Testament he is a covenant God who is always amidst his people to cajole, to punish, or to reward. In the New Testament he pitches his tent among men, he dwells within them as Father, Son, and Spirit. In and through the humanity of the risen Christ, he is with man all days even until the end of this age. Such a way of thinking and writing is normal to man. He always begins by observing and reflecting on the relational aspects of persons and material things as they regard him. He always comes to know reality outside himself by reflecting on the manner in which that reality affects him. Beginning with particular experiences of a person or thing, he moves to generalizations about what is common to those experiences. Thus, the first observers of the moon noted a succession of experiences of the appearances of the moon toward them. Subsequently, they recorded the recurring nature of those appearances in a series of generalizations about the phases of

the moon. In a similar manner Israel realized, first of all, its particular experiences of Yahweh's presence and influence. Only subsequently did it notice a recurring pattern in those appearances;
and hence it eventually was able to write more or less stylized accounts of its relationship to its God. From the etiological character
of Genesis to the formal prayer expressions in the Psalms, we find
the same tendency to generalize the recurring pattern of Israel's
faith relationship to Yahweh.

2. Ontic Aspects

The second type of universal aspect of revelation in Christ is
what I have termed "ontic." Even if things and persons are first
grasped as relational, there will still eventually arise the further
questions of what kind of beings they must be if they are to sustain
these relationships. Man is not satisfied with witnessing and recording the phases of the moon; he must go on to uncover what is the
nature of the relationship between the moon and earth that brings
about the phases that he witnesses. Similarly, he is not content with
knowing the relationship of the humanity of Christ to God, of that
humanity with his own humanity, and ultimately his own personal
relationship to God. He also wants to know the implications these
relationships have for the nature of man, of Christ, and of God.
What must man and visible creation be like if they are called to the
fulfillment of risen existence by their own inner exigence in this
concrete universe? What must Christ be like if he is the mediator
between God and man? What must the Trinity be like if the oneness of God manifested in the Old Testament is to be complemented
by the threefoldness revealed in the Incarnation? In short, the ontic
universal aspects of revelation refer to the enduring natures of man,
visible creation, the risen Christ, and the Trinity which are implied
in the continuing relational character of the risen Christ.

Historically, the recognition of the ontic aspect of universal revelation in Christ came after the New Testament period. Only with
the Fathers do we find questioning about the two natures in Christ,
the inner relationship of the persons in the Trinity, and a philosophical treatment of man in the light of the Gospel message. This
followed not from some special guidance of the Spirit peculiar to
Christianity but from the structure of human understanding as ap-

plicable to Christian faith. The reflection on what God, Christ, and man might be in the light of the Gospel came after the New Testament period because it could not have come before by the very nature of man.[6] Only as corporate Christianity begins to develop its own individual and social potentials does it begin to see more fully, if always analogously, the nature of the reality communicated with and implied in the resurrection of Christ.

3. Dynamic Aspects

The final universal aspect of revelation is what I have termed "the dynamic." It might just as well be called "the developmental." This refers to the enduring processes that mark the present growth of the risen Christ's humanity and the implications of these processes for man *in via*. At first glance, a theorizing about the growth and development of the risen Christ might seem contrary to the acceptance of the perfection of the risen humanity. However, once one grasps that that humanity is forever open to the infinite God while remaining finite, then one can begin to see that there can never be a final stage of that humanity incapable of increase. The risen condition then appears not as the stage when growth ceases but as the stage when growth reaches its perfection. The steady growth on earth of Christ was conditioned by his background, his surroundings, and his limitations as to time and place. As risen, however, he is open to all of creation in all its meanings. As mankind grows and becomes more complex, Christ incorporates into his own humanity all that mankind achieves in an integral way. His very nature as the universal Lord and Saviour thus insures that his present growth will not be piecemeal and halting but utterly universal.

This universal and unlimited growth process in Christ is paralleled by the growth processes in the Church that mark its development. These developmental processes are the present analogue of the normative development that takes place in Christ. They are discovered not at the very beginning of the Church's life but in the course of her history. In the attempt to live out the Gospel in a variety of concrete circumstances the Church stumbles, falls, but invariably moves haltingly ahead. In the course of time she makes headway as a result of mistakes. As a precipitate of that progress, she eventually is enabled to discern the recurring developmental patterns that mark her genuine growth. Thus, for example, she can discern the movement of understanding from the relational to the ontic. This discernment, like all developmental discernment, is possible only after a long period of time. It can take place only after the relational and ontic elements have become clear in a number of instances; for it represents the generic understanding and thematization of what has concretely taken place many times and in many different circumstances and cultures. The relational aspect of revelation must exist in living men over a period of time before it can be thematized in a generalization. Such generalizations must be apparent to large numbers in the Church before ontic questions can arise. Finally, there must be concrete growth in the understanding of both the relational and ontic elements in a number of instances before the Church can begin to appreciate the generic processes of development which lead it toward the fulfillment attained in risen humanity. The developmental is only the forward thrust of the relational and the ontic. It is understandable in terms only of the relational and the ontic, and it can be grasped by men only after they have grasped the relational and the ontic. Experience or performance always precedes understanding; hence the experience of development over a broad range of situations sufficient to ground universal statements must precede any intellectual grasp of the universal developmental aspects of revelation.[7]

INTERPENETRATION OF UNIVERSAL AND PARTICULAR ASPECTS OF REVELATION

The distinction I have made between particular and universal aspects of revelation has been solely for the purpose of clarifying the meaning of the primary object of infallibility. Before moving on to its import for infallibility, I would like to point out several ways in which the aspects I have distinguished concretely interpenetrate.

First of all, the universal aspects of revelation never exist by themselves. Rather, they are only abstract aspects of the universal existence of Christ's humanity which find a present counterpart in a host of particular Christian experiences. The particular and the concrete alone have independent existence. They are in each case the incarnation of many general and universal aspects. They are the matrix out of which the universal aspects of revelation come to the Church's consciousness.

Secondly, particular aspects of revelation are far vaster than universal aspects. Every good aspect of the humanity of every concrete individual is in a real sense revealing of God; it represents a unique path to grasping some facet of the total revelation of God expressed in Christ. Precisely because men are unique and partial manifestations of the fullness of Christ, they do not share with all others much of the good they concretely are. And what they do not share cannot be declared universal revelation. Only when all men are fully united to each other and communicate all that they are to each other in the risen condition will all aspects of concrete human nature also be universal aspects of revelation.

Thirdly, the recognition of universal aspects of revelation in word and action is necessary but not sufficient for full Christian living in this mode of existence. For a man to be a Christian he must witness in his life to all that has been recognized to pertain to the universality of the Christian life. He must profess the articles of faith with his mouth and in his actions. But these articles only encapsulate that which is generic to all Christians of the time. They say nothing about what is particular to each Christian. However, each Christian is called to move forward towards the fullest realization of the risen humanity of Christ possible to him in his unique circumstances. He is to christianize all that he is, not just that which pertains to the generality of Christians of his time. Hence, over and beyond what is implied in the universal relational, ontic, and dynamic aspects of revelation, he must find those particular aspects that pertain to him alone. Not only must he live up to the demands of the Creed; he must live up to them in a way that necessarily goes beyond the abstractions of the Creed. He must live creatively and prophetically in new and different ways if he is to be faithful to the exigency of total relatability placed upon him as a man and as a Christian. In the way he understands Christ, in the manner in which he lives with his brothers, and in the worship he offers to God there must be a unique existential element that goes beyond, though it does not contradict, the general element shared with all Christians. It is this unique element that grounds the possibility, the necessity, and the ambiguity of personal prayer, personal ethical decisions, and even personal beliefs about the Christian message.[8]

Fourthly, both the particular and universal aspects of revelation known to man are subject to development all along the line. The growth of the individual as a human being leads to his having to work out ever more complex decisions in the light of the Gospel. The more he grows, the more demands he faces to use his concrete powers to move towards the total relatability of the risen Christ. "Every one to whom much is given, of him will much be required" (Lk. 12:48). As a result, the unique aspect of Christ that he alone reflects also grows. On the other hand, the development and complexification of many individual and social relationships within the Church over the course of the centuries coupled with the communication between individual Christians and whole Christian communities lead to the expansion of the universal relational, ontic, and developmental aspects of revelation. Because men have been differentiated and have to some extent shared that differentiation over the centuries, they can now become conscious of more nuanced recurring relationships to the God who is present in the totality of human experiences. Because the Church as a whole has more nuanced generalizations about its relationship to God, it can grasp more nuanced generalizations about the nature of God, the nature of Christ, and the nature of man on the way towards Christ. Finally, because of all prior particular and universal developments of its grasp of revelation, the Church can come to a clearer notion of the nature of Christian development as such.

Fifthly, the charismatic and the pluralistic elements in the Church are aspects of the drive towards universal meanings. The charisms, as I indicated in note 4 of chapter 10, are the God-given capacities to live out the ancient tradition in specialized sectors of reality. Initially, charisms are the source of the development of the particular meanings that ground a genuine Christian pluralism. However, after a variety of charisms in different cultures and subcultures have led to diverse realizations of the Christian potential in local Churches, there arises a need to seek unifying threads within the achieved pluralism. Then it is that reflective individuals (hopefully, a few theologians will be among them) frame hypotheses to unify the data furnished by the pluralistic situation. Eventually, the charism of final unification, that pertaining to the episcopal college with the pope at its head, definitively recognizes the new universal meanings in the Church. Thus, the exercise of the charisms leads to pluralism, and pluralism eventually leads to an enriched unity.[9]

The preceding discussion reinforces our basic conclusion on the object of infallibility. The primary object of infallibility is the *per se* revealed doctrine of faith and morals that is *universal*. Particular aspects of revelation simply cannot be infallibly grasped. Because of the limitations of the present condition of existence, no person or persons in the Church can attain the full assurance of being without error with regard to particular aspects of revelation.

THE RESURRECTION AS ORIGIN OF THE CHURCH'S INFALLIBILITY

1. *The Resurrection establishes the definitive Structure of Revelation*

The possibility of such infallibility begins with the resurrection of Jesus Christ; for with his resurrection there is set up for the first time the definitive structure of universal saving reality that is the object of ecclesial infallibility. Before the Resurrection man could be infallible in reflecting on recurring relationships and dynamics of his experience of God. He could know of God's existence, of God's love for man, of man's openness to God. However, he could not know of the fulfillment of man's openness to God in Christ, of the risen condition of existence to which man would be called, of the personal relationship to God by communion with the humanity of the Son, of the Trinity of persons in God. All of these aspects of man's relationship to God came into existence with the Resurrection and hence could be known only when the Resurrection was accepted in faith. At that point the natural infallibility of the human mind came into possession of the definitive object of its exercise. The intrinsic human power to know which grows in differentiation and capacity by its encounter with the situation that surrounds it reached the high point of its knowing capacities when its surroundings included the universal presence and activity of the risen Christ. With the passage of time, it is true, there would inevitably be a growth in the understanding of the implications of the acceptance of the Resurrection as universal. As man becomes more differentiated and complex, he becomes capable of grasping new and deeper aspects of the universal significance and efficacy of the risen Lord. However, such developments will never change the basic Christian revelational fact that came into being on the first Easter. With that fact, the enduring relational, ontic, and dynamic structure of ultimate existence was set up for all time, and with it was established the definitive universal object of infallibility.

2. Revelation Ended with the Last Apostle's Death

We can now see more clearly the meaning of the traditional adage that "revelation stopped with the death of the last apostle." The phrase is perhaps not too felicitous; but it reflects the truth. It combines the two aspects necessary to put us into contact with the supernatural order constituted by Christ's resurrection. On the one hand, it necessarily implies that the period of basic revelation includes the definitive fact of the Resurrection that preceded the death of the apostles. On the other hand, it indicates that something basic to the structure of revelation pertained to the apostolic period. What that basic constituent of the revelation structure was we have already seen. The apostles (who in this connection really stand for the apostolic Church as its chief members) are those who because of their contact with the earthly Christ became capable of grasping his living presence among themselves after his death. They originated the content of the basic message about the Resurrection that was to be passed on by the traditional process throughout the long history of the Church. Without them the faith-acceptance of the Resurrection, an acceptance that is not verifiable by an analysis of experience despite the universal efficacy of the risen Christ, would not have flourished. Our faith in the Resurrection depends upon hearing them. And they have been heard. "Their voice has gone out to all the earth, and their words to the end of the world" (Rm. 10:18; Ps. 19:4).

The word "stopped" or "ended" in connection with the death of the last apostle is, of course, unfortunate. This has given the impression to some that a series of truths were proclaimed right up to the death of the last apostle but that after that moment no new truth of revelation was possible. The only thing possible after the demise of the last of the twelve was a process of bringing to clarity the implications and deductions derivable from the truths they had left behind. In the context I have set up, however, what ceased with the death of the last apostle was the proclamation of the universal presence of the risen Christ by those who experienced it on the basis of their years of living with him before his death. The *primary* witness to the

Resurrection ceased for all time. What did not stop in any sense was the efficacy of the Resurrection itself. It continues to be the living object of universal revelation and, by its continuance, it generates the possibility of ever new facets of its intelligibility being grasped by men who encounter it in the ever changing circumstances of life. Hence it is possible for the Church to pull out of its storehouse things both old and new. The Resurrection is an inexhaustible object of universal revelation; and as such it ultimately is a source of infallible teaching whose limits cannot be determined as long as time shall last and human development take place.

3. Universal Doctrines of Faith

The *per se* universal revealed doctrines of faith that can be infallibly declared are simply thematizations in words of aspects of the Church's encounter with the risen Lord which have achieved a relatively universal existence in the members of the body of Christ at a given juncture of history. These meanings grow with time. Different cultural circumstances give birth to new meanings. Some situations spawn meanings which are proper to one place and time. Other situations lead to meanings which are destined to become universal, although at the given moment they can be found only in a part of the Church. Then there will be stresses and strains until what is only potentially universal becomes actually universal. This was one of the aspects of the struggles that preceded many of the definitions of dogma in the past. It is an aspect which reappears today when the Church enters a primitive culture and attempts to demand of its people an acceptance of doctrines which thematize a stage of human and Christian differentiation they have not yet attained. (Can the demand for monogamy among certain African tribes be an example of such an attempt in modern times?)

A Christian meaning becomes universal when it exists, at least implicitly, in most Christians. It then becomes possible for Church authorities to articulate it explicitly. Such articulations or "definitions of doctrine are not so much innovations as the authentic recognition of collective anticipations and of collective certifications."[10] Therefore, this type of articulation requires a certain development in the very texture of the persons who constitute the Church, and without that development no infallible proclamation is possible because the object of infallibility does not exist as yet.[11] Because of the lack of such a development in the Church of his time, St. Paul could not have infallibly proclaimed a doctrine such as the Assumption of the Virgin Mary. The notion that he and the rest of the apostles had an implicit grasp of all future doctrine and that they could have articulated that grasp if asked is quite difficult to maintain. The grasp and the articulation of the doctrines of future ages by the apostles would have required of them a human and Christian differentiation attainable by other men only after a prolonged history. The apostles would have had to have become men of all centuries, though they lived only in the first Christian century. They would have had to have achieved an experiential continuum capable of grounding all Christian meanings for all time. Given that all development is in community and that their community was totally composed of first-century men, this achievement appears impossible. Only those who think infallibility is an isolated gift by which God miraculously enlightens men to pronounce verbally about objects not grounded in their life experience can believe that the apostles had this kind of global infallibility. The very slowness of the apostolic Church to overcome its restricted Jewish beginning suggests that the twelve did not even immediately grasp the universal mission implied in the acceptance of the resurrection of Jesus.

THE EXERCISE OF INFALLIBILITY AND THE DEVELOPMENT OF UNIVERSAL CHRISTIAN MEANINGS

1. Relational Infallibility

It should now be clear that the exercise of infallibility ought to follow the path of development of universal Christian meanings. The historical evidence indicates this is actually the case.[12] In the beginning the Church lived out its life of belief in the Resurrection for many years before it expressed the meaning of that living in the Scriptures. Moreover, when the Scriptures were written, they gave no evidence of abstract doctrines about the nature of Christ, of Christian man, or of the Trinity. Rather, they basically report the particular relationships of Christians to one another, to the risen Lord, and to God; or they thematize what is generic to these relationships. I suggest that the inerrancy of Scripture (a doctrine that has been too unnuanced, it seems to me) pertains to the universal relational aspects of revelation that so frequently occur in the Bible. The Scriptures are without error to the degree that the particular events they describe exemplify *in concreto* the lasting universal aspects of revelation I have called "relational." Scriptural inerrancy thus becomes a specific form of the expression of infallibility, the form proper to the initial and basic Christian experience.

2. Ontic Infallibility

Infallibility with regard to the recurring relationships in Christian existence has never died out in the Church because these relationships continue in living Christians and have tended to complexify. However, as the Church began to shift towards the expression of the meaning of man, Christ, and God as they are in themselves, it eventually began to speak infallibly about those aspects of universal revelation which I have termed "ontic." This is largely the category into which most of the abstract doctrines of the creeds and catechisms (at least most catechisms until the last ten years) fall. The great councils tended to express themselves about ontic matters.

3. Dynamic Infallibility

The state of the question. Finally, in recent centuries we have entered the period in which the universal developmental processes of Christian existence have begun to appear. I have indicated already why the dynamic and developmental aspects of revelation appear after the relational and ontic aspects. Here I would only indicate that this accounts for the fact that infallibility has hardly ever occurred in developmental matters. The single exception I am aware of is the definition of papal infallibility at Vatican I. This doctrine is really a developmental doctrine because it treats of the process by which the Church in the person of the pope comes to proclaim the universal meanings it has arrived at. Admittedly, the doctrine is quite unnuanced, as these pages have indicated. Nevertheless, a beginning has been made. Further, the mention made at Vatican I of the phenomenon of development of doctrine (D.S. 3020), although no adequate explanation of this process was given, indicates that we may expect something more on this matter in the future.

The crucial matter involving a developmental teaching is that of moral theology. If the relational and ontic universal aspects of revelation pertain to what is usually called "dogma," the dynamic and developmental aspects pertain largely to morals. The question that has come up in recent years has to do with the very possibility of the Church exercising infallibility in moral matters. As one author puts it, "I think that the term 'infallible' does not in fact aptly describe the nature or function of the moral magisterium, and that we should discontinue using that term in describing the moral magisterium."[13]

Evaluation of prior concrete morality. My own view, on the basis of what has gone before, probably differs substantially from that of the author just quoted and from that of the majority of moral theologians. I would admit, first of all, that I do not think that any of the Church's specific moral teaching of the past or present with regard to concrete moral actions has been infallibly proclaimed. I would go further; I do not believe that such specific concrete morality can ever be infallibly proclaimed. Infallibility always has to do with the universal, and infallible moral teaching would have to do with a process of Christian growth common to all Christians in their march to the universal relatability of the risen Christ. However, specific concrete acts can never be universally a source of growth; nor can other specific concrete acts always be a source of Christian retardation. The fact is that concrete acts are inevitably complex and unique. It is true that we can place many acts into a single abstract category like birth control. However, no act fits nicely and perfectly into just one category. Thus, every act of birth control can be many other things—an expression of love for one's spouse, an act of concern for already existing children, and a release of sexual tension. These other aspects may well contribute to the growth of the individual. To claim that every concrete act of birth control leads to a retardation of one's Christian growth is to assume not only that the birth control aspect of the act performed is in some way "wrong" but also that the concrete act has no good aspects to it. It is simply an act of birth control and nothing more. However, this is a manifest oversimplification. Once one grasps this, one can see the utter impossibility of declaring all acts of birth control—or indeed of lying or killing—to be immoral. It is the whole act taken in context of the life of the individual at his stage of development that determines whether he will or will not grow by it. To reduce the concrete act to one abstract aspect is to engage in a fallacy of misplaced concreteness. It is to make the aspect one has abstracted the whole act and the sole determinant of the morality of that act.

However, the morality proclaimed by the magisterium of the Church has invariably been a concrete morality. It has been a morality that has spoken of acts in given concrete circumstances. Thus, usury was long declared immoral because within the context of the agricultural economy in which the prohibition against interest-taking was enunciated, such interest-taking contradicted basic Christian values.[14] The same reasoning, I believe, applies to birth control.[15] No such pronouncements have been nor can be infallible because they do not fulfill the conditions of universality required of infallible pronouncements. At best, they have validity only within the confines of the limited cultural situations explicitly or implicitly (the usual case) assumed by their authors.

It was inevitable that the morality proclaimed by the magisterium would be of this nature in the past. Throughout the Church, as in society as a whole, an aphoristic or rule-of-thumb approach to morality prevailed. People tended to live by the type of maxims we see exemplified in the book of Proverbs, in Sirach, and even in the Gospels. This wisdom could be codified and passed on to future generations; and it worked well as long as society remained relatively stable. Each culture could give birth to common-sense maxims which described how good Christians would act in certain concrete circumstances that tended to recur. It became possible for confessors to prescribe just what the Christian should do in any and all possible situations. In fact, casuists could work out in vast detail just what kind of concrete acts were or were not sins, were or were not mortal or venial sins. Under such conditions, the magisterium that collected and proclaimed the universal experience of the Church could not have been anything but a rule-of-thumb magisterium in morals. Of course, it did not proclaim itself as such. It spoke out of a given level of existence and out of a given Western cultural situation; it proclaimed what had been seen to work for the Christian growth of the members of the Church over a long period. But because it was unaware of the fact that man is culturally conditioned and that different cultures demand different concrete modes of moral growth and development, it could not but assume that the moral wisdom that worked universally in the situations it knew was actually ap-

plicable to all cultures and levels of existence. Nevertheless, because
that wisdom and the decrees that embodied it did not actually speak
for what is normative in all Christian experience in whatsoever
culture, it was not and could not have been infallible. Put simply,
the moral magisterium of the past taught basically a concrete morality; and universality, with the infallibility that can follow only upon
universality, does not pertain to the concrete.

The modern problematic. The modern situation has changed the
conditions under which the moral magisterium operates. In the present, concrete decisions are so complex that no rule-of-thumb can
determine in advance what is morally required. Hence people are
being told to make up their own minds about what they must do.
Of course, after following an aphoristic type of morality for so long
a time, such people find it difficult to exercise independent moral
responsibility. What they lack are the universal principles of wisdom
which would permit them to view the concrete world with Christian
eyes and make decisions that would promote their own growth and
the growth of those about them. In this matter they have much to
learn from non-Christians and Protestants who have long realized
that a rule-of-thumb morality is no longer feasible. The forays by
Catholic moralists into Protestant territory have often been attempts
to get beyond the confines of a rule-of-thumb morality.

It will be replied that the magisterium will furnish such principles
from God if they are necessary; for the magisterium has been divinely
established to enlighten Christians about their moral duties. I believe
that this notion of a magisterium which is inspired with needed solutions apart from the rest of the Church is mistaken. The magisterium
sums up and expresses the working of the Spirit in the whole Church.[16]
It articulates what is meaningful from a Christian viewpoint in the
experience of the whole Christian community. It does not have a
pipeline that allows it to make decisions in utter independence of
the experience of that community.[17] Certainly the magisterium is
not a poll-taker, supposedly following some sort of head-counting
theory. It is no more that than the intellect is a poll-taker following
the primary bent of the emotions. Instead, the charism of the magisterium is to live out of and interpret the living experience of the
Church in the light of the great past. It cannot understand apart from
that experience, just as an individual cannot understand apart from
his own experiential continuum. Hence, if the magisterium is to ar-

ticulate the universal principles of moral wisdom which ground true Christian responsible action, it is necessary that many Church members have lived lives of responsible Christian decisions. Experience comes first; from experience rules and the codifications of laws follow. In the past many different experiences in the same culture gave birth to rules-of-thumb which were eventually codified by the moral magisterium. These codifications did not come first; trial and error, costly blunders, and brilliant breakthroughs by individuals came first and had to come first. Old Testament morality did not come at the beginning of Israel's life, but only after that life had been lived. New Testament morality was not given by Christ *ab initio* but has been the fulfillment of Old Testament morality worked out over the centuries since Christ. If we have reached a stage in which the aphoristic-type morality will no longer work, then the more generic and universal morality which can ground infallibility must now be worked out. It will not be worked out simply by examining the past or by isolated guidance of magisterial figures reflecting solely on texts of the past. Rather, it will be worked out by the whole Church's effort to live out the implications of the Resurrection in a spirit of free decision making. That collective experience will be the soil out of which the magisterium will harvest the universal material for infallible pronouncements.

A sketch of universal moral theology. This is not the place to elaborate what a universal moral theology might be. That would require a separate volume. However, I can sketch the basic framework of that moral theology which emerges from the attempt to live responsibly in the light of the Resurrection. First of all, it would not be a concrete moral theology, a theology that would categorize acts as good or bad. Rather, it would be a resurrectional, subjective, and heuristic moral theology. These terms correspond to the goal, the starting point, and the process of Christian development which are universally valid.

Such a moral theology would be resurrectional or tending towards a goal of total relatability. Each Christian is held by his own nature and inner exigency to move towards the affective, attitudinal, and intellectual attachment to all creatures, to Christ, and ultimately to the Father. He is held, therefore, to grow up to the fullness of Christ, to attain that universality of love and concern which characterizes the Lord's risen humanity. In other terms, he is held to live up to the first and second commandments as a goal to be tended towards in every moment of life. A universal moral teaching would, therefore, have as its first constituent element a clarification of the existential meaning of this goal of universal relatability. It would be continuously engaged in the effort to nuance and develop in the light of the sciences just what universal relatability would concretely mean. It would never exhaust the meaning of that goal because the meaning of goals can be fully grasped only by those who have attained them; for no one understands except on the basis of his own experience. However, in the course of time it will begin to see that the goal is the fulfillment of ever clearer, recurring subjective powers of all persons in the present. It will more and more see the goal as the ultimate extrapolation of the results attained by the continuing faithful implementation of the basic powers to relate now in man.

This brings us to the second element of a universal moral teaching—the subjective. When we speak of morality being "subjective," we refer to the starting point of its exercise. That starting point is always the concrete subject in his unique concrete circumstances. A universal moral teaching would thus seek out the methods by which the subject could know the kind of person he is and the actual capacities he possesses in the light of his unique situation. This aspect of universal morality would thus be concerned with the methodology by which each person discovers who he is. It would thus deal with the thematization of the recurring processes by which all subjects in all cultures come to know and understand who they are in terms of their environment with an eye toward utilizing their capacities in the light of the Gospel for further growth towards the goal of universal Christian relatability.

Finally, the universal moral teaching of which we speak would be heuristic. This means that it would treat of the generic processes of human development by which all subjects can move from their limited subjective starting points towards the goal of humanity achieved in the risen Christ. These processes are to morality what scientific method is to the various sciences. Just as scientific method refers to the enduring processes by which all scientists work on given data in order to reach towards an ultimate goal of totally understanding the universe, so too heuristic moral teaching would refer to the enduring processes by which men work on the given data of their own personalities in order to reach towards the ultimate goal of total Christian realization.

Heuristic moral teaching would deal with a number of problems. It would explain the process by which one accepts and deals with the limitations present in oneself and in one's total environment. It would clarify the method of reasonable moral experimentation; the place of personal prayer, liturgy, and renunciation in Christian growth; the way one checks new moral fruits against the tradition of the past. Above all, it would clearly show the function of basic moral principles. These do not immediately solve concrete cases like abortion and birth control because concrete cases are complex and never fit under a single principle. Rather, basic moral principles represent present understanding of abstract aspects of the goal of morality. They perform their function when they are internalized in a subject along with other basic principles. The subject who has internalized the set of basic moral principles becomes sensitized to all the values these principles represent. As sensitized to these values, he becomes capable of acting wisely in concrete cases where these values are challenged. Only such a sensitized subject, and not abstract bodiless reasoning, can wisely solve concrete cases. Hence the process of internalizing principles which gives birth to the sensitized subject becomes a key aspect for heuristic morality.

Heuristic moral teaching would thus delineate and specify the processes of growth that transcend all differences of concrete cultures and levels of human existence because they are rooted in the enduring dynamism of man to move with all his powers towards the goal of risen existence. Such a moral teaching would further indicate the broad outlines of the results of such an application of growth processes. It would show that gradually a man would move from a narrow integration and attention to self to an ever broader development of his powers to be concerned with all. The delineation of stages of growth would subsequently assist subjects in discovering where they are and what they can reasonably do.[18]

Such, in the barest outline, would be a resurrectional, subjective, and heuristic morality. It obviously would not be a science of concrete ethical rules to be followed; for ethical rules are invariably bound to the cultural situation which spawned them, and they enable men to act well in those situations. Rather, it would be the science by which men could become wise Christians, persons capable of making moral decisions in complex situations pertaining to changing contexts. Only such a morality is equal to the task of equipping men in the Church to deal with the dynamic world of today.

It is obvious that such a morality does not yet exist. I believe we are making the initial stumbling steps towards it. The Church is, as it were, blundering towards a universal morality; and vast confusion exists and will exist until it is achieved. That achievement will come about only by a large-scale effort to work honestly in the light of our Christian tradition with the new problems that face us in varying cultural situations. Only the recurring efforts to make responsible decisions in a variety of circumstances will precipitate the methodological principles that can be the basis of a universal moral teaching. And only when this is done will there emerge the practical possibility of an infallible moral magisterium.

I should note that the kind of morality that can give rise to infallible statements of universal validity is not a morality that will give definitive answers to concrete questions. Rather, it will, if *internalized*, provide the skills that will enable individuals to work out Christian answers to the immense variety of concrete situations that face them. The answers that the applications of these skills will give will never be infallible; for infallibility in concrete cases is not the lot of man in this world. But they will be wisely Christian; and their performer will be ready to revise them in the light of the same infallible principles that gave birth to them when better investigations indicate that the facts of the situation are not what they were thought to be.

What is important is not that the magisterium teach infallible morality but that the living matrix out of which infallible morality may spring should exist. What is needed are large numbers of individuals who are capable of applying lasting principles of morality to ever-changing circumstances. When such individuals exist, the Church will be prepared to pass on, not a traditional aphoristic-type wisdom, but the enduring wisdom of universal developmental principles. Such individuals will be the living font out of which theologians will begin to articulate a universal morality; and such a morality may eventually be infallibly grasped and then proclaimed. Such individuals will also provide the living background, the facilitating personnel, who will make the effective articulation of such a moral teaching possible. Without such persons in the Church, even a magically equipped magisterium could not effectively proclaim a universal morality. An unprepared, aphoristically trained people cannot even begin to grasp a resurrectional, subjective, and heuristic morality unless there are living exemplifiers of such a morality among them. Even with the backdrop of such responsible Christians, men trained in a rule-of-thumb morality will find it difficult to change. They will want to cling to the tried and true, simple way of judging morally. They will be as attached to concrete acts in morality as they have been attached to concrete liturgical ceremonies in worship and stylized formulations in catechetics. They will change only slowly and painfully, if at all; but if they do change, they will do so largely through the presence of vibrant living Christians who responsibly live out their days applying truly universal principles. Abstract teaching of infallible principles does not change men; living persons do.[19]

SUMMARY

According to Vatican I, the primary objects of infallibility are truths of faith and morals *per se* revealed for the whole Church. My effort in this chapter has been to propound a coherent theory that would explain how this teaching of the council corresponds to the basic Christian belief in the Resurrection and the exigencies of the process of human understanding and personal development.

According to the theory propounded, the universally acting risen Christ is the total possible revelation of God to man. He reveals God in human terms. He manifests what is in man grown to full stature. His risen humanity is thus the living epitome of what God is for man and what man can be as a child of God. To know the risen Christ is to know what can be known of both God and man. However, the full knowledge of the risen Christ possible to man comes only with the *eschaton*. In the present condition of existence, man can grasp the intelligibility of the risen Christ only to the degree that he himself achieves full humanity. That which is particular to each man can be grasped only with more or less probability. Only that aspect of Christ's risen humanity which is universally graspable can be understood with any certainty by men; and it is this universal aspect that can be expressed in dogmatic statements.[20] These statements or thematizations of the Church's universal grasp of the risen Christ clarify what was meant by Vatican I when it said that the primary objects of infallibility are truths *per se* revealed for the whole Church. Finally, the theory explains what can ultimately be meant by referring to the truths of faith and morals that are *per se* revealed. The truths of faith are the universal relational and ontic aspects of revelation; whereas the truths of morals are the recurring dynamic principles which characterize the growth of men in all cultures and times. These revealed truths emerge from the universal life of the Church's historical existence. By the nature of things the relational, the ontic, and the dynamic emerge as precipitates of the Church's life in that order. Consequently, the objects of infallibility have tended and will tend to follow the same order. Thus, the earliest expressions of infallibly grasped truth, the Scriptures, are largely thematizations of man's recurring relationships to his fellow man, to Christ, and to the Trinity. The patristic period and those that followed saw the enunciation of statements about the ontic constituency of the reality of man, Christ, and God. All the way through these periods moral rules-of-thumb were enunciated for culturally conditioned man; but now we are moving into a period in which there may finally be precipitated a universal moral teaching, capable of infallible definition.

The Source and Goal of Infallibility

THE HOLY SPIRIT AS SOURCE

1. The Teaching of Vatican I

According to Vatican I, the Holy Spirit is the font and source of the gift of infallibility in the Church. However, the discussion of the council revolved not so much around the meaning of the Holy Spirit as source of infallibility as around the kind of assistance the Spirit rendered to the holders of infallibility. It was eventually said that the Spirit did not give power to proclaim new truths but that he gave assistance to recognize and proclaim the deposit of revelation. Further, his assistance was not given habitually, but only in the moment of exercise of certain qualified functions in limiting circumstances. In short, what Vatican I did was to talk not so much about the Spirit as about the created conditions of the exercise of infallibility that stemmed from him.

In this short section, I would like to put the meaning of the special assistance of the Spirit in the gift of infallibility into a larger context. First of all, it must be recalled that everything is a gift of the Spirit, that all creation is God-given. Though the Father and the Son and the Spirit are all sources of every gift, the Holy Spirit has usually been designated as gift-giver, just as the Father has generally been called the Creator. In fact, however, no specific concrete effect in creation can be strictly said to be the work of any single divine person. Certain effects are attributed to one or the other divine person only because of an affinity between these effects and the operations and properties theology assigns to the persons within the Trinity.[1] What this all means is that it is fruitless to attempt to analyze just how infallibility flows as a gift from the Spirit. What is more to the point is to examine the created qualities of the gift; this is what Vatican I did.

2. Why Infallibility Is Not an Habitual Gift

In the context in which we have been operating, the assertions of

Vatican I take on new meaning. It now becomes clear why infallibility is not an habitual gift of the pope and the bishops but a gift that is accorded only in the exercise of specific acts and in specific circumstances. It also becomes clear in what sense and why infallibility is not an active gift to proclaim new truths but a divine assistance given to recognize and proclaim the deposit of revelation. On the one hand, it is evident that infallibility is not and cannot be an habitual gift. Its exercise requires a prior universality of truth within the Church, at least in an implicit manner. There has to be growth and development in the Church's consciousness in the various areas we have specified—the relational, the ontic, and the dynamic—before there can be an infallible grasp and a subsequent pronouncement to articulate meaningfully what has been taking place. There must be an ecclesial experience throughout the Church to ground such a grasp and pronouncement. Otherwise, such a pronouncement would smack more of the conjuror's trick than of a saving act of God. To think of infallibility as something the magisterium can exercise at will after prayer and fasting is really to think of a magisterium divorced from the rest of the Church. It is to think that the Spirit acts upon the holders of teaching authority independently of his acting on the rest of the Church. It is to envision the process of understanding in the Church apart from ecclesial experience.

3. Infallibility Proclaims only the Deposit of Revelation

On the other hand, the same line of reasoning indicates in what sense and why infallibility is not given to proclaim new truths but to enable the magisterium to recognize and to proclaim the deposit of revelation. That which the Church experiences is the risen Christ. He is the total object of revelation now and forever. Throughout its history the Church more and more comes in contact with him in a host of historical circumstances. It learns more and more about him, the living deposit of revelation. It is forever recognizing him on a thousand roads to Emmaus; it is forever proclaiming its recognition. Infallible pronouncements simply articulate the grasp of universal aspects of these varied recognitions of the risen Christ.

4. Infallibility—A Special Gift

Finally, it should be apparent why infallibility is called a special gift of the Spirit, one so important as to be singled out by a general council. At every moment man is continuously being created by God; he is a continuous gift of God. However, new gifts are always being created so that man can grow and become more than he was. When a person is capable of acting creatively in the Church and society so as to effect growth in a given sector, he is said to possess a charism.[2] Such a charism or gift is operative not continuously but only at the moments when the situation calls for its exercise. Now infallibility is the exercise of the capacity to unify the prior experiential development of the Church by an act of insight into its recurring unities. That insight, like all insight, is a free gift of God which effects an advance beyond one's prior existence. Because that advance in this case is within the Church and because it crystallizes a significant and universal growth of the Church, it is rightly called a special gift of the Spirit to the Church; for this is the gift or charism that sums up and unifies the effects of all other gifts.

THE GOAL OF INFALLIBILITY

Vatican I declared that the goal of infallibility was the maintenance and promotion of the unity of faith and the community of the faithful. It saw the articulation of truth in faith and morals as promoting that twofold goal. The context we have developed manifests just how the process leading to articulation of universal meanings, as well as the articulation itself, brings about the unity of faith and the community of the Church's members.

1. Infallibility Promotes the Unity of Faith

First of all, unity of faith is maintained and promoted by the exercise of the gift of infallibility, as may be seen from an examination of the meaning of unity of faith. That unity can only be a unity in the acceptance of the revelation of God which is the risen Christ. However, that acceptance, as I stated previously, involves elements that are specific to each individual as well as elements that pertain to all members of the Church. Embedded in the concrete acceptance of

each are particular and universal elements. Only the universal elements make possible a unity of faith; for these are the abstract elements that all Christians share or may rightly share. Thus, to have
the same faith as another is to possess the same faith elements as the
other; and the only elements of the faith that one can be expected to
possess in common with all others are universal elements. Since these
are the only elements infallibility can proclaim, this gift is involved
with articulating the very core of the unity of faith.

It is this articulation, whether considered in the process that leads
up to it or in the very act of articulation, that maintains and promotes
the unity of faith. On the one hand, the process leading to the articulation of an infallibly grasped meaning is a process in which the
universal meanings come into existence by the living out of the faith
in a myriad of circumstances. Of its nature this process promotes the
unity of the faith because it is that unity of faith in the condition of
being realized. On the other hand, the articulation of universal
meaning that comes at the end of the process of implicit realization
solidifies the achievement of the unity of faith for those who have
already attained, at least in an implicit manner, the underlying elements of the articulation; for such an articulation makes explicit
and expresses for those who possess the underlying elements just
what constitutes for them the universal faith. Just as a solemn statement of purpose and ideals in the Declaration of Independence
maintained and further unified the signers and those accepting the
document in their common ideals, so too the solemn infallible grasp
and subsequent expression of commonly held aspects of the faith
maintain and further unify both the proclaimers of the document
and those who accept it because they see in it the articulation of
what they already deeply believe. The papal definitions of the Immaculate Conception and the Assumption exemplify this in the
Church. Further, such an articulation can promote the continued
development of those who have not as yet achieved the realization
of the implicit faith underlying the statement of universal meaning.
For them a statement of such meaning can be a spur to additional
growth in the common faith of their brethren.

2. Infallibility Promotes the Community of the Faithful

What has been said about the unity of faith can be applied to the community of the faithful. Community demands more than the existence of shared elements in people. It demands that these elements be *known* as shared. This is best achieved when men grow together. Growth is a process of experience, understanding, judgment, decision, and implementation. Shared growth implies to some degree a common experience, leading to the arrival at common understanding, a common judgment, a common decision, and a common implementation. Now the common elements throughout the Church are the universal meanings relating to the risen Christ, which are the objects of infallibility. All the corporate processes which center around these common meanings build up the community of the faithful. The final articulation of these common meanings, especially when it is arrived at by a process which organically involves the whole Church, will inevitably be a community-building act. Again I must stress that what is crucial is not the proclamation of infallibly grasped meaning but the whole dynamic of building up the community of meanings which underlie and lead to such statements and give them their validity.

3. Doctrine Saves When Accepted

I believe that what I have advanced so far explains why it is as legitimate to speak of saving doctrine as it is to speak of the saving nature of faith as the response to revelation. To be saved is to accept the revelation which is in Jesus Christ risen from the dead in the fullest manner possible[3] To accept infallibly grasped doctrine is to accept that revelation, not in an undifferentiated way, but in a way in which what is universal within revelation is explicitly grasped as such. Accepting doctrine is thus a conscious way of accepting revelation in its universal implications. That is why the acceptance of doctrine has rightly been made the touchstone of membership in the Church and why the denial of doctrine was thought to be such a great sin; for the Church is identified by the universal meanings that doctrine seeks to articulate, and the rejection of doctrine and the meanings doctrine represents is the rejection of that which constitutes the Church and the essence of salvation for all.

Unfortunately, however, there has been too facile an identification of the acceptance or denial of formulas and other expressions with the acceptance or denial of the meanings they represent. On the one hand, this has led to classifying as Catholic those who profess certain verbal formulas, practice certain external rites, and accept certain authority figures in principle. Rather, a Catholic would be one who would accept these expressions precisely as representative of underlying universal meanings. On the other hand, this false identification has led to the too rapid exclusion from Catholic communion (and in theory even from salvation) of those who do not accept Catholic verbal formulas, external rites, and authority figures. Rather, one must ask whether those who reject these various expressions are rejecting the meaning they represent or only the expressions; for it may be that these expressions are rejected because they do not fittingly express the universal meaning for those rejecting them. To reject an expression is not the same as rejecting both the expression and the meaning it represents. Simply rejecting the classic Catholic doctrinal formulas, rites, and authority figures does exclude one from the visible Church; it does not of itself exclude one from salvation.

Further, there has been too facile an identification of temporally conditioned meanings with meanings that ground the Church and salvation for all. This has made it necessary for Catholics to accept as binding many a doctrine that was simply one culturally conditioned teaching. The suffering that many a Catholic exegete and theologian had to undergo for the sake of preserving a cherished belief of one school is well known.

The point about these too facile identifications is that they have led to a discrediting of doctrine in the minds of many. Only right faith is necessary, it is said. Doctrine is something for theologians to fight over. On the contrary, I believe that genuine doctrine, universal doctrine, is crucially important. The acceptance of its meaning is the heart of the saving movement of faith.

THE PRACTICALITY OF INFALLIBILITY

Has the power to define infallibly any practical value? My own view is that it contributes little towards the *immediate* settling of concrete problems that the Church has to face in its encounter with the world. Birth control, abortion, war and peace, and other such matters, *as they appear in modern concrete circumstances*, are not the objects of infallible decisions. On the one hand, infallibility is possible only with regard to universal principles. Such principles do not immediately solve concrete cases, although their internalization makes it possible for men to confront such cases wisely. On the other hand, infallibility with regard to the universal principles that affect such matters as birth control and abortion is not an immediate source from God which automatically furnishes the required principles in new concrete circumstances. Rather, as I have tried to show, such principles emerge only after a long time as a precipitate of the whole Church's growth. Infallibility only sums up a process of understanding that has gradually permeated the Church. Hence it cannot instantaneously produce a definitive answer regarding the principles to be used in difficult cases. I would suggest, for example, that Pope Paul did not produce an infallible statement of principles in the birth control matter because understanding of the issue in the Church had not reached the point where such a decision was possible.

However, infallibility does have practical consequences of another order. Pronouncement of infallibly grasped principles and the steps leading up to them are generic processes by which the Church lives out the common faith and builds itself as a community. The pronouncement that comes at the end is but the crowning expression of a process of ecclesial growth. In its ideal form it is to the implicit understanding of all the faithful what the liturgy is to the interior worshiping attitude of Christians. It is the supreme articulation and expression of universal Christian understanding and is as practical for the further growth of that understanding as true liturgy is for the growth of a spirit of worship. It marks off a stage in the growth of the Church, a solidifying of the assured gains of the past. Thus, it frees the Church for new growth by indicating with certitude the enduring relationships and processes upon which all future growth will depend.[4]

THE NECESSITY OF INFALLIBILITY

A study of the cumulative nature of human and Christian understanding and growth reveals in what sense and why the exercise of infallibility is necessary for the Church's life. I am not saying that there must be a series of statements of the magisterium for the growth of the Church. It is sufficient that there be meanings which all Christians consciously hold and know they consciously hold in union with other Christians. Such universal meanings could be declared definitively by the magisterium, although in most cases there is no need to do so; for the purpose of a statement of infallible understanding is already accomplished by the common acceptance of the meanings in question.

1. Cumulative Versus Accretionary Understanding and Growth

This common acceptance of universal meanings in a conscious way is crucial for growth because of the cumulative nature of human growth in general and of human understanding in particular. Perhaps the best way to clarify the meaning of cumulative personal growth and cumulative understanding is to contrast it with accretionary personal growth and accretionary understanding. By this latter, I mean a kind of increase in being or understanding which is the result of the mere addition in a nonintegrated way of new materials. Thus, the learning of facts in a new field without any effort at all to integrate that learning with one's prior knowledge is an example of accretionary understanding. Accretionary understanding can occur in people with photographic memories if they fail to make the effort to relate each bit of new knowledge with their old knowledge. The ordinary individual has to make some such effort because he can usually remember only by association. Parallel to accretionary knowledge is what might be called accretionary personal growth. This is the extension of the accretionary and nonintegrating phenomenon to the entire field of personal growth. An individual would exhibit accretionary growth if he were simply a congeries of isolated and unconnected experiences and activities deriving from a haphazard pattern of life and thought.

In contrast to accretionary personal growth and understanding is cumulative growth and understanding. Cumulative growth would be one in which each new activity and experience would affect and be affected by the substantial whole of the individual's past growth. The new would be modified by the old into which it would be integrated; and the old would in turn be modified by the new. Cumulative understanding would be the kind that develops continuously, not by piling up new data in separate pigeonholes, but by a progressive expansion of understanding which consistently incorporates into its overall view and each of its subsidiary views all new data. Thus, an historian of the last century might have discovered evidence which proved that the Gospel of John was produced much earlier than the 150 A.D. date he had assigned to it. This bit of knowledge is accretionary upon its discovery; it becomes cumulative for him when he makes the effort to integrate the acceptance of this finding into his whole prior interpretation of John. This effort may entail the changing of many a cherished view about John which was contingent upon the fourth Gospel's late dating. In the end, the view taken of the new finding and the interpretation of the whole field into which that view is inserted must mutually condition one another so that the historian may arrive at as consistent an overall view of the whole and all the parts as possible.

2. Christian Growth is Cumulative—Not Accretionary

The claim made here is that true human and Christian personal growth in general, and growth in understanding in particular, is cumulative rather than accretionary. Accretionary growth leads to personal confusion and inability to understand oneself; for understanding involves the grasping of unity in data, and the accretionary person is by definition one whose growth lacks unity and whose life is unmodified by unifying understanding. Perhaps it is not wide of the mark to say that many of the problems we now face are due to the fact that our society fosters such accretionary growth. Similarly, accretionary understanding leads to disorder; it is the accumulation of facts about the world with no recognition of the intellect's drive towards unity. By its very success it increasingly makes its possessor a wanderer in a hopeless maze. Such understanding was exemplified by the plodding clerk of the 1950s who could win huge sums of money on TV by furnishing unhesitatingly such facts as the population of Thailand in 1828, but who could not grasp the broad issues of the modern world which involved an integration of those facts.

3. Cumulative Christian Growth Requires Infallibility

Christian personal growth, especially growth in understanding, embodies the same cumulative structure I have just described, but it embodies it in the context of faith in the Resurrection. Once one grasps this, it becomes possible to see the necessity of infallible understanding and, at times, of proclamations of that understanding to insure that it is widespread. Cumulative growth in understanding, in an individual and in a society, demands that assured method-ological or structural truths be found along the way that allow us to continue upon the path of growth without fear of a total collapse. These structural or methodological truths are identical with the universal truths which are the object of infallibility.

The chaos resulting from the lack of universal meanings. Why is the assured possession of such universal truths necessary? Perhaps we can best tackle that question by envisaging a situation of growth in cumulative understanding in which there are no assured truths, in which everything is subject to constant revision. In such a situa-tion the initial stage will be marked by an input of data which will be integrated and unified by the individual and his society. The data will be at a minimum and the problem of integration will be minimal. The individual and the society will then, more or less imperfectly, live out the consequences of their cumulative understanding. In time, new data will emerge as the life situation complexifies. These new data will have to be integrated into the old data, modifying the old integration. On the supposition that no lasting truth remains of the old integration, there must be a relatively new integration of material. In turn, there must be a change in the manner in which the individual and the society as a whole live out their respective understandings. Thus, the lack of any lasting truth in the two succeeding integrations of data leads to an overall change in the life that is the expression of the understanding of these integrations. In concrete actuality, of course, no man would completely change his pattern of life. How-ever, the ideal would be to express continuously the changing inte-grated meaning of one's life in society.

Now instead of two integrations of data at the beginning of the life of an individual or of a society, imagine a steady succession of ever more complex integrations that will be necessitated by a rapidly changing, advanced society. Imagine, in other words, the speedy change that prevails today in much of the Western world. If there are no lasting meanings embedded in that developing life and ever increasing data, then there will be a succession of integrations and of corresponding understanding that will be related only as before and after. There will be nothing which in principle will be lasting, although there undoubtedly will be some aspects of the understanding of one situation which will persist *de facto* in the succeeding situation or situations. In the long run, however, there will be no universal meaning that will persist. People will simply have to cope with ever more intricate and complex situations that make them and their understanding a succession of relatively disconnected viewpoints. All new data uncovered by further experience and observation will only force continuous revisions of one's estimate of one's life as an individual and as a member of the Church. Christian integration of life as a whole will become increasingly impossible psychologically for the vast number of individuals and for the Church as a whole. The "future shock" that Alvin Toffler speaks of will be upon us.[5]

To put it in other terms, if there are no universal meanings that can be surely grasped as persisting throughout all changes of concrete life, then the various stages of development are related to one another in an accretionary and not a cumulative fashion. This brings us back to the condition of confusion and lack of self-understanding that we saw as characteristic of accretionary understanding at a fixed moment of time. Both fixed and dynamic accretionary understanding lead to the same hopeless situation. It may not be too far off the mark to state that much of the present difficulty in the Church stems from dynamic accretionary understanding.

The stability deriving from universal meanings. What can give the only stability possible to the individual and to Christian society in a rapidly changing age is a series of meanings that persist through all changes. Such meanings will also give the only unity possible to men of different cultures living in the same chronological time. These meanings—whether relational, ontic, or dynamic—can be termed methodological or structural meanings in the present context. They are methodological in that they furnish not fixed estimates of concrete situations but the fixed landmarks that enable one to assess each new concrete situation. Like any good method, they provide the constant presuppositions and the series of operations that allow one to find one's way amidst ever more complex data. They are structural in that they provide the basic structure for the erection of ever higher and more complex levels of understanding. Because real understanding is cumulative and not accretionary, it is like a building of many stories. Each succeeding story depends for its persistence upon all stories below. Not that the whole physical existence of lower stories has to persist. One can rip out all the walls and floors, but as long as the basic supporting structural skeleton persists, all the upper stories will continue with a solid base. In a similar manner, much of the concrete understanding of the faith of the past can be torn down because it was comparable to the walls and ceilings of our building. But the basic presuppositions and enduring dynamic principles that constitute the skeletal structure of the lower stories must persist if the building itself is to be permanent and one.

The need to grasp universal meanings consciously. Note that these universal meanings must be consciously grasped if they are to provide an active unifying sense at the later stages of a development. In the earlier stages of a development principles can remain implicit. Situations are few and little varied, and one instinctively can do the right thing or be corrected shortly by adverse results. Thus, men were able to live morally in the primitive Church and to worship in a Christian manner without at all explicitly knowing the lasting principles upon which morality and worship are built. They lived out these principles in an implicit manner. At an advanced and complex stage of human existence in which constant concrete changes take place, such implicit understanding is no longer feasible. The fact is that sustained development in its advanced stages demands explicit grasp of the very principles grounding all development; otherwise the individual becomes a maze of unintegrated meanings. Part of growth is always a moving from the implicit to the explicit, as is obvious in the development of child to adult. The later stages of the organism must grasp the significance of earlier stages and the manner in which growth unifies later with earlier stages.

What is true of life is also true of understanding in a given field. Geometry furnishes a convenient example. In order really to grasp the later proofs, one must have internalized the earlier proofs upon which the later rest. One must understand the prior proofs and be able explicitly to recognize their import. Thus, if the student is to master the Pythagorean theorem, he must have internalized the meaning of all prior significant pages of Euclid; otherwise, the proof given will be just so many words on a piece of paper. The attainment of this explicit interiorization of prior material is the reason for working out examples involving the prior theorems. These examples fix the earlier theorems in the living fiber of the student and enable him to make use of the early theorems with ease in the working out of the later proofs. Without these examples a student who simply memorizes the earlier theorems soon discovers that he is lost and can make no headway.

Analogously, the living out of the faith in complex situations such as those of today requires the internalization and explicitation of the basic principles which underlie the development of faith understanding. Since infallibility is the gift involved with the proclaiming of such principles, it is of value still. Once more I stress, however, that what is necessary is not that these universal truths be infallibly proclaimed, but that they be explicitly known by the faithful and implicit in their activity. In many cases, explicit knowledge will emerge without an official proclamation, simply because the matrix of such universal truths is the living universal Church and in an age of communication and free discussion they may become recognized without a proclamation by a magisterial organ. That universal meanings should be known is essential to modern complex Church existence; that they should be proclaimed explicitly by an infallible magisterium is sometimes, but not always, necessary.

The ecumenical significance of infallibility. The ecumenical significance of the foregoing should be obvious. Infallibility, especially papal infallibility, has been considered by many to be the ultimate barrier to the reunion of Christians. As a result, many Catholics with ecumenical interests have attempted to deny it or explain it away.[6] Non-Catholic scholars have also begun to deal with the issue, at times in a creative fashion. Thus, George Lindbeck has made a careful and sympathetic attempt to go over the grounds for infallibility and to propose a theory that might be reconcilable with Roman Catholicism's past and yet open to the needs of the present. Lindbeck sees infallibility as existing precisely for the sake of unity. He believes that this goal of unity should indicate the scope and the limits of infallibility. However, he tends to think that the new cultural situation is rapidly making infallibility a dead letter. In his view, it may have had a genuine unitive function in the past, but at present unity can be maintained only by the intrinsic force of truth, and not by extrinsic proclamations of a magisterium.[7]

I would agree with Lindbeck that the intrinsic force of truth possessed *is* the basic factor in unity. However, as I have stated in these pages, I would see infallibility as a key creative factor in the bringing into being of that intrinsic force; for infallibility highlights the definitive structural and methodological meanings that are necessary for unity in an ever more complex Church. If I am correct, infallibility is not the ultimate barrier to Christian unity; rather, when properly understood, it is one of the essential conditions for the continuing and ever deepening realization of that unity.

4. Summary on the Necessity of Infallibility

To summarize the preceding material on the necessity of the exercise of infallibility, let us recall that God never deserts his Church. This means that the Church persists in time as a created unity; in some way it is always the same Church. It grows and develops, and its later stages are the fulfillment in new and unexpected ways of its earlier stages. However, if it is the same Church in some way, then there must be a common ecclesial intelligibility that marks its total existence over time; otherwise the use of the word "Church" is ambiguous. The Church would be a succession of ever new beginnings related solely as communities that temporally succeed one another. Because the Church is ultimately one over the ages, there is an intelligibility pertaining to it that remains one. It is this intelligibility which is identified with the series of universal meanings that constitute the object of infallibility. As the Church develops and complexifies, it becomes increasingly necessary that these universal meanings become explicitly known; for part of real human development is the development of understanding and the conscious recognition of what one has become. One can develop implicitly only up to a point; then comes the need to explicate that becoming and the principles that have led to it. Without such explication a growing confusion and an incapacity to make Christian decisions in the face of increasing change becomes practically inevitable. The exercise of infallibility provides for the Church as a whole the explication of these meanings. In the measure that these meanings can only be communicated by such an infallible exercise, that exercise becomes necessary in the Church. Under present historical circumstances, however, it seems likely that the level of education and communication may make it possible for many universal meanings to become explicit in a large part of the Church without the exercise of the infallible magisterium. The explication of these meanings is not an obstacle to the ecumenical venture but the essential condition of genuine Church unity.

The Bearers of Infallibility

In speaking of the bearers of infallibility, Vatican I and the theologians who followed in the wake of its pronouncements dealt with two basic questions: first, who the bearers of this infallibility are: and secondly, the conditions under which these bearers exercise such infallibility. As I indicated in my exposition of the official teaching in chapter 9, many lacunae and unresolved questions appear in the treatment of these two questions. It is now time to take up both of them in terms of the context I have been developing.

Infallibility is a quality shared in varying degrees by all members of the Church. On the one hand, the whole body of the faithful (including the hierarchy) possesses what has been called "infallibility in believing," a sense of faith or a consensus of the faithful. In some way there is embedded in the living faith of all a source of infallible truth. On the other hand, the pope alone or the pope in union with the universal episcopate possesses under certain conditions an active or articulatory infallibility, an infallibility in teaching. This standard doctrine did not clarify sufficiently the interrelationship between the bearers of the "infallibility in believing" and the infallible teachers. One could get the impression that the relationship was simply a one-way street in which the infallible pope and bishops were engaged in instructing the faithful, who in turn became infallible. On the other hand, there was a lack of clarity about the relationship existing between the various members of the active or articulatory infallibility. Is the pope an independent bearer of infallibility? Do the bishops derive their power to teach infallibly from him?

THE SHARED NATURE OF INFALLIBILITY

1. The Sense of Faith

These questions can be clarified, I believe, by referring to what has been stated earlier in this work. First of all, the sense of faith,

or the consensus of the faithful or infallibility in believing, refers to
the universal Christian meanings that are implicitly embedded in
the living faith of those who are attached to Christ. These meanings,
since they characterize the universality of Christians, exist at least
implicitly in both the leaders and the ordinary members of the
Church.

2. Reciprocal Relationship Between the Sense of Faith
in all and the Articulators of Infallible Teaching

Secondly, there is a reciprocal relationship between the bearers
of infallibility in believing and the articulators of infallible teaching.
On the one hand, it is the universal Christian meanings existing at
least implicitly in the whole of the faithful which constitute the
source out of which the hierarchy becomes capable of infallibly
understanding and ultimately proclaiming Christian truth for all.
That truth has to have a universal hold in the lived experience of
the Church before it can be meaningfully grasped and proclaimed
by anyone in the hierarchy. The idea that dogmatic statements are
cast down from heaven into the minds of waiting prelates, independently of a concurrent creative action of God in the whole faithful, is basically a magical notion. It is a practical denial of the philosophical concept that man understands only on the basis of his
experience (in this case an ecclesial experience) and of the theological
concept that there is a single plan of God within which he acts in
such a unified way that everything he does relates to everything
else. On the other hand, the infallible understanding and proclamation of universal Christian meanings by the hierarchy makes explicit what previously may have been only implicit in the minds of most
of the faithful; and this serves to strengthen and deepen the sense of
faith of all; for a meaning becomes more operative in one's life for
having been made explicit.[1]

3. Interrelationship Between Articulators of Dogma

Thirdly, the interrelationship between the two articulators of infallible truth—the pope alone and the pope together with the bishops—now becomes clear. It is simply a mistake to consider infallibility to be accorded by God to either one of these two articulators

in some order of priority. What is most basic is the existence of universal meanings. Once they exist, then infallibility of understanding can take place in those who grasp these meanings as universal. Finally, a statement issued by an articulator who has grasped such a universal meaning is a dogmatic statement. In the present issue, what this implies is that under certain conditions the pope actually grasps a Christian meaning that is universal in the Church; and under those conditions he becomes capable of an infallible understanding as an individual who sums up in himself that universal meaning. Hence, any verbal statement that officially expresses his meaning becomes a dogmatic statement. Similarly, under analogous conditions the whole episcopacy including the pope may come to a collective grasp of the same universal meaning. When they officially issue a statement which embodies and represents their collective grasp of that universal meaning, that statement is *ipso facto* a dogmatic statement. What links the pope and bishops together as articulators of infallible statements is not some legal dependency set up by God under which one articulator is in some way derived from the other. Rather, they are linked together as dynamic personal elements in a process that brings to understanding and then to articulation common meanings which identify the Christian.

In concreto, the pope may achieve this understanding of universal meanings by processes that involve consultations with bishops, reading the works of theologians, and examining the tradition. What he has to do is to achieve understanding of universal Christian meanings; and at that moment he becomes capable of a dogmatic statement. The conditions for papal infallibility are simply the conditions that must be realized in order that the pope should grasp universal meanings and proclaim them to all; this we shall take up in the next section. *In concreto* also, the collective episcopate may achieve this universal understanding in a number of ways. Individual bishops in contact with their people and with the living tradition of the past and the theological formulations of the present may come to a personal explicit grasp of universal Christian meanings. When practically all have explicitly grasped such meanings, they constitute a sense of the faith, a consensus of the faithful, in miniature. However, in order to bring that consensus to articulation, there is need for communication among the bishops. This is what led historically to the general councils and to the interaction therein from which a common conscious grasp of universal Christian meanings often arose; and from that common conscious grasp of universal meanings it was possible to frame dogmatic statements. If the general council has been the way in which the common conscious grasp of universal Christian meanings by the whole episcopacy has classically taken place, it need not be so always. If the march of communication allows bishops throughout the world to grasp the same universal meanings, and if they are then able to proclaim those meanings collectively in a statement, that statement will represent definitive meaning.

Hence, it is a mistake to consider the pope acting alone as an infallible articulator apart from the pope acting together with the collective episcopate. Whenever the pope alone speaks infallibly, he is inevitably involved in the same process of achieving consciousness of universal Christian meanings as when he speaks with the corporate episcopate. Hence, even when he speaks on his own authority, he is not unrelated to the bishops, who are integral parts of the dynamic process by which universal Christian meanings emerge to ecclesial consciousness. If the pope as a single individual can come to conscious understanding and articulation of universal Christian meanings, he cannot do so without a process that involves the living activity of the Spirit in the Church in general and the episcopacy in particular.

THE CONDITIONS OF INFALLIBILITY'S EXERCISE

The second basic question involving infallibility has to do with the conditions under which the various bearers of this gift can actually exercise it. Initially, I shall consider the sense of faith or the consensus of the faithful, the so-called infallibility in believing. What is the meaning of this infallibility and what are its limitations?

1. Infallibility of the Faithful

The most fundamental infallibility. First of all, this is the most fundamental of infallibilities. It really should be called the ground of infallibility rather than an infallibility of believing. It refers to those universal meanings that are implicit in the lives of the faithful throughout the world and over the course of history. It is the dynamic source from which the articulators of infallible statements quarry their ore.[2]

An implicit infallibility. Secondly, it is an implicit source of infallible understanding. Although it is quite possible for some of the faithful to arrive at an explicit grasp of the universal meanings present throughout the Church, ordinarily these meanings remain relatively implicit. First comes life in local circumstances; then, after a long time, there may follow reflection on the meanings embedded and implied in that life; and only long thereafter will come reflection on the universal meanings that underlie the more specific meanings of life in various local circumstances. Further, the bringing to explicit understanding and expression of these universal meanings will normally not be the work of the average Christian in a local community but of the theologians and ultimately the magisterium. Thus the doctrine of the two natures in Christ was long implicit in the prayer and worship of the Church's members before it was articulated explicitly by a general council.

A not easily tapped source of infallible doctrine. Thirdly, the consensus of the faithful cannot be easily tapped as a source of infallible doctrine by the method of a poll. This needs to be said because the so-called headcounting theory has been used to indicate that the consensus of the faithful justifies the practice of birth control. Whatever may be said about this particular issue, the notion that any issue can be decided by counting heads is incredibly naïve. As is well known, poll-taking runs into a considerable number of difficulties. The very way a question is framed already prejudices the answer to a certain extent. Thus, to ask whether birth control can ever be allowed or not is to ask a question of the concrete morality of acts that are classified under one abstract aspect which pertains to these acts. It is to assume and to insinuate into the minds of those questioned that whole acts belong to a single category and that one can make moral judgments about that category. It is to assume that if some birth control acts *in concreto* may be morally nonimputable, then birth control itself is morally indifferent. This is similar to asking whether taking life is ever justified or not. When a "Yes" answer is received, one concludes that the taking of life is an indifferent matter that is sometimes permitted by the law of God. Actually, taking life is always an evil and it may never be rejoiced in. That some acts of life-taking may be nonimputable results from the fact that these concrete acts on balance represent a preponderance of human good, even though marred by the negative aspect of life-taking. The point being made is that the way one takes a poll and the way one interprets the answers may bar one from really getting at what the consensus of the faithful really is. The average universal meaning is embedded deeply in the activity of the faithful and is not easily accessible. It is a simple matter for a poll-taker to elicit a response that does not basically articulate the deepest meaning of an individual or a large number of individuals. This is especially true of those whose background with regard to the item being questioned is relatively unsophisticated. Suppose, for example, you had asked the average uneducated peasant of the Middle Ages whether the laity should be consulted in matters of faith. In all probability he would have answered "No." But that would not have been his real answer. The question format and the words used would have seemed to him to be asking whether he would have something articulate to say about Church belief. To that the answer would have been obviously "No." However, the real question should have been whether there was embedded in his experience and his living of the faith significant faith meaning. If the questioner could have helped the peasant to grasp the true meaning of the question in terms he could understand, I suspect that the answer would be a strong "Yes." The problem would be to get the peasant to grasp that meaning. Certainly he could never personally appropriate the question if all he heard was the technical language in which I have couched it. What would be true of the questioner of our peasant is still true of the poll-taker today. He must be careful to avoid asking the wrong question. Otherwise he will fail to elicit what is truly embedded in the experience of the unsophisticated; and he will inevitably provoke the frustration of those who have an articulate, nuanced version of the matter being questioned.

Moreover, even a correctly phrased question that elicits a common response from the whole of the faithful may not be representative of the consensus of the faithful. It is possible for all the men of a given age to agree upon a Christian meaning that will not be universal *tout court* but only universal within the context of a given culture and a given age. The medieval teaching on interest-taking is perhaps an example of this. Further, it is possible for the faithful to agree with practical universality that a given answer is the best available, even though many find difficulties with it. The doctrine concerning limbo, long taught and long held by most of the faithful, was yet held in an uneasy fashion by many. It never reached the definitive status of an infallible dogma in the mind of the faithful, and a poll indicating that practically all the faithful held it would not give it the status of a teaching truly belonging to the consensus of the faithful.

The value of apt articulation. Fourthly, nothing facilitates the recognition that some meaning is truly embedded in the consensus of the faithful more than an apt articulation of that meaning. Who has not had the experience of discovering the deepest meaning within himself because of the clear formulation of another that brought to expression what was already implicit in his mind? I myself have been at a meeting of twenty priests struggling to get out into the open the common meaning they all felt they shared. When finally one man brilliantly and accurately phrased what had until then existed only in a vague and fragmented way in all of us, twenty men rose in unison to shout, "That's it!" Similarly, nothing can so effectively bring about the recognition of the universal meanings implicit in the *consensus fidelium* as an apt articulation of those meanings. Perhaps nothing is so sadly lacking today as are such articulations. To be able to make them requires a gift that does not often appear in the ordinary member of the Church. That gift is one of the charisms that pertain to the office of the bishops of the Church and to the pope as chief bishop. To their charism of explicitly grasping and articulating infallible meanings we now turn.

2. Magisterial Infallibility

The pope and the bishops belong to what has been called the living magisterium or teaching body in the Church. They are the official ecclesial articulators. Before we begin to take up their general role in infallible understanding and articulating, it is important to remember that (1) most magisterial pronouncements are not infallible (as evidenced by the fact that no teaching of Vatican II belongs to this category) and (2) the pope and bishops who compose the magisterium have other than articulatory functions. They are the leaders and chief sanctifiers in the Church. Moreover, the functions of leading and sanctifying are dynamically connected with the articulatory function.

The experience of the whole Church is conditioned by the activities its leadership promotes in the world as well as the liturgy which such leadership promotes in the sanctuary. Further, the so-called non-infallible teaching of the pope and bishops has an important role in the ultimate arrival of the Church at the universal meanings that underlie infallibility.

A general principle. A general principle may be enunciated with regard to the role of the living magisterium of the Church and the historical factors that led to its emergence: *The spread of the Church to diverse cultures and its development in complexity over time necessitated the articulation of universal meanings for the sake of maintaining conscious Church unity. This gave rise to a hierarchical leadership whose articulatory function understandably became more and more dogmatic and less and less prophetic with the passage of time.*

Emergence of the need to expound universal meanings. When the Church was confined to Palestine, it was sufficient that the meanings which characterized its existence should be couched in terms of the Jewish Old Testament background. To unite its members it was sufficient that the leaders should give verbal and liturgical expression to the faith and direct operations solely in terms of the concrete culture of a single people. There was little need to seek transcultural meanings; and even if they had been found, it is doubtful if anyone would have understood what they were all about. However, as the Church spread to different cultures, it became necessary for unity that those elements of Christianity which pertained to all cultures should be distinguished from elements that belonged to the culture of one place and time. Similarly, as the Church developed in complexity over time, it became necessary to distinguish those elements that characterized all stages of its development from those elements that characterized solely its initial stage or any single subsequent stage. Without the articulations that would distinguish universal and perennial meanings from local and time-conditioned meanings, the Church would easily have fragmented into a number of sects. In fact, although this is not the place to give proof, I would suggest that many a heresy and a schism took its origin from the failure to distinguish a universal Christian meaning from a Christian meaning rooted solely in a particular time and place. In short, in order to maintain unity in the Church it is necessary that the common meanings implicitly present in its members should be articulated. When these meanings were only the common meanings of a single time and culture, it was sufficient to articulate these cultural meanings in order to attain conscious unity. When these meanings were the meanings common to all cultures— that is, when they were universal Christian meanings—then it became necessary to articulate such universal meanings.

Emergence of a unifying hierarchy. Now one of the basic functions of leadership in the Church is to maintain and foster unity. This function is implemented by the direction of unifying actions, by the promotion of a unifying liturgy, and by the articulation of common meanings. In the beginning these three functions were all performed by the corporate ecclesial leadership at the level of a single concrete community in a single culture. There really was no need for any true hierarchic operation, and such an operation apparently did not emerge in the Church at Jerusalem in the beginning. Peter was the first among his peers, a natural leader. He did not exercise a true hierarchic function at the outset because it would have been meaningless in the historical context. A hierarchic functioning presupposes that one has some overarching task to perform; but at Jerusalem the leadership task was basically at a single level: it had to unify the membership in terms of the Christian meanings of a given culture; that was sufficient. Thus, its articulations in the beginning were at the level of the meanings common to that one culture.

The need for hierarchic leadership emerged concurrently with the need for expressing higher and more universal meanings. When the Church was only a local Church (albeit a local Church with universal aspirations), it had need only of local leadership. When the Church became expressed in a number of local Churches of various cultures, the need emerged for a more universal leadership that would unify the various local Churches. Thus, what we now term the papacy became operational after the local episcopacy and not before; just as the federal government in the United States emerged after the state and local governments and not before. Further, parallel with the general emergence of more universal leadership, and acting as a stimulus to that emergence, was the need for the articulation of universal Christian meanings. Someone had to express what bound together the Churches of diverse cultures. While such an expression could, and often did, originate with the more reflective laity, it gained unifying force in the Church when it was promulgated by those who had official charge of the work of unity. Moreover, since one cannot appreciate the meaning of an expression unless in some way one arrives at the meaning oneself, the overall unifying leader would have to be a person capable of understanding and articulating universal Christian meanings to perform his office well.

Interrelationship of papal and episcopal functions. In this context the articulatory functions of bishops and pope are interrelated. The bishops are to articulate basic Christian meanings of their respective Churches. The pope, in turn, is to articulate the meanings common to all the Churches. Pope and bishops need one another. The bishops supply, as it were, the raw material for the pope in the concrete meanings that characterize the local Churches. The pope or the whole body of bishops acting with him articulate what is universal in the traditions of local bishops.

The movement from the prophetic to the dogmatic. Thus, hierarchical leadership is parallelled by a hierarchical articulatory power. The higher one goes in the hierarchy, the more universal should be the pronouncements if they are to unify the people for whom they are intended. Moreover, with the passage of time the pronouncements of higher leaders must more and more cease to be prophetic and become dogmatic, at least as a general rule. In the early days of the Church it was possible even for the highest articulating authority to issue statements that were prophetic, that is, immediately applicable to concrete situations. The decrees of the so-called Council of Jerusalem described in Acts exemplify this kind of statement. Such statements, although not utterly universal, were universal for the relatively small and uncomplicated Church of the beginnings. However, with the spread of the Church to many continents and cultures, it is no longer possible for the highest articulatory authority to issue prophetic statements that have applicability to the whole of the Church. The only kinds of understanding that now unify pertain to the universal Christian meanings I have spoken of at length. These universal meanings, when articulated, may be called dogmatic; and such dogmatic meanings are increasingly becoming the only ones the universal articulatory authority can pronounce for all. I would suggest that part of the uproar attending the issuance of *Humanae Vitae*, the encyclical of Paul VI on birth control, stemmed from the fact that the encyclical contained, or appeared to contain, teaching that was below the level of universal Christian meanings. Note that I am not saying the Church must pronounce only at the level of universal meanings. It must engage in the function of articulating those meanings as they apply to concrete contexts. However, this articulating for concrete contexts can no longer be done by a pope whose task is to unify the whole Church. Because there is no longer a single universal concrete context, he can no longer unify by statements which pertain to concrete contexts, but only by statements of the abstract universal kind that characterize the whole Church. The lesser and more particular statements about concrete contexts can emanate only from those who are actively present in those contexts. The bishop and the local pastor are the official Church figures for this task, not the pope.

An objection from history. The development of the magisterium which I have briefly sketched will strike some trained in the old textbooks as attacking the very foundations of the doctrine that Christ instituted a hierarchy for his Church. A first reply would be that modern biblical scholarship among Catholics has shown that there is little historical evidence for the textbook idea that the whole hierarchy of pope and bishops was immediately set up by Christ.[3] This response, though necessary, will not be sufficient to quiet the objectors. Many of them will say that even though there is little biblical evidence for the immediate creation of the hierarchy as we now know it, nevertheless we believe in this immediate establishment because of the Church's tradition. There is a fear that overthrow of the notion that all was personally and immediately established by Christ will be followed by the assumption that the hierarchy is manmade and hence dispensable.

This understandable fear with regard to the overthrow of tradition can be met in a number of ways. In the first place, the idea that the hierarchy came into being as a development does not constitute a denial that it was set up by Christ. To say that an oak was planted by a farmer does not necessarily mean that he thrust a sapling into the ground; he need only have planted the seed. Similarly, to hold that the hierarchy was established by Christ it is not necessary to suppose that he produced the total organizational blueprints. What is required is only the supposition that his resurrection and the need to manifest its universal implications would ultimately give rise to the series of hierarchic unifiers we know as the pope and the bishops. The fear that accepting the idea that the hierarchy evolved in the course of history will rule out the acceptance of its link with the risen Christ is as groundless as was the fear that accepting the theory of man's evolution would rule out his total creation by God. The senseless battle over the question of biological evolution is happily over. It would be a pity if it were replaced by an equally senseless battle over sociological evolution. The origin of the hierarchy in Christ is no more fundamentally affected by the latter than was the origin of man in God by the former.

In the second place, it is difficult to see how the concept of an immediate historical founding of the hierarchical organization of the Church by Christ could be a saving truth. Once we grasp that revealed truth is saving not by some *fiat* of God that makes it so, but by the fact that its acceptance promotes our growth as Christians, the necessity of believing by divine faith that the hierarchy was immediately set up by Christ becomes questionable indeed. One can see how the acceptance of the role of the great unifying figures of bishop and pope is constituent of salvation; for the unity of the faithful with one another and with Christ is an intrinsic part of the condition of being saved. However, the acceptance of the notion that the whole hierarchy originated with the historical Christ long before it was actually needed for the unity of the Church is another matter. It is almost as difficult to see the saving significance of this notion of the historical origin of the hierarchy as it was to see the saving significance of the star of Bethlehem or the three kings. I believe it is as foolish to require *a priori* that the institutional set-up of the Church was immediately formed by Christ as to require *a priori* that the three kings were historical figures. Neither is necessary for the content of the universal saving truth of God. The historical existence of both should be a sheer matter of evidence. To make them of dogmatic import is to create needless problems and to divert attention from matters that pertain to the heart of the faith and to basic Christian living.

Light cast by the basic principle. The above notion of the role of the pope and the bishops as the living magisterium casts light on the solution to a number of questions: the relationship of the magisterium to Scripture and the documents of tradition; the personal requirements of candidates for the hierarchy; and the role of the "loyal opposition" to pronouncements of the hierarchy. First of all, it should be clear that the living magisterium is necessarily of greater importance than Scripture and the subsequent documents of the tradition.

The living people of the Church of a complex age need to be unified by a present grasp of universal Christian meanings. That grasp cannot be obtained simply by reading the Scriptures or medieval ecclesiastical documents because these documents were to a great extent cast in an idiom of another age. More importantly, most of these documents articulated the truth of faith in a manner that applied only to a particular historical context; for they were issued in an age long before the phenomenon of historical conditioning and the need for transcultural meanings were recognized. It is now fairly well-known that the Baltimore Catechism and the various instructional texts of the past are outdated, not because they were false, but because they applied the unchanging and universal truths to the context of a given epoch that is past. However, it is not so well recognized that the same kind of difficulty besets even the Scriptures and the documents of councils. What has to be done is not to prepare every Christian for the task of quarrying from the ancient documents the universal meanings embedded within them; for that would be an almost impossible task. Rather, what is required is a living magisterium that articulates universal Christian meanings and fosters procedures by which those meanings can be grasped by modern Christians in their respective idioms. There has never been a greater need for such a living magisterium. The Scriptures need not be in the hands of all Christians, however desirable that might be. The biblical age would have come after the invention of printing if God's providence had seen the sacred text to be so necessary. However, a living magisterium capable of articulating universal Christian truths in modern terms is and always will be essential.

This does not mean that the biblical and other ecclesiastical texts are unimportant. They will always be necessary as a source for the articulating Church in its theologians and ultimately in its episcopal leaders; without them, present living teaching would tend to be only present teaching, whereas the teaching of the Church must truly be perennial. These texts, especially the Scriptures, will also be of great value for the average Christian as a source of spiritual nourishment when they are read against the background of the universal meanings articulated by a living magisterium.

Light is cast by our notion on at least one of the basic requirements for a hierarchical leader. He must be a person capable of discerning the universal meanings present in the Church of present and past. It is not enough that he should be a good administrator who is knowledgeable in canon law and familiar with the theology of the textbooks. He must have the quality of detecting universal meanings and of making them live both in the thinking and in the activity of the people over whom he is placed. He must be more than a man who insists with simplicity that former ways of expressing orthodox teaching must be now adhered to. He has to realize to the depths of his being that his role is not to get Christians to repeat the formulas of the immediately preceding epoch but to urge, encourage, rebuke, chide, and guide those entrusted to his care to concretize the universal Christian meanings in their immensely varying lives.[4]

Finally, the present context makes a bit clearer at least one of the roles of the "loyal opposition" to ecclesial pronouncements. What we can do without is a tendency to pick and choose among them, to object to this teaching or that one. More productive might be the type of criticism that would concentrate on showing when a present statement issued to the whole Church lacks in some respects the quality of universality. Many of the liturgical formulas which have come from Rome could be criticized on that score, inasmuch as they ask the whole Church to use expressions that are not well adapted to certain cultures, age groups, or professions. Similarly, laws have been formulated—marriage legislation is a good example—that fail to take into account the varying conditions existing in different countries. Some of the legislation of the Roman type made for Eastern rites in the past is an example of this. As I have suggested, the birth control encylical, *Humanae Vitae*, for all its positive content, appears to me to suffer from having appeared to regard certain culturally conditioned meanings as universal. What I am saying here is that opposition to such documents can be of a constructive kind that points out, over and over again, the tendency to impose what is local and culturally conditioned as universal.

The Pope as Bearer of Infallibility

THE BASIC THESIS

Vatican I devoted a good deal of time to the personal conditions under which the pope becomes infallible. However, it achieved little success in showing their inner coherence. The thesis which I wish to advance as a theory unifying all the data is that *the conditions sketched out by the council are simply conditions which, by the very nature of things, any person must realize if he is to achieve infallibility in ecclesial matters.* In other words, the gift of infallibility is not an habitual capacity of the pope but a momentary power, as Vatican I made clear. What the conditions of papal infallibility enunciate are not concrete activities and processes by which the pope achieves the momentary charismatic power of infallible understanding and subsequent articulation; rather, they express the *subjective qualities of personal realization which he must achieve in order that his understanding and the pronouncement that reflects that understanding shall be of their very nature infallible.* Precisely because the interests of the council were in what I might call the ontic personal conditions of infallibility, it refused to enumerate various concrete measures, such as prior consultation with bishops or a pondering of the documents of the tradition, as requirements for the exercise of papal infallibility. There are many concrete ways in which the pope can achieve these ontic conditions of personal realization; for there are many roads to understanding. In fact, as I indicated in the section of this book on interpretation, it is precisely because there are many concrete roads to the same understanding that it is possible for different men with different experiences to arrive by different concrete steps at the same act of understanding. To enumerate a whole series of procedures which must be rigorously followed before the pope becomes infallible is to betray naïvete about the process of understanding. Vatican I exhibited no such naïvete.

DEFENSE OF THE THESIS

1. Defense from the General Teaching of Vatican I

I will attempt to defend this thesis by considerations drawn from (1) the general teaching of Vatican I, (2) the doctrinal past of the Church, and (3) the specific conditions for infallibility set forth by the same council. At Vatican I, two consistently expressed teachings support the notion that the conditions for infallibility are really the conditions of personal realization by which any person, in this case the pope, would become infallible in ecclesial matters. These teachings are: (1) the pope is inseparable from the whole Church when he speaks infallibly; and (2) when the requisite conditions are realized, the pope's doctrine is infallible *ex sese* and not from the subsequent consent of the Church.

The inseparability of the pope from the church. Vatican I went out of its way to make clear that when the pope speaks infallibly, he is at one with the infallible Church. On the one hand, the domain within which the pope can speak infallibly is the same as that within which the Church can be infallible—the domain of revelation. This we have already seen. On the other hand, when the pope speaks infallibly, he is said to be inseparable from the Church. As Bishop Martin of Paderborn put it at the Council:

> The Roman Pontiff cannot be considered as separated from the Church when he acts as head of the Church and draws truths from the deposit of faith, that is, from the Holy Scriptures and divine tradition which shines out of the documents of the Church in all the centuries and which lives in the understanding and the consciousness of the Church itself.[1]

Unfortunately, just what was meant by saying that the pope was inseparable from the Church was never made sufficiently clear and nuanced. According to the theory advanced in these pages, that inseparability would be an inseparability of achieved meaning. Embedded in the ancient tradition of the Church and present now in an implicit way in the whole of the faithful would be one or more universal meanings. When the pope achieves the conditions of infallibility, he becomes capable of making those meanings explicit. By that very fact he is inseparable from the whole Church. He is profoundly one with her in the closest manner that human persons can be one, that is, by the sharing of the same understanding. However, no man achieves understanding in an explicit manner simply by having a set of phrases inserted into his mind. Explicit understanding is always a personal achievement. It implies a corresponding experience and a differentiation of that experience. To understand is to be changed as a person. Einstein was not the same man he had been after he grasped the theory of relativity. Similarly, to understand another person in depth is to be changed oneself. Thus, for the pope to grasp explicitly the universal meanings of the Church's tradition is for him to be changed, and to be changed in such a way that *ipso facto* he is inseparable from the deepest meanings that constitute the Church.

Further, on this reasoning if any other person achieved the same conditions of grasping universal Christian meanings, he would by that very fact have arrived at the capability of infallibility. This, of course, was not expressed by Vatican I. It is, however, in line with a unified theory of infallibility; and its acceptance would go a long way towards eliminating magical notions of infallibility.

The ex sese teaching. The *ex sese* doctrine of Vatican I reinforces the thesis that the conditions of infallibility refer to the personal realization the pope must achieve before he is infallible in Christian understanding and proclamation. This *ex sese* doctrine was aimed specifically at those who claimed that for a papal statement to be infallible it was absolutely necessary that it receive the consent of the whole Church. No one at the council denied that the pope was morally bound to take all steps necessary to achieve understanding of what he was pronouncing on. However, the assembled Fathers rejected the notion that he *had to* consult the Church beforehand or that he *had to* receive its approbation subsequently.[2] Exactly why this consultation was not *absolutely* necessary, however much it might be morally required, was not spelled out. The pope's pronouncement was simply declared to be infallible of itself, *ex sese*. According to the present theory, the pope has to achieve certain personal conditions of being that of themselves render him infallible when they are attained. He has to become capable of an understanding as broad as that of the universal Church. To this end, he has to go through processes which may involve consulting bishops, reading the past documents of the magisterium, dialoguing with theologians, asking the mind of the faithful, or even reflecting on his own past

Christian life in the spirit of prayer and meditation on the Scriptures. Any or all of these means may be employed. However, none of them certainly assures that he will reach a grasp of universal Christian meanings; nor is any one of them absolutely necessary in order that he should reach those meanings. What is absolutely necessary is that he should actually achieve universal understanding on the basis of his experience and that he should go through whatever concrete processes are necessary for him as an individual to achieve that understanding.

Because there are many possible roads to the same understanding and because each individual's achievement of understanding is a unique personal process, no one can spell out in advance the concrete steps by which any and all individuals are to attain a given understanding. When the pope does achieve such understanding, however, he becomes infallible by that very fact. His proclamations possess the quality of being without error *ex sese*. A juridical acceptance by the whole Church can manifest the quality of the proclamation more fully; it cannot confer upon it something it did not possess before.[3] If the pope *had to* take a poll of the bishops and get their collective approval for all infallible statements, he would be reduced to the level of a census taker. At a supreme moment of his life, at a moment when he is most truly universal bishop and churchman, he would be simply repeating formulas derived from a collective other. In the present theory, however, at that supreme moment he incarnates in himself the common meaning embedded in the experience of all the faithful of all the ages, including the bishops. He ontically and personally represents the intelligibility which is present in all. Thus, *ipso facto* he becomes infallible with the infallibility of the whole Church.[4]

2. Defense of the Thesis from the Doctrinal
   Past of the Church

Is infallibility a medieval creation? Can the past history of the Church be shown to support the notion I have advanced? A complete answer would be too lengthy for this book. However, I shall make a number of approaches that will support a positive reply. First, I believe that the doctrine of infallibility can be defended against the attacks of those who assert that it is a medieval creation. For example,

Brian Tierney has shown that this teaching was first formulated by
Pietro Olivi (c. 1248–1298) for what were basically political reasons.
From this he concludes that the doctrine can be discarded; for it is
post-biblical.[5]

In reply to this, I would say that the initial formulation of a doctrine by a theologian and the intrinsic grounds of its justification are
two different things. Tierney assumes that a doctrine has to be present
in some way in the Scriptures for it to belong to the deposit of faith.
The consistent position of this work is that what is revealed exists
often only potentially in the early Church (as an oak in the acorn);
later it exists implicitly in the operation of the Church; and the explication of that deposit may come centuries and even millennia
later. However accurate Tierney's historical research may be, the
dogmatic conclusions he draws about the nonrevealed nature of the
teaching on infallibility do not follow.

Proving the theory from Church history. Secondly, a vast study
of the development of Christian understanding over the centuries
would have to be undertaken in order to "prove" the theory I have
advanced. That study has not yet been made. It has not even been
begun, to my knowledge; and the reason, I believe, for its absence
is not difficult to apprehend. Scholars who work in the history of
theology, like all historians, are guided by their assumptions and
presuppositions. Whether they know it or not, they are sensitized
to certain values; they come to their texts with certain questions
and are prepared to find certain kinds of answers. Now many who
have undertaken to investigate the history of infallibility (like Küng
and Tierney) assume that for a doctrine to be of divine faith it must
be articulated in the sacred books, or it must be reducible to articulation from two or more scriptural articulations, or it must be implicit
in the actions performed by the scriptural Church. Further, one
must be able to trace the understanding of the doctrine through history from the scriptural beginnings. These assumptions, it seems to
me, are too facile. They would rule out what I have called "second-
order dogmatic meanings," that is, doctrines which articulate the
recurring processes by which first-order doctrines such as the Incarnation and the Trinity come into existence.

The contention here is that the teaching on infallibility is such a
second-order dogmatic meaning.[6] It did not appear and could not
have appeared in the beginning. First came Christian experience of

God in Christ and the effort to live out the implications of that basic experience of the Resurrection. Then, after a more or less lengthy period, the recurring relationships between man and man, on the one hand, and between man and God, on the other, were articulated. Only after a further period were the doctrines I have called "ontic" articulated. Finally, doctrines such as infallibility represent summations of the conditions under which relational and ontic teachings have come into being. They are thus thematizations of what are already abstract processes. They articulate what is common to the genesis of all certitude in the Church.

This origin of infallibility means that it could not have emerged early. It is a most general doctrine; and, as is well known, the most general teachings inevitably emerge last. It required almost two thousand years of acting and philosophical reflection for the Church to begin even in a rudimentary way to grasp the conditions of infallibility; and the end is not in sight.

Hence, it is simply a methodological blunder to seek *directly* for the doctrine of infallibility in the sources of the early Church. If one understands the methodological problem as I have set it forth, one knows that what one should seek in the sources is evidence over time of the process by which individual doctrines actually emerged to articulation. This evidence is not to be found in a single source but has to be pieced together from the chain of sources over time, a most laborious task. Then, after one has traced the actual process by which a number of individual doctrines have actually emerged, one can hypothesize as to what is universal in the conditions by which these individual teachings came to articulation. These conditions, I suggest, would be found to check out with the conditions that Vatican I stated to be necessary for the papal exercise of infallibility.

I have offered no historical proof of the foregoing methodological contention; for the proof would obviously require many volumes and be outside the scope of this work. However, I have articulated my method and my assumptions; and they reveal, I believe, why proofs about infallibility from history have not been forthcoming and why works like Brian Tierney's can be questioned. The point is that many works on infallibility have tacitly assumed that this is a doctrine like other doctrines and is to be justified on the same basis as other doctrines. My contention is that this assumption is false; hence historical works on infallibility which proceed from this assumption are vitiated from the outset. Behind all historical works are the assumptions of the historian. He is allowed to have assumptions; but he must know what they are, and he must be prepared to defend them. I would contend that historians of infallibility like Tierney have basic assumptions about the nature of revealed truth in general and about the content of this doctrine in particular that they have not justified. Since I believe these assumptions are false, and since I personally know of no works that proceed from what I consider to be the correct assumptions, I have no difficulty in understanding why good "proofs" from history are lacking.

Justification for the theory. Finally, I should note that while I have not given any *historical* evidence for my contention that infallibility is a second-order doctrine and has to be established by means other than the more direct means used to establish first-order doctrines, yet I have given justification for that contention. That justification is the analysis made of human understanding. Every historian assumes the process of understanding when he analyzes a text and tries to justify his interpretation for the modern reader. He assumes that he can seize the thought of someone in the past—whether he explicitly realizes this or not—precisely because he takes it for granted that the same generic process of understanding existed in men of the past as in men of today. Further, he assumes that his readers go through the same process of understanding that he undergoes; hence they can understand as he does. What I have attempted to do is to exploit processes we all go through and thematize them. Since infallibility has to do with the process of understanding, I have applied the thematizations regarding understanding to this doctrine. Only if my thematizations about understanding and the certitude arrived at by understanding are incorrect will my applications to the exercise of infallibility in the Church be vitiated. If someone accepts my thematizations of understanding and yet denies their applicability to examining a Church doctrine, he either destroys the very grounds on which he operates in doing historical work (i.e., he denies validity to an understanding process which he uses in his work) or advocates the strange view that infallibility has nothing at all to do with understanding. Neither alternative seems inviting.

3. Defense of the Thesis from the Conditions Set Forth by Vatican I

The common simplified understanding. It is now time to turn to the actual conditions of papal infallibility set forth by the council and attempt to show how these conditions, when taken collectively, actually delineate the state any person must realize if he is to achieve infallibility in ecclesial matters. Before undertaking this task, I should state that the conciliar conditions are quite sketchy; they are like an outline, not a detailed drawing. Further, the language used for the conditions and the subsequent manner of expounding these conditions in textbooks have not helped the conciliar teaching. Generations of student priests have been brought up with the belief that God decreed four conditions (the number usually given in the textbooks) under which the pope is infallible. These conditions apparently derive from divine *fiat* and have no assigned rooting in the nature of things. They were not discoverable in the Bible; they were not grounded in the nature of human and Christian understanding; they were simply decreed by the council as four separate conditions that had to be achieved before the pope became infallible. Further, as soon as the pope announced explicitly or implicitly that these conditions had been fulfilled, by that fact he became instantly infallible. If he were going to make an incorrect statement, God would strike him dead or prevent him in some other way from speaking. Hence one could understand how W. G. Ward might hope for a new infallible statement by the pope daily at breakfast, along with his *Times.* The above might seem to be a caricature of the teaching of the textbook theologians. However, it comes dangerously close to the interior understanding of infallibility of many a loyal Catholic layman, priest, and bishop.[7]

Two criteria to be met. From what has been advanced in these pages about human understanding it is to be concluded that a person becomes infallible only when he personally grasps universal meanings. In the Church a person becomes infallible when he personally grasps universal *Christian* meanings. Hence, if we are to show that the conditions for papal infallibility advanced by Vatican I represent the ontic state that any man must realize if he is to be infallible in ecclesial matters, we must show that these conditions delineate (1) the only possible object of infallibility in the Church, universal

Christian meanings, and (2) subjective conditions on the part of the
pope in which he personally realizes a grasp of such universal meanings. Of course, Vatican I did not set up the question in this way; it
would have been impossible at that time. I am simply proposing an
hypothesis that purports to unify and clarify the rather isolated
conditions advanced by the council. This theory does not just repeat
the data of Vatican I; it attempts to unify and explain those data.

Infallibility refers to universal meanings. It seems that the conditions for papal infallibility do refer to universal Christian meanings
as the object of this power. This appears in varying ways in a number of the conditions. First of all, the pope is infallible with regard
to the content of revelation. (I abstract for the moment from the
question of the secondary object of infallibility. I will take up this
question when I deal *ex professo* with the *expressions* of infallible
meanings in chapter 16.) That content refers to truths of faith or
morals *per se* revealed. I have theorized in the section on the object
of infallibility that the only revelation of God that could be infallibly
understood in this life is that aspect which is universal, that is, which
applies to all places, cultures, and times. The stated conditions of
Vatican I for infallibility support this contention. As we saw, the
goal of infallibility is to insure the unity of faith and the community
of the faithful. Hence, this gift deals with what all must believe and
with what unites all. Further, the pope must intend to define in a
universally binding way. Now what is universally binding on all
can only be some truth that pertains to all; otherwise some men
would be required to hold truths that were meaningless to their lives.
Moreover, since the pope must have the intention to define, that is,
to bind the Church in a way that is irreformable for all future time,
the meanings he proclaims must be applicable even for the future.
Finally, I believe that the stipulation of canon law that "nothing is
to be considered as dogmatically declared or defined unless that intention is manifest" indirectly supports the notion that only universal
meanings can be defined. This intention is to be made manifest to
the whole Church. But how can this be done? Even granting that
local teachers are capable of convincing the universal faithful that a
given definition manifestly fulfills the conditions of infallibility,
there is the further problem of manifesting to all Catholics the meaning of the definition. What must be manifest to all believers is not
just that certain conditions of infallibility are fulfilled but also that

they are fulfilled in connection with a given defined meaning. The contention here is that the meaning defined could not be grasped by all the faithful unless it was in some way already incipiently and implicitly present in their being. In other words, we are back to the notion of universal meanings.

The conditions of infallibility are ontic. Secondly, the subjective conditions demanded of the pope in order that he should be infallible are precisely the conditions of personal realization needed in order that an individual should grasp universal Christian meanings. Let us recall these conditions briefly. The basic idea is that the pope is not habitually infallible but only at certain times and under certain limiting conditions. Among these necessary conditions are (1) he must be acting in his capacity as the pastor and teacher of all the faithful; (2) he must be acting in virtue of his supreme apostolic authority; (3) he must be acting personally as an individual who understands what he utters and freely utters it; (4) he must have the personal intention to define in a universally binding way.

Each of these conditions implies in its own way that in proclaiming a universal Christian meaning the pope himself must attain, at least momentarily, a matching universality that enables him to grasp that meaning personally in an explicit way. The first two conditions taken together really say that in an infallible proclamation the pope becomes supremely what his office ideally stands for. The role of the pope is to be the unifier of the Church. He performs this function to the extent that by his governing, liturgical, and teaching roles he makes to live in all the faithful those qualities that bind them together. Ordinarily he performs these functions in a more or less limited way, that is, he governs, enacts the liturgy, and teaches for one or more of the various groupings in the Church. When he speaks infallibly, however, he is acting in his fullest capacity. He personally becomes for a moment not just the pastor of Rome or a friendly bishop to a group of Christians, but the teacher of the universal Church. And for that universal Church he actualizes the limits of his supreme apostolic authority to articulate. In short, what is proper to the papal teaching office is universality. That universality is not achieved habitually in doctrine but only at those supreme moments when the pope actually achieves the supreme apostolic authority of teacher of what is to bind all irrevocably.

What must be stressed above all, however, is that this supreme condition of universal teacher is not simply a condition in which the pope announces that he is acting in virtue of his supreme apostolic authority as universal teacher. I would contend that he must achieve a condition of being in which the universal Christian meanings become so actualized in him that he can proclaim them infallibly to all. This is an ontic condition of existence that is not to be confused with an announced condition of existence. A mad pope could announce he was acting in virtue of his supreme apostolic authority as universal teacher. This would not necessarily mean that he had attained that condition. The same holds true for the pope in ordinary good health. His announcement of his attainment of the universality of understanding proper to infallible statements is not equivalent to his actually attaining that universality. To act as supreme teacher with one's fullest authority is not a legal condition but an ontic condition of existence. No man, not even the pope, can know infallibly when he has attained that condition because this is infallibility with regard to a concrete fact of personal consciousness. And such facts cannot be known with certainty in this life.[8]

Similarly, the third condition enumerated above reinforces the contention that the pope must achieve an ontic condition of existence before he becomes infallible. Vatican I made quite clear that the pope must act personally, that infallibility flowed from the person of a single man acting freely out of his own understanding. However, no one can act freely and proclaim out of his own understanding unless there has been within him the achievement of conditions which enable him to do so. He must be gripped by a universal meaning. He must have it embedded in his own experience before he can proclaim it in a personal way. If the pope were merely a recorder who uttered words given him from on high, then the charism of infallibility would not entail a personal achievement. Once we say that an infallible statement can proceed from him only by a personal act, we postulate that for at least one moment the pope internalizes the universal meanings which he proclaims.

Likewise, the fourth condition indicates the need for the pope to have achieved a condition of being. As I noted when I summarized the conciliar teaching on this condition in chapter 9, the intention to define is not simply an announced intention. Human intentionality is not a matter of proclaiming a given motivation. To intend in a full sense is to direct one's whole being in a given way; the verbalization of one's intention is thus but the outer symbolization and expression and deepening of one's inner understanding and freedom. To intend to marry is not simply to say "I do." It is to have achieved a certain oneness of heart and will that can be the inner basis for a true outer expression of intentionality. Similarly, to intend a celibate life is not just to proclaim a solemn promise at diaconate. It is to have achieved the minimal conditions of celibate existence that can ground an honest external expression of a promise to live in a celibate way for the rest of one's days. Thus, for the pope to intend to define in a universally binding way is for him to have achieved a grasp of what is by its very nature a differentiation of understanding which constitutes a necessary aspect of the growth of every Christian. Anything short of this would make of his definition a purely external legalistic requirement that God's pure *fiat* requires. This would be to strip his defining powers of their saving efficacy.

SUMMARY AND CONTRAST

It may be helpful to the understanding of the theory I have advanced to contrast it with the manualist or textbook interpretation. The manuals content themselves with recounting the conditions for papal infallibility indicated by Vatican I. However, they assume that these are external legal conditions. This means that whenever the pope clearly manifests (whether by explicit words or by surrounding circumstances) that he desires to fulfill all the conditions laid down by Vatican I, at that instant his pronouncement becomes infallible. As long as it is evident that he is uncoerced, that he wants to speak in his capacity of chief shepherd and teacher of all the faithful, that he has decided to use his supreme apostolic authority, that he wants to define a revealed doctrine of faith and morals in such a way as to bind all the faithful irrevocably—then he is infallible in utterance.

The position I have advanced is quite different. It assumes that all the conditions are not merely external and legalistic; they are also internal and ontic. They refer to a state of being that the pope must achieve in order that the understanding he reaches and the proclamations which flow from that understanding will be of their very nature infallible. I have advanced my reasons for this position. I believe that neither my position nor the position of the textbooks can be directly supported by the discussions at the council. However, I also believe that if one approaches the teaching of the council with carefully articulated views on the nature of human understanding, one can find here and there indirect support for the view I have proposed. It seems to me that the holders of the manualist view approach the conciliar texts with unexplicated assumptions about human understanding. I believe these unexplicated assumptions are incorrect.

ADVANTAGES OF THIS VIEW

1. *It Shows the Unity Between Pope and Church*

A number of advantages flow from the view here advocated. First, it shows profoundly the unity that exists between the infallibly pronouncing pope and the whole Church. That unity is not simply willed by God and imposed from without. Rather, it is a unity that comes into creation from God as a sharing in universal meanings. These meanings are the same in head and members in an infallible pronouncement; but the pope is supremely manifested as head because in him those universal meanings come to conscious understanding and articulation. At the moment of pronouncement he is supremely Churchman because he incarnates in himself in an explicit way those universal Christian meanings that I have indicated are the created grounds of the Church's unity and indefectibilty.[9] Just as a man becomes more human when he understands explicitly who he is and what he has become, so too the Church becomes more itself in the explicit understanding (by the pope or anyone else) of the universal Christian meanings that characterize its enduring existence. Thus, the infallibility of the Church believing and the Church teaching is deeply one through the common meanings that are made explicit by interaction of head and members.

2. *It Explains Why Papal Infallibility Cannot Resolve Questions Disputed in the Church*

Secondly, this view explains why the pope cannot decide infallibly disputed questions such as the birth control issue. Only someone with a legal notion of infallibility would expect such a decision from the pope. Only when universal meanings exist implicitly at the level of the universal Church can the pope proclaim them explicitly. He has no immediate pipeline to the Father which bypasses the whole Church. Rather, he is guided by the Holy Spirit to artic- ulate what is already present in the Church. That such meanings did not exist in the Church of the very late 1960s and early 1970s is evident from the failure of the Church universal to recognize them as appearing in *Humanae Vitae*. This does not mean that the teaching of *Humanae Vitae* on birth control is incorrect; it does mean, how- ever, that at the present time such teaching, even if it is correct, has not yet reached the implicit universality required for an infallible pronouncement. Simply put, the gift of infallibility is not a tool to give answers to disputed questions of the present. It is rather a dy- namic through which the assured universal answers of the past come to the surface.

3. It Clarifies the Limited Nature of Infallibility

Thirdly, this view casts light on the necessarily limited nature of infallible pronouncements. There is a popular notion to the effect that infallibility furnishes sharp verbal answers that can in no way be revised. Those who hold this notion have great difficulty accepting the possibility that there may be better ways of referring to the action that takes place in the elements at Mass than "transubstantia- tion." Once, however, one grasps that words refer to meanings; once one sees that meanings represent differentiations of experience and that infallible meanings represent universal differentiations of ecclesial experience—then one can begin to see how not only the words of an earlier formulation but even the meanings they represent can be surpassed without negating the infallibility and irrevocability of past pronouncements.

What has to be grasped is that every answer we give and every answer the Church gives is an answer to a question, even if that question is not explicitly articulated. Moreover, each question pre- supposes a certain level of differentiation on the part of the questioner and therefore a certain level of differentiation in the answer. Thus, when a boy in the first grade asks me what color I prefer, he is asking, really "Within the limits of the color distinctions I can make, what color do you prefer?" Under these circumstances I am completely correct in answering "blue," even if the more precise color is tur- quoise. After a number of years, he may be capable of further distinctions; at that stage I can give a more nuanced answer. However, that more nuanced answer and its representation in a different wording do not deny the fundamental truth of the prior answer. In its own setting it is as correct as it could be.

An analogous situation prevails in infallible pronouncements about universal meanings. These pronouncements necessarily represent those meanings at the level of realization universal in the Church of the time of the pronouncement. That level is the setting for the pronouncement, the implicit question as it were. The answer given at that time is correct for that level of discourse for all time. Thus, it will always be correct for me to say at the child's level of discourse that my favorite color is blue. Similarly, in Christology at a given level of discourse it will always be adequate to say that Christ had a human body, a human mind, and a human will. This would define his creaturehood. Today, however, we might have to state further that he was historically conditioned, that he understood only on the basis of that historical conditioning, that his understanding grew in a cumulative way and thus set limits to his freedom at its lower stages. In other words, we now know a great deal more about what is in man, and when we speak of Christ as man we have a far more differentiated notion of man and ask far more differentiated questions. In such a context the old answers do not become false but only oversimplified for the level of questions that we ask.

The point to all this is that what lies behind infallibility is universal meaning. That universal meaning becomes more explicit and more nuanced with the passage of time because man is subject to unending development. Since dogmatic statements only represent those universal meanings in an articulated way at the level of differentiation attained more or less by the whole Church at the time of their pronouncement, these statements are inevitably of a limited nature. They can and will be refined as time goes on, not simply by a polishing up of terminology but more fundamentally by a development and a sharpening and a nuancing of meaning that stems from a corresponding differentiation in the level of existence of the universal faithful. The implications of this for development of doctrine should be obvious.

While it is impossible for the Church of a given epoch to realize the limitations of its own understanding in a specific way, it is not impossible for it to realize that its understanding is limited in a general way. It cannot realize the specific limitations of its formulations and the living meaning behind them because to realize just what those limitations are is automatically to transcend them. Thus, if the men of Nicea could have realized that their notion of human nature as rational animal was limited because it did not encompass the notion of man as historically conditioned, they would by that realization have surpassed the understanding of man that they expressed. Hence, no age can realize the specific boundaries surrounding its limited notions.

However, the Church can always know that its present understanding and formulations of universal meanings is limited, that such understanding and formulation can and must be surpassed. It is that knowledge which enables the Church to pronounce genuinely the mysteries of faith in a limited infallible manner. The mysteries of faith are aspects of the Resurrection and therefore have an unlimited intelligibility. Any understanding of them is necessarily limited. Yet it is true understanding once one grasps that one's grasp is limited. To understand infallibly is not to understand fully but to understand in a limited way what is universal and to know that one's understanding is limited. This known limitation of understanding was always expressed in the Church when it denominated its credal beliefs as mysteries.

4. Clarification of the Obligation of the Faithful to Accept Infallible Teaching

Fourthly, this view clarifies what is meant by the obligation of the faithful to accept the infallible teaching of the Church. That obligation is not simply one of bowing towards a statement and demanding that our children memorize it. Rather, it is an obligation to commit oneself to recapitulate in one's own life the path followed by the Church in arriving at its dogmatic understanding. It is to commit oneself to develop that Christian experiential continuum capable of sustaining an understanding of past dogma, and then to live out the implications of that dogma so as to internalize it.

Practically, this means that dogmatic teaching has to act as a *reinforcer*, a *stimulus*, and a *challenge*. It acts as a *reinforcer* for those who have already articulated its meaning within their own experiential continua. Each time they express the teaching, especially in a prayer context, they deepen a meaning already within them and acknowledge an obligation to make it more operational in their lives. Thus, to accept the second commandment is to recognize more deeply that all men are our brothers and to renew our efforts to make that brotherhood more vital.

Dogmatic teaching acts as a *stimulus* for those who have its meaning within their experiential continuum but have not yet articulated that meaning for themselves. Their task is to work to discover what doctrine says to them in terms of their life experience so that when they verbalize it, especially at Mass, they are really expressing who they are.

Finally, dogmatic teaching acts as a *challenge* for those who have not yet arrived at the condition of life when the teaching can say something vital to them. It is not yet groundable in their experiential continua. This may be so because they are ignorant, lack background, or are simply stupid. These are the classic *rudes*. They are the people who are akin to boys who recognize only blue in a world which recognizes distinctions such as turquoise. They have every right to be considered good Catholic Christians as long as they are making whatever efforts they can to grasp the doctrine. Often they will not be able to grasp it intellectually and yet will "see" it in its operational implications. This will be sufficient.

However, there are people who are educated and intelligent and yet cannot grasp certain dogmatic teachings because of psychological and personal limitations. I would suggest that even these can be considered Christian as long as they too strive to grow towards possessing the experiential continuum that will allow them to grasp the doctrine of the Church. Hence, there will be Catholics who do not yet effectively grasp that the doctrine of God's universal salvific will implies that all races are equal before the Lord. For the psychological as for the intellectual *rudes* the obligation to accept doctrine thus constitutes a challenge to a development that will permit them to grasp ever more deeply what the doctrine means.

In short, the obligation to accept doctrines is not merely an obligation to acknowledge formulas and to acquiesce in their meanings. It is also an obligation to incarnate those meanings. The recitation of the Nicene Creed at Mass is thus intended to be not an intellectual exercise but a proclamation by God's people of where it has been, where it is, and where it desires to be.

5. Ecumenical Appeal

Fifthly, this view appears to have an ecumenical appeal. Papal infallibility has long been unacceptable in Protestant and Orthodox quarters. However, it seems that many of the objections stem from a fear that the exercise of that infallibility can very well prove to be arbitrary, independent of the rest of the Church, and limited only by certain legal requirements promulgated for the first time by Vatican I. I believe that these objections are understandable but surmountable. They are understandable in the light of the simplified and overlegalistic interpretation of Vatican I current in the average textbook; they are surmountable by a more critical interpretation of Vatican I coupled with a presentation of the underlying faith dynamics that give rise to papal infallibility. Such a presentation I have attempted in these pages. If I am not so unrealistic as to think that my views will immediately solve all outstanding differences, I am sanguine enough to hope that they can constitute the starting point for a far more profitable discussion than has prevailed hitherto. In this matter as in many other matters of dispute, I am of the firm conviction that differences are resolved not simply by clarifying what each side means or has meant but also (and more importantly) by the new explication of as yet unexamined presuppositions and the emergence of higher viewpoints.

To illustrate how the view I have advanced can aid the ecumenical dialogue, I will attempt to show how it can deal irenically and yet honestly with an Orthodox position that has long appeared unacceptable to Roman Catholics. According to this position of Orthodoxy, doctrinal decisions must be accepted by the whole Church if they are to be binding. Unfortunately, Orthodoxy has not made too clear precisely what acceptance by the Church entails.[10] In the interest of clarity and with the intention of facilitating dialogue on the matter, I would like to propose a number of distinctions based on the theory of infallibility enunciated above.

First, I distinguish *anticipatory, implicit,* and *overt acceptance* of a doctrinal decision. *Anticipatory acceptance* refers to a future possibility. It presupposes a condition in which an official teacher in the Church—the pope or a general council—enunciates a truly universal meaning that has not yet become a differentiation of the experiential continuum of the average Christian. Because the meaning,

by hypothesis, is universal, it can be the subject of infallible understanding and verbal proclamation on the part of a teacher; moreover, because the meaning is universal, it can and ought to be personally appropriated by all men as a constituent factor of their
self-differentiation and concomitant saving growth. However,
because the average man, in the hypothesis envisaged, is at present
incapable of personally appropriating the doctrine enunciated despite
its potential universality, acceptance for him can be only a future
possibility. Hence, I call his an "anticipatory acceptance."

Implicit acceptance refers to a present possibility. It presupposes
the enunciation of a universal Christian meaning by Church authority
and the presence in a large body of the faithful of the requisite level
of self-differentiation necessary to recognize the meaning enunciated;
however, in *implicit acceptance* there is no external manifestation
of the fact that the given doctrinal meaning actually resonates with
what is already internally present in the faithful. When this external
manifestation takes place, we then have *overt acceptance.*

It will be seen that these three kinds of acceptance are in ascending
order. *Implicit acceptance* presupposes the stage in which there was
only *anticipatory acceptance;* and *overt acceptance* presupposes the
existence of that self-differentiation which constitutes *implicit acceptance.* Further, it should also be evident that at least *implicit acceptance* is necessary in order that the doctrine in question should
truly be proclaimed infallibly; for such acceptance is but another
way of indicating that universality of meaning which alone can
ground infallible understanding. Hence there is an acceptable Roman
Catholic sense in which one can say that reception of a doctrine by
the Church is necessary in order that a magisterial pronouncement
should be infallible.[11]

Nor is this all. There is even a sense in which one can say that overt
acceptance by the Church is necessary. While it is true that implicit
acceptance is the only *ontic* condition in the Church that is absolutely
required for an authoritative statement to be infallible, yet it is only
when we have *de facto* overt acceptance by the Church—whether explicitly in words or implicitly in acts—that we can be sure that
authority has spoken infallibly. This follows from the fact that there
are not and cannot be any external legal signs by which the Church
can be assured that its authorities have arrived at the condition of
universality that alone can ground infallibility. As I have pointed

out more than once, a mere declaration by authority that it is acting universally and infallibly does not suffice. *A fortiori,* clues in an ecclesiastical document that indicate that the author of the document wanted to speak universally and infallibly do not prove by themselves that he did so. An announced intention is not necessarily a real intention. The only way the Church can be sure that a pope or council has spoken infallibly is by finding the meaning proclaimed actually present in the consciousness of the faithful. Only when the vast numbers of the faithful discover that the meaning of a proclamation resonates with the meaning of the faith within them and, further, make manifest this congruence of meaning explicitly by word or implicitly by action—only then can the Church be assured that its authorities have spoken infallibly. There is no other way by which the Church can be certain her authorities' actions have been truly universal other than the overt manifestation by the faithful that the meaning proclaimed is truly universal. In this sense, then, the overt acceptance by the Church of a teaching can be said to be necessary in order for it to be known that the official Church has spoken infallibly.

It might be objected that this view (1) contradicts the teaching that the pope is infallible *ex sese* and (2) opens the door to subjectivism. I would deny both charges. On the one hand, this view does not contradict the *ex sese* doctrine. When the pope achieves the conditions of infallibility enunciated by Vatican I, he is *ipso facto* infallible. However, by the very unity of the universe and of the Church created by God, he cannot achieve the conditions of infallibility unless there exists in the Church what I have called "implicit acceptance." If the pope were infallible about a matter not already grounded in the whole Church, then his infallibility would be apart from the Church. It would be an isolated gift with no reference to the living Church; and this would contradict the official teaching that his infallibility is inseparable from that of the Church. The *ex sese* doctrine was meant to indicate that when certain conditions were achieved by the pope, he was infallible by their very existence without the legal necessity of explicit approval by the Church either before or after. I have not denied this. Instead, I have clarified the further implications of the conditions laid down by Vatican I for the achievement of papal infallibility.

Nor does this view open the way to unnecessary subjectivism. We have to face the fact that there is a subjective factor in every recognition of papal infallibility. How is any person to know that the pope has spoken infallibly? He can grasp the signs of infallibility only with his own personal subjective powers. If he believes his pastor that the pope has spoken infallibly, then he believes by his own subjective powers. He can accept with infallible certitude that a given teaching of the pope is infallibly true only if he is infallibly sure that the pope has spoken that doctrine definitively. He must know infallibly *what* the pope said and that the pope has spoken infallibly. Yet ultimately he cannot know these certainly unless he himself makes an infallible judgment. There is no way to avoid the need that each person in the Church should possess what has been traditionally called "passive infallibility." Therefore, in order that infallibility should be *effectively* exercised by the pope, the receptive or subjective infallibility of the faithful must also be exercised. The teaching of the pope must have the ring of truth in their minds and hearts if it is to achieve its saving purpose. Hence, a subjective factor is inevitably bound up with infallible teaching. Hence, too, it is not unreasonable and subjectivistic to claim, as I have done, that only when infallible teaching has actually been received by the universal faithful can it be known to have been infallible. The subjective factor is present no matter how one views infallibility, and it does no good to pretend that it does not exist. However, there is a vast difference between the assertion of the existence of a subjective factor and the charge of subjectivism.

In concluding this section on the ecumenical appeal of this view of infallibility, I would add that it partially meets Protestant objections to that teaching. Many Protestants have been fearful of papal arbitrariness, of an imposition of a temporally conditioned belief upon all, of a limiting of the open-endedness of God's truth, and of an attribution to the pope (or to the Church) of an infallibility which belongs to God alone. Each of these fears, it seems to me, has had some basis in the popular manner of presenting infallibility. I acknowledge that the existence of such fears was one of the key factors that led me to rethink the whole question from a Roman Catholic perspective. I trust that the position I have advanced has been sensitive to them.

6. Clarification of Certain Long-standing Catholic Views

Sixthly, the position I have proposed sheds light upon the existence of many long-standing views in the Church which make little sense if one accepts the purely legal textbook notion of the conditions of infallibility. One of these views holds that by heresy that is openly manifested the pope ceases to be pope.[12] Now this view would have no practical import whatsoever if all the pope had to do to counter a charge of heresy was to declare that in his teaching he was fulfilling the conditions for infallibility set down by Vatican I. But if the conditions of Vatican I represent the ontic personal conditions the pope must achieve before his pronouncements can attain the level of infallibility, then the notion that the pope becomes deposed by openly manifested heresy begins to make sense. For in the position which I have advanced, the role of the pope is to be the unifier of the whole Church. This he fulfills in a supreme way when he proclaims that universal teaching which lies at the foundation of the Church's unity. When he pronounces *ex cathedra*, he is supremely pope precisely because such a pronouncement has to do with the universal meanings by which the Church realizes its unity. If, however, the pope manifestly proclaims heresy—that is, if he proclaims as universal Christian truth something that is not—then he betrays the very meaning of his office. By that very act, and to the degree that that act persists, he ceases to be pope. Hence it was thought that if the pope persisted in his overt heresy, he would be *ipso facto* deposed.[13]

Similarly, in the light of the position I have advocated, one can see why a strong minority at Vatican I wanted to specify that the pope should consult the Church before making any infallible definition. If such a consultation is not absolutely necessary in order that the pope should attain the ontic condition required for infallible pronouncement, it is yet a practical necessity if a papal pronouncement is to have any saving effect. Unless the doctrine the pope intends to proclaim already exists universally in the contemporary faithful in some way, his proclamation will fall on uncomprehending ears. A statement of universal meaning must explicate what is already at least implicit in the minds of the faithful if it is to be understood. Hence the pope must in some way consult the people—e.g., through their leaders, the bishops—if what he has to say is to achieve its saving purpose. He must know "where the Church is at" if he is to teach in such a way as to be understood.

Finally, it should now be clear why the fear that the definition of infallibility of the pope would make the bishops and other teachers superfluous is utterly groundless. In the next chapter I will speak of the role of the bishops. Here I would only mention the role of the ordinary laity and of the theologians in the teaching office of the Church.

The ordinary laity have an irreplaceable teaching role because their lived faith and the explanations of it that they give to their children and their peers constitute the corporate experiential continuum of the Church upon which all official teaching depends for its effectiveness. Moreover, it is the laity who encounter the problems of everyday life that raise new questions and demand new answers from the Christian tradition. The corporate experience of the laity is the initiating source for development of dogma.

The theologians have a different but equally significant role. Their task is to reflect upon the past experience and understanding of the Church and to confront it with the new questions posed by modern experience and understanding. Further, they propose new meanings in the hope of unifying the ancient tradition and the modern experience. Their teaching, while not definitive or binding in any official sense, is yet an indispensable part of the process (1) by which the body of the faithful become more aware of the Christian meaning of their increasingly complex modern experience and (2) by which the official teachers are enlightened so as to be able to come to new authoritative or definitive teaching. Without the theologians, the pope and the bishops at Vatican II would have undoubtedly remained in the perspectives of the past, and the ordinary members of the Church would have remained at the stage of the Baltimore Catechism.

The Bishops as Bearers of Infallibility

As I previously indicated, most of the official Church teaching regarding infallibility has pertained to the infallibility of the pope. Comparatively little has been said about the other infallible articulators of doctrine—the bishops. It is generally conceded that the objects of infallibility—both primary and secondary—are the same for both. It is also admitted that the Holy Spirit is the source of this gift in both pope and bishops and that the goal of papal and episcopal infallibility is the same, the unity of the Church. Differences emerge when one begins to speak of the manner in which the two infallibilities are achieved and articulated. Vatican I spent a good deal of time indicating the conditions under which the pope is infallible; it spent little time clarifying the conditions under which the bishops achieve infallibility. It did say, as I have pointed out, that a solemn decree of a general council enjoys the same quality of infallibility as a solemn decree of the pope (i.e., a papal decree fitted out with the requisite conditions defined by Vatican I). However, it did not clarify the conditions for a solemn decree of a general council, and subsequent theology has not advanced this question to any notable degree. Furthermore, the council attributed infallibility to the ordinary and universal magisterium of the bishops scattered throughout the world, whereas it made no such assertion of infallibility for the ordinary and universal magisterium of the pope—i.e., his teachings in encyclicals, bulls, speeches and other forms which do not achieve the conditions required for solemn definitions. In this case, too, the council failed to set forth the conditions under which the bishops throughout the world are actually infallible in their ordinary and universal magisterium.

The foregoing paragraph indicates the basic division of this section on the bishops as the bearers of infallibility. First, I shall discuss the infallibility of the ordinary magisterium of the bishops scattered throughout the world. I shall attempt to indicate why this ordinary and universal magisterium of the bishops is infallible whereas the corresponding magisterium of the pope is not; and I shall set forth the conditions under which the ordinary and universal episcopal magisterium can be said to be infallible. Secondly, I shall treat of the infallibility of the bishops gathered in a general council, and I shall speak of the problems involved in their exercise of infallibility as well as the conditions under which this infallibility is achieved.

INFALLIBILITY OF THE BISHOPS SCATTERED GLOBALLY

1. Two Senses of Ordinary Teaching

At first sight it may seem strange that the bishops scattered throughout the world are said to be infallible in their ordinary and universal teaching whereas the corresponding papal teaching is not held to be endowed with this infallible quality. The problem arises, I believe, because the words "ordinary and universal" are actually being used in two different senses. With regard to the pope these words refer to the part of his teaching that falls short of possessing the qualities enunciated by Vatican I for his extraordinary and solemn teaching. If the theory I have advanced is correct, then the conditions for the solemn teaching are really the ontic qualities the pope must achieve in order that his pronouncements might be *of their very nature* infallible. If these conditions are lacking, a teaching might be correct; however, it will not have that correctness *per se* but only *per accidens*. Hence, it is not an infallible teaching. Thus, the ordinary and universal teaching of the pope would not be of its very nature infallible— namely, that teaching of the pope which goes out to the whole world but does not possess the intrinsic qualities of universality that we have seen are necessary for infallibility.

However, the words "ordinary and universal" mean something else when they are applied to the teaching of the bishops scattered throughout the world. They refer, I believe, precisely to the universal Christian meanings that are embedded in the teachings of the various bishops of the Catholic Church. Once this is said, however, there comes to the surface not only the reason why this teaching is infallible but also the reason why it is so difficult to determine precisely. On the one hand, this teaching is necessarily infallible since it refers to the universal Christian meanings that ground ecclesial infallibility. On the other hand, however, this teaching is not presented in any clear and unadulterated and easily discernible form. Instead, it is manifested in a whole range of expressions that indicate in a non-differentiated manner both the enduring universal meanings which ground infallibility and a host of temporally and culturally conditioned meanings which adapt that universal meaning to particular circumstances. To clarify this a short digression on the prophetic teaching of the bishops is necessary.

2. The Local Bishop as Prophet

A local bishop is not basically a dogmatic figure whose task is to manifest the universal teaching of the Church in statements which refer to that universality in its naked abstractness. Rather, the bishop is primarily a prophetic figure who applies the lasting meanings of the Church to the local situation. His task is to make that meaning come alive in a particular way in the group of people he leads and represents. He is to do this by his direction of the Church entrusted to him as well as by his explicit teaching. As a result, the universal meanings of the Church appear in his words and actions, as a general rule, embedded in particular applications to particular circumstances. Further, there is rarely a distinction made between what is totally universal and what is simply the present application and culturally conditioned dress in which the universal now appears. Thus, for example, the necessity of baptism was often clothed in teachings about limbo that manifested practically to the faithful their obligation to have their children baptized. Limbo was theological teaching that conveyed the necessity of baptism in the best manner then possible. It was a theoretical construct that seemed to explain the data of faith. It was not a perfect explanation, for it was difficult to reconcile with the universal salvific will; but it effectively conveyed the necessity of baptism. It was authorized, at least implicitly, by bishops in much of the Catholic world. Yet it now appears that this teaching on limbo does not pertain to the universal Christian meanings as does the teaching on the necessity of baptism.[1] (Of course, one would have to nuance the teaching on the universal necessity of baptism. This would carry us far beyond the limits imposed by the present question.) Now what is true for limbo is largely true of most episcopal teaching. It is a prophetic effort to make the lasting ecclesial meanings come alive in a particular place and time. In the more homogeneous Church of the past that local effort often involved using the same temporal expressions and the same theoretical constructs that were used else-where. In the more heterogeneous Church of the present (and of the future), the efforts of local bishops to teach will undoubtedly involve a pluralism of expression and theoretical construct unknown in the past. Much of the recent writing of Karl Rahner is concerned in one way or another with this phenomenon.[2] In both past and present, the universal teaching of the Church tends to be manifested by local bishops in forms that express in an undifferentiated manner both that universal teaching and a temporally conditioned set of theoretical constructs.

3. Discerning the Infallible in Ordinary Episcopal Teaching

What this means for the discerning of the infallible teaching of the Church in the ordinary and universal teaching of the bishops scattered throughout the world should now be clear. That discernment, practically speaking, can never be certain. What is universal will be so embedded in a multiplicity of forms and so overlaid with what is temporally and culturally conditioned that its isolation will only be possible by an actual communication and dialogue between the bishops. The situation is actually quite close to that of the determination of the *sensus fidelium*. As we saw in treating that *sensus,* it is an *implicit* source of infallible teaching; but it cannot be quarried by simplistic poll-taking procedures precisely because the universal embedded in the consciousness of the faithful does not appear in isolated and distinct form.[3] In the present context we can say that the teaching of the universal episcopate can be compared to a concentrated *sensus fidelium.* It contains in an implicit fashion the universal ecclesial meanings that ground infallible recognition. Such meanings may exist for a long time before they are explicitly distinguished and isolated. Normally this comes about, however, only when an attempt is made by the pope or by the bishops in communion with him and with one another to get at what is truly universal. It is this implicit nature of the universal teaching of the Church as it appears in the teachings of the scattered bishops that has made the theological attempts to call any given teaching of the Church *de fide* by the ordinary and universal magisterium of the bishops such a hazardous venture. We simply do not have the techniques to uncover the universal intentionality that exists in an implicit way in the multifaceted teachings of bishops in the various parts of the world and over the many centuries of the Church's life. Only the man who already knows what is universal in ecclesial understanding has the chance of uncovering that understanding.

4. Individual Bishops Speak for the Whole Church

The foregoing may help clarify the meaning of the contention that individual bishops in some way speak for the whole Church. They do so by making the universal teaching of the Church appear in a visible and concrete way in the faithful entrusted to them. The Church can be said to be the concrete locus of universal Christian meanings. It is present whenever those meanings are present in a more or less global way in concrete persons. Insofar as the bishop leads in the work of this concretizing of revelation, he can be said to "speak" for the whole Church. This is his role as bishop; in the measure that he fulfills that role, he does speak for the entire Church.

INFALLIBILITY OF THE BISHOPS IN A GENERAL COUNCIL

If the universal meanings that ground the possibility of explicit infallible understanding exist in the episcopacy as scattered throughout the world, the assembly of the bishops in a general council is one (not the only one) manner by which that implicit ground can be brought to conscious and explicit awareness and even to articulation. This conscious and explicit awareness can occur in a single individual such as the pope whenever he achieves the requisite universality set forth in the conditions of Vatican I. It can even exist in an individual bishop if he actually does achieve those conditions in his own life, although the nature of his office does not demand that he should be capable of such explicit consciousness when he operates within the context of the people he serves. However, a general council is of such a nature as to facilitate the emergence of universal meanings to the explicit consciousness of the assembled bishops.

In this section I will attempt to set forth: (1) that the individual is the sole possible locus of infallibility; (2) that a general council achieves infallible understanding only insofar as the individuals who compose it achieve the ontic conditions of infallibility; (3) that the infallible decrees of councils are statements that represent the individual and collective explicit understanding of the assembled bishops; (4) that in a modern age there may be other ways of achieving the kind of infallible statement once achievable only in a general council; (5) that there is need for nuanced distinctions about the meaning of the ecumenicity of councils; (6) that the interpretation of conciliar decrees involves far more than tracing the genesis of texts through various stages; (7) that the recognition of the dogmatic ecumenicity of a council is really a re-cognition of its universal teaching; and (8) that all the foregoing factors shed light on the significance of non-infallible ecclesial teaching in general and non-infallible conciliar teaching in particular.

1. The Individual as Locus of Infallible Understanding

First of all, the individual person is the sole possible locus of infallible understanding. This statement must be made initially because unhappily there is an implicit acceptance by many of the view that the infallibility of a council is something diffused among large numbers of bishops. Somehow, it is supposed, they may be fallible individually, but they are infallible collectively. I would contend, however, that infallibility refers to the achievement of understanding of universal ecclesial truth and that such understanding either exists in an individual or not at all. To understand is to grasp the unities implicit in experience; to understand infallibly in the Church is to grasp those abstract unities that are, or should be, present in the legitimate development of all Christians. Such a grasp of the unity in experience cannot, by its very nature, exist partially in a number of individuals who only understand as a collectivity. It can exist only in a single person who is the subject of the appropriate experiences and who sees explicitly in them that which unifies them. A group of individuals can possess all the data which ground an act of understanding in such a way that one individual possesses some of the data, a second individual some more, and a third more again; yet the actual grasp of the unity in the data that constitutes the explicit act of understanding can occur only in a single person because understanding is grounded only in personal experience. To understand is to have the requisite data in one's possession and to have noted the unities therein.[4]

2. The General Council and Individual Infallibility

Secondly, from this it follows that a general council which achieves infallible understanding is really a group of men who individually have arrived at a condition of infallibility. This means that individually they have achieved that ontic state of existence that Vatican I indicated was required of the pope as a prerequisite of infallibility. This apparently startling claim flows from all that we have said so far; but if it is accepted, it will shed light on the value of a general council and upon certain past teaching regarding such a council.

On the one hand, this conclusion sheds light on the value of a general council from a dogmatic view. Such a council is not simply a meeting to which bishops come in order to make dogmatic statements about what is already universally known. (I am abstracting here from the pastoral value of general councils and concentrating on their doctrinal purposes. Of course, the two functions are far more closely allied than is often thought, as should be obvious to anyone who has read these pages; however, I cannot take up the pastoral question.) Rather, a general council is also, as a study of the history of councils will reveal, a place where the ontic conditions of infallibility that previously did not exist in any explicit manner in the bishops scattered throughout the world are now developed in these men by a process of interaction. In a council that utters infallible teaching the bishops are invariably changed; their horizons are broadened; by their communication with one another they come to see, at least unreflexively, that their own teaching to their flocks is wrapped up in temporally and culturally conditioned words and concepts; in their mutual confrontation and in their study of the past traditional teaching of the Church, they gradually begin to grasp that which transcends the application of divine revelation to their own dioceses; eventually there emerges in their respective consciousnesses a more or less explicit understanding of that which is truly universal in the Church's understanding. In short, the council provides a place where a process of conversion of bishops can occur; and as a result of that conversion to a condition in which the ontic conditions of infallibility are realized, the bishops are enabled to issue a statement or statements that represent universal ecclesial meanings and by that fact are necessarily infallibly true.

On the other hand, the statement that a general council becomes infallible only when the individuals who constitute it personally achieve the ontic conditions of infallibility sheds light on a number of teachings that pertain to a general council. Thus, it clarifies why much of the teaching of councils—such as the whole of Vatican II— never attains the level of infallibility. This does not occur because the bishops benignly decide not to issue any burdensome, irreformable decrees. Rather, it occurs usually because individual bishops at the council do not achieve the ontic conditions of infallibility, owing either to insufficient development of meaning in the Church prior to the council or to a failure to achieve sufficient dialogue, confrontation, communication, and conversion at the council.[5] Again, this statement clarifies the meaning of the ancient notion that infallible statements of councils require practical unanimity of the assembled bishops.[6] If such unanimity was expected, the underlying reason is that the teaching of the council has universal validity, and that if this is so, then it should be recognized by those whose mission it is to make the universal faith live in various parts of the world. A council is not, at least in the matter of doctrinal teaching, a political struggle about practical decisions which of their very nature must breed disagreement. Rather, it is an effort to attain a grasp of what is truly universal and to proclaim that to the whole Church. Should such a proclamation lack practical unanimity of support among the assembled bishops, its proclamation as universal would be in evident contradiction to its very nature. The coercion of bishops to accept a decree against their consciences likewise contradicts the nature of an infallible decree.[7]

3. Conciliar Decrees Represent Collective Understanding

Thirdly, the infallible decrees of general councils are statements that represent the individual and collective explicit understanding of universal ecclesial meanings by the assembled bishops. Hence these statements are merely pointers to meanings that exist in men. Strictly speaking, they are not infallible, because infallibility refers basically to understanding. That understanding can and must be universal, but no expression can have universal significance. All expressions are temporally and culturally conditioned, at least to some extent. All this has bearing on the concluding section of this book, which deals with expression. I mention it here because it has significance for the interpretation of general councils that I will take up in my sixth point below.

4. Extra-conciliar Dogmatic Decrees

Fourthly, in the modern age there may be other ways of achieving the kind of dogmatic statement by bishops once achievable only in a general council. This follows from the fact that a dogmatic statement by bishops is simply one that represents and symbolizes their mutual achievement of the ontic conditions of infallibility. In the past such an achievement for the most part necessitated the assembly of bishops in one place in order that the give-and-take, the confrontation, the mutual exchange and communication, and the personal conversions necessary for the widespread realization among the bishops of universal ecclesial meanings might occur. Now, however, with the advent of improved communication at a distance through such means as closed circuit television and conference telephone calls and with the possibility that large numbers of bishops in the future will begin to grasp explicitly the meaning and necessity of a transcultural theology, the likelihood arises that the conditions prevailing at a general council which permitted, at least in some cases, the emergence of explicit universal ecclesial meanings will be achievable by other means.

5. The Ecumenicity of Councils

Fifthly, there is need for nuanced distinctions about the meaning of the ecumenicity of councils. Here I distinguish *absolute ecumenicity*, *cultural ecumenicity*, and *dogmatic ecumenicity*. *Absolute ecumenicity* of a council refers to a condition in which every faith meaning in the entire Church is represented and expressed at a council. This is evidently an ideal goal that never has been achieved and never will be achieved in this eon. The Communion of Saints is the only "council" that will ever possess absolute ecumenicity. All councils prior to this eschatological council are necessarily partial and imperfect; they represent degrees on a continuum; they can only issue statements of partial truth. Against the scale of absolute ecumenicity, each of the so-called general councils of the past has varying degrees of ecumenicity, although the precise measure in which they approach the ideal is known only to God.

Cultural Ecumenicity (which is another way of speaking about geographical ecumenicity) refers to the more or less *external* manner in which the various culturally conditioned ways of expressing the Christian and universal faith are represented at a council. A council becomes a general council in the cultural sense to the degree that it includes men who represent *all* of the diverse manners of realizing the faith that exist at the time of the council. In terms of cultural ecumenicity, we are again faced with the fact that councils belong on a continuum. No council has ever represented every cultural realization of the universal Christian faith, not even any of the first seven general councils. Vatican II, with its vast attendance of Roman Catholic bishops and its efforts to extend hospitality to many non-Catholic Christians, still failed to represent fully every manner in which the universal faith had been realized in concrete culturally conditioned contexts.

Dogmatic ecumenicity refers to the condition in which a council of bishops from various parts of the world actually achieves, by a process of give-and-take, the ontic conditions of infallibility and manifests that achievement to the world in a statement. Thus, a council possesses dogmatic ecumenicity when it permits the emergence and expression of universal ecclesial meanings. Such an emergence is possible even if the episcopal participation is not widespread and relatively universal in cultural terms, because it is possible to grasp the universal in only a few culturally conditioned particulars. It is true that, all other things being equal, a council which possesses cultural ecumenicity of a relatively high degree has a better chance of achieving dogmatic ecumenicity; however, all other things are not usually equal, as the failure of Vatican II to achieve dogmatic ecumenicity proves. I might add that the Orthodox tradition recognizes in its own way what I have tried to say here. For Orthodoxy the standard or criterion of ecumenicity is truth. By this is meant what I have called universal ecclesial meanings—the truth for the whole Church.

6. The Interpretation of Conciliar Decrees

The goal of all interpretation is to uncover the understanding of the author of a document. The interpreter attempts to achieve, on the basis of his own experience, the same understanding achieved and expressed by the author of the document he is interpreting. As I indicated in chapter 1, he tries to grasp through the text what the author explicitly, implicitly, or incompletely understood.

The difficulties encountered in interpreting the text of an individual author are compounded when one attempts to interpret a document produced by a group of men. For when one seeks to interpret a document produced by a group, one is seeking the shared understanding existing in the minds of the individuals who composed it. Thus, the goal of interpretation of a conciliar decree is that of uncovering the common understanding in the minds of the bishops who assented to the decree. This is true both for infallible decrees that proclaim universal ecclesial meanings and for lesser statements. However, if the interpreter is seeking this shared understanding, two problems emerge which complicate the interpretative venture. These problems concern the existence and the depth of this common or shared understanding.

Lack of shared meaning. The first problem centers on the existence of shared meaning and understanding among the assembled bishops. It is quite possible for a group of bishops to agree on the phrasing of a document without coming to shared understanding. They agree on the words, but they do not agree on their meaning. If this were not so, congressional members would never disagree on the meaning of laws they have passed; and members of religious chapters would never disagree on the meaning of the constitutions they have promulgated. If these relatively small bodies have difficulty in establishing common meaning, how much more difficult is that task for a vast body of men of different cultures who assemble for a general council.

This difficulty in achieving shared understanding among the bishops at a council stems basically from the fact that each bishop necessarily considers any view, and a text purporting to express it, from his own perspective and from the matrix of meanings constituted by his past history. A tailor will view people according to the clothes they wear; a fight manager will look at them according to their pugilistic ability; a scholar may evaluate them according to their knowledge. In the same way, despite all explanations given for a text at a council, each bishop will look at it and understand it *to some extent* in his own way.

It is true that there will be some aspects of a document that have been so long and so seriously discussed that a large core of agreement will have been reached by the time of the document's passage. However, there will be other aspects in which only minimal agreement will have been reached in the area of meaning. Thus, the passage of a document by a large majority of bishops present should not deceive us into thinking that they have all thereby agreed to the totality of meanings which the authors of the document intended to express. Agreement to accept an expression, such as a document, is not *ipso facto* agreement to all its intended meanings.

Lack of shared existential depth of meaning. The second problem centers on the varying depth of the acceptance of common meanings. It is possible for two men to agree on a principle and yet for their agreement to differ in existential depth. To grasp the significance of this a few clarifying distinctions may be helpful.

As I have often repeated, one understands only on the basis of experience; in fact understanding, the attainment of a meaning, is nothing but a heightening of the unities in experience. Further, particular culturally conditioned meanings can thus be present only in particular culturally conditioned experiences because they represent heightening of elements which tend to be found only within those experiences. So it is that chemists discourse easily with one another about the composition of various materials, and economists bandy terms that are the stock-in-trade of their profession. Both groups possess particular meanings grounded in common areas of experience. Nevertheless, interchange between members of the two groups is difficult because the areas of experience are differently specialized and the experiences of one group cannot ground the meanings of the other group.

However, universal meanings can be grounded in a variety of experiences because it is their nature to be a possible and necessary aspect of the development of all men of whatsoever culture and specialization. Such meanings are highly abstract. Accordingly it is possible for almost any man, despite the specialized and limited nature of his experience, to come to a realization of such meanings. Even a limited and evil Christian can therefore assent to a universal Christian meaning, despite the lack of existential breadth and depth in his life.

All this suggests that men can grasp and assent to universal meanings in ways that vary in existential depth and breadth. Here I would make a distinction between *anticipatory* and *resumatory* assent to a universal meaning. These represent two ends of a continuum. Acceptance towards the anticipatory end of the continuum is based on a bare minimum of experiences. The person accepting in this way has never attempted to live out the meaning to any extent; he has never encountered the difficulties involved in internalizing it and making it come alive in concrete life. Thus, a man accepting in an anticipatory way the principle that "people have to be taken where they are and helped from there" will never have tried to reach people of another background and culture. He will never have realized the pain involved, the stumbling steps, the misunderstandings, and the personal conversion needed when one attempts to implement the principle. Hence his acceptance of the principle by no means involves the explicit acceptance of all these things which accompany the attempt to implement it in the concrete. These are off in the vague and indefinite future.

On the other hand, resumatory acceptance is one which summarizes and crystallizes actual experience with the implementation of a principle. One thus proclaims a meaning which has been embedded in the warp and woof of one's concrete life. Such acceptance implies the co-acceptance of difficulties implied in putting the meaning into operation. In assenting to the principle that "people have to be taken where they are and helped from there," one also assents more or less explicitly to facing the problems connected with its implementation. In short, anticipatory acceptance tends to be naked conceptual acceptance; resumatory acceptance is the proclamation of a personal conviction. Anticipatory acceptance will demand a personal conversion and development if one attempts to carry through its implementation; resumatory acceptance implies that this conversion and development have already taken place.

The situation is further complicated by the fact that questions asked subsequent to a council often involve two or more conciliar principles, each of which was accepted at different degrees of existential depth by the assembled bishops. Thus, if one asks about the nature of the Church according to *Lumen Gentium,* one may receive a reply that involves such elements as the hierarchical structure and the people of God. Now it is safe to say that the acceptance of the hierarchical element in the Church by most bishops was at the resumatory end of the spectrum, whereas the acceptance of the Church as the people of God was more toward the anticipatory end of the spectrum. Moreover, these two elements were more juxtaposed than synthesized at the council. The problems involved in the existential living out of the acceptance of both were not explicitly envisioned and worked out.

This type of problem is compounded in instances where two groups of men at the council independently worked out principles that are in tension in the concrete. Thus, the rights of authority are stressed in one context and the liberty of individual conscience in another. How these principles are to be reconciled in concrete life is not clarified; for no overall reconciliation and synthesis of the total output of the council was attempted.

Three principles of conciliar interpretation. In the light of these two problems, how is one to interpret conciliar texts? A first method is to read the text and attribute to the words the meanings one habitually attributes to those words. Basically, this is what fundamentalism is all about. For some time the texts of councils were read in this way; fortunately, however, this method has been given a quiet funeral by professional theologians, although it is not uncommon to find others in the Church who employ it from time to time.

A second method of interpretation, the one currently in vogue, is the genetic textual method. The interpreter traces the development of the text through the various stages of its evolution. He follows it from its inception in a theological commission, to the discussions on the council floor, to the changes that appear in the various revised texts, and finally to the passage of the finished document. He seeks for the meanings that were intended by the various authors of the original document and the subsequent revisions.

Such a procedure, it appears to me, is quite valid for the determination of the conceptual intent of the theologians who framed the document and the bishops who sponsored it after thoroughly examining it. But of itself it does not necessarily indicate the common meanings that entered into the minds of the assembled Fathers and were promulgated by their votes. I believe that it is possible for many bishops to assent to the promulgation of a document without assenting to certain meanings the framers of the document intended to convey. Many a bishop did not read the text carefully, did not attend all the discussions that refined its meaning; many a bishop did not grasp the import of what he heard with regard to parts of the text for reasons that ranged from tiredness, to boredom, to lack of the background necessary to grasp the material discussed. It is possible, for example, that a number of the bishops at Vatican II did not understand the meaning of subsidiarity and collegiality in the same way as certain theologians who framed the documents which contain these teachings.

One may counter with the claim that the teachings of a council are precisely what the authors of the documents intended and explained on the council floor, whether the Fathers grasped that teaching or not. To hold this, however, would be to hold that the bishops can proclaim a teaching without even understanding and accepting it. It would be to attribute to bishops a purely juridical, even magical, teaching authority by which they could point to something as Church teaching without personally appropriating it and recognizing its meaning as something to be witnessed to. At the logical extreme, this would mean that some devious theologian working in committee could conceivably foist upon the bishops in council, and subsequently on the Church as a whole, a teaching the bishops really would not agree with if they did understand it. The only reasonable viewpoint, it seems to me, is to recognize that the meaning arrived at by the framers of conciliar documents becomes official Church teaching only to the extent that this meaning is understood and accepted by the universal Church as represented by the vast majority of the bishops at a council.

These considerations bring to light some of the limitations of the genetic textual method for determining what the conceptual meanings promulgated by a council really were. Further limitations become apparent when we consider the fact that the meanings assented to were accepted existentially at levels of intensity that ranged from the anticipatory to the resumatory. The genetic method is of little value in determining the level of existential depth with which principles were accepted. This, in turn, makes it difficult for this method to evaluate whether one can attribute to a council practical conclusions which appear to flow from a conciliar principle or a combination of conciliar principles. Thus, one might infer from the conciliar teachings on freedom of conscience and the personal value of sexual activity of spouses that the practice of birth control was left by the council to the responsible free choice of couples. But can this be said to be the understanding of the bishops? While I do not intend to solve this particular problem, I do think a general principle can be stated to cover this type of case. *The more conclusions are drawn from principles accepted by the bishops in an implicit and anticipatory way, the less one can attribute these conclusions to the council. On the other hand, the more such conclusions were directly envisioned by the bishops or the more they are derived from principles that were explicitly and resumatorily accepted, the more these conclusions can be attributed to the council.* However, if one accepts this principle, one also accepts the basic limitations of the genetic textual method in the determination of whether practical conclusions or implementations ought to be attributed to a council.

These limitations of the textual method suggest that a third and complementary method of interpretation should be employed, namely, the test of fruits. This method is based on the principle that what one believes and accepts is better expressed by how one acts than by what one says. Words are expressions that can be attached to an almost infinite variety of meanings in different people; actions tend far more to actualize the same aspects of the experiential continua of men; hence they tend, especially when interpreted in context and genetic sequence, to reflect better than words the meanings that are implicit in a person.

I believe that we can best fix the meaning of a council by tracing the activity after the council of each bishop who composed it. We may discover that in the activity of a given bishop certain conciliar principles were implemented from the outset and the difficulties involved in their implementation were boldly confronted and worked out. This would give good grounds for saying not only that he had accepted the principles but also that he had accepted them in depth and at the resumatory end of the spectrum. Secondly, we may discover with regard to another conciliar principle that there were initial attempts to implement it, but after a series of difficulties such attempts were abandoned. This would give grounds for saying that the principle had been accepted but that its acceptance had been towards the anticipatory end of the spectrum. Thirdly, we may discover that after the council no activity occurred in the implementing of a given principle even though there were occasions that clearly called for it. In this instance, we may assume that the principle had not been accepted at all. Fourthly, we may discover that soon after the council a principle was briefly implemented but that activity of this nature was abandoned after a few difficulties emerged; later, however, there was a return to the implementation of the principle and a confronting of all the difficulties entailed. This would give grounds for saying that the principle had been accepted at the council only in an anticipatory fashion, but that subsequently the bishop underwent a personal conversion that enabled him to accept it in a resumatory way. These four cases and their variations and combinations give some idea of how we may arrive at the meanings intended by individual bishops at a council through tracing the development of their activity after the council. If such a procedure were followed for all of the bishops, combining the results would enable us to arrive at the range of common understanding that was expressed by the conciliar documents.

The practical limitations of this method are all too evident. How is one to go about the process of tracking down the actions of bishops after a council? The work involved would be prohibitive. At best a statistical sampling might be attained, and one could detect trends or patterns in the actions of individual bishops or episcopal conferences. I mention this method, however, not just because of its theoretical validity but also because its presentation helps to bring out the enormous dimension of the problem we face when we attempt to determine the official meaning of a council.

Interpreting the official teaching of a council in the light of these principles. The official teaching of a council consists in the shared meaning that the bishops intended to express by the conciliar documents. But just what are these shared meanings? In the light of the foregoing discussion on the achievement of shared meaning, the varying depth of existential possession of meaning, and the methods of interpretation, I would suggest the following principle. *Official conciliar teaching consists primarily in those principles that were explicitly accepted in at least an anticipatory manner by the majority of the assembled bishops, or in the immediate logical deductions from such principles. It consists secondarily in the practical conclusions bound up with the implementation of principles that were accepted by the majority of the Fathers in a resumatory fashion.* The shared meaning referred to by this principle becomes official Church teaching in the measure that the Fathers intended to express and teach it through the documents of the council. It becomes infallible teaching insofar as the meaning taught is a universal Christian meaning and is grasped and proclaimed by the majority of bishops with the same degree of personal achievement of meaning and intentionality to teach that characterizes the exercise of papal infallibility.

The goal of interpretation is to uncover this official (or infallible) teaching of a council. This is done by the application of the genetic textual method and the test of fruits. These methods, as I have indicated, have grave limitations. It is for this reason I believe that any honest interpretation of a council must necessarily be minimal in scope. Only that teaching will be called official which reflects the central core of meaning that would have been agreed upon by anyone seriously considering the document passed. What that central core is can be determined, in the first place, by the genetic textual method. For example, in a long document this central core will consist largely in the basic thrust of the material. Further, some sections will have been discussed at length; as a result, specific meanings will most certainly have entered into the thought pattern of the majority of bishops. Such meanings also belong to this central core. Finally, concise statements framed solely to eliminate certain erroneous teachings, provided this elimination is so discussed as to be clear to all who vote, will almost surely represent the common understanding of the bishops attending the council. That central core can be determined, in the second place, by the test of fruits. Are there meanings apparently expressed by the council which have subsequently been expressed in a growing way by the majority of the bishops? These, too, can be considered to be official conciliar teachings.

The determination of infallible teachings follows along similar lines. However, this determination is not only subject to all the difficulties that surround the determination of any official conciliar teaching; it is also subject to the difficulties involved in discovering with certitude that all the conditions pertaining to infallibility have been achieved. It is this compounding of difficulties that has led to the numerous revisions about the extent of the infallible teaching of the councils of the past. A cursory study of the history of the manual presentation of the infallible teaching of the Council of Trent over the last century would be quite instructive in this matter.

The real problem. This brief and oversimplified treatment of the interpretation of conciliar teaching indicates where the real problem of the Church lies with regard to a council. The problem is not primarily one of interpreting the council. Rather it is *one of continuing the development of Christian meanings set in motion by the council.* By its very nature, a council is not a producer of a rounded and complete set of meanings. It is true that some meanings are gradually accepted by most of the bishops and are taught by the council. But many more meanings gain only partial acceptance; moreover, these partially accepted meanings, and even the generally accepted and taught meanings, are grasped with varying degrees of existential depth. Finally, many meanings taught are particular ecclesial meanings which constitute the starting point towards the eventual achievement of universal meanings. Because of all this, conciliar teaching is inevitably incomplete. It is much more like a large uncut diamond than like a small polished gem. It demands completion, and that completion can come about only by the expansion of the Church's corporate experiential continuum beyond the stage reached at the council. Such an expansion requires more than the exegesis of documents; it requires a continuous conversion and growth not only on the part of the bishops but also on the part of the rest of the Church.

7. Recognition of the Dogmatic Ecumenicity of a Council

Impossibility of grasping dogmatic ecumenicity directly. Seventhly, the subsequent recognition of the dogmatic ecumenicity of a council is really based on a re-cognition of its universal teaching *as universal.* Note that I am referring here to dogmatic ecumenicity. Such ecumenicity pertains to the achievement of the ontic conditions of infallibility, an achievement which can never be identified by a single external sign or by any number of external signs in combination. The whole Church has no infallible way of recognizing *directly* that a given council of the past actually achieved the ontic conditions of dogmatic ecumenicity. It is for this reason that theological books have had constantly to revise theological notes upon given theses that were once supposed to have been infallibly proclaimed by a general council. One has only to peruse any of the old textbooks' treatments on original sin and to note what the Council of Trent is said to have infallibly taught on this question. Only those who hold that the conditions of infallibility proclaimed by Vatican I are legal and external conditions subject to visible identification can think that infallible conciliar (or papal) teaching is easily identifiable. Even then, however, a close examination of the conditions that prevail in the concrete order will reveal that the identification of merely external and visible signs purported to pinpoint infallible meaning is not so easy as believed.

The basic point is that one attains infallible understanding only when one achieves a certain universality of being that allows one to grasp the truly universal ecclesial meanings. However, no one can ever attain such understanding simply by willing it or by proclaiming to the world that one has fulfilled the conditions laid down by Vatican I. Simply willing the ontic conditions by virtue of one's teaching office does not assure that one attains them. Nor does the following of certain external procedures assure this goal. Internal understanding in an individual and in a group is never necessarily connected with certain external procedures; if that were so, we would long ago have evolved perfect teaching methods to bring about understanding. Further, even granted that a pope or a council attains the conditions of infallibility, there is no direct infallible way by which they can indicate to the rest of the Church that they have attained these conditions. They can use no means different from those which would be used by a comparable group of bishops who honestly believe that they are pronouncing infallibly when, in fact, they are not. In short, there is no combination of external signs that will infallibly identify the achievement of the internal ontic conditions of infallibility.

The indirect path of recognition. How then can the Church know that a council has achieved dogmatic ecumenicity at a given moment and with a given teaching? My answer is that the Church as a whole recognizes the stated council as having been dogmatically ecumenical by an *indirect* path. This involves two steps. First of all, the Church as a whole, and especially in its representatives, actually grasps the meaning of the truth attained by the council and signified in its verbal pronouncements; this is absolutely necessary because no one can assent to a truth as having been proclaimed by a council if he does not know what the truth is. Secondly, the Church becomes conscious of the fact that this meaning actually characterizes the living out of the faith in a universal way. In other words, the Church comes to know more or less explicitly that a given meaning is a universal ecclesial meaning. What this all boils down to is that the recognition of the ecumenicity of the doctrine proclaimed by a council is simply the re-cognition of that teaching by the whole Church. That re-cognition establishes directly for the realizing Church the truth of the dogma under discussion. Indirectly, it establishes that the council which originally taught it had achieved the conditions of dogmatic ecumenicity when it produced that teaching. I might note that the present Church can never be infallibly sure of this indirect identification because it can never ascertain with infallible truth that the council Fathers did teach what it now sees to be a universal ecclesial meaning. The Church can only have high moral certitude in these matters.

Ecumenical import of this view. This way of looking at things, it seems to me, will help to reconcile the Roman Catholic teaching on the infallibility of councils with the teaching of the Orthodox. Roman Catholics hold that a council is infallible *ex se*. By analogy with the conditions laid down for the infallibility of the pope, Roman Catholic theologians would hold that a council's teaching is infallible when the requisite conditions are fulfilled, even without subsequent approval by the Church. With this I am in hearty accord, as the reader will have seen. On the other hand, at least one Orthodox view puts immense stress on the subsequent acceptance of a council.[8] A council does not become ecumenical unless it is received as such by the whole Church.

I believe that the present approach brings out what is true in both positions. By stating that dogmatic ecumenicity is attained when certain ontic conditions are realized, it clarifies why Roman Catholics insist that a council is ecumenical *in se* when certain conditions are achieved, even before subsequent acceptance by the Church. On the other hand, by stating that a council cannot be known to have achieved dogmatic ecumenicity until the Church recognizes its teaching as such, it indicates that a council does not achieve effective ecumenicity until that re-cognition takes place. Only with that re-cognition does the teaching of the council truly have ecumenical saving effects, because only with the re-cognition of universal truth itself is the individual actually saved. Truth saves by being known, not by one's knowing that someone else has proclaimed it. A council effectively becomes ecumenical when the universal Church appropriates that saving truth whose possession constitutes the ontic foundation of the council's dogmatic ecumenicity. That appropriation becomes possible only when the universal truth that was implicitly present in each local Church reaches the state of explicit awareness in these Churches, at least in their chief representatives, the bishops.

The preceding discussion indicates the value of the distinction we have made between absolute, cultural, and dogmatic ecumenicity.

Absolute ecumenicity pertains only to the fulfilled Communion of Saints. Roman Catholics tend to emphasize cultural ecumenicity and to rate a council as ecumenical when it contains representatives of the various cultures that make up the Church in a more or less full way. The Orthodox tend to emphasize what I have called dogmatic ecumenicity; hence for them truth is the standard of ecumenicity. I believe the failure to recognize that two different yardsticks are being used has led to unnecessary differences. Further, the failure to grasp that ecumenicity of truth exists in various degrees has likewise muddied the waters. There is a vast difference between the naked dogmatic ecumenicity that exists when only the members of the council grasp a truth explicitly and the comparatively full dogmatic ecumenicity that exists when the vast majority of Christians grasp that same truth in a lived way. One can make out a case that the Church is on the march towards full dogmatic ecumenicity, towards absolute ecumenicity; and that march is often initiated by the minimal dogmatic ecumenicity that has appeared in general councils.

Is this view dangerous? This view of re-cognition of universal meanings by the Church as the means towards grasping that a council (and a pope) have spoken infallibly will strike not a few as being dangerous for the welfare and security of the Church. If one cannot be sure that the magisterium has spoken infallibly until after the universal Church has begun to incarnate the meanings referred to, then the comfortable security that Catholics once had in the authority of the magisterium would seem to vanish. To a certain extent the charge is correct. The old confidence that the magisterium, at least, has the answers was false and misleading. It does the Christian little good that his leaders have the truth unless he himself appropriates it. Truth saves intrinsically by its very possession. The more the truth is rooted in the whole of a person's thoughts, words, actions, worship— the more he ontically *is* as a person. The magisterium exercises a broad ecclesial function which is of value not in that it knows the truth or proclaims the truth in some formula, but in that it works to have the truth grasped. When a Catholic believes the one thing necessary is that the magisterium has issued an infallible statement and one has merely to exegete it to understand it, or that one has merely to accept the fact that the magisterium has spoken infallibly—then he fails to grasp that truth saves *ex sese*. Certainly he must have confidence and respect for what the magisterium says even before he grasps it. However, he benefits from that proclamation only when he grasps its meaning; and when this occurs, he is in a position to contribute to the widespread recognition of ecclesial truth which constitutes true ecumenicity. The four conditions Vatican I laid down for the infallibility of the pope maintain their value—but as ontic rather than legal conditions. However, they must be complemented by a growth in Christians that internalizes meanings. Only then will the saving value of infallible teaching be achieved. Only then will the meaning that has been proclaimed be actually heard. The older notion which seemed to assume that meaning could be made audible simply by the fact that the four conditions had been achieved at a council appears to be naïve. The limited security a Christian can have in this world is not a security which rests finally upon the truth that is possessed and proclaimed by another. Rather, it rests ultimately upon the truth that he himself possesses. It is the truth that makes one free; it is the truth that saves; but just as freedom and salvation are personal possessions, so, too, truth makes free and saves only when it is a personal possession. The claim here is that the function of the magisterium is to facilitate that possession. In a statement that reflects an abstract universal meaning, the teaching office prods the Church to a development which enables it to grasp that meaning and to begin the process of ever more deeply internalizing that meaning in its life. This way of looking at things does bring out difficulties in recognizing the truth of the teaching of pope or council, as compared with the easy recognition assumed in the old way of presenting things. However, this condition is not dangerous but valuable. It overthrows a false security in order to point out where the more precarious but real security lies.

8. Importance of Non-infallible Teaching

Eighthly, non-infallible conciliar (and papal) teachings have great significance for the Church. They are non-infallible precisely because they are not universal; they do not have the resonance of truth in every age and culture. They may well be true, at least for certain limited circumstances. However, they are not what I have called universal ecclesial meanings.

At times they are not infallibly proclaimed because the Church as a whole has not grown to the stage in which such meanings actually

characterize its existence; the passage of time will enable the magisterium, if circumstances warrant it, to declare such previously non-
infallible meanings in an infallible way precisely because they have
attained a *de facto* universality they formerly did not possess. At
other times, Church teaching is non-infallible because what is proclaimed is only a truth that applies to one epoch or culture, even
though the men at the time of the proclamation are unable to see its
limited applicability. I believe, for example, that the current magisterial teaching on birth control is an amalgam of culturally conditioned meanings and universal meanings that have not been sufficiently distinguished, although I cannot attempt to clarify this here.
Of course, this does not mean that such teaching is worthless. It may
be quite valuable for Christians of a given epoch or culture and it
may also be a significant aspect of the process by which a truly
universal meaning emerges. In fact, this last may be the most important reason for paying attention to non-infallible teaching. If it is
listened to intently enough, there may eventually come to consciousness the truly universal elements that are embedded in it. Thus, one
can listen to Paul's injunction that women should keep their heads
covered in Church and discover within it the universal ecclesial
meaning that people in the Church should express an attitude of
reverence towards God in worship in their whole comportment and
according to the mores of their respective cultures. The fact of the
matter is that local or restricted meanings inevitably emerge first;
universal meanings always arise later. It is precisely these local or
restricted meanings that are often the subject of non-infallible teaching. But it is also their utterance that eventually leads to the realization and then proclamation of universal meanings. Whitehead once
said that men should study the more particular sciences first. These
constitute the proper entry into the more general and abstract sciences
such as philosophy. The same dynamic that makes Whitehead's
statement sensible also clarifies why non-infallible and restricted
truths come first, whereas the infallible and universal truths come
last, in the order of discovery. To ignore non-infallible teaching, or
simply to refute it without asking for the circumstances in which it
appeared to be (and very probably was) true, is to eliminate the
necessary prior stage in the process of achieving universal meanings.
One never arrives at the universal except in and through the particular. The Church never arrives at universal teaching except in and

through its grappling with particular circumstances and arriving at particular understandings. For the student, consequently, the attentive study of what was provisional and culturally conditioned can be an almost indispensable way of attaining the universal. This has long been recognized in the natural sciences. Theological practice should make it recognized in the science of theology. If this were done, denials of teachings like the value of infant baptism, the existence of secondary objects of infallibility, and the attribution of the state of original sin to a first sinner in history would be replaced by imaginative efforts that would uncover in each of these a culturally conditioned way of pointing to a more lasting and universal aspect of revelation.

Dogma as Enunciated—Dogmatic Expressions

SUMMARY AND PROSPECTUS

My basic division has been threefold: dogmatic meaning, dogmatic understanding, and dogmatic expression. In chapters 5 through 8, I took up dogmatic or universal ecclesial meanings; in chapters 9 through 15, I treated dogmatic understanding or the explicit grasp of these universal meanings. I now move to the consideration of dogmatic expression.

It should be clear, however, that this neat threefold division is largely analytic and conceptual. In concrete actuality, dogmatic meaning, understanding, and expression do not exist as separate entities; rather, they are integral aspects of a continuous process. Dogmatic and universal meanings never emerge without some concomitant explicit understanding; and explicit dogmatic understanding is never without some concomitant expression. Thus, I found it impossible to treat dogmatic understanding without constantly referring to dogmatic statements. This was inevitable because the achievement and manifestation of dogmatic understanding demands dogmatic expression. Hence too, in this section, although I explicitly treat dogmatic expression, I must refer constantly to the dogmatic meanings and the dogmatic understanding which dogmatic expression springs from and points back to.

GENERAL MEANING OF ENUNCIATION OR EXPRESSION

An enunciation or expression in the present context is simply a word, a symbol, a gesture, or an action that bodies forth and empirically represents in an imperfect, concrete, and relative manner an interior meaning. This definition implies the *universality, incompleteness, concreteness,* and *relativity* of expressions.

1. Man Universally Expresses Himself

Expressions are *universal*. Any and all activity can be an expression of meaning. The words we speak, the gestures we make, the involuntary emotions we express, the changes in temperature we experience, the ritual we practice—all these activities and many more express the explicit or implicit meanings operative in us. They are the prolongation of meaning into the world, and they exist as such because of the unity of man. A good case can be made that man always in some way expresses his significant interior meanings in his activity, whether he is conscious of that expression or not. Thus it is that no matter how hard a man tries to change his voice, it retains certain empirical characteristics that distinguish it from the voice of every other man. And it is no exaggeration to say that given the proper tools of empirical observation, a competent observer could distinguish any man on the planet by noting his ordinary expressive activity over a very short period of time. Man is forever expressing the meaning that is himself in all his activity. He is by nature an expressive being.

2. Man's Expressions are Incomplete

Man's expressions are inevitably *incomplete*. In making this assertion I do not mean to say that all observers are necessarily limited and that they therefore fail to detect all that is contained in any given expression. This is undoubtedly true. Rather, I mean that, because of his limited nature, no man can pour his whole self, his whole present meaning, in any one expression or chain of expressions. Man is an historical being, and he acts and becomes only in a succession of temporal moments. He never appears fully in any single expression; nor does any aspect of his being get bodied forth totally in any one expression. Only if he totally possessed and mastered himself in a single and integrated unity could the possibility of a complete expression even be considered.

Man says more than he intends to say. This imperfection of expression appears concretely in the fact that in every expression a man inevitably says both more and less than he intends to say. First, he says more than he explicitly intends to say. Suppose I wish to convey to a student that his paper is inadequate. In the process of speaking to him I reflect the fact that I had little sleep last night (I yawn), that I am displeased with him (the tone of my voice gives that away), and that I am bored with marking papers such as his own (the careless way I criticize his paper and the manner in which I toss it at him across the desk reveal my attitude). The point is that my whole concrete comportment says far more than I explicitly intended to say. It is this recurring phenomenon that permits psychiatrists to learn more about a man than he intends to tell them; and it is this that permits a good historian to know more about the real motivations of past ages than the men of these ages themselves knew.

Man says less than he intends to say. Secondly, he says less than he intends to say. This follows from the fact that no man ever fully grasps (at least in all but the simplest cases) the constituent elements of the understanding that he wishes to express; nor does he find at hand an appropriate expressive medium for every constituent element that he does grasp. On the one hand, all but the most elemental acts of understanding are cumulative. They are made up of a chain of constituent elements that build upon one another. Thus, if I understand the Pythagorean theorem, I do so only because I genuinely understand the prior theorems which constitute the basic elements of that understanding. Now if I attempt to express my understanding of the Pythagorean theorem in a complete way, I must consciously grasp all the elements that have gone into that ultimate understanding. I would have to grasp explicitly and express the whole process that leads to the theorem. This would be a formidable task, and in practice no teacher ever consciously adverts to all the elements that go into the theorem. He relies on the habitual understanding of his pupils to fill in the gaps of his present expression. Now what is true of abstract geometry is far more true of the expressions of complex circumstances of everyday life. We never fully advert to all the factors that go into our understanding of any complex situation. Hence we never fully pack our implicit understanding into our explicit expressions.

On the other hand, we frequently do not find an appropriate expression for one or more of the constituent elements that we do explicitly grasp. How often do we find ourselves in the situation in which we do clearly see how what we are trying to convey fits together; and yet we do not find available to us a symbolic system appropriate to the expression of the grasped meaning. The man who cannot tell his wife that he loves her, the scholar who utterly fails to communicate his rich understanding to his students, and the mystic who finds ordinary religious language woefully inept for imparting his experiences to others—all these illustrate in the extreme what to some extent happens in every effort we make to express ourselves.

3. Man's Expressions are Concrete

Man's expressions are *concrete*. All expressions—whether written or spoken words, gestures, actions—are products of concrete activity of which they are the terminal aspects. They are the result of concrete activity and are the terminal part of that activity. Because they are concrete, expressions inevitably body forth and represent more than one abstract meaning, although this may not be the intention of the individual who produces them. In other words, because expressions are concrete, it is possible for them to convey a multiplicity of abstract meanings; it is possible for them to say both more than the author intends to say and less than he intends to say. If a pure abstract expression were possible, then it would convey in an undiluted and simple way a single abstract meaning. There would be a one-to-one correspondence between abstract meaning as grasped by the subject and his expression. This, however, is impossible because our expressions are invariably concrete.

4. Man's Expressions are Relative

Finally, expressions are *relative*. By this I mean, in the first instance, that they are relative to the individual or social beings that produced them. They reflect the meaning consciously intended or subconsciously manifested by the beings that produced them. They reflect the imperfection, the incompleteness, and the concreteness of these beings.

The utter uniqueness of each concrete expression. This relativity of all concrete expressions leads to a number of consequences. First of all, it means that each expression is utterly unique in that it is reflective of a unique person or persons in a unique situation. The words I utter or write body forth in their concreteness a panoply of meanings that have never before existed as they do now. The tone of my voice, the curves in my writing, the emotions that lie behind my expression and the gestures that accompany it constitute as a whole a nonrepeatable event. No expression, *taken in its concrete entirety,* is ever exactly the same as any other expression.

The impossibility of duplicating concrete expressions. Secondly, any purported duplication of an expression is, therefore, only the duplication of one or more abstract aspects of the original concrete expression. I can duplicate the sounds you utter to the extent that a listener can identify your words and mine as manifestive of a reference to the same word in Webster's dictionary. But I cannot duplicate the whole range of emotions, attitudes, and meanings that your words in their concreteness body forth. I can reproduce on paper the text of a council, but that text as produced by me does not manifest the total connotation of meaning that existed in the minds of the council members. I can duplicate the features of your external moral acts to some extent; but no concrete act of mine will ever totally duplicate your act; nor can my concrete act actualize to the last detail the same array of human potentials that were actualized in your expression.

Attachment of an expression to a variety of meanings. The uniqueness and impossibility of duplication of concrete expressions are intensified by a third consideration. Expressions, especially verbal and symbolic ones, have a kind of independent existence insofar as they take shape on paper or are recorded on tape. In the limited abstract aspect in which they exist in these conserving media, they achieve a quasi-permanence. They are given the opportunity to live on. However, the meanings that are bodied forth by men tend to change as men and civilizations change, develop, and decline. The persistence of expressions, however, leads to the phenomenon by which the same expressions (I mean, of course, the external form of the expressions) manifest new sets of meanings. So it is that dictionaries record archaic meanings for words which now manifest different abstract meanings. So it is that certain forms of religious dress once symbolized piety but now, at least for some people, signify humorous anachronism.

I might add that the more arbitrary the form of an expression, the more it can be reflective of diversified meaning. Thus, words can reflect a whole range of meanings. It is possible for the same verbal form to actualize one set of meanings in one epoch and the contrary set in another epoch. However, bodily acts, in that they necessarily actualize basic experiential capacities of the person, do not admit of the same flexibility. Hence, while physical sexual expression obviously varies in its total concrete meaning from one person to another, yet the fact that such expression necessarily actualizes certain capacities common to all men means that there is an irreducible aspect of meaning that such activity must express at all times to some degree.

The consequent impossibility of universal expressions. This relativity of expression and the consequences that flow from it lead to the basic contention that while there can be universal abstract meanings, there cannot be any universal expressions. There are no concrete expressions that always and everywhere body forth the same set of abstract meanings. Universality belongs to the abstract, but all expressions pertain to the concrete.

This rather simple and innocuous statement has a number of implications of major importance. It implies, for example, that there are no words on paper, stone, or tape that have universal validity as relevant expressions of lasting meanings. Such expressions are necessarily relative. Hence there are no catechisms whose verbalizations constitute relevant expressions for every age and time. One simply cannot canonize the Baltimore Catechism or even the Catechism of the Council of Trent. Further, there are no verbal statements of the magisterium—even the verbalizations of an infallible pope or council—that, *as expressions*, have universal validity. In other words, such verbal formulas do not in every age and culture body forth and express the universal meaning that once produced them. Moreover, even the Scriptures are subject to this relativity of expression.

The same line of reasoning pertains to liturgical and moral expressions. There simply is no one lasting form of liturgy that always and everywhere bodies forth the universal meanings that underpin worship. Liturgy is a concrete expression, and as such it is relative to its time and place. It must body forth the universal Christian meanings in a given time and place; hence its form will always have to relate to that time and place. In like fashion, there are no concrete moral acts that always and in every context manifest the basic Christian moral drive towards total perfection. Taking interest on loans may be a relevant expression of universal Christian meanings in one historical context; it may be an immoral expression in another context. There are no concrete activities which in their concreteness always express the same universal meaning or set of universal meanings.

Admittedly this recognition of the relativity of all concrete expression poses major problems for the catechist, the theologian, the liturgist, and the ethician. I believe these problems can be solved, although this is not the place to attempt a solution. However, the solution cannot come about by absolutizing the expressions of the past—even the expressions of the Bible. It can only come about by recognizing explicitly the relativity of all expressions and by seeing these expressions as so many paths of entry to universal meanings. Christianity will be saved from absolute relativism only when it explicitly and wholeheartedly recognizes that its stability does not rest on the shaking reed of concrete expressions but on the solid rock of universal meanings.

FUNCTIONS OF ENUNCIATIONS OR EXPRESSIONS

In general, expressions have two functions: that of *directly* developing the subject; that of *indirectly* developing the recipient. Both functions occur simultaneously and both have individual and social facets or consequences.

1. *Expressions Directly Develop the Subject*

On the one hand, insofar as an expression bodies forth and projects an interior meaning or an already existing set of relationships, it leads *directly* to the further constitution and development of the subject or social body that produces it. Just as the interior word of understanding leads to the creation of further interior meaning and development, so too in its own way does the exterior word, symbol, gesture, or action. When an individual speaks his thoughts, the flow of words and the bodily mechanisms the flow actualizes inevitably call forth and activate a host of images, associations, feelings, and attitudes that are too fleeting and too subliminal to be explicitly grasped. This actualization of the capacities of the person necessarily leads to a change in him; and if that change is the fulfillment of already existing capacities, it constitutes a development. Thus it is that the expressive lover finds himself becoming a deeper lover, and the expressive teacher discovers, in the very course of his writing or speaking, facets of an explanation that previously had been veiled from him. Further, when a subject expresses himself in the presence of other subjects, their responses invariably trigger or occasion in him diverse constituent changes.

What is true of the words of the individual is also true of his other forms of expression. A man's gestures, his artistic expressions, and his varying symbols lead to the constitution of his being by the very fact that they body forth, however imperfectly, the meaning system that at present constitutes him. Above all, the concrete actions by which he expresses himself towards the world about him deepen, broaden, and, in the limit, transform his very being. To the degree that a man creatively grasps the potentials in his own being that can be expressed in society and finds appropriate actions to actualize these potentials in unity, to that degree does he grow through the constructive use of freedom.

Further, what is true of individual expressions is also true of social expressions. In the course of time a society develops its own language, its own symbolic systems, its own organizational patterns, and its own governmental structures. These expressions cut across individual differences and constitute means by which the society as a whole expresses itself. In the context in which I am now writing, such social expressions are simply means by which the interrelated persons who constitute the social body express themselves and thereby develop, distort, or transform their beings. These expressions are to the social body what individual expressions are to the individual; they lead to the development (or disintegration) of the subject society. In the measure that they actualize the genuine potentials of the members of the society in a rounded and integrated way, they promote the growth of the society. In the measure that they actualize the root potentials of the men concerned in a distorted way, they promote their retardation.

2. Expressions Indirectly Develop Their Recipient

On the other hand, expressions *indirectly* promote the development (or retardation) of the recipient towards whom they are directed. Expressions—whether verbal, symbolic, or concrete actions—communicate meaning to others by conditioning and altering their sensitive apprehensions, by provoking or retarding their understanding, by facilitating the making of new judgments. In the individual, this is obvious from the effects the activities of parents have on their children and teachers have on their students. However, this is also true of social expressions. The language spoken in a country, the social customs that prevail, the recurring features of the environment and the structures of government invariably affect each individual encountering them. Further, insofar as these structures mark one generation in the marrow of its bones, they also mark succeeding generations which are affected by those who have gone before. And insofar as the expressions of one generation are encased in traditional symbols, rites, and formulas, they can be catalysts for the growth and development of future generations which are exposed to them.

Thus, expressions as means of communication facilitate the change in the objects of the expressions. When they adequately express the subject and effectively communicate the meaning of the subject to the recipient persons, then they facilitate the unity of persons.

APPLICATION TO ECCLESIAL EXPRESSIONS IN GENERAL

The expressions of the Church I envision are its doctrinal formulas, its liturgical rites, its laws, and its governmental structures. Each of these in its concreteness bodies forth in an imperfect, relative, and unique way the living meanings that were constituent of the Church that produced them.

1. The Twofold Function of Ecclesial Expressions

As expressions they performed, and still perform, a twofold function in the Church. On the one hand, they contribute to the development of the body of Christ that expresses itself through them; on the other hand, they communicate the meanings expressed to others upon whom they have an effect. It is this latter function of communicating meaning to others (and hence helping transform them) that will preoccupy us in this study, although the former function is undoubtedly of equal importance. Thus, Scripture is not merely the means by which all subsequent ages in the Church come into more or less direct contact with the meanings of the primitive Christian community; it was also one of the great expressions by which that community constituted itself.

2. Classifying Ecclesial Expressions

What can be said about ecclesial expressions of the past and present viewed from the perspective of their nature as mediators of meaning to us? What relationship do these expressions have to the matter of infallibility?

First of all, it is improper to ascribe to expressions the attributes of fallibility or infallibility, of truth or falseness. These attributes apply properly to a grasp of meaning by a mind. When a mind asks a limited question of reality and subsequently apprehends all the data pertinent to that question, it can then become differentiated in a manner that corresponds to the unities and relationships present in the data; it grasps truth. Further, when the truth that is grasped constitutes a universal meaning, a meaning that would constitute a differentiation proper to the full development of all men, then the truth involved is subject to being grasped infallibly. When such an infallible grasp pertains to matters of faith, there then emerges the area of infallible religious truth.

Expressions are for their recipient in the Church only pointers to meaning. They more or less adequately represent the meaning or meanings present in the persons who produce them. They are intended to act as catalysts which facilitate the acquisition of meaning by the recipient. Truth is a quality of mind; expressions are markings on paper, in wood, on stone; they are sounds that are uttered, symbols that are utilized, actions that are performed. Neither the words, nor the symbols, nor the acts can be said to be true or false. Their adequacy or inadequacy will depend not only on the skill with which they are produced but also upon the capacity of their prospective audience to be catalyzed by them. Hence words once great can lose their existential moving power; symbols such as the cassock can evoke reactions ranging from awe to ridicule; and concrete actions such as interest-taking can be morally blamed and then subsequently accepted.

Secondly, expressions may be more meaningfully classified according to the range of meanings they represent and the differentiation of that range which they allow us to glimpse. Regarding the range of meanings, at one extreme are the expressions that represent a single abstract meaning. Mathematical statements are perhaps our best exemplification of this extreme; and this accounts for the fact that such statements are subject to minimal misinterpretation. In the Scriptures, the second of the two great commandments is somewhat like this type of statement (Mk. 12:31 and parallel passages). However, the second commandment allows for an almost unlimited expansion because it is heuristic in nature. At the other extreme are stories, symbols, and concrete acts—all of which body forth a host of meanings and hence are subject to a variety of interpretations. With regard to these expressions that represent a wide range of meanings, further distinctions can be made. Some manifest in their individual existence and surrounding context the intention of their author to point explicitly to one or more of the meanings bodied forth; many statements of councils fall into this category. Others indicate no such conscious intentionality because the person or Church which produced them had not come to conscious differentiation of meaning. However, at times the circumstances permit the perceptive observer to grasp in the expressions meanings that were actually operative in the author of the expression, even though he was not conscious of them and hence did not explicitly intend them.

APPLICATION TO SCRIPTURE'S EXPRESSIONS

On the basis of the foregoing distinctions about expressions, we can evaluate in a general way the Scriptures, the statements of the magisterium of subsequent epochs, and the expressions that pertain to the so-called secondary objects of infallibility. First of all, it is simplistic to refer to Scripture as the *norma non-normata* or as an infallible document. The Scriptures cannot be infallible because they are expressions, and infallibility is a category that does not pertain to expressions. Further, that which is a norm is not a text but a universal meaning. Hence, Scripture can only be a norm in the sense that it represents and bodies forth universal Christian meanings. However, it is clear that the Scriptures fall largely into the category of texts that represent a multiplicity of meanings of varying degrees of universality and in an undifferentiated manner. Rarely were universal Christian meanings grasped explicitly by authors of the Bible; never did these authors distinguish explicitly between meanings that were universal and meanings that pertained to their historically conditioned culture, because biblical man had not arrived at the stage of differentiation that would have made such distinctions possible.

If through the text we can now discern the universal religious meanings operative in the two testaments, this is largely due to the differentiation of consciousness made possible by the course of history. Thus, the resurrection of Christ referred to a universal meaning operative in the primitive Church; covenant referred to an operative meaning also. However, just what was universal in both concepts was not explicitly grasped because the question about universality had not been explicitly placed. If the biblical texts are a source for our grasp of such meanings, they are that source only in conjunction with the explicit differentiation of Christian consciousness that has taken place over the ages. If there is a *norma non-normata* of faith, it is the living grasp of universal meanings made possible by that conjunction of text and differentiated Christian consciousness. This, I submit, is what is ultimately meant by the dictum that the rule of faith is Scripture as read in the Church.

However, there are further limitations on the claims of Scripture as *norma non-normata*. These flow from the development of universal meanings in the post-biblical period. As I have indicated in the section on universal meanings, such developments are not merely logical prolongations of meanings represented in the Scriptures. Rather, they are also free and unpredictable developments of meanings universal to men who are touched by the Resurrection. Such meanings were contained in the New Testament Church only to the extent that the New Testament Church possessed the risen Christ and a humanity with potential structures that were universally developable. The biblical text could only represent the universal meanings then existing; it could not represent meanings not yet present in man. Hence it can function as a norm with regard to such future developments only in the restricted sense that it points out overriding heuristic categories that all future development must conform to. However, it should be stressed that Scripture can function even in this limited sense only because of a differentiated use of Scripture that emerged after the biblical epoch.

APPLICATION TO LATER MAGISTERIAL STATEMENTS

The statements of the magisterium of the Church differ markedly from those of Scripture. In the first place, the range of meanings pointed to by these statements is generally far more restricted and focalized. Scripture is full of concrete statements, that is, statements that refer to concrete beings or activities. Hence the Gospels abound in actions attributed to Christ, in parables, and in speeches delivered in unclarified context. The parables admit of innumerable interpretations and even more numerous applications. They are designed to make people think, and their meaning is usually not precisely narrowed down. The actions of Christ, like all concrete actions, can be read and interpreted from a multiplicity of viewpoints. Finally, the speeches, in that they are often disassociated from any known context, admit of a variety of implications. In contrast to this, the official teaching of the magisterium is couched in far more abstract, and hence restrictive, terms. Further, the range of possible meanings is narrowed down by the contextual nature of these statements, a context that is far better preserved than the context of scriptural utterances. Thus, we know there is only one possible meaning to be ascribed to many texts of Vatican II precisely because the speeches, the *modi*, and discussions that describe the context of these texts are available to us. Finally, because of a further and sharper differentiation of consciousness that had taken place subsequent to the biblical age, the men who produced the conciliar documents often clearly distinguished or explicated the basic meaning they intended in their utterances. Hence, while the reader can grasp other meanings in their expressions, yet he can know that one or more central meanings are what were explicitly intended by the authors. In most cases such explicit differentiation is not evidenced by the biblical texts.

However, even magisterial statements cannot *tout court* be labelled with the word "infallible." This is so, as we have seen, because infallibility properly applies to meanings and not to statements; it is so because much of magisterial teaching does not proceed from the fullest exercise of the Church's teaching office; finally, it is so because the vast bulk of magisterial teaching in the past was really a teaching that proclaimed the faith within the limited context of one culture. It enunciated meanings that were true within the context of that culture and given that culture's presuppositions. Thus, the matter and form of the sacraments as presented at Trent largely reflect what was truly the Church's official way of expressing the lasting meanings behind the sacraments within the context of its given historical existence. However, the meanings referred to by these statements on matter and form did not have validity in every possible culture.

Hence they are not universal meanings; and even a correct apprehension of the texts that point to them does not grasp universal meanings.

Further, if today we can grasp universal meanings that lie behind the intended meanings in magisterial statements, this does not directly follow from the expressions of the magisterium taken in isolation. It follows from the fact that these texts assist us, who have benefited from a further differentiation of meaning, to grasp the universal meanings that were operative but unexplicated and undifferentiated in the magisterial minds that produced the texts. It is the symbiosis of past texts as pointers to past meaning *and* further present ecclesial differentiation that allows us to grasp now those universal meanings which lie at the roots of infallibility.

APPLICATION TO SECONDARY OBJECTS OF INFALLIBILITY

1. The Kinds of Secondary Objects

One last set of expressions must be considered. I refer to what theology has called the "secondary objects of infallibility." In recent years this topic has rarely been treated in Roman Catholic writing. Formerly, however, it was a standard topic in the manuals. The basic notion was that the primary object of infallibility was the ensemble of truths *per se* revealed. This I explained in the section dealing with the teaching of Vatican I. The secondary objects of infallibility were said to be "other truths which are necessarily connected with revealed truths."[1] These other truths include (1) speculative truths which are logically connected with revealed truths; (2) dogmatic facts, especially of a doctrinal nature; (3) certain general disciplinary decrees; (4) solemn canonization of saints; (5) the definitive approbation of religious orders by the Holy See.[2]

A few explanations of these categories are in order. Speculative truths which are logically connected with revealed truths are of two kinds. Some are in the area of presuppositions. Thus, the very possibility of speaking about revealed truths presupposes the capacity of reason to know *in some way* truths that are beyond reason. Others are in the area of logical deductions from revealed truths.[3]

Dogmatic facts are also of two kinds. First, there are *simple* dogmatic facts like the legitimacy of the Council of Trent. The Church is said to be capable of infallibly declaring that Trent was a general council because, if it could not do this, its whole teaching office would be put in jeopardy and revelation itself would be imperiled. Secondly, there are *doctrinal* dogmatic facts. This refers to the determination of the meaning intended by a post-biblical author in a given text. The magisterium of the Church was said to be capable of infallibly deciding that the meaning intended by such an author was either orthodox or heretical.[4]

General disciplinary decrees refer to laws universally imposed by the supreme authority of the Church as a means of ordering the lives of Christians throughout the world. Such laws may be in the area of Christian discipline (e.g., universal laws of fasting); they may have to do with the liturgical rites of the Mass and the other sacraments; finally, they may be in the area of means for promoting the preaching of the Gospel. In each case, infallibility is said to be operative to the degree that the laws in question imply doctrinal truths.[5] This does not mean that these laws are the best possible. It only means that they contain nothing contrary to faith, morals, or the salvation of souls.[6]

The solemn canonizations of saints are the definitive decrees of the universal Church by which certain Christians are declared to have been received into heaven. These saints are then proposed to the veneration and imitation of the faithful. The precise aspect under which these decrees are said to be infallible is difficult to ascertain in the manuals. It is generally claimed that grave harm would be worked in the Church if men were venerated as saints who *de facto* were sinners. The historical difficulties with a number of men who were long venerated as saints, the ambiguity and sinfulness of all men (the saints included), the precise meaning of veneration of men long dead—all these constitute areas that the manualist tradition failed to treat or lightly brushed over.

Finally, the definitive approbation of a religious order by the Holy See is said to be infallible in that it guarantees that the way of life commended is *apt* for living out perfection according to the evangelical counsels. In other words, the general set-up of the order so approved implies nothing contrary to the Gospel directives for the attainment of Christian perfection.

The reader who is unaccustomed to these categories will doubtlessly feel himself propelled back into another age. It is difficult to imagine that this terminology was used universally in standard Roman Catholic works well into the fifth and even the sixth decade of the twentieth century. It must be recalled, however, that no claim ever was made that these five categories (there are other ways of dividing the material) had been proclaimed by the magisterium to be within the scope of its prerogative of infallibility. Theologians did the proclaiming, and this became common theological doctrine. Only in the sixth decade of this century was there any questioning of the propriety and scope of infallibility with regard to the secondary objects, and such attempts were sporadic and largely of a superficial nature.

2. Theorizing about the Secondary Objects

The general argument. I would like to suggest that a rethinking of the whole matter in terms of the framework I have set up will reveal both the validity and the limitations of the past teaching on secondary objects of infallibility. The basic point I would make is that the secondary objects do not lie in the realm of meaning but in that of expression. The Church can be infallible only in the area of the universal meanings that are associated with living faith in the risen Christ; this is always the area of the primary object of infallibility. However, the Church lives in a concrete ambiguous world, and it cannot exist and preach only in the realm of abstract meaning. It must proclaim its message in a relevant manner and in terms that make sense to the milieu in which it operates. The secondary objects of infallibility constitute an aspect of this relevant proclamation.

We have come to realize that neither the texts of Scripture nor those of the solemn magisterium of the Church of subsequent ages are to be identified with the revelation of God. Rather, they are theological expressions in which the official Church manifests its realization of the truth out of which it lives. In varying degrees, they are shot through with all sorts of temporally conditioned meanings that do not transcend the boundaries of the situations in which the texts were formulated. Even though these expressions take the form of words (and hence tend to be more in the area of the abstract and the universal), yet they bear aspects that are concrete and particular and, therefore, perishable.

Application of the argument to speculative truths. What must now be realized is that the so-called secondary objects of infallibility represent a variety of even more concrete expressions in which the Church attempts to manifest to the modern world those lasting meanings that constitute her identity. In pointing out speculative truths that are logically connected with revealed truth, the Church shows its recognition of the presence of its universal patrimony in the various areas touched by the human sciences. In the past, the one area touched was the area of philosophy, although there were some forays (perhaps unfortunate ones, at times) into such areas as human origins and evolution. At present, it is becoming evident that the Church will more and more move into the areas studied by psychology, sociology, economics, and politics. What must be noted in each case is that the Church *can* bear infallible judgments in all cases only to the extent that the questions touched manifest or deny aspects of *universal saving truth*. However, since the issues the complex human sciences deal with are invariably penetrated with the conditioned, the problematical and the time-bound, it is inevitable that Church pronouncements regarding them will have to reflect a host of assumptions and attitudes which, of their nature, do not pertain to the universality of saving truth. No one can meaningfully enter into the area of the concrete and the temporally conditioned— even in the name of universal truth—without becoming involved to some extent with the nonuniversal. Hence the pronouncements of the Church in these areas will necessarily contain a good deal of perishable wrapping around the core of universal truth. That wrapping was unavoidable even in the Scriptures, which dealt with a relatively simple environment; how much more is it unavoidable in pronouncements about complex modern questions. The key point is that the Church looks upon human situations as so many attempts to live out the universal patrimony that she bears. In judging such situations, she attempts to point out what she sees in them which either manifests or contradicts that patrimony. She is convinced, even infallibly, of the validity of that patrimony. However, she cannot make an infallible judgment about its presence in any given situation; for there is no infallible prophecy. Ultimately what she is saying is that some given situation or teaching either adequately or inadequately expresses her universal teaching in a modern context. She can be infallible only about that patrimony and not about the present concrete circumstances. To put this in other words, we can set up a comparison between past ecclesial statements of Scripture and the magisterium *and* present ecclesial statements touching on speculative truths related to revelation. Both kinds of ecclesial statements are attempts to express universal saving ecclesial meanings. The first more or less adequately points to these meanings in faith expressions that reflect a host of other less universal meanings; the second more or less adequately points to these meanings as they are embedded in speculative scientific concepts. In both cases, the complexity and the ambiguity of the media within which the Church seeks to point out universal saving meaning preclude that the judgment of infallibility should attach to the evaluation of these media. Only when a so-called speculative truth actually coincides with or contradicts a universal saving meaning can the Church pronounce infallibly upon it.

Application of the argument to dogmatic facts. Similar reasoning pertains to the secondary objects known as dogmatic facts. What the living Church can do with regard to a general council is not to recognize infallibly that it fulfilled certain juridic conditions for a council but to recognize that its decrees more or less adequately manifest the Church's present possession of universal saving truth. The living Church, in effect, re-cognizes the presence of its patrimony in the expressions of the past. Similarly, in judging the text of an author to be orthodox or not, the Church is saying that the text in question more or less adequately represents or misrepresents universal saving truth in a given context. This follows from the fact that no expression—even that of Scripture—can be said to express the faith infallibly. To accord to Church officials the power to read infallibly an author's intention or to declare infallibly the validity or nonvalidity of forms of expression in given historical contexts is to grant to these officials a prophetic infallibility that belongs to God alone, and it is to attach to a judgment on an expression a note of certitude that pertains properly only to meaning. Infallibility is a quality that attaches only to the act of understanding. It can no more be predicated of an expression than love can be predicated of water.

Application of the argument to other secondary objects. The canonization of saints, the definitive approbation of the way of life of a religious order, and universal disciplinary decrees accord with the same reasoning. In them the Church recognizes a more or less adequate concretization of certain lasting aspects of her tradition. If she can recognize these aspects in verbal formulations, then she can also recognize them when they appear in a way of life, in a legal decree, and in the concrete history of a saintly individual. What canonization of saints and "canonization" of rules have in common is that they are enfleshments of universal saving truth. Both are concrete, though the former is obviously more concrete than the latter. Both are relevant; for they attempt to point out in rules or persons the universal saving norms that pertain to the modern age.[7]

Summary of the argument on secondary objects. In summary, the so-called secondary objects of infallibility pertain to the area of expression. They manifest universal saving meaning. Because these expressions are concrete and multifaceted, they are not simply identified with that saving meaning. Their acceptance by the Church only means that in them the Church sees expressed in a more or less adequate manner the universal truths by which she lives and by which she is identified. These expressions cannot be called infallible truths, any more than Scripture can be called an infallible document. Infallibility should be restricted to the grasp of universal meanings. Hence the very term "secondary objects of infallibility" is, I suggest, misleading. I believe that it would be better to speak of "secondary expressions" of revealed truth in contradistinction to the primary expressions of Scripture and the solemn decrees of the magisterium.

Suggested new distinctions and terminology. If the foregoing is accepted, I believe that it will not be long before new terminology representing a different division of meaning will come into use in theology. In place of the distinction dividing truths into natural and supernatural, there will be a distinction between meanings and their expressions. The supernatural-natural distinction will be eclipsed because the *de facto* universe is intrinsically called to one end, the vision of God in Christ. Further, all truth in this one universe in which the risen Christ as Lord is fully present to all reality is what might be called in the older terminology "supernatural truth." In the meaning-expression distinction, both meaning and expression will be differentiated. Meaning will be divided into universal meaning and limited meaning; the former will refer to those aspects of self-differentiation that constitute a part of the good development of all persons; the latter will refer to good aspects of self-differentiation that pertain only to some persons. Finally, expressions will be recognized as falling on a continuum. At one extreme will be those expressions such as words referring to abstract concepts that tend to manifest a single meaning. At the other end will be those expressions that by their very concreteness manifest a multiplicity of meanings. With this shift in terminology it will be easier to explicate the fact that infallibility pertains to the area of meaning and not to that of expression.

Reconciliation of this view with the past. While all this would appear to shift away from the path that theology has taken in the days since the Council of Trent, I would suggest that the shift basically accords with the ancient past of the Church. In this connection I would recall that the past tended to look upon dogma and heresy in a far broader way than we currently do. At various times dogma embraced (1) a doctrine founded on the Christian faith or (2) a disciplinary decision. Heresy embraced even practices that were contrary to Church usage.[8] I would suggest that this state of affairs arose from the deep-seated recognition that dogma and heresy were not simply affairs of conceptual knowledge but aspects of a lived-out faith. However, in the absence of clear distinctions between meaning and expression and in the failure to distinguish the culturally conditioned from the transcultural, the natural tendency was to group together all expressions of faith-meaning or its denial under the heading of dogma or heresy. It was only the Franciscan Philippe Neri Chrismann (1751–1810) who gave to the term "dogma" its more limited modern sense. "A dogma of faith is nothing other than a doctrine and a divinely revealed truth, doctrine and truth which the public judgment of the Church proposes to be believed by divine faith in such a way that the contrary is condemned by the same Church as heretical teaching."[9] Unfortunately this modern notion has tended to make dogma a largely conceptualistic item in the life of the average Catholic, something the older and broader notion of dogma did not do. I do not believe that we can return to the past. However, we can have the best of the old and the new by recognizing that there are (1) universal transcultural, enduring dogmatic meanings and (2) an unlimited number of possible culturally conditioned expressions of those meanings in word, symbol, and action. By dividing the pie into meanings and their expressions and by acknowledging distinctions in the kinds of meanings and expressions, we preserve both the all-inclusiveness of the older way of viewing things and the scientific precision of the modern way.

Epilogue

A NEW SITUATION—VAST PLURALISM

A new situation exists in the Church. We have a pluralism of both meaning and expression to a degree that the past never knew. On the one hand, there is pluralism of meaning. It results from the attempt to root the lasting meaning of the Christian tradition in a multiplicity of cultures and subcultures. This attempt inevitably brings new aspects of the old tradition to light because each culture questions that tradition in a new way. Since different questions are asked, new and different answers are given. These new answers may not fulfill the ancient tradition in going beyond it; in this case they are false and must be rejected. However, they may be legitimate fulfillments; in this case they should be accepted. To set forth the criteria for judging such developments is beyond the scope of this book. Here I would state only that the effort to enroot the old tradition in a multiplicity of cultures constitutes the basic condition that makes our time a matrix of pluralistic Christian meanings.

On the other hand, there is a pluralism of expression. This occurs not only because each culture and subculture tends to have different words, actions, and symbols for the same meanings; it occurs also because the different meanings brought to light in different cultures tend to breed their own particular expressions. Moreover, there is a tendency for different cultural groups to attribute to the same external word or action or symbol a partially different meaning; and this, in reality, changes the expression. This multiplication of both meaning and expression in our time constitutes an enormous problem for the Church. What formerly occurred slowly over the centuries is now occurring simultaneously all over a world made aware of differences by rapid transportation and instantaneous communication. How can the Church maintain its unity in such diverse circumstances?

MEETING THE PROBLEM OF PLURALISM

I believe that the problem of reconciling pluralism of meaning and expression with the need for unity in the Church can be solved on the basis of what I have indicated in this treatment of infallibility. This solution can take place in what can best be termed an hierarchical manner. At the broad base of the hierarchical pyramid are the particular culturally conditioned meanings of individual local Churches and their appropriate cultural expressions. These meanings and their expressions, precisely because they enroot the one faith in a given historically conditioned cultural context, are not and cannot be universal. They pertain, and rightly so, only to the Church of a given place and time, not only because they contain elements of meaning and expression that arise from a concrete situation, but also because the universal elements they embody are ordinarily not consciously envisioned at the high degree of abstraction that makes them transcultural and universal. Thus, in the agricultural economy of the early Middle Ages, taking interest was seen to be a sin. Practically no one could explicitly grasp the transcultural conditions that made this type of activity sinful in that particular cultural situation. The understanding of the average Christian was local and limited; it was for a given time and place; yet it embodied the faith for that time. It was a relevant expression, as all professions of faith should be.

However, it is not enough that there should be a multiplicity of local realizations and expressions of universal Christian meanings. There must also be *some* men who are capable of seeing that these varied local meanings and local expressions are actually manifestive of what is transcultural and universal. Further, they must be capable of articulating their understanding, so that it can be made manifest that a true Christian unity does exist. Such men should be the bishops of the Church; and men who cannot perform this function should not be selected as bishops. For the bishop should be the symbol of the unity of the Church; and he can no longer be that unless he can grasp the unity of faith as it exists in many cultures and subcultures. When bishops, aided by others who speak for the Church—both clerical and lay persons—are capable of seeing that the culturally conditioned understandings and expressions of the faith in their respective dioceses are so many concrete projections into new situations of more abstract and universal traditional meanings, then the basis of a unity in pluralism will be established.

This solution frankly recognizes that in practice there cannot be a single *operative* creed, a single moral code, and a single liturgy for the whole Church. By an operative creed I mean a statement of Christian meanings that expresses for the men of a given situation the faith that is alive in them. Such a creed would have to be a culturally conditioned expression because the average Christian could not see an attempt at a transcultural creed as reflective of the faith that lives in him. Instead, such a creed would appear to him as a jumble of words divorced from his living context, something like the Nicene Creed we recite at Mass. That Nicene Creed is not an operative creed because it embodies transcultural meanings in the language of another day; it does not express for the average Christian what his faith life means to him.[1] Further, what is true of an operative creed is also true of a moral code and a liturgy. These have to have roots in the concrete life of a people of a specific culture if they are to enable men to grow towards God by expressing their relationship to him from where they are. Differences in the practical conditions of life and in the stock of symbols of a people make it imperative that the moral code and the liturgy be adjusted for them.

However, I do not mean to assert that it is impossible for the Church to articulate a transcultural creed, a transcultural moral teaching, and transcultural principles of liturgy.[2] I believe that men in the Church can come to transcultural understanding by recognizing as embedded in their historically conditioned experiential continua those elements that are universal and transcultural. Further, I believe that they can point to these elements by a series of words, a formula. Such a formula, considered precisely as an expression, would of necessity have nothing of the transcultural about it. However, it would point to what was lasting and could be identified as pointing to it by those who had achieved the requisite level of abstraction. The belief that we cannot achieve supracultural understanding and corresponding supracultural formulations springs from a failure to grasp the distinction between *heuristic* formulations (which indicate the universal relationships and processes that generate all cultural formulations) and *conceptual* formulations (which indicate the results of the implementation of generic heuristic relationships and processes in a given culture). There cannot be any universally valid conceptual understanding and formulation; there can be a universal heuristic grasp and formulation. It is true, however, that no one can ever grasp a universal heuristic relationship or process (and *a fortiori* the meaning of their corresponding formulations) except in the concrete experiential continua of a given culture. In fact, it is only by the process of

living and thinking in the context of two or more cultures that a man
ordinarily comes to a grasp of what is transcultural. Our age has
facilitated that process because even men who live their lives in a
single geographical context find that they have passed through a
number of different cultural situations.

I would see the situation in which both pluralism and unity are
maintained as one which includes: (1) a group of culturally conditioned Churches expressing the universal patrimony of the Church
in their own language, symbols, and particular actions; (2) a number
of men clustered around the bishop of each diocese who grasp what
is truly universal in the traditional meanings of the Church and are
capable of judging when the Church in their area is living out (or not
living out) that tradition in its own distinct concrete manner; and
(3) communication between these men under the pope with regard
to their common possession of transcultural Christian meanings,
effected through transcultural formulations which indicate to them,
and through them to their respective flocks, that all are part of the
same universal Church.

THE PRESENT VALUE OF DOGMATIC DEFINITIONS

The overriding importance of dogmatic statements should now
be clear. These are formulations that are recognized by the Church
to represent its conscious grasp of the transcultural meanings that
constitute its unity over space and time. They symbolize all that
makes for unity in the created reality that is the visible Church. As
such, they have undimmed importance for the maintaining and deepening of unity; for the way to deepen a value is to express it, and the
expression of the substratum of unity in verbal terms is a valuable
form of such expression, even if it is not the only form of it.

Nor should we be deterred by the fact that in former times the
articulation of dogmas came about largely at the instance of heretics.
This has led a number of theologians to say that the Church should
define only when there is definite heresy to be opposed. Definitions
are thought to be limiting factors in the life of the Church, if not *per
se*, yet in their historical circumstances and their concrete effects on
the life of the Christian people. I believe that this objection, though
correct in its evaluation of the historical consequences of many past
definitions, does not reach the heart of the matter. On the one hand,

it misses the main positive intrinsic reason for a definition; on the other hand, it fails to see the liberating qualities that can flow from a definition rightly conceived and promulgated.

On the one hand, the ultimate reason why the Church must define dogma is not in order to put down heretics but in order to express itself and its unity over the ages. Man is so constituted individually and socially that he must express himself if he is to grow out towards the infinite God. Infallible definitions are only the definitive ecclesiological implementation of this basic dynamic. Now it is true that the Church becomes aware of the truth it possesses (or better, that truth which possesses the Church) only when it is challenged in some way. We see an answer only after we are aware of the question to which it corresponds; and the Church sees a particular facet of the truth it lives by only when that facet is called into question by historical circumstances. In the past, that questioning largely came about through the efforts of men who pushed forward the frontiers of understanding by asking new questions and proposing new answers. Inevitably, by the very nature of experiments with new aspects of truth, a number of these efforts were heretical; statistically, many of these efforts could be counted on to fail; and because of the personal attachment of innovators to their creations, the propounders of erroneous new theories could often be counted on to refuse to acknowledge their failure. In addition, the tendency of the champions of orthodoxy to back prospective heretics into corners did not help matters. Finally, the past situation was complicated by the fact that the culturally conditioned nature of ordinary concepts and formulations was hardly recognized. Hence, by and large, the story of heresy is not so much one of good men versus bad men as it is one of confused and struggling men attempting to articulate new thoughts from a variety of matrices.

However, the past is not the present. There is now at work a new dynamism pushing the Church towards dogmatic articulation. That dynamism derives from the *recognized* existence of various culturally conditioned formulations, activities, and symbols. The recognition at first reveals great differences, for we tend as human beings to notice first the respects in which men and situations differ. However, after the differences are recognized, one gradually comes to see those things that persist through all differences. This is the peaceful and nonpolemical way in which transcultural universal Christian meanings come to consciousness. In other words, that consciousness of the common patrimony of the Church which was formerly occasioned by heretical formulations is now being occasioned by the living out of the faith in many cultures and subcultures which are in communication with one another. In either case, the recognition of common transcultural meaning needs to be expressed by the very dynamism of human living. Just because such articulations of the Church in the past also (and even primarily) tended to be the means of identifying heretics and heresies does not mean that this must always be so. A definition can be and should be, first of all, a proclamation of the truth that is in the whole Church. Only *per accidens* should it be the means of indicating heretics.

On the other hand, a definition that is rightly conceived and promulgated should be a liberating factor in the Church and not a restricting one. Once it is realized far and wide that the Church can define only universal aspects of truth, and not culturally conditioned ones, the faithful can begin to see this liberating characteristic. Such a definition can act as a spur and a challenge to men of each age to appropriate that which necessarily pertains to the good Christian development of all men of all ages. Such an appropriation would enable Christians to unlock the store of spontaneity in their innermost natures; for in realizing those values that pertain to the universal structure of Christian development, persons are freed for further growth in the dimension of values. It should be noted, however, that this liberating effect does not take place by the mere conceptual grasp of transcultural truth. It is only when such truth is deeply internalized by concrete implementation and a spirit of prayer that it transforms the whole of a person and makes him into a deeper and more integral Christian. The more one actualizes the basic normative values of Christianity that have been articulated in the creeds, the more one realizes in himself that personal Christian existence that constitutes the foundation of a genuine Christian spontaneity. By internalizing in a concrete way, in one's own place and time, the enduring values of the Christian tradition, a person *becomes* that truth which makes one free. To be ignorant and maldeveloped, to be disunified and unintegrated in one's realization of Christianity, is to be unfree and unspontaneous; for one is limited and confined by the inner lack of realization of the faith. To have internalized the truth of Christianity in a global way; to have emotionalized it, attitudinalized it, understood it, willed it, expressed it in word and symbol and action—this is the road to freedom. "The truth will make you free" (Jn. 8:32).

A BROADER FUNCTION OF THE MAGISTERIUM

This liberating capacity of internalized and integrated truth (but not of truth that is largely of a conceptual nature) points the way to a broader function of the magisterium of the Church. That magisterium should not be satisfied with articulating the truth in conceptual terms. Rather, it must explicate the truth for the service and development of persons. It must make use of our present knowledge of how truth is communicated and personally assimilated; it must utilize, where appropriate, such techniques as feedback, group discussion, and the invitation of criticism by informed persons. It must encourage the participation of the members of the Church in the formulation of doctrine itself. The reason for this is not that each member of the Church is as competent as the hierarchy in the matter of understanding and articulating the tradition; if this were so, then we obviously would not have been choosing the right people as bishops. Nor is the reason that we must have democracy in the Church; once one realizes that the Church is built on a tradition, the notion that each man's opinion (quite apart from the degree in which the tradition shapes his life) is as good as that of the next man becomes nonsense. Rather, all must share in the formulation of doctrine to the extent that this is necessary for the common internalization of truth, which is the goal of all doctrinal teaching. The magisterium does not exist in order that Christian truth shall be verbally proclaimed; it exists to serve the function of promoting the internalization of the truth in all the faithful; and it is morally bound to use whatever means are necessary to promote that end.

Notes

CHAPTER 1

1. Gustave Thils, *Orientations de la Théologie* (Louvain: Éditions Ceuterick, 1958).
2. *Problemi e Orientamenti di Teologia Dommatica* (Milan: Marzorati, 1957), I, II. See also the briefer, though more up-to-date, German work of the same period: Johannes Feiner, Josef Trütsch, and Franz Böckle, eds., *Fragen der Theologie heute*, 2nd ed. (Zürich and Cologne: Benziger, 1958).
3. The literature on historical method and hermeneutics is quite considerable. For the Protestant theological development of the subject consult the following: James M. Robinson and John B. Cobb, Jr., eds., *The New Hermeneutic* (New York, Evanston and London: Harper and Row, 1964); Van A. Harvey, *The Historian and the Believer* (New York: Macmillan Co., 1966); Robert Funk, *Language, Hermeneutic, and Word of God* (New York: Harper and Row, 1966); Langdon Gilkey, *Naming the Whirlwind: The Renewal of God-Language* (Indianapolis and New York: Bobbs-Merrill Co., 1969), especially pp. 191–203 which summarize and criticize recent Protestant developments. For a brief present-day introduction to the question see Paul Achtemeier, *An Introduction to the New Hermeneutic* (Philadelphia: Westminster Press, 1969). For treatment of the hermeneutical question by Catholic theologians see R. Lapointe, *Les Trois Dimensions de L'Herméneutique* (Paris: Gabalda, 1967); René Marlé, *Le Problème Théologique de L'Herméneutique* (Paris: Éditions de l'Orante, 1968); Edward Schillebeeckx, "Towards a Catholic Use of Hermeneutics," in his *God the Future of Man* (New York: Sheed and Ward, 1968), pp. 3–49; Otto Muck, "Zum Problem der existentiellen Interpretation," in *Zeitschrift für katholische Theologie*, 91 (1969), 274–288; Joseph Möller, "Hermeneutisches Denken als Problem und Aufgabe," in *Theologische Quartalschrift*, 149 (1969), 392–398. Behind these more theologically oriented writings and the many others of which they are but a small sampling lie a host of more basic philosophical works. Among these are Thomas Kuhn, *The Structure of Scientific Revolutions* (Chicago: University of Chicago Press, 1962); Israel Scheffler, *Science and Subjectivity* (Indianapolis, New York and Kansas City: Bobbs-Merrill Co., 1967); Abraham Maslow, *The Psychology of Science* (Chicago: Henry Regnery Co., 1969); Stanley Jaki, *Brain, Mind and Computers* (New York: Herder and Herder, 1969); Peter L. Berger and Thomas Luckmann, *The Social Construction of Reality* (Garden City: Doubleday & Company, 1966); Maurice Mandelbaum,

The Problem of Historical Knowledge (New York: Harper and Row, 1967);
R. G. Collingwood, *The Idea of History* (London: Oxford University Press,
1956); Bernard J. F. Lonergan, *Insight* (London: Longmans, Green and Co.,
1957); Michael Polanyi, *Personal Knowledge* (Chicago: University of Chicago
Press, 1958); Henri Marrou, *The Meaning of History* (Baltimore: Helicon,
1966); Hans-Georg Gadamer, *Wahrheit und Methode*, 2nd ed. (Tübingen:
J. C. B. Mohr, 1965); J. V. Langmead Casserley, *Toward a Theology of His-
tory* (New York: Holt, Rinehart and Winston, 1965); Michael Polanyi, *The
Tacit Dimension* (Garden City: Doubleday & Company, 1966); Emilio Betti,
Allgemeine Auslegungslehre als Methodik der Geisteswissenschaften
(Tübingen: J. C. B. Mohr, 1967); Ray L. Hart, *Unfinished Man and the
Imagination* (New York: Herder and Herder, 1968); Emerich Coreth,
"Hermeneutik und Metaphysik," in *Zeitschrift für katholische Theologie*, 90
(1968), 422–450; Emerich Coreth, *Grundfragen der Hermeneutik* (Freiburg:
Herder, 1969); Gordon Leff, *History and Social Theory* (University of Ala-
bama Press, 1969); Richard E. Palmer, *Hermeneutics* (Evanston: Northwestern University Press, 1969). I would like to acknowledge the formative influence of many of the pages of the works cited above on my own thought.
As the body of this volume will indicate, however, there are varying degrees
and kinds of dependence on past authors and one often cannot acknowledge
that dependence by citing specific pages. Where this is possible, I shall do so.
I should remark here that the work of Bernard Lonergan has had greater
influence on these pages than that of any other writer.

4. Actually, as I shall attempt to demonstrate, present understanding must
be superior to past understanding if texts are to be interpreted correctly.

5. Hence there are crucial times in life for certain experiences. If a baby is
not caressed at a certain stage, he may be irreparably damaged. See the
summary of the results of studies of babies made by R. A. Spitz in L. Joseph
Stone and Joseph Church, *Childhood and Adolescence: A Psychology of
the Growing Person* (New York: Random House, 1957), pp. 62–66.

6. In point of fact, no word *only* represents prior understanding. In the
concrete context that each word in a text finds itself, it is always productive
of some experiential effect. Poe's *The Raven* is an example of a poetic combination of words that as words convey more than a specific past meaning.
However, the ability of words to convey more than past meaning is not confined to poetry, though it is best exemplified in that medium. Some of the
reasons why this is so will become clear in the course of this work.

7. Lonergan, *Insight*, pp. 25–30.

8. *Ibid.*, pp. 19–25.

9. For remarks pertinent to mythological expression see *ibid.*, pp. 530–546.

10. *Ibid.*, pp. 553–558.

11. For a brief summary of views on the *sensus plenior* and pertinent bibliography see Raymond Brown, "Hermeneutics," in *The Jerome Biblical*

Commentary (Englewood Cliffs, N.J.: Prentice-Hall, 1968), Section 71:56-70.

12. See Albert Mehrabian, "Communication Without Words," in *Psychology Today*, 2 (September 1968), 53-55. According to Mehrabian, 55 percent of the impact of communication is facial, 38 percent is vocal, and only 7 percent is verbal. For a longer treatment see M. Wiener and Albert Mehrabian, *Language Within Language: Immediacy, a Channel in Verbal Communication* (New York: Appleton-Century-Crofts, 1968).

13. By this sentence I distinguish implicit from explicit errors by the recipient with regard to meanings implied in another's communication. I implicitly err when I "feel" or vaguely intuit in another's expression meanings that are in no way there, not even implicitly. I explicitly err when I conceptualize such implicit errors.

14. In the concise terms of Bernard Lonergan, *Insight*, p. 582, this is set forth as follows: "The proximate source of the whole experiential component in the meaning of both objective and subjective interpreters lies in their own experience; the proximate source of the whole intellectual component lies in their own insights; the proximate source of the whole reflective component lies in their own critical reflection."

15. I believe that it is the failure of many authors to steep themselves in the subject matter of their investigation that has weakened their treatments of infallibility. Infallibility has to do with the way men of the Church of the past came to certitude. If the present interpreter wishes to grasp what they meant when they described the process of coming to the certitude of faith, then he must first make a self-critical study of how he himself comes to understanding and certitude. Mere exegetical techniques, though necessary, are not sufficient. No one believes that an historian of the nineteenth century can faithfully interpret Gauss without having first acquired an experiential continuum differentiated by mathematical understanding. Yet it is often taken for granted that a Church historian can write a history of the origins of the doctrine of infallibility or conduct an investigation of the meaning of Vatican I on the subject without spending a good deal of effort in differentiating his own experiential continuum in the area of how men come to understanding and certitude.

16. It is said that the interpreter comes to an understanding of the meaning of his text by reading it in context. However, what reading a text in context might mean is often not clarified. I would say that to read a text in context is to grasp its meaning against the background of the constellation of insights (also represented in the texts) that are preliminary to and contributory to the meaning of the specific text under consideration. Thus, to grasp what Euclid meant in his exposition of the Pythagorean theorem is to grasp the genetic sequence of meanings expressed in other theorems that lead up to and make understandable the proof in this theorem about right-angled tri-

angles. One does not have to grasp all the feelings that Euclid had in the process of writing his geometry, even if Euclid had expressed those feelings in the margins of his text; for such feelings are not pertinent to the context of the Pythagorean theorem. Similarly, in interpreting a given historical or theological text, I need not relive the whole life experience of the author of the text as that experience shines through the corpus of his work. I must, however, duplicate in my own person the complementary and genetic insights that grounded and made possible the terminal insight behind the text I am studying. Only then do I know the author's context. From this it becomes apparent why it is often difficult to approximate the more profound meanings of the texts of the past. Such meanings are embedded in a vast complex of interdependent insights that must first be grasped as the context within which they emerge. For an interesting modern approach to this question see Jean-Marc Laporte, "The Dynamics of Grace in Aquinas: A Structural Approach," *Theological Studies*, 34 (June 1973), 203-226.

17. Explicit error can spring from the fact that one has not experienced certain elements pertinent to the question at hand or from the fact that one does not advert to elements present in one's experiential continuum which are relevant to that question.

18. In his *Autobiography*, which is not presently available to me, R. G. Collingwood held that we can only understand what a past figure really thought if his thought was true. His reasoning is summed up by T. M. Knox in his preface to Collingwood's *The Idea of History* (London: Oxford University Press, 1956), pp. xi-xii. "It is impossible to understand what Plato thought without discovering what problem he tried to solve; and if the problem can be identified, that is proof that he solved it, because we only know what the problem was by arguing back from the solution. It follows that it is impossible to discover what Plato thought without simultaneously discovering whether his thought was true. . . . If this analogy be pressed, the inference would seem to be that we can understand a philosopher's problem only when he has solved his problem correctly, so that all philosophical writings are either true or unintelligible."

Knox rightfully objects to this point of view because it seems to him that we are able to detect errors and erroneous views in past texts and to understand why they are errors. The present discussion indicates why this is so and why Collingwood went wrong. Collingwood correctly saw that the human mind can understand only that which is intelligible, unifiable, coherent. Regarding past texts, the mind can supply only coherent hypotheses that make consistent sense of the marks on paper. It is the coherence of a man's thought that enables the future interpreter to grasp what it might have been. If, *per impossibile*, a man's writings were totally inconsistent, so that a given thought did not correspond to any other and he constantly varied the symbols used to represent his thought, then no one would be able to supply an interpretation. The case is analogous to that of a code in which, arbitrarily and without consistency, a set of symbols are substituted for sentences in a book. If a different symbol is used for the same meaning each time that meaning occurs, then it will be impossible to crack the code. It is consistency that permits one to crack a verbal code, and it is also consistency in thought that enables one to "crack" a past meaning.

However, a series of past meanings may be coherent and intelligible without being correct. They will be coherent if they unify the data they envision. They will be correct only if the data they unify correspond to *all* the data pertaining to the question in hand as those data appear in the external world. Hence, it is possible for a present interpreter to grasp a past meaning insofar as he grasps the data perceived by the former writer and the unity that that writer saw in the data. But it is also possible for the present interpreter to see the error in the past writer in that he supplies data that the past writer missed and hence arrives at a different unifying explanation. Collingwood's mistake, therefore, was to confuse the intelligibility and coherence required of a past text with its correctness.

I might add that the present analysis of why Collingwood went wrong is in itself an example of the manner in which the subsequent interpreter can grasp the meaning of a coherent but false past view.

19. See Leslie Dewart, *The Foundations of Belief* (New York: Herder and Herder, 1969), pp. 302–334, for another view of this question.

20. The works of Gadamer and Hart cited in note 3 of this chapter deal extensively with what I have called the "stimulative" power of classic and paradigmatic texts. So, of course, do the writings of Heidegger, upon whom Gadamer so evidently depends. For a good summary of the thought of Heidegger and Gadamer in this regard, see Richard E. Palmer, *Hermeneutics* (Evanston: Northwestern University Press, 1969), pp. 124–217. I might add that it seems to me that a great deal of the disagreement between Gadamer and Betti (see note 3) over the meaning of interpretation stems from the fact that Betti and other "objective" historians stress the first of the three interpretive functions I have described, whereas Gadamer and Heidegger stress the "stimulative" power of texts, a function I would prefer to disassociate from that of interpretation. The failure to indicate clearly that texts have a whole series of purposes has produced unnecessary disagreements between men who are differently oriented. Betti's effort to uncover the intelligibility of the past is as legitimate a task as Gadamer's attempt to unlock present potentialities.

21. It is this process that accounts for the continuing reinterpretation of Scripture that is evidenced in Scripture itself. The New Testament is not simply a drawing out of the implications of the Old Testament. It uses the

Old Testament with a liberty that goes beyond the attempt to find the exact understanding of the original author. In this connection, one might consult the following: Pierre Grelot, *Sens Chrétien de l'Ancien Testament* (Tournai: Desclée & Co., 1962); Barnabas Lindars, *New Testament Apologetic* (London: SCM Press, 1961); E. Earle Ellis, *Paul's Use of the Old Testament* (London: Oliver and Boyd, 1957), esp. pp. 147–149; Edwin D. Freed, *Old Testament Quotations in the Gospel of John* (Leiden: E. J. Brill, 1965), esp. pp. 126–130; Robert Horton Gundry, *The Use of the Old Testament in St. Matthew's Gospel* (Leiden: E. J. Brill, 1967). For a summary of views on the relationship of the New to the Old Testament up to 1964, consult Roland E. Murphy, "The Relationship between the Testaments," in *The Catholic Biblical Quarterly*, 26 (July 1964), 349–359. For a more modern view see Prosper Grech, "Interprophetic Re-interpretation and Old Testament Eschatology," in *Augustinianum*, 8 (1969), 235–265 as summarized in *Theology Digest*, 18 (Summer 1970), 154–163. None of the authors here cited expressly supports the view I have advanced. They do not relate the New Testament interpretation of the Old Testament to a basic dynamism of the human mind as I have done. However, the detailed evidence they adduce is not inconsistent with the more general theory proposed in the text above.

22. The scriptural quotations in this book are from the *Revised Standard Version and the Apocrypha*, copyrighted 1957 by the Division of Christian Education, National Council of the Churches of Christ in the U.S.A.

CHAPTER 2

1. What I have said here regarding Scripture applies also to all subsequent authoritative texts of the Church, including the definitions considered to be infallibly proclaimed. Usually such authoritative statements are less comprehensive, less concrete, and less suggestive of further meanings than the Scriptures; for they are generally more abstract and more reflective of generic understanding than are the biblical texts. However, these magisterial documents also manifest implicit beliefs of their authors. Such beliefs can be explicitly formulated by later Church teachers; they can be complemented and even corrected; they can serve as catalysts for the generation of new meanings. What is curious is that we have long recognized that subsidiary and implied aspects of such magisterial documents are not to be taken as the infallible teaching of the Church. Yet we have too slowly come to see that the same dynamic that militates against the global infallibility of subsequent ecclesial documents also militates against the global inerrancy of Scripture.

2. See Bernard Lonergan, "Theology in Its New Context," in *Theology of*

Renewal, ed. L. K. Shook (New York: Herder and Herder, 1968), I, pp. 34–46. An interesting contrast is reflected in the older approach of Yves Congar, "Theology's Tasks after Vatican II," *ibid.*, pp. 47–65.

3. That there must be an accord between the meanings of theology and the meanings expressed in Scripture is agreed to by all; it is the nature of that agreement that is debated. My own view is that Scripture is largely a prophetic document that contains a host of temporally conditioned meanings. These meanings by their nature pertain to one culture and one time; hence, they cannot be normative for all times. However, Scripture also contains embedded within its culturally conditioned affirmations a framework of truth that transcends the limitations of any culture in pertaining to all historical cultures. These truths are norms that all succeeding ages must conform to by making them concrete in ever differing circumstances. Unfortunately, there is no clear delineation in Scripture of these transcultural norms. How they are to be identified is a prime concern of my treatment of infallibility in subsequent chapters.

4. The classic work of this kind is Oscar Cullmann, *The Christology of the New Testament* (Philadelphia: Westminster Press, 1963). Other books of the type include Vincent Taylor, *The Names of Jesus* (London: Macmillan & Co., 1953); Reginald Fuller, *The Foundations of New Testament Christology* (New York: Charles Scribner's Sons, 1965); Ferdinand Hahn, *The Titles of Jesus in Christology: Their History in Early Christianity* (London: Lutterworth Press, 1969). Hahn attempts to show that the Christological titles which he treats independently of one another do lead to a convergence of results.

5. Fuller, *The Foundations of New Testament Christology*, p. 251.

6. The problem of unifying various accounts of the same reality in the mind of the interpreter is met by Bernard Lonergan with his notion of a "universal viewpoint" (*Insight*, pp. 564–568). While I do not make use of Lonergan's terminology, I believe that the notion as he describes it rests on the same analysis that I employ in the text.

7. Cf. Karl Rahner, "L'avenir de la Théologie," *Nouvelle Revue Théologique*, 93 (January 1971), 3–28, esp. 19–20.

8. For other views on the divisions of the theological enterprise and the task of the various divisions see Bernard Lonergan, *Method in Theology* (New York: Herder and Herder, 1972), pp. 125–368; David Tracy, *Blessed Rage for Order* (New York: Seabury Press, 1975), pp. 237–240.

9. For appropriate bibliography and a summary view of the thought of modern Church historians on the role of the findings of the human sciences in the Church history enterprise, consult Anton Weiler, "Church History and the Reorientation of the Scientific Study of History," in *Concilium*, British edition, 6, vol. 7 (September 1970), 13–32. In the same issue, which

is given over in its entirety to Church History, C. W. Mönnich writes on "Church History in the Context of the Human Sciences" (*ibid.*, pp. 42-52). Unfortunately, neither author comes to grips with the basic problem of how understanding of past understanding is possible at all.

10. For two good overviews of the rapid societal changes that affect the quality of personal existence see Peter Drucker, *The Age of Discontinuity* (New York: Harper and Row, 1968), and Warren Bennis and Philip Slater, *The Temporary Society* (New York: Harper and Row, 1969).

11. A failure to appreciate the significance of the present even for the interpretation of the word of God in Scripture was one of the factors in the demise of neo-orthodoxy in Protestantism. See Langdon Gilkey, *Naming the Whirlwind* (Indianapolis and New York: Bobbs-Merrill Co., 1969), pp. 80-106.

12. I have attempted to exemplify this view of theology as thematizing the enduring relational elements and dynamic processes resulting from the presence of the risen Christ throughout history in a series of apparently unrelated articles: "Tension, Morality, and Birth Control," *Theological Studies,* 28 (June 1967), 258-285; "One Church: What Does It Mean?" *Theological Studies,* 28 (December 1967), 659-682; "Theological Method and the Nature of Ministry," *Proceedings of the Catholic Theological Society of America,* 24 (June 1969), 1-9; "Christian and Jew Today from a Christian Theological Perspective," *Journal of Ecumenical Studies,* 7 (Fall 1970), 744-762.

13. See Herbert Butterfield, *The Origins of Modern Science, 1300-1800* (New York: Free Press, 1965).

NOTE TO THE INTRODUCTION TO PART TWO

1. The approach I will take is not intended to deny that in the concrete development of the theological teaching on dogma and infallibility there has been triumphalism. Anyone conversant with the theological history of the last three centuries knows that such an attitude has been present. However, I believe that an overconcentration on this facet can vitiate a theological approach to dogma and infallibility. It seems to me that Hans Küng's *Infallible? An Inquiry* (Garden City: Doubleday & Company, 1971) suffers from being primarily an attack on triumphalism. It is more a prophetic proclamation than a theological study. Insufficient effort is made to get at the philosophical and theological roots of the claim to infallibility. The presuppositions of the study of history go uninvestigated. In its own genre, Küng's book is excellent; it has provoked a discussion of infallibility. If I do not make much reference to it, it is not that I do not appreciate what Küng has tried to do; rather, it is that I believe the questions he raises have to be answered at a far more fundamental level than the one at which he has worked. Hence my work is in no important sense a response to the content of Küng's book.

Rather, it is a response to a problem he has highlighted. For those interested in a summary of Küng's approach and of the debate it precipitated I would suggest a series of condensations that appeared in *Theology Digest,* 19 (Summer 1971), 104–132. Neither these articles nor several books that have appeared in response to *Infallible? An Inquiry* seem to me to be related to the approach I am following in this book.

CHAPTER 3

1. Why the presence and activity of the risen Christ is not perceivable by those who have not received the Christian witness will be clarified in the next chapter.

2. In actuality we are dealing with a continuum. Some men are profoundly affected by the Christian witness to the risen Christ. Others may be totally unaffected, especially if they live in remote corners of the world. However, most men have been touched in some degree by activity stemming from belief in the Resurrection, even where they have not grasped Christian preaching on this central article of faith in any meaningful way.

3. It should be apparent that I am setting up a series of distinctions that do not correspond precisely to the old natural-supernatural distinction. In the categories I am using, the world has seen two existing orders. The first order lasted from the beginning until the incarnation, death, and resurrection of Christ. The second follows on and fulfills this first order. It is inaugurated by the Incarnation, and especially the Resurrection, and it will have no end. It is ontically different from the prior order precisely because of the presence within it of the God-man who in his humanity affects all of creation. These two orders exist whether men acknowledge them or not, just as the distant galaxies exist whether men know of them or not. However, within each order the creative work of God brings various men to differing degrees of under-standing of that order. Thus, in Israel the creative providence of God brought about a consciousness that he was the Lord of history and of all the nations. That realization constituted the basic selection of Israel as God's chosen nation. In other words, within the one order that existed before Christ there was a people who came to an understanding of the basic contours of that order; and that understanding made them to be God's elect. On this, see Eric Voeglin, *Israel and Revelation* (Louisiana State University Press, 1956). Similarly, in the new order constituted by the universal presence of the risen Christ, there are some who are brought to a consciousness of that presence. These are the ones whom I designate as pertaining to the *experiential-witness* level because their initial recognition of the risen Christ derives from the witness of the Apostolic Church. On the old distinction between the natural

and the supernatural order see Karl Rahner, "Concerning the Relationship between Nature and Grace," in *Theological Investigations*, vol. 1 (Baltimore: Helicon, 1961), pp. 297–317.

4. See Jerome Bruner, *The Relevance of Education* (New York: W. W. Norton & Company, 1971), p. 4.

5. Quoted in Bruner, *The Relevance of Education*, p. 148.

6. To raise the question of the existence of universal meanings is to raise the question of communicable objectivity. I cannot treat the topic of such objectivity within these pages. Let me say that the notion of some kind of objectivity apart from the human subject is unthinkable for man. The only kind of objectivity he can know is that proper to the subject that he is. There can be a common objectivity for all subjects precisely because there can be a common universal development of all subjects in this world. This does not mean that there are no objects. But objects as known can only be known according to the capacity of the knower. What objects are for God is not and cannot be what they are for man. God knows according to his subjectivity; and because his subjectivity is total, his objectivity is total. Man can know only according to human powers. If he lacked sight, his standard of objectivity could not include color; if he lacked hearing, it could not include sound. One can legitimately speculate that there are untold aspects of objects that are beyond man's ken. This does not mean that his knowledge is not objective. It merely means that he can possess only human objectivity; and the standard of objectivity is the fully developed subject who internalizes all the universal meanings possible to human development. Particularistic meanings common to a given culture, but not all cultures, cannot be called objective as such, although they may incarnate aspects that are universalistic and hence objective in the sense that we use objective. On this view, subjectivity and objectivity are not opposed; in fact, they are correlatives. The most subjective person—that is, the one who most completely realizes the universal potential of all subjects and is most involved in interaction with the world—is at once the most objective of observers; he is, in fact, the standard of human objectivity.

In the above view truth is a quality of the subject as he develops his openness to all objects, including other subjects. Truth is in its terminal ideal the total realization in the subject and his concreteness of every universal self-differentiation. To live fully in the truth would be to have reached the stage of personal development in which total relatability of all creation would be matched by a commensurate self-differentiation. In Christian terms this would be to have grown up to the fullness of Christ. This view accords well with the Gospel notions of Christ as the Truth, of the need to do the truth in charity. It accords well, too, with the scholastic notion that one understands only on the basis of one's experience. To achieve the fullness of truth is to achieve the fullness of concrete self-differentiation and self-realization in the context of this world.

7. See Johannes Lotz, "Problématique du 'Semel Verum—Semper Verum,' " in *L'Infaillibilité: Son Aspect Philosophique et Théologique* ed. Enrico Castelli (Paris: Aubier, 1970), pp. 455-469, especially 464-465; in the same volume see Sergio Cotta, "Le Droit à l'Infaillibilité et la Faillibilité du Droit," pp. 27-35.

8. On the existence of a natural infallibility in philosophers like Descartes and Rousseau see Henri Gouhier, "Infaillibilité et Nature," *ibid.*, pp. 229-235.

9. See D. O. Hebb, *The Organization of Behavior* (New York: John Wiley & Sons, 1949), pp. 17-37, for a presentation of the psychological evidence for the subjective factor in every perceptive experience. Though old, Hebb's work is still valuable.

10. Alphonse De Waelhens, "Réflexions Philosophiques sur l'Infaillibilité," in *L'Infaillibilité*, ed. Castelli, pp. 399-407.

11. The whole question of the paradigm shift in scientific generalizations is treated at length in Thomas Kuhn, *The Structure of Scientific Revolutions* (Chicago: University of Chicago Press, 1962).

12. This accords well with the classic notion that infallible truth inevitably goes back to a kind of vision. Thus, in the Greek demonstration one ran everything back to axioms that were not proved by reasoning but shone of themselves. They could only be pointed to as self-evident. Whitehead advances a similar notion. What I have attempted to do here is to "point" not to something external to man but to recurring aspects of his interior experience. On the general notion of infallibility through vision see Ernesto Grassi, "L'Infaillibilité, un Problème Philosophique: Langage et Vision," in *L'Infaillibilité*, ed. Castelli, pp. 329-355.

13. Antoine Vergote, "L'Infaillibilité entre le Désire et le Refus de Savoir," in *ibid.*, pp. 375-390, especially p. 385.

14. The problem with objections to infallibility deriving from a desire to maintain freedom generally stems from a false notion of freedom. For a profound discussion of the nature of freedom see Yves Simon, *Freedom of Choice* (New York: Fordham University Press, 1969).

15. Warren Bennis and Philip Slater, *The Temporary Society* (New York: Harper and Row, 1968); Peter Drucker, *The Age of Discontinuity* (New York: Harper and Row, 1968); Alvin Toffler, *Future Shock* (New York: Random House, 1970).

16. That a special claim to infallibility should arise in a Church that attempted to maintain unity while spreading over diverse cultures and civilizations is almost to be expected.

CHAPTER 4

1. The effort to expound a transcultural Christology is closely associated with the question of the absoluteness of Christianity. On the latter one might consult the classic of Ernst Troeltsch, *The Absoluteness of Christianity and the History of Religions* (Richmond: John Knox Press, 1971). Troeltsch's work suffers from attempting to establish the absoluteness of the Christian religion by evidence drawn from a study of comparative religion. Such a method presupposes that one can establish what could only be a datum of faith by empirical observation. See Walter Kasper, "Absoluteness of Christianity," in *Sacramentum Mundi*, vol. 1 (New York: Herder and Herder, 1968), pp. 311–313. I personally believe that it is misleading to speak of the absoluteness of Christianity; this terminology implies that the defective historical form in which the Christian belief has taken shape has something absolute about it. I think it preferable to speak of the absoluteness of Christ. On this see Lesslie Newbigin, *The Finality of Christ* (Richmond: John Knox Press, 1969); Charles Davis, *Christ and the World Religions* (New York: Herder and Herder, 1971), especially pp. 124–132. Two works that indicate a centrality of Christ and simultaneously a valued estimation of non-Christian religions are John Dunne, *The Way of all the Earth* (New York: Macmillan Co., 1972); Robley Edward Whitson, *The Coming Convergence of World Religions* (New York: Newman, 1971). I have treated the issue of the absoluteness of Christ and the comparative relativity of Christian forms in two articles: "One Church: What Does it Mean?" *Theological Studies*, 28 (December 1967), 659–682; and "Christian and Jew Today from a Christian Theological Perspective," *Journal of Ecumenical Studies*, 7 (Fall 1970), 744–762. Quite helpful in the formulation of a transcultural Christology are Peter Hodgson, *Jesus: Word and Presence* (Philadelphia: Fortress Press, 1971), esp. pp. 220–291; Gerhard Lohfink, "The Resurrection of Jesus and Historical Criticism," *Theology Digest*, 17 (Summer 1969), 110–114; Edouard Pousset, "La Resurrection," *Nouvelle Revue Théologique*, 91 (December 1969), 1009–1044; Rudolf Schnackenburg, "On the Expression 'Jesus is risen (from the dead),'" in *Theology Digest*, 18 (Spring 1970), 36–42. A whole issue of *Lumière et Vie*, no. 107 (March–May 1972), is given over to the many facets of Resurrection theology. An excellent recent study is Edouard Pousset, "Croire en la Resurrection," *Novelle Revue Théologique*, 96 (February 1974), 147–166 and (April 1974), 366–388.

2. Karl Rahner, "The Concept of Mystery in Catholic Theology," in *Theological Investigations*, vol. 4 (Baltimore: Helicon, 1966), pp. 36–73; Bernard Lonergan, *Insight*, pp. 634–686; Emerich Coreth, *Metaphysics* (New York: Herder and Herder, 1968), pp. 170–196.

3. Regarding the theology of death, consult Karl Rahner, *On the Theology*

of Death (Freiburg: Herder, 1961); Ladislaus Boros, *The Mystery of Death* (New York: Herder and Herder, 1965).

4. For an account of the way in which the various elements of a man's history are so preserved that nothing is ever lost see Karl Rahner, "Ideas for a Theology of Childhood," in *Theological Investigations*, vol. 8 (New York: Herder and Herder, 1971), pp. 30–50.

5. Cf. Acts. 2:36; Rom. 10:9–13; 14:9; Phil. 2:5–11. The theme *Lord* is treated in all the biblical dictionaries.

6. Bernard Lonergan, *"Insight:* Preface to a Discussion," in *Collection: Papers by Bernard Lonergan, S.J.*, ed. Frederick E. Crowe (New York: Herder and Herder, 1967), pp. 152–163.

7. Implicitly we even recognize that any object that would actualize the same generic potentials of our nature would be of the same kind as this object. This process is what grounds our capacity to generalize.

8. One could say that the Christian order begins with the Incarnation. However, because Christ becomes universal in fact only at his resurrection, I tend to refer the establishment of the Christian order to that moment. Nevertheless, as the subsequent discussion of this fifth thesis will indicate, there are grounds for referring to the moment of the Incarnation as the beginning of the Christian order. The reason for this seeming ambiguity is the fact that resurrection is the term of a process that begins with the conception and birth of Christ. The risen state is the mature state of the Incarnation.

9. A failure to recognize that our present relationship to Christ is not a strict personal relationship often leads to disillusionment among certain beginners in prayer. They hear that in prayer we are personally related to Christ and expect something more than the kind of in-faith relationship to Christ I have been speaking of.

10. Of course, I have no intention of denying a genuine grace in the Old Testament period. That grace, however, was by definition not a Christian grace effected through the presence of Christ. Rather, it was that change in man brought about by God's free creative action by which man moved towards the condition of being able to accept the Resurrection before it occurred.

11. See Lonergan, *Insight*, pp. 564–568, on the subject of the universal viewpoint.

12. Although I have been using the terms "intellect," "will," and the like, I do not intend to canonize any way of conceiving man. I merely wish to state that faith affects every part of man, no matter how one subdivides man's operations. I use conventional subdivisions as a handy way to refer in a more specific manner to the totality of man.

13. Küng, *Infallible? An Inquiry*, p. 185. This, of course, is not my only disagreement with Küng. As must be obvious by now, I would disagree with the whole context or horizon within which he has set the question of infallibility.

CHAPTER 5

1. The distinction made here approximates the classical distinction between supernatural truths *quoad modum* and *quoad substantiam*, but it is not identical with it.

2. *Commonitorium*, II, n. 22., P. L. 50, 640.

3. See L. Malevez, "L'invariant et le divers dans le langage de la foi," in *Nouvelle Revue Théologique*, 95 (April 1973), 353–366. This article situates the invariant in the faith in the universal and the transcultural, especially in pages 354–359.

4. All this is too well-known to demand defense. The Council of Trent officially proclaimed much of what is summarized here. See *D.S.* 1642, 1652, 1739, 1740, 1751 from Trent and *D.S.* 1320 and 1321 from the Council of Florence.

5. For a standard manual presentation see Joseph de Aldama in *Sacrae Theologiae Summa*, IV, 2nd ed., by Joseph de Aldama and others (Madrid: La Editorial *Católica*, 1953), pp. 317–356.

6. On the subject of sacrifice in Israel consult Roland de Vaux, *Ancient Israel: Its Life and Institutions* (London: Darton, Longman and Todd, 1961), pp. 415–456.

7. On the general question of the institution of the sacraments and their symbolic constituents see E. Schillebeeckx, *Christ the Sacrament of the Encounter with God* (New York: Sheed and Ward, 1963), pp. 112–132.

8. Karl Rahner, "The Theology of the Symbol," in *Theological Investigations*, vol. 4 (Baltimore: Helicon, 1966), pp. 221–252.

9. I am at present working on a book that will illustrate the method with regard to a transcultural notion of vocations.

CHAPTER 6

1. I do not intend to say that concrete knowledge of facts will never be of necessary saving value. I believe that in the universal condition of the blessed every facet of one's life and of the neighbor's and *a fortiori* of Christ's is seen as a link in a chain of events each of which affects each other. In that kind of existence there is a sense in which every concrete fact becomes a dogmatic meaning that is shareable and to be shared by all; everything about everything constitutes an abiding aspect of existence and of salvation. In the present flesh-and-blood existence, however, our incomplete grasp of ourselves and of concrete facts makes an obligatory self-differentiation with regard to such facts impossible. Of course, by this I do not intend to deny that the experience

and non-infallible knowledge of concrete particular beings is an essential aspect of the present salvation of each of us. While all of us must have experience and knowledge of some concrete present beings, there is no concrete present being that must be experienced and known by all.

2. See Bernard-Dominique Dupuy, "Le magistère de l'Église, service de la parole," in O. Rousseau, J. J. von Allmen, and others, *L'Infaillibilité de l'Église* (Gembloux: Chevetogne, 1963), pp. 53–97, esp. pp. 54, 84.

3. This way of looking at things clarifies how men not in the state of grace can pertain to the Church. At the same time I would stress that only a highly abstract thinker could come to the conclusion that man can arrive at a Christian differentiation of consciousness without a good measure of co-operation with the grace of God. Understanding grows out of a life process; and universal Christian understanding can exist only within the framework of a life process that is significantly Christian. I am suggesting here that membership in the Church is not simply the external acceptance of certain norms and formulas. Even an honestly intended acceptance of this sort may not ground genuine Church membership; for such membership is based on the objective possession of dogmatic meanings, and these can be lacking in a man of good will. Of course, membership is always a question of degree. What is required is that one should possess the most basic universal meanings in a more or less explicit fashion plus an implicit willingness to accept those further differentiations which the Christian community has arrived at in the course of time.

4. This is not to deny that there can be an enduring basis for a hierarchical structure in the Church. However, as I will try to show in the section on the emergence of the hierarchy (chap. 13), that enduring basis is to be located in the universal hierarchical nature of personal reality. In other words, what is lasting in the hierarchy is due to an element of dogmatic meaning embedded therein and not to some imagined concrete structure willed, somewhat arbitrarily, by God to last forever.

5. To clarify and amplify this statement would require a separate volume on development of dogma. This second condition denies that development of dogma is *only* a matter of making explicit what formerly was implicit in being and activity. History and the freedom that is associated with it have to do with the emergence of the new and the unexpected. That emergence, of course, has to fulfill the old. For some further explanation of this, see chapter 11, especially the sections dealing with the particular and universal aspects of revelation.

6. Küng, *Infallible? An Inquiry*, pp. 181–185.

7. Nicolas Afanassieff, " L'Infaillibilité de l'Église du point de vue d'un théologien orthodoxe," in *L'Infaillibilité de l'Église*, ed. Rousseau and others, pp. 184–185.

CHAPTER 7

1. For the underlying philosophical aspects relating to the process of conceptualization see Bernard Lonergan, *Verbum: Word and Idea in Aquinas* (Notre Dame: University of Notre Dame Press, 1967).

2. Of course, I am not saying that there is never a movement from the universal to the particular. I am simply saying that the *first* emergence of a universal meaning and the *first* emergence of a universal structure built on understanding and freedom come after particular meanings and structures. A teacher can teach universal meanings or principles first, and by force one can impose universal structures first. This, however, is not the path of discovery and spontaneous emergence.

3. It may help to clarify what a history of dogma would be in the context which I have set forth in this book. First of all, such a history of dogma and its growth would take into account the history of the Church as lived. That history as lived is the development of the corporate experiential continuum of the Church. Embedded in that history, though far from the whole of it, is the development of universal Christian meanings. That development would be marked by the emergence of implicit culturally conditioned meanings, then explicit culturally conditioned meanings, and finally by explicit universal meanings. To trace the emergence of these meanings the historian of dogma would have to look back over the past from the vantage point of one who has developed transcultural universal hypotheses. Then he would have to master, at least in its broad outlines, the history as lived in the Church and the various contexts in which that history was lived out. He would then be in a position to make explicit the process by which universal Christian meanings had developed in the Church. His history would include not only what the past expressed in documents but also, and above all, what it expressed in life. For one who desires this kind of history of dogma, much of what has been written would have to be complemented. The reader who desires another view of the task of a history of dogma might consult two works of erudition by Jaroslav Pelikan: *Historical Theology: Continuity and Change in Christian Doctrine* (New York: Corpus Instrumentorum, 1971); *The Christian Tradition: A History of the Development of Doctrine*, vol. 1 (Chicago and London: University of Chicago Press, 1971).

4. The tradition supports the notion that only those who live the faith can participate in the process of grasping Christian truth without error. See William Thompson, "Sensus Fidelium and Infallibility," *The American Ecclesiastical Review*, 167 (September 1973), 454–457.

CHAPTER 8

1. "Furthermore, Catholic theologians engaged in ecumenical dialogue, while standing fast by the teaching of the Church and searching together with separated brethren into the divine mysteries, should act with love for truth, with charity, and with humility. When comparing doctrines, they should remember that in Catholic teaching there exists an order or 'hierarchy' of truths, since they vary in their relationships to the foundation of the Christian faith." (*Unitatis Redintegratio* or The Decree on Ecumenism of Vatican II, #11.)

2. John R. Sheets, "Teilhard de Chardin and the Development of Dogma," in *Theological Studies,* 30 (September 1969), 446.

3. Dogmas are both mysterious and meaningful to us because of the characteristics of the Resurrection from which they stem. On the one hand, the Resurrection represents a condition of human existence that is beyond our capacity to experience or understand directly; hence dogmas which stem from the Resurrection are necessarily mysterious. On the other hand, the Resurrection represents the fulfillment of human existence. Hence we can meaningfully speak of it as the final extrapolation or projection from the present processes by which men grow. Dogmas, in effect, point to essential aspects of the kingdom of God and the aspects and processes by which that kingdom is realized. Because we now experience only the Church and not the fulfilled kingdom, dogmas must be mysterious; because the Church is already the kingdom in its initial stage of realization, dogmas are meaningful. I might add that the specifically Christian dogmas which refer to the human nature of Christ and the conditions of our humanity which will stem from our rising with him will be cleared up when we attain risen existence and risen experience. The unlimited mystery of God—Father, Son, and Holy Spirit—and the mystery of how God could become man will forever remain; for we shall never attain the strictly divine mode of existence or experience. It is for this reason that when speaking under the category of mystery I would divide dogmas into (1) unlimited mysteries—the Trinity and the process of the Incarnation and (2) limited mysteries—those implicit in the acceptance of the risen humanity of Christ.

4. Karl Rahner, "The Concept of Mystery in Catholic Theology," in *Theological Investigations,* vol. 4 (Baltimore: Helicon, 1966), pp. 36–73; Juan Alfaro, "Cristo Glorioso, Revelador del Padre," in *Gregorianum,* 39 (1958), 244–250.

5. Because of their mysterious and eschatological nature, dogmas point to an ideal. Thus, the dogmas of the roles of the popes and bishops as teachers and rulers indicate what they ideally are to be. The dogma of infallibility points to an ideal achievement of Christian teaching, not to what *de facto*

ordinarily is. The Church has to be constantly on guard against the tendency to think that what ought to be actually is. A case could conceivably be made that the great temptation of the Catholic Church has been to immanentize the eschaton. A healthy view of dogmas would see them as lasting challenges to grow.

CHAPTER 9

1. I do not intend to deny that the very articulation and expression of dogmatic meaning *in concreto* contributes to that meaning. Expression and meaning have a reciprocal effect. Meaning tends to be expressed in word, symbol, and act. In turn, these expressions modify, amplify, and develop meaning in the subject who utilizes them. However, as a finished product set before us in a conciliar statement, a written text is simply a clue to a prior meaning that existed only in living minds. I shall take up the question of dogmatic statements in chapter 16.

2. My fundamental disagreement with Hans Küng's whole approach in *Infallible? An Inquiry* is his failure to distinguish dogmatic meanings and dogmatic understanding from dogmatic statements in a clear way. This leads him to put his stress on the difficulties involved in making dogmatic statements that have enduring validity. See especially pages 157–162. Precisely because of my completely different approach, I have not attempted to distinguish my position from Küng's at each point of the argumentation. It makes little sense to underline differences in detail when the whole framework in which the question is cast is different.

3. For the teaching of Vatican I on the source of infallibility see Gustave Thils, *L'Infaillibilité Pontificale* (Gembloux: Éditions J. Duculot, 1969), pp. 125–141. Thils' work will be basic for the teaching of Vatican I on infallibility.

4. *Ibid.*, pp. 223–226.

5. L. Choupin, *Valeur des Décisions doctrinales et disciplinaires du Saint-Siège,* 3rd ed. (Paris, 1929), pp. 46–47 as quoted in *ibid.*, p. 160. The translation is mine.

6. For detail on the object of infallibility see *ibid.*, pp. 234–246.

7. See Thils, "L'Infaillibilité de l'Église dans la constitution 'Pastor aeternus' du premier Concile du Vatican," in *L'Infaillibilité de l'Église,* ed. Rousseau and others, pp. 147–159.

8. Thils, *L'Infaillibilité Pontificale,* pp. 141–145.

9. Karl Rahner and Joseph Ratzinger, *The Episcopate and the Primacy* (Freiburg: Herder, 1962), pp. 92–101.

10. Thils, *L'Infaillibilité Pontificale,* p. 148.

11. *D. S.* 3074.

12. *Ibid.* For a discussion of this and the first requirement as they were artic-ulated at Vatican I see Thils, *L'Infaillibilité Pontificale,* pp. 204–207.

13. *Ibid.,* pp. 212–216.

14. *Ibid.,* pp. 167–175. See also Georges Dejaifve, "Ex sese, non autem ex consensu Ecclesiae," in *Le Premier "Symposium" International de Théologie Dogmatique Fondamentale,* ed. Gustave Thils (Turin: Società Editrice Internazionale, 1962), pp. 69–81.

15. The basic inevitability and soundness of the position of Vatican I ap-pears when we begin to analyze what was said there in the light of the dynamics of human understanding. For the pope to proclaim infallibly in a personal way, he must personally grasp the doctrine in question and also grasp that that doctrine is certainly embedded in the long tradition of the Church on revelation. However, such understanding cannot be attained by the following of a set of juridical procedures. In the concrete, human under-standing follows diverse paths that cannot be predetermined beforehand by some legal body. That is why teaching so often fails; for the process of understanding cannot be structured for each individual in the same way; nor does the same individual follow the same path to understanding at all moments of life. Once one says that the gift of infallibility is a *personal* gift of the pope, then one must deny set legal procedures for the actualization of infallibility. Of course, one may deny that infallibility is a *personal* gift of the pope, and fall back into some notion that the Church in some vague way remains in the truth, although no one infallibly appropriates that truth. This latter view has its own inconsistencies, as I shall point out later on.

What must be countered here is the kind of interpretation of Vatican I put forth, for example, by Hans Küng. In *Infallible? An Inquiry* he says: "Even the qualifications of Vatican II do not prevent the pope in any way from issuing infallible and of course still less fallible proclamations, when-ever and wherever he wishes, exactly as Vatican I wanted and decided" (p. 104). "It must be recognized without any illusions that, according to Vatican I (and II), no one can prevent the pope from proceeding arbitrarily and autocratically in questions of doctrine—fallible or infallible. . . . if he wants, the pope can do everything, even without the Church" (p. 105). The polemical nature of these statements makes them one-sided. They manifest that Küng has failed to grasp a crucial point. The pope *cannot* pro-claim doctrine infallibly whenever and wherever he wishes on his mere whim. He must first actually inform himself and achieve the conditions for infal-libility. These conditions are not achieved by his mere saying that he has achieved them. Küng's basic fear is of irrational and totally centralized control: "The problem is still papal absolutism" (p. 103). Because of that fear he desires to set up legal structures to prevent the pope from making any and all statements for the whole Church without express prior consultation set forth in legal safeguards; and he desires that this be done even for doctrinal statements. Such legal machinery would appear very desirable for pastoral statements. However, the desire for such machinery should not blind one to the fact that Vatican I was treating the problem of infallibility on a level other than the juridical. It was dealing with the plane of ontic realization, of the actual achievement of certain conditions of understanding by the pope; and it realized, vaguely it is true, that one cannot structure the conditions of understanding by law. To so misread the intent of Vatican I as to imply that it said the pope by mere whim can be infallible is to caricature the council. For Vatican I every infallible definition of the pope is necessarily in its inner reality a collegial act, even though the exterior conditions manifesting that collegiality cannot be set out in predetermined legal structures. (See Thils, *L'Infaillibilité Pontificale*, pp. 216–221.) Should that inner collegial reality be lacking, there is no infallible statement. And no assertion by the pope out of mere whim can create that collegiality.

16. Thils, *L'Infaillibilité Pontificale*, pp. 149–153.

17. *Ibid.*, pp. 162–166.

18. *Ibid.*, pp. 210–211.

19. Cardinal Newman noted that the simple laity were not bound to accept the technical formulas against Arianism as a condition of communion as long as they introduced no novelties of belief of their own. But he does not clarify just what kind of acceptance of orthodoxy the ordinary laity are bound to. See *The Arians of the Fourth Century* (London: Basil Montagu Pickering, 1876), pp. 150, 254.

20. "Declarata seu definita dogmatice res nulla intelligitur, nisi id manifeste constiterit" (Canon 1323, no. 3).

21. *D. S.* 3011.

22. Umberto Betti, *La Costituzione Dommatica "Pastor Aeternus" del Concilio Vaticano I* (Rome: Pontificio Ateneo "Antonianum," 1961), pp. 645–647.

23. Joachim Salaverri in *Sacrae Theologiae Summa*, I, 2nd ed., by Joseph de Aldama and others (Madrid: La Editorial Católica, 1952), pp. 663–664.

24. For a summary overview of the teaching of Vatican I on papal infallibility and for an appropriate bibliography see Gustave Thils, "Précisions sur l'infaillibilité papale à l'occasion d'un centenaire," in *Revue Théologique de Louvain*, 1 (1970), 183–190.

CHAPTER 10

1. See chapter 3.

2. See Bernard Lonergan, *Insight*, pp. 319-332.

3. Following this line of reasoning, one can see that there is a sense in which one can speak of theory as being a substitute for greater immediate awareness. The race that could not see would concoct a theory that would translate the effects of light into elements that it could immediately perceive, e.g., into sound. The moment that race acquired a capacity to see, a whole host of theories would be sent to limbo. The more a being can immediately perceive reality, the less it has need of theories. God does not theorize; he simply immediately "knows." The fact that man enjoys the capacity to employ an understanding process is both his glory and the mark of his limitation. In that man understands, he outstrips the rest of visible creation; in that in him understanding is a process and not an immediate awareness, he is marked by limitation.

4. I use the term "charism" here to refer to the God-given capacity to live out the ancient tradition of the Church into a new context. In this view the various charisms refer to the special sectors of reality in which the Christian can operate creatively. Thus, a person who has the charism of teaching is capable of presenting the Christian tradition in such a way that his audience can grasp that tradition in its own terms; a person who has the charism of unifying would be one who had received the gift of bringing together in a new present context the Christians of our time; a person who has the charism of healing would be one through whom the ever available power of the Spirit to heal comes to bear upon modern man. The charisms presuppose a Church on the march towards an ever greater kingdom, a Church not totally delineated in the past but growing out of a past creatively towards a not completely known future, a Church in which the new and the unexpected is ever to be looked for. In this perspective it will be seen that charisms are necessary to the Church; further, they are necessary not just to the prophetic members but also to those who belong to the episcopacy. Karl Rahner has written fairly extensively on charisms in the Church. See, for example, his *The Dynamic Element in the Church* (Freiburg: Herder, 1964), pp. 42-83; "Observations on the Factor of the Charismatic in the Church," *Theological Investigations*, vol. 12 (New York: Seabury Press, 1974), pp. 81-97. For a summary treatment see the article on "Charisms" in *Sacramentum Mundi*, vol. 1 (New York: Herder and Herder, 1968), pp. 283-284. Vatican II made several references to the widespread charismatic element in the Church. See *The Dogmatic Constitution on the Church*, no. 12; *The Decree on the Apostolate of the Laity*, no. 3; no. 30; *The Decree on the Missionary Activity of the Church*, no. 23.

5. A. Tanquerey, *Synopsis Theologiae, Dogmaticae,* II, 26th ed. (Paris: Desclée, 1950), p. 697.

6. See Karl Rahner, "Dogmatic Considerations on Knowledge and Consciousness in Christ," in *Dogmatic vs. Biblical Theology,* ed. Herbert Vorgrimler (Baltimore: Helicon, 1964), pp. 241–267.

CHAPTER 11

1. Karl Rahner, "On the Theology of the Incarnation," in *Theological Investigations,* vol. 4 (Baltimore: Helicon, 1966), p. 116.

2. It is the lack of certain kinds of self-realization that grounds the phenomenon of the *rudes* mentioned in the textbooks. These are the simple folk who cannot grasp the meaning of certain doctrines. I might add that it is this same lack of self-realization that grounds the great difficulty, and even the impossibility, some educated modern people experience in accepting certain Church teachings. The simple and the unlettered have no monopoly over the inability to grasp one or more doctrines. It is possible for a man to be highly differentiated in one area of human experience and yet to be totally undeveloped in a number of other areas.

3. In this context sin becomes the refusal to grow out towards the fulfillment of the Communion of Saints; sin would thus be intrinsically opposed to salvation. The full acceptance of this notion of sin and its implications would, I believe, lead to a genuine development of a Christian morality suited to the needs of our times.

4. It may shock some to hear it said that since Christ is the Revelation of God who sums up all of creation, all of creation becomes revelatory. On this view every true understanding in physics, chemistry, psychology, and sociology would be revelatory and thus saving. Yet this follows from the very nature of salvation as being the condition of union with the whole of creation, with Christ at the apex of creation, and in and through him with the Father. However, Christ's specific mission is not to reveal to us the secrets of the material universe as such. Rather, he came to unite all that we are, including our relationship to creation, to God in a personal way. All that was categorized under the rubric of "natural revelation" is taken up by him and invested with new meaning that does not destroy it but fulfills it.

5. Genuine understanding, love, and integration demand a going out of oneself and an increase of one's being which implies a creative act of God. This is basically what anonymous faith is. See Matthew 25:31–46.

6. For a clear analysis of the movement of understanding from God as he is for us to God as he is in himself see John Courtney Murray, *The Problem of God* (New Haven: Yale University Press, 1964), pp. 5–66.

7. The threefold division of the universal aspects of revelation refers, of course, to the emergence of *possibilities* in the Church. For an account of the actual kinds of forms that so-called dogmatic statements have taken historically, see Josef Nolte, *Dogma in Geschichte: Versuch einer Kritik des Dogmatismus in der Glaubensdarstellung* (Freiburg: Herder, 1971). Avery Dulles, in *Theological Studies*, 34 (June 1973), 304, summarizes the results of Nolte's investigation as follows: "Nolte distinguishes three basic forms of dogmatic statement. In Scripture and the early Church one finds confessional formulas that express the faith in summary form; although they have something of the character of dogmas, these formulas are not intended as exclusive or definitive. Closer to the modern concept of dogma are the definitions of the ancient councils; these are exclusive, in the sense that they intend to protect the faith against a heresy, but they are regarded as emergency measures rather than as eternal statutes. Many of these ancient definitions succeeded so well that they continue to fulfill a paradigmatic role with regard to posterity. The modern period is characterized by explicative-tendentious dogmas, as N. calls them. These are extensive in character and are not drawn up in response to any grave crisis. N. finds dogmas of this third type tainted with dogmatism, and he welcomes the decision of Vatican II not to enact any new dogmas of this kind. He hopes that the Church in our day may be passing into a meta-dogmatic phase, in which dogma would be purified of the defects of dogmatism."

Nolte indicates that historically official Church statements have not clearly followed the path of universal meanings. In other words, the historical dogmas (as I have suggested in chapter 5) often intermingled the universal with the culturally conditioned. I would add, however, that from our vantage point we can point out the emergence of relational, ontic, and dynamic meanings that are universal even if the ancient Church did not consciously identify these meanings. That identification will now enable us to pass into Nolte's "meta-dogmatic phase, in which dogma would be purified of the defects of dogmatism."

8. See Karl Rahner, "On the Significance in Redemptive History of the Individual Member of the Church," in *Mission and Grace*, vol. 1 (London: Sheed and Ward Stagbooks, 1963), pp. 114–171.

9. Pluralism is inevitable in the present condition precisely because particular meanings always precede universal meanings, sometimes by centuries. Yet pluralism must not be viewed as an end in itself; rather, it is a stage towards the richness of eschatological unity. This means that all meanings or actualizations of human potential are ultimately shareable and hence universal, but not now. Pluralism has become a problem of greater magnitude in our time because of the rapid and diverse development of particular sectors of meaning without a corresponding development of the capacity to unify.

10. Maurice Blondel, "History and Dogma," in *The Letter on Apologetics and History and Dogma* (London: Harvill Press, 1964), p. 287.

11. As I shall indicate in chapter 16, it is only the grasp of a universal meaning to which infallibility can be referred. Articulations only represent that grasp.

12. I do not mean that the path of *statements* considered normative follows the path of the development of universal meanings. Historically, normative statements resulted largely from the challenge of heresies; these statements are not rounded expressions of what the faithful clung to most certainly. I am talking about the development of the kinds of meanings that, in retrospect, we can see were held to tenaciously by the Church.

13. Daniel Maguire, "Morality and Magisterium," in *Cross Currents*, 18 (Winter 1968), 47. Gerard J. Hughes, S.J., in "Infallibility in Morals," *Theological Studies*, 34 (September 1973), 415–428, propounds an updated view of the notion that infallibility does not describe the function of the moral magisterium. Hughes states that "no moral principle in normal form . . . can be either a timeless or a necessary truth" (p. 425). Later on the same page he says: "In the sense of 'irreformable' which I have proposed, then, it would appear that moral principles of their very nature cannot be completely irreformable." Hughes' article is informative because it indicates that the kind of moral principles he is dealing with are not the kind of principles I have called universal meanings. Hence I would agree with what Hughes affirms. However, I shall argue that there are moral principles that transcend the limitations of Hughes' ethical norms and reach the level of universality. These can be infallibly grasped.

14. See John T. Noonan, Jr., *The Scholastic Analysis of Usury* (Cambridge: Harvard University Press, 1957), pp. 11–20.

15. See my article "Tension, Morality, and Birth Control," in *Theological Studies*, 28 (June 1967), 258–285.

16. Stanislas Breton, " 'Lumen naturae' et 'Lumen gratiae' dans le concept théologique d'infaillibilité," in *L'Infaillibilité*, ed. Castelli, p. 278, puts it this way: "l'infaillibilité, dans la conscience qu'une Église s'en donne à un moment de son histoire où elle condense la leçon de son passè, recueille la fonction régulatrice d'un 'sens commun' qui ne peut se tromper dans la mesure exacte où sa vérité dogmatique sert l'unité du corps ecclésial."

17. If one accepts the notion of a single plan of God for the universe and the correlative notion that what God wills is manifested in creation, then it will be expected that all God's gifts are intrinsically related in the order of creation.

18. Lawrence Kohlberg has done interesting work in the stages of trans-cultural growth. See, for example, his "Education for Justice: A Modern Statement of the Platonic View," in a collection of lectures by five experts, entitled *Moral Education* (Cambridge: Harvard University Press, 1970), pp. 57–83, especially pp. 71–78. Also see, more conveniently, his "Indoctrina-

tion versus Relativity in Value Education," in *Theology Digest,* 21 (Summer 1973), 113–119. Kohlberg speaks here and elsewhere of six invariant stages of moral development that are present in all cultures. I would see his six stages as points on a continuum of man's growth from self-centeredness to total relatability.

19. This whole discussion indicates the need for what I would term an "operational dogma." This would be an understanding and teaching of the recurring emotions, attitudes, and modes of operation that would characterize a person who believed the truths of faith. Thus, a man who believed in the Communion of Saints would make that belief operative by ever going out towards his neighbor with the hope of final achievement of understanding and love. He would know that he had an obligation, and even the ultimate capacity, to overcome every contrary attitude, emotion, and hang-up towards each other person. He would never rest content with the limited attachment he now has to his neighbor. He would know, too, the genuine basis of lasting commitments and the need to become a committed person. I believe, in short, that Christian morality is simply dogma operationalized.

20. Again I must insist that strictly speaking statements are not infallible. Infallibility is a quality of understanding. Statements only represent that infallible understanding; thus, only in a loose sense can statements be called "infallible."

CHAPTER 12

1. Even the Incarnation is caused by all three persons acting through the one divine nature. However, that the three persons act as a single cause does not mean that there cannot be special relationships between the individual persons and the beings created by the three. The Incarnation is an obvious case. Many theologians believe that there are other cases. On this see my *The Divine Indwelling and Distinct Relations to the Indwelling Persons in Modern Theological Discussion* (Rome: Gregorian University Press, 1960).

2. See note 4 of chapter 10 for the meaning of charism.

3. See the subsection on "Man's Subjective Appropriation of Revelation in Christ" in chapter 11 for the explanation of the equation of the acceptance of revelation with salvation.

4. With regard to the connection between infallibility and freedom, the remarks I made in the beginning of the subsection "Concluding Remarks" in chapter 3 are applicable.

5. Alvin Toffler, *Future Shock* (New York: Random House, 1970).

6. See Francis Oakley, *Council Over Pope?* (New York: Herder and Herder, 1969); Leonard Swidler, "*The* Ecumenical Problem Today: Papal Infallibility," in *Journal of Ecumenical Studies*, 8 (Fall 1971), 751–767; Brian Tierney, "Origins of Papal Infallibility," *ibid.*, 841–864; Brian Tierney, *Origins of Papal Infallibility, 1150–1350* (Leiden: E. J. Brill, 1972); Hans Küng, *Infallible? An Inquiry*. Characteristic of the views of these men are the final words of Brian Tierney in the article cited above: "The doctrine of papal infallibility no longer serves anyone's convenience—least of all the pope's. It gives scandal to Protestant and Orthodox Christians. The papacy adopted the doctrine out of weakness. Perhaps one day the church will feel strong enough to renounce it." (p. 864.)

7. George Lindbeck in *The Infallibility Debate*, ed. John Kirvan (New York: Paulist Press, 1971), pp. 107–152.

CHAPTER 13

1. The interrelationship existing between the articulators of Christian meanings and the whole body of the faithful helps explain why Vatican I spoke of only one infallibility. See Thils, *L'Infaillibilité Pontificale*, pp. 145–148. For a philosophical analysis of the reasons why infallibility must be present in all the persons of a system if it is to be effective, see Raymond Panikkar, "Le Sujet de l'infaillibilité: Solipsisme et Vérification," in *L'Infaillibilité*, ed Castelli, pp. 423–445.

2. For the primacy of the lived faith of the Church as the basis for subsequent magisterial teaching see Karl Rahner, "Ist Kircheneinigung dogmatisch möglich?" in *Theologische Quartalschrift*, 153 (1973), 103–118, especially pp. 105–111.

3. See, for example, Raymond E. Brown, *Priest and Bishop* (New York: Paulist Press, 1970); André Lemaire, *Les Ministères aux origines de l'Église* (Paris: Éditions du Cerf, 1971).

4. I would suggest that the basic objection to the pope and the episcopate on the part of many non-Catholic Christians stems from their perception that these leaders do not manifest the unifying qualities which their office demands. One may legally possess an office without possessing to a marked degree the qualities that office requires. Legally one may be bishop or pope, but ontically—that is, in the very composition of one's being—one may be far from what that office implies. Thus, there is inevitably a gap between one's official position and one's personal realization, just as there is a gap between one's Christian profession and one's degree of Christian realization. When the gap between office and personal realization is great, there will

be objections to episcopal leaders. We should candidly admit the need for critics of the gap. However, despite all the inadequacies of officeholders in the very qualities of their office, there remains the ecclesial need for unifiers. That need is built into the very nature of man and Christian society. It cannot be eradicated by the inevitable failures of those who attempt to meet it by assuming the burden of office.

CHAPTER 14

1. Quoted in Thils, *L'Infaillibilité Pontificale*, p. 230.

2. *Ibid.*, p. 173.

3. For an interesting and informative account of the meta-juridical nature of infallibility see Vittorio Mathieu, "Infaillibilité et Autolégitimation d'un Système Juridique," in *L'Infaillibilité*, ed. Castelli, pp. 45–48.

4. The view advanced here has the further advantage of being reconcilable, it seems to me, with the Orthodox view propounded by Nicolas Afanassieff in "L'Infaillibilité de l'Église du point de vue d'un théologien orthodoxe," in *L'Infaillibilité de l'Église*, ed. Rousseau and others, pp. 183–201, especially pp. 199–200. Much of the objecting of Orthodoxy to papal infallibility has been to a concept of that infallibility which is, at least in my view, unreasonably legalistic in tone. Such an infallibility derives simply from the placing of certain external legal conditions; it has no reference to the ontic conditions required of the man of faith if he is to arrive at certitude. Orthodoxy has naturally objected to such legalistic textbook treatment of infallibility, the only one with which it could be expected to be familiar.

5. Brian Tierney, *Origins of Papal Infallibility, 1150–1350*. Tierney summarizes his findings as follows: "There is no convincing evidence that papal infallibility formed any part of the theological or canonical tradition of the Church before the thirteenth century; the doctrine was invented in the first place by a few dissident Franciscans because it suited their convenience to invent it; eventually, but only after much initial reluctance, it was accepted by the papacy because it suited the convenience of the popes to accept it." (*ibid.*, p. 281). Tierney does not consider the possibility that there may have been a dynamic at work throughout the history of the Church leading her to certitude in doctrinal matters. Subsequently, a reflection on this dynamic led to the doctrine of infallibility at Vatican I. Well before Vatican I, however, initial attempts at articulating this dynamic were made, often for reasons of convenience. However, the fact that the early articulations were poorly motivated and poorly expressed does not necessarily vitiate the doctrine of infallibility. Almost invariably the initial articulations of a

truth are inadequate. Witness the initial articulations of the doctrine of God in human history. Tierney's belief that the Church can dispense with the doctrine of infallibility if it wishes is not simply the product of his historical research. Rather, it is the product of that research *and* his theological presuppositions about the nature of revelation. Those presuppositions are largely implicit in his work. If they were made explicit and defended, then it would become apparent, I believe, that we differ not on historical facts but on our views of the deposit of revelation and the way understanding that deposit develops.

6. That the doctrine of infallibility is at a different level from the doctrines of the Incarnation, Trinity, and other credal teachings is indicated by Karl Rahner, "Zum Begriff der Unfehlbarkeit in der katholischen Theologie," *Schriften zur Theologie*, vol. 10 (Einsiedeln: Benziger, 1972), pp. 315–317. On the same point see also George Lindbeck in *The Infallibility Debate*, ed. John Kirvan (New York: Paulist Press, 1971), pp. 107–152.

7. For the kind of textbook treatment most priests have been exposed to see A. Tanquerey, *Synopsis Theologiae Dogmaticae*, I, 26th ed. (Paris: Desclée, 1949), pp. 585–603. Hardly two pages are given to an explanation of the conditions of infallibility, and no attempt is made to explain why these conditions are required. Tanquerey's treatment is typical of the education of priests on the subject in most parts of the world prior to 1960. This is the approach which practically all bishops in office in today's Church have been taught, since most of them were in the seminary prior to 1960.

8. Cf. *D. S.* 1534.

9. See chapter 6, the section entitled "Three Reasons Indicating the Necessity of Dogmatic Meanings."

10. See R. P. Nicolas Afanassieff, "L'Infaillibilité de l'Église du point de vue d'un théologien orthodoxe," in *L'Infaillibilité de l'Église*, ed. Rousseau and others, pp. 183–201. There is no single Orthodox view on infallibility since Orthodoxy has not developed its theology with regard to this category in any definitive fashion. The Orthodox Church prefers to speak of the Category of "Truth." Infallibility is the result of Truth. In general, however, Orthodox theology does not accept even the teachings of a general council as infallible unless these teachings have been received by the Church. Afanassieff attempts to explain what this reception by the Church means. Cf. Yves Congar, "Reception as an Ecclesiological Reality," in *Concilium*, 8, vol. 7 (September 1972), 43–68 in the British edition.

11. For historical background on the reception of a council in the Catholic Church see Alois Grillmeier, S.J., "Konzil und Rezeption," *Theologie and Philosophie*, 45 (1970), 321–352.

12. See the discussion in Hans Küng, *Structures of the Church* (New York: Thomas Nelson and Sons, 1964), pp. 249–268, especially pp. 260–262.

13. See Paul de Vooght, "Esquisse d'une enquête sur le mot 'infaillibilité' durant la période scholastique," *L'Infaillibilité de l'Église*, ed. Rousseau and others, pp. 99–146, especially pp. 101, 115, 117, 138, 142. In particular, I refer the reader to Raoul Manselli, "Le Cas du Pape Hérétique, vu à travers les courants spirituels du XIVe Siècle," in *L'Infaillibilité*, ed. Castelli, pp. 113–130. This author indicates that the position of Pietro Olivi was that when the pope is truly pope he cannot err as common teacher of the faithful. A pope "who maintains a thesis that is erroneous and diverse from that of the Church with the obstinacy that characterizes the true heretic by that very fact is no longer the true pope nor the true head of the Church" (*ibid.*, p. 116). Note that the question of the automatic deposition of the pope by his public heresy runs into the further question of who is to decide that the pope has lapsed into heresy. The answer is that there is no satisfactory answer. No one, neither the pope nor a general council, can make infallible decisions in concrete cases. The conditions of infallibility are enumerations of the qualities that must be possessed by those who pronounce infallibly. Whether such conditions are realized or not is a matter of fact, and there is no infallibility about matters of concrete fact. It is the common recognition of universal Christian meaning that brings peace and unity to the Church. When that common recognition does not exist—that is, when the pope disagrees with the rest of the Church on a matter of doctrine—there is no arbiter who can definitively decide that the pope is in error, and has thus ceased to be pope, or that the pope is correct. Only the suffering struggle of the Church can resolve the impasse. No dogmatic principle can. Thus, the ancient problem of whether the pope is superior to a general council or vice versa is a misplaced problem. It is manufactured by those who are trying to resolve a crisis by dogmatic means. It cannot be answered in the terms proposed because they assume that ultimately there is one essential part of the Church which can definitively judge in a concrete case that another essential part has been derelict in its basic functioning. Dogmatically, however, there is no superiority of pope or council in the value of their concrete judgments. Neither has some ultimate capacity to judge the performance of the other. Hence, crises of division can only be resolved by creative attempts to bring about unity. Inevitably, structural means taken to bring about unity in times of crisis are temporally conditioned means. They cannot have a dogmatic status.

CHAPTER 15

1. For the long tradition on limbo see William A. Van Roo, "Infants dying without Baptism," *Gregorianum*, 35 (1954), 406–473.

2. Karl Rahner, *Theological Investigations,* vol. 6 (Baltimore: Helicon, 1969) has a number of articles dealing with pluralism. The theme comes up in many of Rahner's writings on a diversity of subjects.

3. See chapter 13.

4. Because the individual is the sole locus of understanding, it is simplistic to think that the whole Church can be infallible but that no individual can enjoy this quality. Ultimately, papal infallibility is grounded on the possibility and necessity of individual infallibility.

5. This is the reason why Vatican II could make no infallible statement. The assembled prelates knew implicitly that they had not reached the level of transcultural understanding needed for dogmas today. It was defensible in the past to have culturally conditioned doctrines, although we must reinterpret them in a transcultural way now; however, we cannot justify issuing such culturally conditioned dogmas in the present. Hence, in the inability to issue the kind of dogma that makes sense today, Vatican II issued no binding statements demanding definitive acceptance. Of course, the bishops would not have articulated the matter in this way.

6. See Hilaire Marot, "Conciles anténicéens et conciles oecuméniques," in *Le Concile et les Conciles,* ed. D. O. Rousseau (Paris: Éditions du Cerf, 1960), pp. 19–43, esp. 37–43.

7. It is interesting to note that a bishop who cannot see the universal validity of what is proclaimed by his brother bishops is really the equivalent of the classical *rudes.* He too must work to develop his experiential continuum so that he can find the meaning proclaimed by his fellow bishops in the context of his faith life.

8. See R. P. Nicolas Afanassieff, " L'Infaillibilité de l'Église du point de vue d'un théologien orthodoxe," in *L'Infaillibilité de l'Église,* ed. Rousseau and others, pp. 183–201. Afanassieff uses a terminology which differs from my own. However, I think his meaning approximates what I have to say here, although he has no epistemological references.

CHAPTER 16

1. Ioachim Salaverri in *Sacrae Theologiae Summa,* I, 2nd ed., by Joseph de Aldama and others (Madrid: La Editorial Católica, 1952), p. 712.

2. *Ibid.,* p. 716.

3. *Ibid.,* pp. 713–714.

4. *Ibid.,* p. 714.

5. *Ibid.,* p. 715.

6. A Tanquerey, *Synopsis Theologiae Dogmaticae,* I, 26th ed. (Paris: Desclée, 1949), p. 625.

7. With regard to the canonization of saints there is a further question. How can the Church know with certitude that a person has joined the living Christ and thus become part of the lasting truth of reality in Him? The answer to this question, given the historical difficulties surrounding the very existence of a number of saints, goes beyond the scope of this work.

8. Thils, *L'infaillibilité Pontificale*, p. 154. Cf. Peter Fransen, "The Authority of the Councils," in *Problems of Authority*, ed. John Todd (Baltimore: Helicon, 1962), pp. 72–78.

9. Quoted in Walter Kasper, *Dogme et Évangile* (Tournai: Casterman, 1967), p. 35.

NOTES TO THE EPILOGUE

1. I cannot take up here the question of whether the creed said at Mass should be an operative creed. This question, I believe, has many more ramifications than appear at first sight.

2. Cf. Avery Dulles, *The Survival of Dogma* (Garden City: Doubleday & Company, 1971), p. 160. Dulles says that we "cannot hope to achieve supracultural formulations." However, his context is not the same as my own. I believe that if he were to consider the context within which I am operating he might well agree that a certain type of supracultural formulation is possible. The point I am making is that it is possible to propose a formula that points to heuristic supracultural aspects embedded in ever changing concrete situations.

Glossary

This Glossary has a number of purposes. First, it will enable all readers to find quickly the meaning of terms that I have coined because, to my knowledge, no terms exist for the meanings I propose. Secondly, it furnishes a list of terms that are current in theology but for which I have given definitions utilizing the thought patterns of this book. Finally, it contains a few terms that are well known to theologians but which may be unknown to the intelligent lay reader. The italicized words and phrases appearing within the definitions below are defined elsewhere in the glossary.

Absolute ecumenicity: A condition of a council in which every faith meaning in the entire Church is represented and expressed. *Absolute ecumenicity* represents an unachievable ideal.

Accretionary growth: Growth that is marked by a series of isolated and unconnected experiences and activities deriving from a haphazard pattern of life and thought.

Accretionary understanding: Understanding that is constituted by the mere addition in a non-integrated way of new data. An example would be the learning of new facts in a field without any effort to integrate that learning with one's prior knowledge. *Accretionary understanding* contrasts with *cumulative understanding.*

Anticipatory acceptance of a doctrinal decision: This kind of acceptance refers to a future possibility. It presupposes a condition in which an official teacher in the Church enunciates a *universal Christian meaning* that has not yet become a differentiation of the *experiential continuum* of the average Christian. Because this meaning, by hypothesis, is universal, it can and ought to be appropriated by all Christians, but, because most Christians cannot at present appropriate or accept the decision as reflecting who they already are, their acceptance is said to be anticipatory. In contrast we have *implicit acceptance* which refers to a present possibility. This kind of acceptance presupposes the enunciation of a universal Christian meaning by Church authority and the presence in a large number of the faithful of the requisite level of self-differentiation necessary to recognize the meaning enunciated; however, in *implicit acceptance* there is no external manifestation that the doctrinal meaning proclaimed actually resonates with what is already present internally in the faithful. When this external manifestation takes place, we then have *overt acceptance.*

Anticipatory assent to universal meaning: This is an understanding and assent to a universal meaning that involves practically no internalization of that meaning. The person assenting has not attempted to live out that meaning; he or she has not had the meaning penetrate the emotions and attitudes. The person has been only superficially changed by the meaning. *Anticipatory assent to universal meaning* contrasts with *resumatory assent to universal meaning.*

Basic Christian fact: This is the incarnation, life, death, and resurrection of the Son of God.

Catalytic function of texts: This is the capacity of texts, while remaining ever the same, to facilitate a new and creative actualization of the *experiential continuum* of the present reader.

Charism: The God-given capacity to live out the ancient tradition of the Church in a new way in some specialized context of life. *Charism* implies an habitual capacity that is a disposition for receiving new impulses of the Spirit.

Christian faith: The condition of the explicit human acceptance of the existing Christian order. See *existing order.* In other terms, *Christian faith* refers to a life lived at the *experiential-witness level.* Such faith is a gift of God.

Christian Order: See *existing order.*

Christian transcultural meaning: This is the equivalent of *universal Christian meaning* and *dogmatic meaning.*

Communication: This is a process between one who acts and one acted upon. The actor so acts that a meaning within his *experiential continuum* is actualized within the *experiential continuum* of the person acted upon. For genuine communication it is not necessary that the meaning be explicitly grasped by either party, although such explicit grasping is helpful to communication.

Conceptual formulations: Those that indicate the results of the implementation of generic heuristic relationships and processes in a given culture. See *heuristic formulations.*

Consensus of the faithful: The faith agreement, sometimes explicit but usually implicit, that is constituted by the presence of *dogmatic meanings* in Christians. It is also called the *consensus fidelium* or the sense of the faithful.

Cultural ecumenicity: A condition at a council in which in a more or less external manner all the various culturally conditioned ways of expressing the universal faith are represented.

Cumulative growth: A growth in which each new activity and experience would affect and be affected by the substantial whole of the individual's past growth. The new would be modified by the old into which it would be integrated, and the old would in turn be modified by the new. *Cumulative growth* is to be contrasted with *accretionary growth.*

Cumulative understanding: Understanding that develops continuously, not by piling up new data in separate pigeonholes, but by a progressive expansion of understanding which consistently incorporates into its overall view and each of its subsidiary views all new data. *Cumulative understanding* is to be contrasted with *accretionary understanding.*

Differentiation: A specific actualization of an *experiential continuum.*

Dogma: A formula solemnly sanctioned by the Church as an expression of *dogmatic meaning.* A dogma is, therefore, a composite of an enduring *dogmatic meaning* that has been explicitly grasped and a more or less adequate verbal expression of that meaning. Dogma is irreformable though developable in its meaning component; it is subject to a wide variety of revision in its expressive component.

Dogmatic ecumenicity: A condition in which a council of bishops from various parts of the world actually achieves the ontic conditions of infallibility and manifest that achievement to the world in a statement.

Dogmatic meaning: An actual or potential *differentiation* of the human *experiential continuum* that (1) has been achieved in Christ as the universal perfect man and (2) which is demanded, at least as a goal, as an achievement of all men in this life by their very nature as creatures made to reach out to and encompass all creation and the Creator. A *dogmatic meaning* is equivalent to a *universal Christian meaning,* and a *Christian transcultural meaning. Dogmatic meanings* are divided into *first-order dogmatic meanings* and *second-order dogmatic meanings.*

Dogmatic statement: A verbal expression that points to and represents a *dogmatic meaning.*

Dogmatic understanding: The Church's explicit awareness of its possession of *dogmatic meaning.*

Dynamic aspect of universal revelation: See *universal aspect of revelation.*

Dynamic infallibility: See *universal aspect of revelation.*

Ecclesial expression: Doctrinal formulas, liturgical rites, laws, and governmental structures which body forth in an imperfect, relative, and unique way the living meanings that were constituent of the Church that produced them.

Error in communication: A condition in which the recipient of an expression of another (1) assigns to that expression an act or acts of understanding not in accord with the act expressly intended by the communicator; or (2) misreads, at least in part, that which is implied in the total concrete expression (the sound of the voice, the facial attitude and gestures, the connotation of individual words and the succession of words, etc.) of the communicator, whether that misreading remains implicit in the recipient's being or becomes expressed by him in a concept; or (3) errs by a combination of both (1) and (2).

Ex cathedra: This phrase refers to the indispensable conditions of the exercise
of papal infallibility as set down in Vatican I. The pope is said to speak
ex cathedra when (1) he acts as supreme teacher and pastor of all the
faithful; (2) in so acting he exercises his supreme apostolic authority;
(3) he defines a doctrine of faith and morals; (4) he defines in such a way
as to bind the universal Church in faith. In this book I have accepted
all the conditions summed up in the phrase *ex cathedra.* However, I
have tended to group these conditions under the object of infallibility
(condition 3) and the limiting conditions on infallibility's exercise (condition 1, 2, and 4). See pp. 141–148.

Existing order: The total network of relationships that can unite present flesh
and blood persons with the surrounding world and the Creator. There
have been two existing orders. The pre-Christian order consisted in a
network of relationships that excluded Christ; the Christian order is a
network in which Christ is an integral part. Within the Christian order
there are two levels of conscious life. See (1) the *simple experiential level*
and (2) the *experiential witness level.* The Christian order IS the *existing
order* whether people know it or not. This, at least, is the faith stance
of this book.

Experience: The actualization of any human potential. One experiences
when there is such an actualization even when one is unaware of what
has occurred, e.g., when one is asleep, distracted, or focused on another
aspect of a global experience.

Experiential continuum: The totality of actualization undergone by an
individual in his or her lifetime.

Experiential-witness level: The level of existence of those who recognize
through the Christian tradition that they are affected by the risen Christ.

Expression: A word, a symbol, a gesture, or an action that bodies forth and
empirically represents an interior meaning in an imperfect, concrete,
and relative manner. The actual speaking of a word, the actual using
of a symbol, and the actual performance of an action are all expressions
in a primary sense. In a secondary sense, expressions are the non-personal
results of primary expression — the words on paper or tape, the symbols
as existing apart from the person using them, and the concrete results
of actions.

Ex sese, non autem consensu ecclesiae: Literally, this means "of itself, and
not because of the consent of the Church." This famous phrase is used
to indicate that when the pope fulfills the conditions of infallibility
indicated by the term *ex cathedra,* he is infallible by that very fact. Prior
or subsequent consent by the Church in some legal fashion, however
desirable that might be, is not an additional necessity for infallibility.

Factual universality: This refers to any condition of the concrete universe of creation and its relationship to the Creator which will persist *de facto* throughout this present mode of existence before the parousia. *Factual universality* differs from *presuppositional universality* in that the latter is a species of factual universality whose universality can be known with certitude even now.

First-order doctrines: See *first-order dogmatic meanings.*

First-order dogmatic meanings: Meanings directly and immediately present in the experience of all Christians, at least potentially.

General aspect of revelation: An aspect of the realization of the full humanity of Christ that is achievable in the present eon by all human beings.

Heuristic formulations: Those that indicate the universal relationships and processes that generate all cultural formulations. See *heuristic view or notion.*

Heuristic view or notion: This is a view that is indicated by listing the pattern of recurring generic processes whose implementation leads to its realization. Thus one could indicate the total intelligibility of the universe heuristically by indicating the pattern of recurring processes by which humans grow in understanding. Similarly, one indicates perfect humanity heuristically by indicating the pattern of generic growth processes by which a present human being would move toward it.

Implicit acceptance of a doctrinal decision: See *anticipatory acceptance of a doctrinal decision.*

Implicit or subliminal meaning: A differentiation of an *experiential continuum* that could be explicitly grasped or understood but which has not yet been so grasped or understood.

Infallibility: The recurring generic process by which the Church, because of the universal nature of the witnessed saving reality which *dogmatic statements* express, can come to a certitude in the understanding of that reality that is equal to the certitude that a person has of his or her own existence.

Interpretation: Primarily, this is the process of grasping the *meaning,* whether intended or not, that derives from the author of a text or other expression. This grasp is always in terms of one's present *experiential continuum.* Secondarily, an interpretation is a statement which refers or points to the results of that process. In this work texts are seen not only as expressions to be interpreted for old meanings but also as catalysts for new meanings. See *catalytic function of texts.*

Irreformability of dogma: See *stability of dogma.*

Limited universal meanings: Meanings that exist universally within a situation, e.g., a civilization or a culture, that is less than the total human situation over all of time and space.

Magisterium of the Church: In this book the magisterium of the Church is

restricted to the pope and bishops seen as official teachers. This is not
to deny that others, such as theologians, have an important teaching
function. (see Yves Congar, "Pour une histoire Sémantique du terme
'Magisterium' " in *Revue des Sciences Philosophiques et Théologiques*,
60 (1976), 85–98; Yves Congar, "Bref Historique des formes du 'Magistère' et de ses Relations avec les Docteurs" in *Ibid.*, 99–112.)

Meaning: In the subjective sense, a meaning is a unified differentiation of the
experiential continuum that potentially or actually may be consciously
understood. This is the usual use of meaning in this work. However,
meanings also exist apart from conscious subjects, at least in a derived
sense. Such a meaning is the aspect of intelligibility in the universe of
objects (which includes other subjects) which can become through
experience intelligible to a subject.

Methodological meanings: These are *universal Christian meanings* viewed
as the basis of a methodological approach to new reality. When *universal
Christian meanings* are internalized by a subject, they facilitate the ability
of that subject to engage new reality with a "normative pattern of re-
current and related operations yielding cumulative and progressive
results." (Bernard Lonergan, *Method in Theology*, p. 4). These same
meanings are called *structural meanings* insofar as they constitute the
enduring structure around which all further meanings cluster.

Norma non-normata: This classical term is used of Scripture. It indicates
that Scripture is the absolute norm and cannot be judged by any superior
norm. The theory set forth in this work indicates that this classical term
and its meaning need to be carefully nuanced. See pp. 280–281.

Ontic aspect of universal revelation: See *universal aspect of revelation.*

Ontic infallibility: See *universal aspect of revelation.*

Operational dogma: An understanding and teaching of the recurring
emotions, attitudes, and modes of operation that would characterize a
person who accepted a truth of faith.

Operative creed: A statement of Christian meaning that realistically expresses
for persons in a given cultural situation their particular participation in
the faith of the Church. An operative creed would be contrasted with
a dogmatic creed. A dogmatic creed would be one whose expressions
referred exclusively to *dogmatic meanings.*

*Ordinary and universal teaching of the bishops scattered throughout the
world:* This refers to those *dogmatic meanings* present in the teaching of the
bishops of the world in some way. Such teaching is by its nature infallible teaching. However, it is difficult to determine. See, in contrast,
ordinary and universal teaching of the pope.

Ordinary and universal teaching of the pope: This refers to teaching by the
pope which, though addressed to the whole Church, lacks one or more

of the conditions required for papal infallibility.

Overt acceptance of a doctrinal decision: See *anticipatory acceptance of a doctrinal decision.*

Particular aspect of revelation: An aspect of the realization of the full humanity of Christ that is presently achievable by a limited number of persons at most.

Personal relationship: A relationship founded upon communication and sharing of operations that flow from what is specific to a personal being. A personal relationship in the strict sense requires a fundamental equality of natures of the two parties. Hence, we can have a strict personal relationship with God only because God has shared our nature in the Incarnation. See pp. 80–81.

Pluralism: This is a legitimate diversity of Christian individual and social realization. Pluralism is of two basic kinds. First, pluralism of meaning refers to the realization by diverse Christians of differing sets of *universal Christian meanings* or of Christian meanings of a less than universal kind. Pluralism of expression refers to a diversity in language, symbols, concrete actions, etc. which express the same shared meanings.

Presuppositional universality: This is a species of *factual universality* which can be known with certitude. It refers to aspects of creation and its relationship to the Creator which are presupposed in the twofold acceptance of (1) the universal presence and activity of the risen Christ, who now fulfills the incipient exigency for total relatability that was his when he walked this earth, and of (2) the recurring exigencies and relationships of all human subjects. See pp. 130–131.

Primary objects of infallibility: These are truths of faith and morals which are *per se* revealed for the whole Church. They are to be contrasted with the *secondary objects of infallibility.* This traditional terminology would have to be greatly nuanced in the light of distinctions made in this book. In general, the *primary objects of infallibility* are equivalent to what I have called *dogmatic meanings.* In turn, *dogmatic meanings* are subdivided into *first-order dogmatic meanings* and *second-order dogmatic meanings.*

Prophetic meaning: This is a Christian meaning applicable only to concrete local contexts. It is contrasted with *universal Christian meaning* which is abstract and applicable to all contexts. See *universal Christian meaning.*

Prophetic statement: The articulation of a *prophetic meaning.*

Reception of a doctrinal decision: See *anticipatory acceptance of a doctrinal decision.*

Relational aspect of universal revelation: See *universal aspect of revelation.*

Relational infallibility: See *universal aspect of revelation.*

Resumatory assent to universal meaning: Conceptual assent to a meaning that crystallizes and summarizes prior struggle with, personal involvement in, and internalization of the meaning. In such assent the meaning is emotionalized, attitudinalized, intellectually grasped, and freely willed. Such assent should be contrasted with *anticipatory assent to universal meaning.*

Resurrection: The arrival by Christ at the condition of full growth of his humanity, the condition in which he realizes in his humanity the integral and universal relatability that each human nature is intrinsically called to.

Revelation: God's making himself known to us. The risen Christ is the supreme locus of revelation. See *particular aspect of revelation, general aspect of revelation.*

Salvation: As used in this book, salvation refers to the condition of sharing the *resurrection* of Christ. It is that condition in which the human person fully relates to all other persons, to the risen Christ, and in and through him to the Father. Salvation is thus more than the condition of having one's sins forgiven.

Secondary objects of infallibility: Classically these are truths other than *primary objects of infallibility* which are necessarily connected with these primary objects. In the theological manuals the secondary objects of infallibility included (1) certain speculative truths; (2) dogmatic facts; (3) certain general disciplinary decrees; (4) the solemn canonization of saints; (5) the definitive approbation of religious orders. See pp. 283ff. for clarification of the meaning of these terms.

Second-order doctrines: See *second-order dogmatic meanings.*

Second-order dogmatic meanings: The generic relationships, processes, and implications that characterize all *first-order dogmatic meanings* and their emergence. The *dynamic aspects of universal revelation* give rise to *second-order dogmatic meanings.*

Simple experiential level: In the *existing order* the *experiential continuum* of each individual is affected by the risen Christ. Those who are existentially unaware of being affected by the risen Christ are living at the *simple experiential level.*

Stability of dogma: This refers to the enduring validity of *dogmatic meaning.* Strictly speaking, dogma is not stable insofar as it is a composite of an enduring dogmatic meaning and a more or less adequate expression. The instability of the second aspect of the composite, expression, makes it misleading to speak of the stability of dogma. The more accurate phrasing would be the stability of dogmatic meaning. Stability of dogma is also referred to as the *irreformability of dogma.*

Structural meanings: See *methodological meanings.*

Surd: That part of an *experiential continuum* that is *ex se* unintelligible. See pages 13–15.

Symbol: A sensible expression (word, story, event, etc.) which is the product of the actualization of human potentials, which represents those potentials, and which can occasion the actualization of these same potentials or other potentials in other persons or even in the author of the symbol. A symbol is a sign to the extent that it leads to the actualization in the present recipient of the same potentials it expressed and represented in its author. It is a symbol in the strict sense to the degree that it leads to the actualization of new potentialities in the present recipient.

Transcultural Christian meaning: See *dogmatic meaning.*

Transcultural meaning: A *meaning* which of its very nature pertains to all cultures. Transcultural meaning is *universal meaning.* However, the term *transcultural meaning* refers more directly to the resulting capacity of *universal meanings* to bridge differences in cultures. The term *universal meanings* refers more directly to universal potentialities intrinsic to human nature.

Understanding: This is *primarily* a heightening of experience that allows one to grasp one or more unities or connections in one's experiential continuum. Understanding is thus a higher level experience. Because of the necessarily assumed isomorphism between the experiencer and what is externally experienced, understanding is *secondarily* a grasp of the corresponding unities of any object experienced. There are, however, acts of understanding of purely internal processes.

Universal aspect of revelation: An enduring aspect of the risen Christ which is in some way graspable by all Christians in the present condition of existence. Universal aspects of revelation are divided into (1) relational aspects, (2) ontic aspects, and (3) dynamic aspects. For an extended notion of relational aspects see pages 173–175; for ontic aspects, pages 175–176; for dynamic aspects, pages 176–177. Infallibility as exercised with regard to each of these aspects is called (1) relational infallibility, (2) ontic infallibility, and (3) dynamic infallibility.

Universal Christian meaning: This is the equivalent of *dogmatic meaning.*

Universal ecclesial meaning: This is the equivalent of *dogmatic meaning.*

Universal meaning: A *meaning* that exists or can exist as a moment of legitimate and necessary human development in every person of every age and culture.

Index of Subjects

Abortion, 190, 199–200

Absolute ecumenicity of a council, 253, 265–266

Abstraction, 9

Accretionary understanding, 201–204

Anticipatory acceptance of a doctrinal decision, 239–240

Anticipatory assent to a universal meaning, 256–257, 259, 260, 261

Approbation of the way of life of a religious order as a secondary object of infallibility, 283, 287–288

Assumption, doctrine of Mary's, 88, 126, 183

Birth control, 129, 185, 186, 190, 199–200, 212, 217, 221, 234, 235, 259, 268

Canonization of saints: 327; as secondary objects of infallibility, 284, 287–288

Charism: 85, 164, 179, 196, 317; of the Church's magisterium, 187–188

Christ: 236; experiencing him as risen, 71; growth processes of, 72–75, 167–168; his human knowledge, 164; our knowledge of his resurrection, 76–80; personal relationship to God in him, 80–83; as the supreme locus of revelation, 166–169; see Resurrection of Christ, Death of Christ as an aspect of his growth

Christian fact, the basic, 66–83

Christian experiential-witness level, see Experiential-witness level

Christian order: 80–83, 309; see Existing order

Christian truth, saving nature of, xvi

Church: membership in, 311; as a Universal Christian meaning, 88

Communication: 10–23; conditions governing, 16–18; elements of, 18–22; function of expression in, 278

Communion of Saints: 88, 126, 171; defined operationally, 321

Community of the faithful, as promoted by infallibility, 197–198, 200

Conceptual formulations, 292

Consensus of the faithful: as defined by the possession of universal Christian meanings, 208–209; determination of its meaning, 212–214; nature of, 211–212; its relationship to the papal and episcopal articulators of infallibility, 209; see Infallibility of the faithful, *Sensus fidelium*

Creed, 291–292

Cultural ecumenicity of a council, 253–254, 265–266

Culturally conditioned meaning, 89–91, 92, 93, 94, 95, 97, 98, 99, 100, 291, 306

Cumulative growth, 200–207

Cumulative understanding, 200–207

Death of Christ as an aspect of his growth, 73–75

Development of dogma, see Dogma

Index of Authors